YALE HISTORICAL PUBLICATIONS
MISCELLANY 81

David Horne, Editor

PUBLISHED UNDER THE DIRECTION
OF THE DEPARTMENT OF HISTORY

The Political Thought of Pierre d'Ailly

THE VOLUNTARIST TRADITION

BY FRANCIS OAKLEY

NEW HAVEN AND LONDON, YALE UNIVERSITY PRESS, 1964

In Memory of My Father

Preface

Book titles are not always satisfactory media for the communication of intentions, and the title of this book is no more satisfactory than most. It means, nevertheless, what it says. The book is a study in the *political* thought of Pierre d'Ailly. As such, it is both less and more than a study of his ecclesiology. It is less in that it ignores, brackets, or fails to do justice to those elements in his thinking that are relevant to the Church alone and not even indirectly to other political societies—as, for example, his views on the *locus* of infallibility within the Church. It is more in that it concerns itself not merely with d'Ailly's Conciliar views but also with those political and legal ideas which he formulated independently of his more famous ecclesiastical theories and prior to them.

The book speaks the language of an historian and it is directed chiefly to historians, perhaps not only to medieval historians. It is my hope, however, that it will also have something to say to those whose primary interests center on philosophy or political theory—at least to those among them who, unlike the philosophy student of my acquaintance, do not "read Aristotle only in order to refute him," but believe that the long history of Western thought is something more than a dreary repository of "quasi-answers to pseudo-problems," or a collection of outmoded arguments congruent only to the pressing needs of philosophers in search of therapeutic straw men.

It would make lengthy and, I fear, tedious reading if I were to acknowledge individually all the obligations incurred in the course of preparing this study. But some debts are outstanding. I must thank the Prime Warden and Wardens of the Worshipful Company of Goldsmiths for the award of the travelling research scholarship which enabled me to spend two fruitful years at the Pontifical Institute of Mediaeval Studies, Toronto, and I must thank the Faculty members of the Institute, particularly Professor J. Reginald O'Donnell, for their unfailing kindness to me. I must thank Professors Roland H. Bainton and Alexander Passerin d'Entrèves of Yale University and my colleague at Williams, Daniel D. O'Connor, for reading in whole or in part one or other of the versions of the book and for giving me the benefit of their help, criticism, and advice. I must thank the Editors of the *Journal of British Studies* for permitting me to include in the final chapter of the book material originally published in article form in that journal. I must thank the President and Trustees of Williams College for grants from the Class of 1900 Fund towards the cost of preparing the manuscript for the press. I must thank my wife for the countless reasons and more for which husbands who try to write books should thank their wives. Finally, I welcome the chance to acknowledge the heavy debt I owe to the patience, generosity, and understanding of my mother and of my late father.

F. O.

Williamstown, Massachusetts
April 1964

Contents

Abbreviations and Citations

Abbreviations have been used only for those works to which frequent reference has been made in more than one chapter. Complete references for all other works are given in the footnotes when they are first cited.

Arquillière   H. X. Arquillière, *Le plus ancien traité de l'église. Jacques de Viterbo, De Regimine Christiano (1301–1302)*, Paris, 1926.

Carlyle, *History*   R. W. and A. J. Carlyle, *A History of Medieval Political Theory in the West*, 6 vols. London and Edinburgh, 1903 ff.

Chastenet   H. Bourgeois du Chastenet, *Nouvelle Histoire du Concile de Constance*, Paris, 1778.

C Med H   The Cambridge Medieval History, 8 vols. Cambridge, 1911 ff.

C Mod H   The Cambridge Modern History, 13 vols. Cambridge, 1909 ff.

Conc. Trid.   *Canones et Decreta Sacrosancti Oecumenici et Generalis Concilii Tridentini sub Paulo III, Julio III, Pio IV, Pontificibus Max. Celebrati*, ed. J. Le Plat, Antwerp, 1779.

Denifle   H. Denifle and E. Chatelain, *Chartularium Universitatis Parisiensis*, 4 vols. Paris, 1889–97.

D'Entrèves, *Aquinas*   A. P. d'Entrèves, *Aquinas: Selected Political Writings*, Oxford, 1959.

Dupin   Jean Gerson, *Opera Omnia,* ed. Louis Ellies Dupin, 5 vols. Antwerp, 1706.

Ehrle   Franz Ehrle, *Martin de Alpartils Chronica Actitatorum, 1* Quellen und Forschungen aus dem Gebiete der Geschichte, 7, Paderborn, 1906.

Figgis, *Studies*   J. N. Figgis, *Studies of Political Thought from Gerson to Grotius,* 2nd ed. Cambridge, 1931.

Gierke-Maitland   Otto Gierke, *Political Theories of the Middle Age,* trans. F. W. Maitland, Cambridge, 1938.

Goldast   Melchior Goldast, *Monarchia s. Romani Imperii,* 3 vols. Frankfort, 1668.

Hardt   H. von der Hardt, *Rerum concilii oecumenici Constantiensis,* 6 vols. Leipzig, 1697 ff.

Hefele-Leclercq   C. J. Hefele, *Histoire des Conciles d'après les documents originaux,* trans. and ed. H. Leclercq, 11 vols. Paris, 1907 ff.

Hinschius   P. Hinschius, *Decretales pseudo-Isidorianae,* Leipzig, 1863.

Kantorowicz, *King's Two Bodies*   Ernst H. Kantorowicz, *The King's Two Bodies: A Study in Medieval Political Theology,* Princeton, 1957.

Kern, *Kingship*   Fritz Kern, *Kingship and Law in the Middle Ages,* trans. S. B. Chrimes, Oxford, 1939.

Lagarde, *Naissance*   Georges de Lagarde, *La Naissance de l'esprit laïque au déclin du moyen âge, 4-6,* Paris, 1942 ff.

Leclercq   J. Leclercq, *Jean de Paris et l'ecclésiologie du XIIIe siècle,* Paris, 1942.

Lettenhove   Kervyn de Lettenhove, *Chroniques relatives à l'histoire de la Belgique sous la domination des ducs de Bourgogne, 1,* Brussels, 1870.

Lewis, *Political Ideas*   Ewart Lewis, *Medieval Political Ideas,* 2 vols. London, 1954.

Mansi   J. Mansi, *Sacrorum conciliorum nova et amplissima collectio,* 31 vols. Florence, 1759 ff.

Martène et Durand   E. Martène et V. Durand, *Veterum scriptorum . . . amplissima collectio,* 9 vols. Paris, 1724 ff.

McIlwain, *Growth*   C. H. McIlwain, *The Growth of Political Thought in the West,* New York, 1932.

Meller, *Studien*   B. Meller, *Studien zur Erkenntnislehre des Peter von Ailly,* Freiburg i. Breisg., 1954.

Oakley, "Laws of Nature" Francis Oakley, "Christian Theology and the Newtonian Science: The Rise of the Concept of the Laws of Nature," *Church History, 30* (1961), 433–57.

Ockham, *Sent.* William of Ockham, *Super Quatuor Libros Sententiarum*, Lyons, Jean Trechsel, 1495.

PL J. P. Migne, *Patrologiae Cursus Completus . . . series latina,* 221 vols. Paris, 1844 ff.

Roberts, "Pierre d'Ailly" A. E. Roberts, "Pierre d'Ailly and the Council of Constance: A Study in 'Ockhamite' Theory and Practice," *Trans. Royal Hist. Soc.,* 4th ser. *18* (1935), 123–42.

Salembier, *Alliaco* L. Salembier, *Petrus de Alliaco,* Insulis, 1886.

Salembier, *Cardinal* L. Salembier, *Le Cardinal Pierre d'Ailly,* Tourcoing, 1931.

Salembier, *Schisme* L. Salembier, *Le Grand Schisme d'Occident,* 5th ed. Paris, 1921.

Scholz R. Scholz, ed., *Aegidius Romanus De Ecclesiastica Potestate,* Weimar, 1929.

Sent. Pierre d'Ailly, *Quaestiones super I, III et IV Sententiarum,* Lyons, Nicolaus Wolff, 1500.

Sermones Pierre d'Ailly, *Tractatus et sermones,* Argentinae, 1491.

ST St. Thomas Aquinas, *Summa Theologica,* Rome, 1889 ff.

Tierney, *Foundations* Brian Tierney, *Foundations of the Conciliar Theory,* Cambridge, 1955.

Tschackert, *Ailli* P. Tschackert, *Peter von Ailli,* Gotha, 1877.

Ullmann, *Origins* Walter Ullmann, *The Origins of the Great Schism,* London, 1948.

Ullmann, *Papalism* Walter Ullmann, *Medieval Papalism: The Political Theories of the Medieval Canonists,* London, 1949.

Valois, *France* N. Valois, *La France et le grande schisme d'occident,* 4 vols. Paris, 1896 ff.

For the many references to the canon and civil laws I have used the standard editions of A. Friedberg, *Corpus Juris Canonici,* 2 vols., Leipzig, 1879–81, and P. Krueger, Th. Mommsen, and R. Schoell, *Corpus Juris Civilis,* 3 vols., Berlin, 1899–1902.

For references to the *glossa ordinaria* to each of the books of the canon law I have used the following editions: *Decretum Divi Gratiani,* Lyons, 1560; *Decretales D. Gregorii Papae IX,* Lyons,

1583; *Liber Sextus Decretalium D. Bonifacii Papae VII, Clementis Papae V, Constitutiones Extravagantes tum viginte D. Joannis Papae XXII tum Communes,* Lyons, 1584.

References to the two laws conform to a uniform and accepted system, the divisions of the collection concerned being given in descending order of magnitude. Thus X, 5, 31, c. 8, *in v.* potestati refers to *Decretales Greg. IX,* Book 5, Title 31, Chapter 8, the gloss on the word *potestati.* Similarly C. 5, 59, 5 refers to *Codex Justiniani,* Book 5, Title 59, Section 5.

In quoting Latin works printed after 1500 I have usually retained the punctuation and capitalization of the edition used. In the rendition of non-English proper names no attempt has been made to attain linguistic consistency. I have simply employed the form that seems to be most commonly used in the English-speaking world; hence, "Aegidius Romanus" rather than "Giles of Rome," but "John of Paris" rather than "Jean de Paris."

Introduction

Political philosophy [1] comes into existence only when men who have asked why they should obey their rulers fail to be silenced by Thrasymachan arguments or satisfied with appeals to prescriptive right. For the central problem of political philosophy is the necessity of finding rational grounds for political obligation. [2] This is the problem that brings the pragmatic scrutiny of

1. For current uses and abuses of the terms "political philosophy" and "political theory" see J. C. Rees, "The Limitations of Political Theory," *Political Studies, 2* (1956), 242–52, esp. 242 n. 1; also John Plamenatz, "The Use of Political Theory," *Political Studies, 8* (1960), 37–47. Like Rees, I shall use these terms in a frankly traditional sense to cover such cognate questions as "the relation between order and freedom, the justification of political authority, the limits of political obligation, and the purpose of political power as well as those questions that arise in the normative study of political institutions."

2. It has become fashionable in the English-speaking world to dismiss such questions as unanswerable pseudo-problems and to downgrade accordingly the traditional political theories concerned with them. Our political scientists do not always seem to realize that there are important philosophical issues at stake, but, as historians, we must confine ourselves to noting the issue, and must make the most of the reassurance that even "the critics of the traditional theories . . . do not deny the great practical influence exerted by the theories despite their logical defects," (Rees, p. 233 n. 1); cf. T. P. Weldon, *The Vocabulary of Politics* (Harmondsworth, Middlx., 1953), p. 100. The historical importance of these traditional theories, if not their philosophical significance, remains, it would seem, immune both to the hyperbole of their critics and the timidity and confusion of their defenders.

political processes into uneasy conjunction with the imperatives of moral philosophy. This is the problem that lay—few would deny it—at the heart of ancient political speculation. This is the problem that has served as the conscious focus of its modern counterpart. It can hardly be said, however, to have exercised the majority of medieval political thinkers. Theirs was a conception of society as pledged to the pursuit of an other-worldly ideal but equally bound to regulate the behavior of mankind in this world, and the bulk at least of the early medieval literature was dominated, therefore, not by questions relating directly to political obligation, but rather by problems concerning the relations which should exist between *regnum* and *sacerdotium*.[3]

Two incidents served to reinstate the question of political obligation as the focus of all political philosophizing. The first, occurring around 1260, was the translation from the Greek of Aristotle's *Politics*. The second was the election in 1378 of the rival pope, Clement VII. The significance of the first of these two disparate events needs no elaboration here. It is the second with which we shall concern ourselves, for the relevance of the Great Schism of the West to the problem of political obligation is not immediately apparent.[4]

The first papal election after the long-awaited return of the Papacy from Avignon to Rome took place in April 1378, to the accompaniment of rioting outside the conclave and sharp dissension within. It ended with the election of the Archbishop of Bari, a compromise candidate who took the title of Urban VI. The Roman mob had clamored noisily for the election of a Roman. The cardinals, unwilling to accede to this demand, but divided among themselves, had been forced, for the first time in over half a century, to choose a non-French pope. The Arch-

3. These problems themselves involve the problem of political obligation, but they do so at one remove. Thus McIlwain, *Growth*, pp. 146–47, can comment that "the peculiar problem of Church and State" was "the greatest perturbation which has ever drawn men's thoughts about the state out of their proper political orbit, and for many ages the most powerful stimulus to all political speculations."

4. For a recent account of the events that culminated in the Great Schism see Ullmann, *Origins*. For the history of the Schism itself, see Salembier, *Schisme*, and Valois, *France*.

bishop of Bari may have been an Italian, but at least he was no Roman, and many of the French cardinals had come to regard him almost as one of their own race.[5] They were able, therefore, to agree on his candidacy. But his subsequent behavior led to a rapid worsening of relations, and in the May and June of 1378 all the cardinals, with the exception of the four Italians, made their way to Anagni. There, by the end of September, they had not only repudiated Urban's election as made under duress and therefore invalid, but had also gone on to choose in his place Robert of Geneva, one of the French cardinals. He assumed the name of Clement VII and took up residence at Avignon. Since neither of the rival claimants was able to displace the other or to command the allegiance of all the Christian nations, the Schism thus engendered was of a far more serious nature than its many predecessors, and despite all efforts by churchmen and temporal rulers to terminate it was to endure for almost forty years. Both claimants obdurately refused to withdraw, either individually or concurrently, and their rival curias strove to perpetuate their claims—Benedict XIII was elected at Avignon to succeed Clement VII, and Boniface IX, Innocent VII, and then Gregory XII to succeed Urban VI at Rome. Finally, in 1409, the abortive attempts of the Council of Pisa to end the Schism led to the addition of a third line of papal claimants, in the persons first of Alexander V and then of John XXIII.

These years of grave constitutional crisis within the Church gave rise to much anxious questioning about deficiencies in the machinery of Church government and also to a good deal of far-reaching speculation about the very nature and location of ecclesiastical authority. In the writings of a group of lawyers, theologians, and administrators—notable among whom were the *curialis*, Dietrich of Niem, the canonist, Franciscus Zabarella,

---

5. Sixteen cardinals took part in the conclave. Of these, one was Spanish, four were Italian, and eleven were French. The French, however, were unable to act as a body for they were themselves divided, the Limousin cardinals seeking to elect for the fifth successive time a pope from their own region. This the other French cardinals were determined to prevent, but to do so they had to secure the support of the Italians, and the candidacy of an Italian was a means to this end. See Ullmann, *Origins*, pp. 9 ff.

and the theologians, Conrad of Gelnhausen, Henry of Langenstein, Pierre d'Ailly, and Jean Gerson [6]—such speculations crystallized into a set of related theories of Church government which made possible a resolution of the Schism and which has come to be known as "the Conciliar theory."

Basic to this theory was the central insistence that the final authority of the Church lay not with the Pope but with the whole body of the faithful (*congregatio fidelium*) and that the Pope possessed, therefore, not an absolute but merely a *ministerial* authority, delegated to him for the good of the Church. This belief was supported by canonistic and theological arguments as well as by analogies drawn from the history of the ancient ecumenical councils, and it opened the way for an appeal from the obduracy of the rival pontiffs to the decision of the faithful as expressed through their representatives assembled in a general council of the whole Church. Such a possibility was realized at the Council of Pisa and, more strikingly, at Constance, where the Conciliar theory found expression, not only in the judgment and deposition of popes, but also in the promulgation of the decree *Sacrosancta,* which declared:

> This sacred synod of Constance forming a General Council . . . represents the Catholic Church and has immediate power from Christ which anyone, of whatsoever status and condition, even if holding the Papal dignity, is bound to obey in matters pertaining to the Faith, extirpation of the schism and reformation of the said Church in head and members.[7]

Events such as these had an importance that redounded far beyond the limits of purely ecclesiastical history, and Laski, perceiving this, claimed that the Conciliar theory should be viewed "not merely as a theory of ecclesiastical organization" but as a

6. Niem, Gelnhausen, and Langenstein were Germans; Zabarella, Italian; d'Ailly and Gerson, French.

7. Sidney Z. Ehler and John B. Morrall, eds., *Church and State through the Centuries* (Westminster, Md., 1954), p. 105; Latin text in Hardt, *4,* 98.

4

political theory in its own right, and not merely as one more
medieval political theory but as perhaps the most influential one
of all—for it was "the one universal expression to which medieval constitutionalism attained." The road from Constance to
the Glorious Revolution of 1688 was in fact "a direct one." The
Conciliar thinkers constructed "a whole armoury of civil principle," and they were "the ancestors, through pamphlets like the
Vindiciae contra Tyrannos, of Sydney and Locke." [8]

Laski was not alone in adopting this position. Janet, before
him, had not regarded the Conciliar movement as relevant to
his subject,[9] but Gierke had, and few historians of political
thought writing after him failed at least to acknowledge its significance.[10] For Gierke spoke of the Conciliar movement as
forming "an important chapter in the historical development
of 'Nature-Right' theories of the State," and as contributing
"immensely to the success of the political doctrine of popular
sovereignty." [11] In this, as in other matters, he was echoed by
J. N. Figgis, who suggested that the Conciliar arguments were
important because they were "more purely political than those
of the earlier Middle Ages," being concerned not with conflicts
between rival authorities "but with the depositary, the function
and the limits, of sovereign power in a perfect society." [12] R. H.
Murray, similarly, commented that "the Conciliar movement
was the first to raise the problems of the state in their present
form"; [13] McIlwain, in his discussion of the Conciliar issue and

8. Harold J. Laski, "Political Theory in the Later Middle Ages," *C Med H, 8,*
638; Frederick B. Artz, *The Mind of the Middle Ages* (New York, 1953), pp.
303–04, has echoed both Laski's sentiments and his words.

9. P. Janet, *Histoire de la science politique* (3rd ed. Paris, 1887), *1,* 471 n. 1.

10. Carlyle, *History, 6,* is a notable exception.

11. Otto von Gierke, *The Development of Political Theory,* trans. B. Freyd
(New York, 1939), pp. 147–48.

12. Figgis, *Studies,* p. 49. Figgis added elsewhere that "the claim of the Council to be superior to the Pope was always at the service of advocates of the rights of
the people against the despotism of Kings" ("Political Thought in the Sixteenth
Century," *C Mod H, 3,* 736). Similarly Ullmann, *Origins,* p. 6: "Monarchy versus
oligarchy was the real issue of the Schism, or, seen from a different angle, absolute
versus constitutional monarchy."

13. R. H. Murray, *The History of Political Science* (2nd ed. New York, 1930),
p. 101.

its historical importance, was in the main content to summarize the analysis of Figgis; [14] and Sabine concluded that

> The controversy in the Church first drew the lines upon which the issue between absolute and constitutional government was drawn, and it spread the type of political philosophy by which in the main absolutism was to be contested. . . . From the Conciliar theory of the fifteenth century there is a directly developing line of thought to the liberal and constitutional movement of the seventeenth and eighteenth centuries.[15]

With the exception of Figgis, however, none of these writers makes much of an effort to document his assertions, and even the evidence proffered by Figgis is somewhat scanty. It could hardly, indeed, be otherwise, for despite the current interest in the Conciliar period little attempt has yet been made to analyze and elucidate the political thinking of any of the leading Conciliarists other than Nicholas of Cusa.[16] The pioneer work of Figgis, admittedly only a general introduction, remains, in McIlwain's words, the "most brilliant and valuable summary extant." [17]

Despite the admitted importance of Conciliar theory, considerations such as these suggest making no general evaluation of its place in the history of European political thought until we know a good deal more about the political thinking of the indi-

---

14. McIlwain, *Growth*, pp. 326 ff.

15. G. H. Sabine, *A History of Political Theory* (2nd ed. New York, 1950), pp. 326–27.

16. A short monograph on Gerson—Carl Schäfer, *Die Staatslehre des Johannes Gerson* (Cologne, 1935)—constitutes something of an exception to this generalization. Nicholas of Cusa has attracted a good deal of attention. See Andreas Posch, *Die "Concordantia Catholica" des Nikolaus von Cusa* (Paderborn, 1930); Jean-Joseph Vilmain, *Les principes du droit public du Cardinal Nicholas de Cues* (Strasbourg, 1922); R. Schultz, *Die Staatsphilosophie des Nicholaus von Kues* (Meisenheim am Glan, 1948); Paul E. Sigmund, "Cusanus' *Concordantia*: A Re-Interpretation," *Political Studies, 10* (1962), 180–97, and now his *Nicholas of Cusa and Medieval Political Thought* (Cambridge, Mass., 1963).

17. McIlwain, *Growth*, p. 348 n. 2.

6

vidual Conciliarists themselves, about the sources of such thinking, and about the subsequent fate of their ideas. I have chosen, therefore, to analyze the political theory put forward by one of the most famous of these Conciliar thinkers—Pierre d'Ailly, scholar, diplomat, bishop and cardinal, philosopher, theologian, astronomer, geographer, and eminent protagonist, both in theory and practice, of Conciliar principles. Three main reasons dictated this choice: the first, that no complete study of his political theory or even of his ecclesiology has yet been attempted;[18] the second, that d'Ailly was a philosopher as well as a publicist and formulated his political ideas in such a way that they are relevant to any "rightly-ordained" political association and not merely to the Church or to the particular constitutional crisis which the Great Schism had engendered; the third, that these ideas were expressed in numerous tracts, both academic and publicistic, and exerted an enduring influence in the centuries which followed—not only, it seems, upon theories of ecclesiastical government.[19]

18. D'Ailly has not lacked biographers but no separate treatment of his ecclesiology exists and to date the most complete published examination of his political ideas has been the article of Roberts, "Pierre d'Ailly."

19. For the bulk and scope of d'Ailly's writings see below, pp. 13–14. For the subsequent printings of his works and the influence of his ideas see below, pp. 216 ff.

1.
Pierre d'Ailly:
Student, Churchman, Theologian

Pierre d'Ailly was born in 1350 of bourgeois parentage at Compiègne in the Ile de France.[1] Little or nothing is known of his childhood years but it is recorded that in 1364 he entered the University of Paris as a bursar of the College of Navarre. This college had been founded in 1304 by Jeanne de Navarre, wife of Philip IV, thus postdating the more famous Sorbonne, and with it during the following three centuries were to be associated a notable series of Conciliarists and Gallicans, among them d'Ailly himself and his pupil, Jean Gerson, as well as Jean Courtecuisse, John Major, Jacques Almain, and the famous Bishop Bossuet.

I

D'Ailly began his academic career as a student in the Faculty of Arts and as a member of the "French" nation,[2] and after becom-

1. This brief biographical sketch is based mainly upon the most recent biography, Salembier, *Cardinal.* See also the more recent sketch by A. Coville in *Dictionnaire de biographie française,* s. v. Ailly, Pierre de.

2. The University of Paris was composed of the four Faculties of Arts, Theology, Law, and Medicine. The Faculty of Arts consisted in turn of four "nations,"

ing a Bachelor of Arts in 1367 he taught for a year in that Faculty. In 1378, however, he was admitted to the higher Faculty of Theology and was faced with the successive hurdles of the long and arduous "postgraduate" course in theology. Like all of his fellows he was obliged to spend the first six years studying the Bible and the *Sentences* of Peter Lombard—the standard textbook of theology during the later Middle Ages—and after examination he was admitted to the rank of *baccalaurius cursor.* As a cursor, he now became a teacher of theology and was required to lecture on the Bible to the junior students of his own Faculty. The next rank, that of *baccalaurius sententiarius,* came in 1377, and with it the duty of lecturing on the *Sentences*—his commentary on each book being preceded by the requisite formal discourse known as the *principium.* In 1378, after he had finished his course on the *Sentences,* he was admitted to the rank of *baccalaurius formatus,* and in 1381, having battled his way through the necessary series of formal disputations, he was granted the *licentia docendi* and became a Doctor of Theology.[3] Already in 1372 he had been chosen as proctor of the "French" nation, and in the years that followed he became successively canon of Noyon (1381), rector of his old College of Navarre (1383), chaplain to the King (1389), and Chancellor of the University of Paris (1389).

The closing years of d'Ailly's theological studies and his entry into public life coincided, therefore, with the opening years of the Great Schism. Under pressure from the French king, Charles V, the University had recognized the Avignonese pontiff, but the "English" and "Picard" nations of the Faculty of Arts had chosen to remain neutral, and, as early as 1379, two members of the "English" nation—Conrad of Gelnhausen and Henry of Langenstein—had boldly advocated the summoning of a general

---

known as the French, the English, the Picard, and the Norman; none of the designations coincide with modern national affiliations.

3. These disputations were three in number and were known as the *Vesperiae,* the *Aulica,* and the *Resumptio.* As d'Ailly chose to discourse in his own disputations on matters concerning ecclesiastical polity we shall have occasion more than once to refer to them.

council to put an end to the Schism. With the death of Charles V in 1380 and the succession to the throne of a minor, the University itself shifted its position. In 1381 it openly indicated its preference for the Conciliar solution and in that year d'Ailly himself seems to have defended this position before the royal court.[4] Such a position was by no means in accord with the policy of the regent, Louis of Anjou, who hoped for Avignonese assistance in furthering his own ambitions in Italy, and it is perhaps because of this that d'Ailly retired for a while to his canonry at Noyon. During the course of the same year, nevertheless, in his *Epistola diaboli Leviathan,*[5] he once again advocated the Conciliar solution, and despite later shifts and hesitations this seems to have been the solution closest to his heart. He never seems to have wavered in his conviction of the superiority of the whole Church to the Pope, and in the years after 1403, when other solutions had failed and when the obduracy of the rival claimants was becoming increasingly apparent, he recurred once again to his earlier advocacy of the Conciliar position.

In the years that intervened, however, d'Ailly became one of the leading prelates of his day. During the course of his rise to fame, he fluctuated in his attitudes to the Avignonese Papacy and the problem of ending the Schism. In 1383 he returned to the University as Rector of Navarre and busied himself with matters academic until 1394, when, after a referendum had revealed it to be overwhelmingly the opinion of the University, he openly committed himself to supporting the *via cessionis,* or simultaneous abdication of the rival pontiffs, as the most practicable way for ending the Schism and the one most likely to succeed. This approach, adopted by the French court, served for the next few years as the focus of the national ecclesiastical policy, and led in 1398 to the unilateral French withdrawal of obedience from the Avignonese pontiff in an unsuccessful attempt to coerce him into abdicating.

4. Valois, *France, 1,* 340–41, has thrown some doubt upon d'Ailly's rôle in this matter.
5. This work appeared anonymously. It is to be found in Tschackert, *Ailli,* Appendix V, pp. [15]–[21].

D'Ailly himself, though sent to Avignon both by the University and the King, and charged on successive embassies with the task of securing the adoption of the via cessionis, seems to have become somewhat less than enthusiastic in his advocacy of the cause—possibly because of a succession of favors heaped upon him by the Avignonese popes. Only the refusal of the royal permission had prevented Clement VII from making him Bishop of Laon as early as 1389, and, to a series of minor benefices, Benedict XIII was able to add in 1395 the bishopric of Puy,[6] and in 1397 the more important bishopric of Cambrai. These favors were interpreted by d'Ailly's former colleagues at Paris as an attempt—regrettably successful—to purchase his support; and when he became Bishop of Puy at least one of the nations of the Faculty of Arts decided to exclude him from its meetings, especially those in which the ending of the Schism was to be discussed.[7] It is difficult to assess the extent to which such suspicions were justifiable, but it is certain that d'Ailly opposed the withdrawal of obedience in 1398, was active in bringing about a partial restoration of obedience in 1403, and was willing to speak in defense of Benedict XIII at the Council of Paris in 1406.

During the years 1399 to 1402 he withdrew from the French ecclesiastical and political scene and concerned himself with diocesan duties at Cambrai, devoting much of his attention to the implementation of wide-ranging reforms, anticipating in practice many of the ideas he was to include in the program of reform presented in 1416 at the Council of Constance. The end of 1402 brought renewed involvement in matters of high ecclesiastical policy, and though d'Ailly was still willing to defend Benedict XIII against his most violent detractors at Paris, his conviction of that pope's sincerity was gradually being eroded. The subsequent years of fruitless negotiations, negotiations in which he himself was deeply involved, finally led him in January 1408 to break with Benedict and to return to his own diocese. This break became definite in the course of the following year.

6. A diocese which d'Ailly never visited.
7. See Valois, *France*, 3, 70–71.

By that time, the collapse of negotiations between the Roman and Avignonese popes had led dissident cardinals from both camps to forswear their allegiance to their respective pontiffs and to summon a general council of the whole Church to meet at Pisa. This news d'Ailly had welcomed, and aligning himself formally with the dissident cardinals, he had set off for Pisa. He had sent ahead of him an important series of letters and suggestions, but he cannot be said to have played a prominent part at Pisa for he was absent on the business of the Council during the two fateful sessions which witnessed the attempted deposition of the Roman and Avignonese popes and the election of their successor, Alexander V. In the troubled years that followed, however, d'Ailly became increasingly prominent in ecclesiastical affairs. In 1411, John XXIII, successor to Alexander V, made him a cardinal, and there can be no doubt about the importance of his position when the Council of Constance met. His rôle during the early sessions of the Council was clearly a dominant one. From his opening sermon on December 2, 1414, until the election of the new pope, Martin V, in 1417, d'Ailly was involved in many, though not all, of the great events of the Council—and, notably, in the condemnations of John XXIII, of John Hus, and of the propositions of Jean Petit, the apologist of tyrannicide. At the close of the Council, Martin V sent him as a legate to Avignon, and there he died on August 9, 1420.[8]

Despite the extent of his involvement in practical affairs, d'Ailly had been able to write a great deal, and he left behind him over one hundred and seventy works—books, tracts, letters and sermons—concerning an astonishing variety of subjects.[9] The largest group of these is devoted to matters relating to the Schism, and sandwiched between this and quite a large group of philosophical and theological works are to be found works on Biblical matters—such as his *Epistola ad novos Hebraeos*—some rhetorical, pietistic and poetical works—such as his *Le jardin amoureux de l'âme dévote*—and an imposing set of tracts on

8. For the establishment of this exact date see Salembier, *Cardinal*, pp. 360–61.
9. The most recent and complete listing is that of Salembier, *Cardinal*, pp. 368–76.

13

geography and astronomy. This last set includes his *Imago mundi* (1410), perhaps the best known of all his works because of its alleged influence on Christopher Columbus,[10] and his *Exhortatio super kalendarii correctione* (1411), in which he advocated in vain the reform that was later to be adopted by Gregory XIII.

Our principal concern will be with his philosophical, theological, and publicistic works. Those devoted to purely philosophical matters are few in number, and with the possible exception of his *Tractatus de anima* are mere opuscules. His theological works are more numerous and more substantial, but one work— the *Quaestiones super primum, tertium et quartum Sententiarum*—stands out as the most complete and authoritative statement of his views. These philosophico–theological works were written during his early years as a teacher at Paris and present us with his general philosophical and theological positions and his fundamental views about political society as they stood in the years before he became personally involved in practical and theoretical problems of ecclesiastical politics. It should be possible, therefore, to distinguish those of his political views which were simply the product of his grappling with concrete problems from those which were more intimately related to his general philosophical and theological positions. It will, in any case, be advisable to devote some time at the outset to a brief examination of these positions.

II

In the nineteenth century, there used to be a tendency among historians of philosophy to regard the philosophical disputes of the whole medieval period as pivoting upon a single recurring problem, that of the status of universal concepts—that is to say, in more medieval terms, the problem of the precise relations between genera and species, on the one hand, and individuals, on the other; or again, to put the same question in a different way,

10. *Ymago mundi*, ed. and trans. Edmond Buron (Paris, 1930). The editor's introduction (*1*, 1–113) discusses the matter of this alleged influence.

the problem of the mode of existence to be ascribed to genera and species. Viewed in this light, the history of medieval philosophy tended to assume the character of a recurrent dialectic between the Realist and Nominalist schools, between those philosophers who claimed that universals possess something more than merely conceptual existence, and ascribed, therefore, some degree of extra-mental reality to them, and those who believed that only individuals truly exist and that universals correspond to no extra-mental reality. Thus the radical differences between the philosophies of the thirteenth and fourteenth centuries, respectively, were seen to flow from the familiar realist-nominalist divide; the thirteenth century distinguished by the triumph of moderate realism, and the fourteenth by the recrudescence of nominalism in the philosophy of those who followed the so-called *via moderna*.[1] Thus William of Ockham could be seen in opposition to Duns Scotus, in very much the same way as the early nominalist Roscelin had been placed in opposition to the famous realist, William of Champeaux.

The influence of this general approach to the history of medieval philosophy was most pervasive and it has left as its legacy the lingering belief that the fourteenth century was an age of destructive scepticism and irresponsible criticism. Against the background of such an interpretation, it is understandable that d'Ailly, admittedly a follower of Ockham, has customarily been regarded as above all one of the more eminent partisans of the revived nominalism and as a man undaunted by its destructive corollaries.[2] It is less easy, however, to understand Manser's representation of him as being, in some sense other than the merely chronological, a forerunner of Descartes, or the contention of Sertillanges that his views bordered on agnosticism.[3] Such in-

1. For a discussion of the *via moderna* see Etienne Gilson, *History of Christian Philosophy in the Middle Ages* (New York, 1955), pp. 489–540.

2. Salembier, *Alliaco*, pp. 144–45; Maurice de Wulf, *Histoire de la philosophie médiévale* (Paris, 1947), *3*, 150.

3. G. M. Manser, "Drei Zweifler auf dem Kausalitätsprinzip im XIV Jahrhundert," *Jahrbuch für Philosophie und spekulative Theologie*, 27 (Paderborn, 1912), 291 ff.; A. G. Sertillanges, *Traité de Dieu*, *1* (Revue des Jeunes edition of the *Summa theologiae*)—both cited in M. Patronnier de Gandillac, "Usage et valeur

terpretations, nevertheless, have been reiterated, and we have also been assured that d'Ailly is at once a follower of Ockham and an anticipator of Luther, an agnostic, a philosophical sceptic, and even an Averroist.[4] Indeed, it now seems that this truly many-sided thinker, so ill-treated by modern neo-Thomists, was not lacking even in Thomist sympathies. For it has recently been claimed that Thomist influence is apparent not only in the psychological foundations of his epistemology, but also in his teaching on the relation of truth and knowledge, with its rejection of the Averroist doctrine of the double truth.[5]

There is, clearly enough, considerable confusion and disagreement concerning the fundamental import of d'Ailly's theological and philosophical thought. No doubt some of this confusion can be ascribed to the continuing lack of any definitive treatment of his philosophy. Much of it, however, is the result not only of the pioneer stage in which historical study of fourteenth-century thought still lingers, but also of that whole anachronistic historical approach which strove to comprehend the diversity and novelty of late medieval philosophy in terms of the early scholastic disputes between realists and nominalists. Admittedly there is a radical difference between the thought of the thirteenth and fourteenth centuries, but this difference can hardly be subsumed under the traditional categories. The dominant characteristic of fourteenth-century thought, as Leff has correctly insisted, is not its nominalism—for that would be to put the philosophical cart before the theological horse—but rather its desire "to disengage faith from reason," [6] a desire shared by Ockham and the nominalists as well as by their realist predecessor, Duns Scotus. For both Ockham and Scotus lived "in very different circumstances

---

des arguments probables chez Pierre d'Ailly," *Archives d'hist. doct. et. litt. du M.A., 8* (1933), 44, notes 2 and 3. Cf. Salembier, *Alliaco,* pp. 150–51, 352; Tschackert, *Ailli,* pp. 303 ff.

4. Tschackert, *Ailli,* pp. 303 ff. Salembier accused d'Ailly of leaning toward the Averroist doctrine of the double truth (*Alliaco,* pp. 164–65, *Cardinal,* pp. 297–98); cf. Gandillac, p. 44.

5. Meller, *Studien,* pp. 11, 285–87.

6. Gordon Leff, *Medieval Thought from St. Augustine to Ockham* (Harmondsworth, Middlx., 1958), p. 258; see also his article, "The Fourteenth Century and the Decline of Scholasticism," *Past and Present, 9* (1956), 30–41.

from Abelard and William of Champeaux—in the aftermath of the 1277 condemnations and the conflict over Thomism." [7] It is, therefore, in the light of these events that their thought should be considered.

The condemnations, which denounced as contrary to the Christian faith a host of philosophical propositions, several of which were Thomistic, were promulgated by Etienne Tempier, Bishop of Paris, and Robert Kilwardby, Archbishop of Canterbury. In so acting they reflected a fear, already widespread among theologians, that the metaphysical necessitarianism of Aristotle and his Moslem commentators, Avicenna and Averroës, endangered the Christian doctrine of the freedom and omnipotence of God. The doctrinal act of 1277, as Gilson points out, traced the condemned errors to their very root, "namely, the Aristotelian identification of reality, intelligibility and necessity, not only in things, but first and above all in God." [8] The honeymoon of philosophy and theology was over, and this marked the beginning of the theological reaction that was to vindicate the freedom and omnipotence of God at the expense of the ultimate intelligibility of the world.[9] But though this may well explain the note of scepticism characteristic of so much of the philosophical endeavor of the fourteenth century, in what way does it

7. Leff, p. 260, where he also says: "Though Duns and Ockham worked from opposite poles, they devoted themselves to realigning faith and reason rather than to any single problem of cognition."

8. Gilson, *History*, p. 407. The whole of Part IX, pp. 385–427, is devoted to an analysis of the significance and effects of the condemnations.

9. This amounted to an abandonment of any attempt to reconcile the Greek conception of a necessarily existing universe, ruled by strict necessity, with the Biblical notion of a freely created world, ruled by a free and omnipotent divine will. Moslem thinkers had already faced the same problem and had adopted a comparable solution. Al Ash'ari (d. 936) and his followers vindicated the Semitic notion of God by adopting an atomistic view of the world as constituted of disjointed moments of time and points of space, connected together only by the will of God and possessing, therefore, no natural necessity. They held to this position so strictly that they were driven into a thorough-going occasionalism—see L. Gardet and M.-M. Anawati, *Introduction à la théologie musalmane*, Études de phil. méd., 37 (Paris, 1948), pp. 52–66. This viewpoint was also adopted by some Jewish thinkers—see Ernest Renan, *Averroës et l'Aerroisme* (Paris, 1861), p. 106, and Isaac Husik, *A History of Medieval Jewish Philosophy* (New York, 1958), p. xli.

throw any light on the nominalism of Ockham and his successors? A closer look at the condemned Greek views will serve to indicate the answer to this question.

Collingwood has told us that the Greeks regarded the universe as "saturated or permeated with mind," and that they did this because they drew an analogy "between the world of nature and the individual human being." For the individual comes to think of himself as a union of mind and body, the mind directing the body according to its own desires, and he goes on to think of nature as possessed of similar characteristics.[10] Plato sought to vindicate philosophically this pervasive belief in the presence of mind and therefore of intelligibility in the universe by postulating eternally subsisting "Forms," essences, or "Ideas," and by asserting (in the *Timaeus*) that these Ideas served as exemplars, patterns, or blue-prints in accordance with which the Demi-urge or World-Maker fashioned out of preexistent matter an intelligible world.[11] Early Christian thinkers disagreed among themselves concerning the extent to which such a doctrine was compatible with the account of creation contained in Genesis,[12] but at least from the time of St. Augustine onwards, Christian theologians constantly made use of it in their explanations of the creation of the world by God. The presence of intelligibility in the world demanded, they believed, that the creative act must be an intelligent one, and they went on to argue that if the creative act was to be an intelligent as well as a free act, then it must presuppose in the divine agent some intellectual model or exemplar. What they did, then, was to follow the Neo-Platonists—and, more particularly, the Jewish philosopher Philo of Alexandria—not only in denying the autonomous existence that Plato seemed to have ascribed to the Ideas, but also in "locating" these Ideas in the divine mind. The Ideas of Plato thus became the divine ideas. They were in no way regarded as distinct from

10. R. G. Collingwood, *Idea of Nature* (Oxford, 1945), pp. 3, 8.

11. *Timaeus*, esp. sec. 27–37.

12. Thus Irenaeus (b. ca. 140) could oppose to the Platonic Ideas the Christian doctrine of a free creation *ex nihilo*, whereas Eusebius of Caesaria (d. ca. 340) could affirm that the picture of creation in the *Timaeus* is similar to that contained in Genesis—see F. Copleston, *A History of Philosophy* (London, 1946 ff.), 2, Ch. 2, esp. 22 and 30.

God, but simply as being the eternal objects of the divine contemplation and the exemplars or patterns which God followed in the erection of the universe.[13]

This doctrine, consecrated by its association with the name of St. Augustine, was adopted by the vast majority of medieval theologians and occupied a central place in their thought. On this general point, Abelard was at one with Anselm, and Bonaventure with Aquinas. For our purposes, however, it must suffice to note two of its more important consequences. In the first place, if, for example, we are to regard man as having been created in accordance with God's idea of human nature and not simply by arbitrary fiat, then the natural moral law must similarly be regarded not as a mere mandate of the divine will, but rather as necessarily flowing from God's idea of human nature. In the second place, it is clear that this theory of the divine ideas entailed, or was entailed by,[14] some realist type of solution to the problem of universals. For if there were in fact no such entity as humanity or human nature, there would be no reason to postulate in God an idea or exemplar of human nature.

This doctrine of the divine ideas and metaphysic of essences raises some formidable difficulties for the Christian, and medieval theologians were, in fact, very careful to hedge it around with cautious qualifications.[15] But it is clear from some of the

13. Thus Augustine can say that the Ideas are "certain archetypal forms or stable and unchangeable reasons of things, which were not themselves formed but are contained in the divine mind eternally and are always the same" (*De Ideis*, 2; as cited in Copleston, *History*, 2, 73). For a recent discussion of the changes which the theory underwent in the Hellenistic period, see Harry A. Wolfson, "Extradeical and Intradeical Interpretations of Platonic Ideas," *Journal of the History of Ideas*, 22 (1961), 3–32.

14. Modern analytic philosophers have naturally preferred this latter formulation—cf. Stuart Hampshire, *Spinoza* (Harmondsworth, Middlx., 1951), pp. 218–19: "Most metaphysical systems can be in part interpreted as exaggerated projections upon reality of some obsessive difficulty of logic and of the interpretation of the forms of language . . . . Plato's metaphysical theory of a real world of Ideas or Forms which he contrasts with the actually perceived world of phenomena, has its logical root (or one of them) in a puzzle about the use of general names and abstract terms."

15. Thus Aquinas "was careful to state it in such a way as not to imply that there are ontologically separate ideas in God, a doctrine which would impair the divine simplicity" (Copleston, *History*, 2, 73).

19

propositions condemned in 1277 that they had not been careful enough.[16] Gilson has spoken of Ockham's thought as being a post-1277 theology "in a more than chronological sense," and as being dominated "by the first words of the Christian creed: I believe in one God, the Father Almighty." It is hardly surprising, therefore, that Ockham should have rejected the doctrine of the divine ideas not only as dissolving the unity of the Christian God into a heathen multiplicity,[17] but also as implying a qualification of the divine omnipotence and freedom. Nor is it surprising that he should have viewed the divine liberty as similarly compromised by the realist connection of the natural moral law with the doctrine of the divine ideas, for the moral law, just as the whole of creation, must, he insisted, be utterly contingent upon the unhampered fiat of the divine will. And believing this, he had no choice but to dismiss the doctrine of the divine ideas and the whole related "metaphysic of essences" as "a non-Christian invention which had no place in a Christian theology and philosophy.[18]

Respect for the authority of St. Augustine, however, softened the impact of this dismissal, for Ockham was careful to retain the language of the traditional doctrine even while emptying it of its traditional content. It is permissible, if we will, to speak of the divine ideas, but when we do so, we must remember that we are speaking, not of any universal ideas, but merely of the ideas which God has of creatures themselves. For since outside the mind only individual things are producible, these divine ideas must be ideas of actual or possible individual creatures. They are, in fact, only individual creatures *as known by God*,[19] and, thus conceived, constitute no threat either to the simplicity

16. Gilson, *History*, pp. 728–29, lists some of these propositions. One of them is: "That God necessarily produces what immediately follows from him." The direct quotations following in the text are on pp. 410, 498.

17. He was willing to admit no plurality or distinction in God except those necessitated by the doctrine of the Trinity.

18. Copleston, *History*, 3, 51.

19. Ockham, *Sent.*, I, dist. 35, qu. 5, G. This whole question is devoted to the problem. For a useful analysis of Ockham's arguments see Lagarde, *Naissance, 5,* 101–24.

of God or to the untrammelled freedom of His act of creation.[20]

Such a position involves, as Georges de Lagarde points out, something more than a simple elimination of the Platonic Ideas. It entails a denial of the necessity of postulating any "bond of participation" between created things and "the first intelligent principle which is God." The Christian faith teaches us that things are created by God, but we are not required to believe that they in any sense "participate in the divine being" or "the divine intelligible" or that any "metaphysical bond links them with God." This position consorts very profoundly with Ockham's belief that the world is a collection of singular existents "isolated in the absoluteness of their existence." [21] It is a stark world in which a free and omnipotent God boldly confronts, without any *necessary* intermediaries, the multiplicity of singular entities which He has created and which are radically contingent upon Him. Hence the dismissal of any necessary relations or connections in nature between distinct things, even between cause and effect.[22] Hence, too, the belief that if we are to know the order of the world we can only examine what is de facto, for being completely dependent on the divine choice it cannot be deduced by any a priori arguments.[23] Thus, linked with Ockham's fundamental insistence on the omnipotence of God and at least in part dependent upon it is, not only his nominalism, but also his empiricism.

20. As L. Baudry says, Ockham was determined to deny that "les essences eternelles constituent une sorte de monde qui s'impose à la raison de Dieu et sur lequel se règle son action creatrice."—*Le Tractatus de Principiis Theologiae attribué à G. d'Occam*, Études de phil. méd., *23* (Paris, 1936), 21.

21. Lagarde, *Naissance*, *5*, 120–21, 124.

22. Ockham, *Quodlibeta septem una cum tractatu de sacramento altaris* (Strasbourg, Jordanus de Quedlinburg, 1491), Quodl. VI, qu. 2 and 6; *Opus nonaginta dierum* (Lyons, Jean Trechsel, 1495), cap. 95 at *Hereticum est dicere omnia de necessitate evenire.*

23. And God often does by a greater number of means what he could do by fewer so that not even Ockham's famous razor, his principle of economy, is of assistance here. Hence Paul Vignaux, *Philosophie au Moyen Age* (Paris, 1958), pp. 180–81: "Ne mettons pas le principe d'économie de pensée sur le même plan que le principe de la toute-puissance, maître en ontologie: ce qui est règle de notre intellect ne l'est point de l'action divine."

In the light of this approach to Ockham's general philosophical principles,[24] the positions of his nominalist, or, more properly, his *voluntarist* successors—among whom d'Ailly should certainly be numbered—become less inaccessible. In their day the tocsin had clearly not ceased to sound, for in the opening pages of his commentary on the *Sentences* of Peter Lombard, d'Ailly himself refers to the condemnations of 1277.[25] The basic tenet of his thought, as of Ockham's, is the unity, freedom, and omnipotence of God. Witness to this are his assertions of the familiar principle that God can do anything that does not entail a formal contradiction,[26] and also his reiterated attacks on those "ignorant jurists" who betray their unfamiliarity with Holy

24. This is the approach which has become increasingly common among recent historians of later medieval thought. Gilson, Copleston, and Vignaux all incline to it (Vignaux with some qualifications), but its most firm exponents have been Baudry and, more recently, Heiko A. Oberman, "Some Notes on the Theology of Nominalism with Attention to Its Relation to the Renaissance," *Harvard Theological Review, 53* (1960), 47–76. Even Philotheus Boehner, who once firmly rejected the charge of having endorsed Baudry's characterization of Ockham's philosophy as a "philosophy of the divine omnipotence," has not proved to be unsympathetic to this general approach—see the introduction to his edition *Ockham: Selected Philosophical Writings* (London, 1957), pp. xvii–xxii, and his *"In propia causa:* A Reply to Professor Pegis," in *Collected Articles in Ockham* (New York, 1958), p. 302. For a very different point of view see Ernest Moody, *The Logic of William of Ockham* (London, 1935), and George Lindbeck, "Nominalism and the Problem of Meaning as Illustrated by Pierre d'Ailly on Predestination and Justification," *Harvard Theological Review, 52* (1959), 43–60. Lindbeck's is the more sweeping but less convincing statement. For some criticisms of it see my article, "Pierre d'Ailly and the Absolute Power of God: Another Note on the Theology of Nominalism," *Harvard Theological Review, 56* (1963), 59–73.

25. *Princ. in I Sent.*, E, F. 21v, where he cites the condemned article: "Quod creatio non est possibilis, quamvis contrarium tenendum sit secundum fidem"; cf. P. Mandonnet, *Siger de Brabant et l'Averroism Latin au XIIIme siècle* (2nd ed., Louvain, 1908), 2, 189, art. 189.

26. *Sent.* I, qu. 13, art. 1, C, f. 159r: "omne quod fieri non implicat contradictionem deus possit de sua absoluta potentia facere"; cf. Ockham, *Sent.* II, qu. 8, O. Boehner, *Ockham: Selected Philosophical Writings*, pp. xvii–xxii, regards this insistence that "God can do (or make or create) everything which does not involve a contradiction" as the fundamental "guiding principle" of Ockham's philosophy. He points out that it was because of this that Ockham was so badly in need of a "refined and powerful logic" since he was "always looking beyond facts and the actualities towards absolute being and absolute possibility."

Writ by imagining that God is limited or in any way bound by "created laws." [27] Similarly, his preoccupation with the unity and simplicity of God, and his rejection—Trinitarian questions apart—of any distinction in God, either real or formal, whether it be between the divine intellect and will [28] or between the divine essence and ideas.[29] The only distinction that can validly be drawn between creatures, he says, is a *real* distinction between things that are separate or separable in such a way that one cannot in any way be said to be the other. Such a distinction cannot be applied to God, and if the Scotistic formal distinction which is inapplicable to creatures is valid in the special case of the Trinity, it cannot, properly speaking, reveal any other non-identity in God.[30] D'Ailly rejects, therefore, the old argument that the existence of distinct creatures presupposes the ex-

27. *Sent.* I, qu. 12, art. 2, J, f. 147r: "Unum signum est magnae ruditatis et ineruditionis in scripturis facere magnam difficultatem in hoc, sicut communiter faciunt rudes juristae qui imaginantur Deum esse obligatum legibus creatis."

28. *Princ. in II Sent.*, F, f. 28(B)r: "Voluntas divina et divinus intellectus seu ratio sunt omnibus modis idem, tam formaliter quam realiter, nec distinguuntur inter se aliqualiter"; cf. *Princ. in I Sent.*, R, f. 26r; I *Sent.*, qu. 6, art. 2, L–M, f. 97r.

29. *Sent.* I, qu. 6, art. 3, U, f. 100r: "Essentia divina est unica et non plurificabilis, *nisi in Tribus suppositur* . . . . Unde unimaginabile est quod divina essentia esset realiter plures ideae creaturarum, nisi ponendo illas ideas esse distinctas formaliter. Quae distinctio formalis supra satis reprobata est."

The "formal distinction" referred to is, of course, that of Duns Scotus. For an analysis, see M. J. Grajewski, *The Formal Distinction of Duns Scotus* (Washington, D. C., 1944).

30. *Sent.* I, qu. 6, art. 1, B–C, f. 94r: "Essentia divina tam idem est personae vel relationi sive personali proprietati quod idem est sibi ipsi . . . . Secunda conclusio est quod inter essentiam et personam vel relationem sive proprietatem personalem non est aliqua non idemptitas quam proprie debeamus vocare distinctionem formalem . . . quia inimaginabile est quod sit aliqua non idemptitas sive distinctio nisi plurium, et [in]imaginabilis est pluralitas nisi rerum"; E, f. 95r: "quaecumque distinguuntur realiter sunt plures res"; F, 95r–95v: "distinctio . . . ex natura rei potest intelligi dupliciter. Uno modo proprie, et tunc distinctio ex natura rei non est nisi plurium realitatum quarum una non est alia . . . . Alio modo improprie [etc.]. Primo modo, nulla res distinguitur ab aliquo quod est ipsa, et sic essentia non distinguitur a persona vel relatione etc. . . . Talis distinctio formalis nunquam est in creaturis. Patet quia ibi nunquam una res est plures, et quaelibet earum, sed bene in divinis, *nec est ibi concedenda nisi ubi credita nos compellunt*" (italics mine). Cf. *Princ. in II Sent.*, F, ff. 28(B)r–28(B)v.

istence of some real or formal distinction in the Creator, commenting that to the question "why He [God] produces distinct things, I say that His liberty suffices for a reason." [31]

It is hardly surprising, then, that on the specific question of the divine ideas, d'Ailly should refer us to Ockham's *Sentences*. Ockham, he tells us, handled this matter "very nicely" (*valde pulchre*),[32] and d'Ailly's own teaching amounts to a reiteration of the position adopted by his chosen master. Accordingly, respect for the authority of St. Augustine dictates the retention of the language of the traditional doctrine, but careful qualifications remove its sting. There is but one God and the unity of the divine essence resists all attempts to dissolve it into a profane plurality. Thus we cannot properly speak of the divine ideas as being *things* really present in God. St. Augustine did not mean to suggest this, and even had he done so, it would be proper not to follow him in this matter, but rather, with reverence, to reject his teaching.[33] The divine ideas, then, can only be said to be in God in an intellectual fashion, just as things known by us can be said to be in our own minds. For they are, in fact, nothing other than creatures. They are simply actual or possible creatures as known by God.[34]

This position involves, furthermore, a firm commitment to nominalism. Being simply actual or possible creatures as known

31. *Sent.* I, qu. 6, art. 1, S, f. 99v: "Idem et omnino indistinctum potest producere distincta, nec ex distinctione productorum potest concludi in deo distinctio realis, nec potest concludi in deo distinctio formalis rationum causalium. . . . Et si quaeras quare producit distincta, dico quod sufficit pro ratione ejus libertas." Gilson, *History*, p. 407, points out that one of the propositions condemned in 1277 was that God, being one, cannot immediately and freely produce a plurality of effects "quod ab uno primo agente non potest esse multitudo effectuum."

32. *Sent.* I, qu. 6, art. 3, T, f. 99v.

33. Ibid., CC, f. 101v: "non intendit Augustinus quod omnes ideae sunt in deo realiter et proprie. Et sic hoc intellexisset Augustinus non esset in hoc sequendus, sed cum reverentia negandus."

34. Ibid., Y, f. 100v: "in deo non sunt plures ideae . . . realiter et proprie, sed bene sunt in eo infinitae intellectualiter et objective . . . . Patet quia . . . infinitae sunt ideae sicut sunt infinitae res producibiles, et illae non sunt in deo, realiter et proprie, sed solum intellectualiter et objective, scilicet tanquam quaedam cognita ab ipso, et non aliomodo"; cf. U, f. 100r: "ipsius creaturae idea sit creatura."

by God, the divine ideas can only be ideas of singulars and not of universals, for despite Plato only singular entities exist outside the mind and there are no universals.[35] The firmness of this commitment becomes very clear when d'Ailly attempts to handle the doctrine of the Trinity. In all his attacks upon the postulation of any distinction in God, he was careful to make an exception of the Trinity,[36] but he is now constrained, nevertheless, to admit that the doctrine is difficult to defend.[37] This does not, however, dispose him to embrace any form of realism, for he tells us that those who believe in the reality of universals "are not worthy of the name of philosophers." Indeed, to accept realism would be to adopt a position harder to sustain than the doctrine of the Trinity, for the authority of the faith, decisive in the one question, is irrelevant to the other.[38]

D'Ailly presents us with a universe similar, in its broad outlines, to that of Ockham. The metaphysic of essences banished, we are left with an utterly free God and a fragmented world of isolated singular entities radically contingent upon Him. And, as in Ockham's case, this entails the acceptance of some form of empiricism. It is not by chance that two of d'Ailly's favorite phrases are *experientia docet* and *patet inductive*,[39] for if one believes, as he does, that the order of the world depends entirely on the divine

35. Ibid., Z, f. 100v: "Ideae solum sunt singularium. Patet quia sola singularia sunt [ad] extra producibilia et nulla alia. Et si Plato aliter senserit, non eum in hoc sequendus, nec in hoc eum approbat Augustinus . . . . Ideae non sunt universalium. Patet quia nulla sunt—nisi ponatur quod universalia sint quaedam res in anima simpliciter existentes rebus extra communes et per praedicationem universales."

36. See above, n. 29, p. 23.

37. *Princ. in II Sent.*, F, f. 28(B)r: [The proposition that] voluntas divina et intellectus divinus seu ratio non sunt omnibus modis idem sed distinguuntur formaliter est ita difficilis ad sustinendi, sicut positio de trinitate."

38. *Sent.* I, qu. 5, art. 2, R, f. 89v: "Concedentes aliquod unum esse plura individua unius generis vel speciei non sunt digni vocari philosophi . . . . Aliquod genus vel speciem aliquam esse realiter plura individua et quodlibet illorum est ita difficile ad sustinendum sicut essentiam divinam esse tres personas et quamlibet illarum. Immo videtur aliquo modo difficilius quia fides non ponit personas distingui essentialiter, et tamen duo individua ejusdem speciei distinguuntur essentialiter. Et tamen ad hoc non cogit auctoritas fidei, immo forte magis ad oppositum, ut posset declarari."

39. See, for example, the tract *Utrum conscientia erronea excuset a culpa*, in Dupin, *1*, 637 and 639.

choice, and if one denies the existence of any metaphysical bond between things, there can be no hope of deducing that order a priori. There is, he tells us, no analytic link between cause and effect. Every secondary cause acts contingently.[40] Everything that the divine will produces indirectly through the agency of secondary causes, it could produce directly itself,[41] and "God does many things by a greater number of means that he could do by fewer." [42] Gandillac is correct, therefore, when he concludes that the very manner in which d'Ailly handles the divine ideas "forces him to see in nature, that is, in the realm of secondary causes, merely a relative order which can be the object only of empirical inductions." [43]

Such a view of the universe might also be expected to commit a theologian to a fideistic position, or even to some form of occasionalism.[44] Not only, as we shall see, did d'Ailly avoid occasionalism, but he was also far from rejecting the use of reason in theology and specifically condemned those "imprudent Catholics" who adopted a fideistic position even on a dogma as difficult as the Trinity.[45] No doubt this may seem somewhat inconsistent, for what can the human reason tell us of God when God has been set in somber contradistinction to His creatures, and the world stripped of its ultimate intelligibility? But the confusion which has arisen on this point disappears when due value is accorded to two fundamental distinctions which d'Ailly drew. The first concerns the will of God. The second concerns the reason of man.

40. *De libertate creaturae rationalis,* in Dupin, *1,* 632: "Quaelibet causa secunda, sive libera, sive non libera, aeque contingenter agit."

41. *Princ. in I Sent.,* K. f. 23v: "Notandum est quod sicut voluntas divina quicquid potest producere, mediante causa secunda, potest producere se sola, sic ipse de potentia absoluta posset rationalem creaturam obligare se sola."

42. *Sent.* I, qu. 9, art. 3, QQ, f. 129v: "Dico quod deus multa facit per plura quae posset facere per pauciora, nec hoc est frustra."

43. Gandillac, p. 87.

44. As in the case of the Moslem thinkers cited above, II, n. 9, p. 17.

45. *Sent.* I, qu. 5, art. 3, X, f. 91r–91v: "Sequitur quod valde utile est studere in materia trinitatis . . . . Immo apparet blasphemia quorundam imperitorum catholicorum, maxime juristarum, prelatorum et aliorum, qui dicunt inutile esse de hac materia disputare, sed sufficit simpliciter credere. Sed anathema sit qui hoc dixerit."

D'Ailly distinguished, in the first place, between the *absolute* and the *ordained* powers of God (*potentia absoluta* and *potentia ordinata*). Lest he be accused of inconsistency, it should be noted that he assures us that "this is not to say that there are in God two powers, one absolute and the other ordained." It is, rather, merely a way of speaking about God's modes of action, and thus "God is said to be able to do by His absolute power what He can do simply and absolutely." In other words, when we consider the power of God in this way, we are considering it without keeping in mind either the truths made known to us by revelation or the indications apparent in the order of nature; so considered, it must be regarded as "limited" only by the principle of non-contradiction. When, on the other hand, we speak of God as acting according to His ordained power, we can mean two things. In the first place, and more strictly speaking, we can mean that so long as God permits to endure the presently-ordained world-order, He can do only those things which by His ordination are to be done. In the second place, and less narrowly, we can mean that God may do anything that His absolute power permits Him to do, provided only that it does not contradict any truth revealed in the Sacred Scriptures.[46] Of these two *ordained* modes of divine action, which might be called the

---

46. *Sent.* I, qu. 13, art. 1, D, f. 159r: The question is: "Utrum omne possibile fieri, sive omne quod fieri non implicat contradictionem deus possit de sua absoluta potentia facere," and in replying d'Ailly posits several distinctions. Thus: "Tertia distinctio est circa istum terminum *potentia absoluta* . . . . Deum posse aliquid facere solet dupliciter intelligi: uno modo secundum *potentiam absolutam*, alio modo secundum *potentiam ordinatam*—non quod in deo sint duae potentiae, una absoluta et alia ordinata, sed deus dicitur illud posse de potentia absoluta quod simpliciter et absolute potest. Et sic intelligitur deus omnipotens et de tali potentia semper loquar in praesenti articulo . . . . Sed deum aliquid posse de potentia ordinata potest dupliciter intelligi: uno modo stricte, quod potest stante sua ordinatione qua aeternaliter voluit se sic vel sic esse facturum, et sic solum potest illa quae ipse ordinavit se facturum; alio modo potest intelligi magis large, quod potest stante veritate legis seu scripturae divinae. Et sic possibile ordinate potest dici illud quod est possibile absolute et non obviat alicui veritate legis ordinatae vel scripturae sacrae." This distinction was by no means the monopoly of d'Ailly or even of the nominalists, but Oberman, "Some Notes on the Theology of Nominalism," pp. 55–56, has correctly insisted upon its central position in nominalist theology. It crops up again and again in d'Ailly's works even in a discussion of the possibility of human knowledge of the end of the world—see *Sermo de quadruplici adventu domini*, in *Sermones*, f. t5r.

natural and supernatural ordained orders,[47] the natural is more stringent than the supernatural because it imposes greater restrictions on the absolute power of God. There are things impossible by the natural ordained order which are possible by the supernatural, because they are possible by God's absolute power and not excluded by any divine revelation. For something that is contrary to the divine ordination is not necessarily forbidden by the Scriptures, but the converse always holds true.[48]

This teaching is not as complex as it may at first appear to be. What d'Ailly is in fact saying is this: that God's absolute power, subject though it can be to no limitation, *normally* expresses itself, nevertheless, in accordance with the supernatural or natural order which has been ordained. Thus, as Christians, we must believe that God guarantees to fulfill the divine promises contained in revelation, and, even as mere philosophers, we can safely assume (though not with the certitude that only revelation can ensure) that the order apparent in nature betrays certain constant rules according to which God will *normally* act. The big reservation assumed in all this, and underlined by the use of such qualifications as "by the ordained law" (*de lege ordinata*) or "by the common course of nature" (*de communi cursu naturae*),[49] is that God did not ordain the present economy in any necessary fashion, and, of His absolute freedom and power, can always transcend it, as He does in the case of miracles.[50] For once it is admitted that God can Himself directly effect, of His absolute power, whatever He normally effects indirectly by means of secondary causes,[51] it must also be admitted, for example, that He can produce in us an intuition of a non-existing

47. The terminology is that suggested by Gandillac, p. 57, n. 1.

48. *Sent.* I, qu. 13, art. 1, D, f. 159v: "Quia quicquid obviat scripturae sacrae repugnat ordinationi divinae, sed non e converso."

49. *Sent.* I, qu. 12, art. 3, CC, f. 153v: *De libertate creaturae rationalis*, in Dupin *1*, 632; cf. also *Sent.* IV, qu. 2, art. 2, N (*de lege communi ordinata*); *Sent.* I, qu. 9, art. 3, JJ (*stante ordinationi dei*).

50. Thus although fire is normally the cause of heat it is not so necessarily but only in a contingent fashion, for God can always suspend the operation of the laws of nature, as indeed he did in the case of Mishach, Shadrach, and Abednego, whom King Nebuchadnezzar committed to the flames of the furnace, but who emerged unscathed. *Sent.* IV, qu. 1, art. 1, E, f. 185r.

51. See above, n. 41, p. 26.

object; [52] or, in the moral order, that he can obligate us directly, and not as He normally does, by means of some revealed law; [53] or again, in the order of salvation, that He can save men without an infusion of supernatural grace, even though it is true to say that "by the ordained law" the possession of such infused grace is necessary for salvation.[54]

The echoes of this fundamental distinction between the absolute and ordained powers of God reverberate throughout d'Ailly's theology and are to be heard even in the more remote reaches of his philosophy, impinging upon his political thinking both directly [55] and also by means of his ethical doctrines and his teaching on the natural law.[56] It is in his theory of knowledge, however, that these echoes are loud enough to generate the second important distinction with which we are concerned. This distinction—between "absolute evidence" (*evidentia absoluta*) and "conditioned evidence" (*evidentia conditionata vel secundum quid*)—is, by implication, somewhat ambivalent in that it serves both to restrict and to enhance the rôle of reason. Those who have accused d'Ailly of fideism and scepticism have done so because they have concentrated almost exclusively upon its negative implications. D'Ailly ascribes absolute evidence only to such knowledge as is true under any circumstances, even in the event that God, of His absolute power, intervenes to suspend His ordained economy.[57] The realm of this type of knowledge is

52. *Sent.* I, qu. 3, art. 1, M, f. 72v: "Notitia intuitiva tam sensitiva quam intellectiva potest simpliciter et absolute esse de re non existente; probatur . . . quia omnis res absoluta distincta loco et subjecto ab alia re absoluta potest per divinam potentiam absolutam existere sine illa."

53. *Princ. in I Sent.*, K, f. 23v: "Notandum est quod sicut voluntas divina quicquid potest producere mediante causa secunda potest producere se sola, sic ipsa de potentia absoluta posset rationalem creaturam obligare se sola. . . . Sed tamen ipsa de potentia ordinata non posset rationalem creaturam obligare nisi mediante aliqua lege creata."

54. *Sent.* I, qu. 9, art. 2, H, f. 188r: "Prima conclusio, nullus potest esse amicus dei de lege ordinata non habendo in se aliquam qualitatem infusam, quae sit charitas vel gratia. Secunda conclusio, aliquis potest esse amicus dei de potentia absoluta non habendo aliquam qualitatem infusam, quae sit charitas vel gratia."

55. See below, Ch. 3.

56. See below, Ch. 6.

57. *Sent.* I, qu. 1, art. 1, E, f. 44r: "Dico quod duplex est evidentia: quaedam est *evidentia absoluta,* qualis est evidentia primi principii vel reducibilis ad eam.

clearly extremely restricted. The only "limitation" on the absolute power of God is the principle of non-contradiction; therefore the type of proposition possessing absolute evidence can only be one the rejection of which would violate that "first principle." For example, it would be contradictory to suggest that God, even by a miracle, could bring it about that one should be made cold by warmth, or that one should be deceived in the apprehension of one's own existence.[58]

It follows, therefore, that by far the greater part of knowledge, from that of the existence of the world to that of the existence of God, cannot be absolutely evident to us. But it can, d'Ailly assures us, possess a conditioned or relative evidence, or at least be probable to us in natural reason.[59] Such knowledge is valid or

---

Alia est *evidentia conditionata,* qualis est evidentia nostri ingenii quae est circa primam. Evidentia absoluta simpliciter potest describi quod est assensus verus sine formidine causatus naturaliter, quo non est possibile intellectum assentire et in sic assentiendo decipi vel errare."

58. *Sent.* I, qu. 1, art. 1, O, f. 48r: "Aliqua humana notitia de necessario et impossibili aliter se habere, sicut de primo principio et similibus est infallibilis. Patet quia non stat ipsam esse et aliter esse quam significat, nec est possibile talem notitiam aliter significare . . . . Et ideo licet Deus posset ipsam facere non esse aut non significare, tamen non potest facere eam significare oppositum sui significati quomodo significat, sicut quod non posset facere quod caliditas frigefaceret seu produceret frigiditatem. Tertia est quod aliqua humana noticia de aliquo contingenti vero est infallibilis. Puta noticia qua scio me esse vivere"; cf. ibid., E, f. 44r.

59. *Sent.* I, qu. 1, art. 1, E, f. 44r: "Evidentia autem secundum quid potest describi quod est assensus verus sine formidine causatus naturaliter, quo non est possibile, *stante dei influentia generali et nullo facto miraculo,* intellectum assentire et in sic assentiendo decipi vel errare"; ibid., F, f. 44v: "Evidentia secundum quid seu conditionata vel ex suppositione, scilicet: *stante dei influentia generali et cursu naturae solito nullo facto miraculo"* (italics mine). See also *Sent.* I, qu. 3, art. 3, DD, f. 78r, where d'Ailly defines *ratio naturalis* as "rationem sumptam ex hiis quae nobis apparent de communi cursu naturae," and adds: "sic ergo sumendo, patet quod multae rationes naturales possunt fieri et factae sunt a philosophis concludentes tantum unum deum esse, licet *non evidenter tamen probabiliter* et probabilius quam posset concludi oppositum" (italics mine). Gandillac, p. 47, incorrectly equates *ratio naturalis* with *evidentia conditionata;* this is to overlook the difference between probability and evidence, and d'Ailly himself warns us that "quantumcunque augeantur rationes probabiles in apparentia, nunquam posset generare certitudinem aequalem certitudini noticiae evidentis, igitur talis est certitudinis infinitae" (*Sent.* I, qu. 1, art. 1, A, f. 42v); cf. art. 3, RR, f. 58v. For the precise meaning attached to "probable" see *Sent.*

possesses a probable validity only in the present economy, or in other words may not be proof against a possible incursion of the absolute power of God. Nevertheless, it is only this fundamental consideration of the divine omnipotence that forces us to ascribe to the information communicated to us by the senses merely a relative validity,[60] and we are not, therefore, entangled in any stultifying scepticism. Miracles apart, and given the common course of nature, we have no rational grounds for doubting such relative evidence. Foolish indulgence of such a doubt would only serve to betray us into many absurdities and to destroy all possibility of reasoning about the world of nature.[61]

We should not, then, expect all truths to possess the highest evidence. Taken together, the realms of absolute and conditioned evidence cover a broad area and embrace many degrees of evidence, for evident propositions possess greater or lesser validity in direct proportion to their greater or lesser intimacy with the first principle.[62] The realm of absolute evidence may be a narrow one, but that of relative or conditioned evidence is

---

I, qu. 1, art. 2, Z, ff. 52r–52v. Gandillac also misinterprets *lumen naturale*, a related term, by equating it with *evidentia absoluta*, whereas d'Ailly himself defines it as "lumen sive cognitionem sine errore intellectui possibilem de communi cursu naturae"—viz.: only in the presently-ordained economy (*Sent.* I, qu. 3, art. 3, DD, f. 78r).

60. *Sent.* I, qu. 1, art. 1, F, f. 44r: "Tertia conclusio est quod impossibile est viatorem aliquid extrinsecum ad eo sensibile evidenter cognoscere esse evidentia simpliciter et absoluta, sed bene evidentia secundum quid et conditionata . . . quia quicquid deus potest facere mediante causa secunda, vel mediantibus causis secundis, potest per seipsum."

61. *Sent.* I, qu. 1, art. 1, F, f. 44v: "loquendo de evidentia secundum quid seu conditionata vel ex suppositione . . . talia possunt esse nobis sufficienter evidentia sic quod de ipsis non habemus rationabiliter dubitare. Probatur hoc, quia stante dei influentia etc. non stat talia nobis apparere et non sic esse. Unde quamvis talis apparentia possit esse, ipsis objectis non existentibus, per potentiam dei absolutam, tamen propter hoc non habemus rationabiliter dubitare. Nam ex hoc multa inconvenientia et absurda sequerentur . . . . Secundo sequitur quod non posset sufficienter inferri ex una re alia, nex ex causa posset concludi effectus, nec e contra. Et sic perirent omnes demonstrationes naturales."

62. *Sent.* I, qu. 1, art. 1, K, f. 46v: "de facto, non est necesse evidentiam de aliquo esse summam. Immo, in evidentia sunt gradus quia primum principium est evidentissimum, et deinde alia magis vel minus secundum quod magis vel minus appropinquant ad primum principium."

31

much wider, and wider still is the region beyond it in which the probable or dialectical arguments of natural reason hold sway. It is in these second and third zones that we may rediscover discussions of many issues which d'Ailly had banished from the sphere of absolute evidence. Some of these issues were a specific rejection of occasionalism,[63] arguments for the existence of God, and rational corroborations of many of the central articles of the Christian faith, including, appropriately enough, the divine liberty itself.[64]

This treatment of d'Ailly's philosophical and theological positions, while it has tried to avoid the arbitrary, has certainly not been inclusive. It has, indeed, been extremely selective. The criterion on which certain aspects of d'Ailly's thought have been singled out for examination has been simply their relevance to his political ideas. Georges de Lagarde has made a formidable case for believing that Ockham's political thinking responded, in more than one of its phases, to the profound exigencies of his nominalism.[65] In the first place, then, it is important that we should at least be alive to the possibility that d'Ailly's denial of any metaphysical foundation to universal concepts, and his concomitant reduction of the world to an agglomeration of singular entities, utterly distinct from one another, may have exercised a corresponding influence upon his political thinking. In the second place, it is ethics which forms the buffer state between the-

63. He does this by distinguishing between *natural* and *voluntary* causality. The latter, being wholly and immediately dependent upon the will of God, is proper to the sacraments but not to the natural world (*Sent.* IV, qu. 1, art. 1, D–F, ff. 184v–185v). For a full discussion, see Gandillac, pp. 70–72.

64. See Gandillac, pp. 72–84. Thus d'Ailly can say (*Sent.* I, qu. 1, art. 2, V, f. 50v): "naturaliter possibile est viatorum de multis veritatibus theologicis habere opinionem. Probatur: naturaliter possibile est viatorem de illis veritatibus habere opinionem ad quas probandas naturaliter potest habere rationes dyalecticas seu probabiles inducentes ad assentiendum intellectum indifferentem; sed sic est de multis veritatibus theologicis." Hence (*Sent.* I, qu. 13, art. 1, J, f. 161v): "probabile est naturali ratione quod quicquid deus agit, ipse agit libere. Patet quia nobilissimus modus agendi, scilicet per intellectum et voluntatem, est deo attribuendus. Ergo deus agi libere."

65. Lagarde, *Naissance,* 5 and 6, esp. 5, Ch. 6.

ology and metaphysics on the one hand and political philosophy on the other; and the distinction between the absolute and ordained powers of God occupied so fundamental a position in d'Ailly's thought that it informed the whole character of his ethical teaching.[66] In the third place, an appreciation of his related distinction between the spheres of absolute and conditioned evidence is necessary if we are to know what exact status d'Ailly the philosopher can have accorded to the ideas expressed in the writings of d'Ailly the politician and publicist. Of the several types of knowledge which he distinguishes, the narrowest—that possessing an absolute evidence—can clearly claim priority. Of the others, that revealed to us by faith is prior to that which is merely probable in natural reason, for the certitudes of faith triumph over the uncertain opinion to which alone probable reason gives birth.[67] Recognizing, however, the extreme limitations imposed upon absolute evidence, and recognizing, too, the ambiguity of the political teaching explicit in revelation, we may safely expect, when finally we turn to d'Ailly's political thinking, to be listening to arguments which for the most part demand no more exalted a status than that of being probable in natural reason, or, at the most, of possessing "a conditioned evidence."

66. See below, Ch. 6.
67. Thus *Sent.* I, qu. 1, art. 2, T, f. 5or: "Noticia non evidens est duplex. Quaedam cum formidine quae vocatur *opinio*. Alia cum certitudine quae vocatur fides." Thus he can say later on (*Sent.* 1, qu. 13, art. 2, K, f. 161v): "Licet antecedens sit probabile naturali ratione . . . tamen secundum fidem est impossibile, et ideo" etc.

2.
Regnum, Sacerdotium, and Politia Ecclesiastica

The value of d'Ailly's political thinking lies, I would suggest, in his attempts to grapple with the central problem of political obligation; it is with these attempts that we shall, for the most part, be dealing. Nevertheless, as McIlwain has said, "for the half-millennium between the eleventh and seventeenth century . . . the bulk of all the writings which we may term political were directly and primarily concerned with the great controversy between the spiritual and secular authority." [1] D'Ailly's writings, though they form, along with those of most of the principal Conciliarists, something of an exception to this generalization, are not completely outside its scope. The problem of the relations between *regnum* and *sacerdotium*—between the kingship and the priesthood—was still a very real one in his day, and it was possibly only the more pressing problem of the very survival of the unity of the Church that relegated it to a subordinate position in his works. What little he has to say on the subject should not be ignored, if only because it helps to reflect the traditional background against which his more "modern" approach to the basic problems of political theory was made.

1. McIlwain, *Growth,* pp. 146–47.

I

The theoretical problem—of the relations which should exist between the regnum and the sacerdotium—was rooted in the actual fact of conflict between the two offices, the boundaries between which were not, and perhaps could not be, clearly drawn. Even in the later Middle Ages it was usually formulated, not so much in modern terms of a conflict between two distinct societies, Church and State, as of a dispute between twin spheres of authority in a single society—the Christian commonwealth—a problem analogous to disputes between the branches of modern democratic governments in which the executive, legislative, and judicial powers are constitutionally separated.[2] Gierke has stressed that the general medieval belief in the ultimate unity of the universe, in the priority of the One over the Many, exercised a profound influence even over the formulation of this particular problem. All partial wholes—and mankind is one of them—had to be subordinated to that principle of unity which is "the aim and object of the universe." [3] If the social order of mankind was to be regarded as informed with a metaphysical unity, Christendom could not but appear as a single universal commonwealth. Thus, even if man possessed a two-fold destiny, and even if such a duality entailed the existence of two distinct social orders, spiritual and temporal, it still was normal to assume that this duality could be dissolved into a higher unity.[4]

But if theoretical considerations such as these helped to determine the way in which the problem was formulated, the

2. J. N. Figgis, *Churches in the Modern State* (2nd ed. London, 1914), pp. 190–91, argues that throughout the earlier part of the Middle Ages "Church and State in the sense of two competing societies did not exist . . . . Such a notion would be possible only if the sense of corporate personality in Church and State had been fully developed. This was not the case." This whole essay, included in his book (pp. 175–226) as an appendix entitled "Respublica Christiana," is valuable.

3. Gierke-Maitland, pp. 9–11.

4. For examples of this type of argument see Gierke-Maitland, pp. 101–02, n. 3. Aquinas is prominent in this context.

problem itself can only be understood in terms of those repeated and bitter clashes between the temporal and spiritual powers upon which centers so much of the drama of medieval history. The ascription during the early Middle Ages of a sacred character to the royal office, the concomitant tendency to regard kings as in some sense priests (a tendency reflected in and strengthened by quasi-sacramental coronation ceremonies), the growth in practice of a considerable degree of aristocratic, royal, and imperial control over the churches of the West—all of these helped to postpone for several centuries the onset of any major conflict between the regnum and the sacerdotium. It was only in the last quarter of the eleventh century that the first great outburst of polemical writing on the problem occurred, touched off by the dramatic and revolutionary Gregorian attack on the control exercised over ecclesiastical appointments by the laity in general and by the German Emperor in particular. This outburst was to be paralleled in importance during the Middle Ages only by the great efflorescence of publicist literature in the first half of the fourteenth century, which, initiated by the clash between Boniface VIII and Philip IV of France, drew sustenance from the bitter strife between the Avignonese papacy and Lewis of Bavaria. It endured for several decades until, in the fateful year of 1349, along with countless lesser figures, William of Ockham was swept from the scene.

During the years between these two great outbursts, the lawyers and theologians, invigorated by the recovery of the *Corpus juris civilis* and the works of Aristotle, and spurred on by the elaboration of the canon law and the scholastic theologies, had devoted enough of their attention to this crucial problem to exercise a deep and transforming influence on the positions characteristic of the papalist and antipapalist camps. This influence is apparent in the works produced during the second great outburst of polemical writing which will be our primary concern.

In the course of these long centuries of tangled controversy, three solutions to the problem crystallized. Two of these were monistic and had a certain persuasive logic. The first and less common involved the bold assertion of the supremacy of the temporal power and the subordination to it, or amalgamation with it, of the spiritual. Marsilius of Padua, to whom Lewis of Bavaria extended his grateful protection, was alone in drawing the full implications of this argument, but vague and confused anticipations had occurred in earlier writers. Indeed, in the *York Tractates* produced during the height of the Investiture Contest by the English or Norman "Anonymous," these anticipations had been somewhat less than vague or confused; but the thesis propounded by the *Tractates* was really a reiteration of the political ideas current in the already-doomed era of "Priest-Kings and Emperor-Pontiffs," ideas which drew their inspiration not from any incipient secularism but rather from the early medieval pattern of "liturgical kingship." [5]

The second and far more common monistic solution drew a very different conclusion. It asserted that the unity of mankind must find its logical expression in an external jurisdictional unity and that this entailed the supremacy of one of the two powers. This dominant power was the spiritual, a power wielded first and foremost by the Pope—for the whole universe is ordained to God, Who is the supreme ruler, and it is the Pope and not the Emperor or any other secular ruler who is the Vicar of God on Earth and who may even be called "the celestial emperor." [6] The Pope, therefore, has a direct power in temporals and it is the duty of the temporal ruler to wield on behalf of the Church, and under its direction, the sword entrusted to him. This view, unambiguously expressed by the propapal publicists of the early fourteenth century, had its roots in the theories of some of the most famous of medieval canonists, theories which can be traced back beyond the pontificate of Innocent III but which found their clearest expression in the glosses of his contemporary—the English canonist, Alanus—and later on in those of Innocent IV, Hostiensis, and William Durantis, the Speculator. [7] It has been common to regard this view as the canonistic

5. The expression is that used by Kantorowicz in the course of his illuminating discussion of the *Tractates* (*King's Two Bodies*, Ch. 3); cf. George H. Williams, *The Norman Anonymous of 1100 A.D.* (Cambridge, Mass., 1951), pp. 127–99.

6. This expression occurs in a gloss of the canonist Bernardus Parmensis to X, 1, 7, c. 3; cited by Ullmann, *Papalism*, p. 118.

7. Alanus taught at Bologna early in the thirteenth century; Innocent IV (d. 1254) not only issued decretals as Pope, but also wrote an important com-

view par excellence, but such an interpretation, though force-fully reiterated in recent years, has been called into question by the discovery in less well-known texts of Alanus, Hostiensis, and Durantis, of positions more compatible with our third solution.[8]

This third and most common solution—if, indeed, it can properly be treated as a single solution—was dualistic in nature and received very many diverse formulations, some of them papalist in inspiration, some imperialist. Its ultimate origins can be found in the famous statement of Pope Gelasius I in 494 to the effect that the world is ruled by two coordinate powers, that the duties of the spiritual are the weightier of the two, and that if, therefore, priests should obey kings in matters pertaining to the public order, so also should kings be subject to the priestly power in matters concerning salvation. This statement, incorporated during the twelfth century by Gratian into his *Decretum* and paralleled by one of his own dicta elsewhere in that work,[9] was not far removed in sentiment from the view expressed by Justinian in one of his *Novellae* [10] and constituted ground common to medieval views widely differing in their import. The Gelasian division of functions was far from being a precise one. At the one extreme, it was able to provide the foundation for the

---

mentary on the Decretals; Hostiensis (Henry of Segusia, d. 1271), one of the most distinguished of medieval canonists, wrote glosses both on the Decretals and on Innocent IV's *Novellae;* William Durantis (d. 1296) was famous especially for his *Speculum Judiciale.* Alanus, for example, could say: "papa judex ordinarius est et quoad spiritualia et quoad temporalia"; text cited in S. Mochi Onory, *Fonti canonistiche dell'idea moderna della Stato* (Milan, 1951), p. 191, n. 2.

8. Ullmann, *Papalism,* Ch. 6, lays great stress on the rôle of Alanus who, he says (p. 142), "marked the turning-point in the development of canonistic politi-cal thought." Mochi Onory, however, is able to present Alanus in a very different light (*Fonti canonistiche,* pp. 191–94); see also Alfons M. Stickler, "Concerning the Political Theories of the Medieval Canonists," *Traditio,* 7 (1949–51), esp. 454–63. In the course of a severe criticism of Ullmann's contentions, Stickler makes it clear that the whole issue remains, and is likely to remain for some time, a *quaestio disputata.*

9. D. 96, c. 10; cf. the *dictum* after C. 2, qu. 7, c. 41: "Notandum est, quod duae sunt personae quibus mundus iste regitur, regalis videlicet et sacerdotalis. Sicut reges praesunt in causis saeculi, ita sacerdotes in causis Dei. Regum est corporalem inrogare penam, sacerdotum spiritualem inferre vindictam."

10. *Novella* VI, Praefatio.

canonistic tradition which was to be dominant at least until the early thirteenth century, and which continued to find echoes later on, even in the writings of those canonists who asserted a thorough-going papalist monism. Huguccio of Pisa, the teacher of Innocent III, is probably the best representative of this tradition.[11] At the other extreme, the Gelasian formula, because it at least admitted the divine origin of the imperial authority, was made to serve the purposes of those pro-imperialist publicists who insisted on the rigid confinement of the priestly power to a strictly defined spiritual sphere. Dante's *De monarchia* may perhaps be regarded as the summation of this particular strand in the dualist tradition.

In between these extremes, the same ancient formula remained the point of departure of those more moderate dualistic solutions which were put forward by representatives of both camps, but which, formulated in the wake of the reception of the *corpus Aristotelicum* in the West, bore also the clear impress of Aristotelian modes of thought. For the Aristotelian concepts of political life as natural to man and of a social order as based on a hierarchy of ends exercised a transforming influence on them. This influence can clearly be seen even in some of the fragmentary remarks on the problem which were made by Aquinas, since his political philosophy was predicated, as was the rest of his system, on the principle that "grace does not destroy nature but perfects it." Thus, though he did not entirely abandon the older view of political authority as a "remedy for sin," he was able to follow Aristotle in ascribing a natural basis and a positive moral value to the state. At the same time he was able to teach that the pursuit of the natural end of man, which it is the duty of the state to supervise, remains subordinate to his supernatural destiny, to which he can attain only through the mediation of the Church: "in those matters which affect the salvation of the soul . . . the spiritual power is to be obeyed before the temporal." [12] If we are to admit the witness of the text which

11. Huguccio (d. 1210) was perhaps the greatest of the Decretists. He taught at Bologna and finished his great *Summa* about 1190.

12. *Commentum in quatuor libros sententiarum*, II, dist. 44, qu. 3, art. 4; in d'Entrèves, *Aquinas*, pp. 186–87.

within a few decades of his death was regarded as the definitive statement of his position, Aquinas went on to claim that "those who are concerned with the subordinate ends of life must be subject to him [i.e., the Pope] who is concerned with the supreme end and be directed by his command." [13]

By concentrating upon this text, and by subordinating the other texts to its "exacting requirements," the Parisian theologian, James of Viterbo, was able in 1301–02 to claim Thomistic support for his own position of extreme papalism.[14] Other writers, however, were less sure about the precise import of Aquinas's teaching. The use made of Thomistic principles by one of the moderates, John of Paris,[15] was perhaps more charac-

13. *De regimine principum*, I, cap. 14; in d'Entrèves, *Aquinas*, pp. 76–77. See I. T. Eschmann, "St. Thomas Aquinas on the Two Powers," *Mediaeval Studies, 20* (1958), 177–205. In this penetrating study, the author makes a strong case for excluding the witness of this work from any assessment of Aquinas's doctrine because its authenticity, though "really probable" is "juridically indemonstrable" (p. 196). The central text, he argues, is that which is to be found in *Sent.* II, dist. 44, which Thomists and historians alike have found to be such an embarrassment. If, however, it is analyzed methodically in the light of its sources, it will be seen to be a reflection not of any extreme papalist monism, but rather of "the Gelasian dualism of c. 10, D. 96," which thus must be regarded as "a doctrine of definitive Thomism" (p. 200).

14. In his *De regimine christiano* (Arquillière, pp. 83–310), James followed Aquinas in regarding the state as natural and as possessing a positive ethical value, but argued from the superior end pursued by the Church to its actual control of the temporal power, believing that only in this way could nature be perfected (see McIlwain, *Growth*, pp. 260 ff.). Eschmann, p. 177, n. 4, indicates the way in which James conflated the two principal Thomistic texts.

15. In his *Tractatus de potestate regia et papali*, Leclercq, pp. 172 ff.; cf. Richard Scholz, *Die Publizistik zur Zeit Philipps des Schönen und Bonifaz VIII* (Stuttgart, 1903), pp. 275–333. We shall often have to refer to this tract and a few biographical details about John of Paris may be in order. His family name was Quidort; he was born ca. 1269, and he died in 1306 while under threat of ecclesiastical censure because of the line of argument he had taken in a tract defending the doctrine of the real presence of Christ in the Eucharist. He was a member of the Dominican order, and, at the turn of the century, was one of the best-known exponents and defenders of Thomism at the University of Paris. His *Tractatus de potestate regia et papali* appeared at the end of 1302 or the beginning of 1303, and at the height of the struggle between Boniface VIII and Philip IV. It was not a polemic but was nevertheless directed, at least in part, against the extreme papalism of his fellow theologians Aegidius Romanus and James of Viterbo. Though little known for some years, it attracted the attention of the

teristic and more influential, for his arguments fostered a tradition followed not only by antipapalists such as Ockham but also by later supporters of papal absolutism in spiritual matters such as Torquemada and Bellarmine, men who were willing to restrict the Pope's claims to temporal authority to that of an attenuated indirect power entirely consequent upon his complete supremacy in spiritual matters. Although he started out from the same Thomistic assumptions of the relations of nature and grace and of a hierarchical articulation of social groups, each taking its superior or inferior place in accordance with the ultimate importance of its purpose, John of Paris drew from them different conclusions than had James of Viterbo. While admitting that the values served by the spiritual power were superior to those served by the secular, he insisted that both powers were derived independently of each other from God, and that the natural political life supervised by the secular power needed no perfecting by means of Church control. While admitting, also, that the Pope was supreme in spiritual matters, he denied that he had any *direct* power in temporal affairs or over temporal goods.[16] The only means of coercion, therefore, that remained to him was the exercise of the spiritual weapon of excommunication; and this being rightly applicable only in spiritual causes, its temporal results, however great, could only be indirect.

And it is with John of Paris that we shall end our brief introduction to d'Ailly's treatment of the problem. For although it is Ockham's theory which has been said to be "almost the last important contribution to the medieval discussion of Church and State relationships," [17] and although d'Ailly is so often a faithful follower of Ockham, his own most coherent remarks on the question approximate most closely to the position taken by John of Paris, from whose tract, indeed, they are often directly drawn.

French Conciliarists during the latter years of the fourteenth century, and enjoyed an enduring popularity among later Gallican writers.

16. Except by the grant or concession of princes (*Tract. de pot.*, Proemium; Leclercq, p. 175).

17. Lewis, *Political Ideas*, 2, 551.

II

The first glimpse of d'Ailly's thought on this subject may well engender the suspicion that it provides, at the most, a somewhat unpromising piece of field work for an experienced archaeologist of ideas, an excavated site in which the recent and the primitive have carelessly been heaped together—perhaps by a clumsy amateur, or by an impatient and philistine contractor. Nor is such a suspicion totally unfounded. The repetition of traditional formulas may be remarked even in his later writings. In a discourse delivered in 1406 at a Council held at Paris, he is even capable of evoking memories of the long-dead era of "Priest-Kings, and Emperor-Pontiffs," for in a burst of courtly rhetoric he describes the French King not only as sovereign in his own kingdom in temporal affairs, but also, by virtue of his royal consecration, as "une personne moyenne entre spirituelle et temporelle." [1] In perhaps a more characteristic mood, he can lecture Christian princes on their duty to set a good example to their subjects, to eschew immorality, blasphemy, the practice of the magic arts, and heresy, to attack the Saracens and to keep the Jews in their place—to rule their peoples, in fact, not for their own selfish ends but on behalf of Christ.[2] Similarly, in a letter written in 1414 to John XXIII, he can echo the old theory of the sword which was to be wielded by the regnum on behalf of the sacerdotium. Turning rhetorically to the Emperor and the secular princes for help in the matter of the Schism, he says to them: "because of this have you received the sword from God, that you may be defenders of the Church, to the punishment of evildoers." [3] Indeed, what are perhaps his longest disquisitions

1. Chastenet, "Preuves," p. 163. The context in which the statement appears makes clear that it was no more than a piece of rhetoric, and d'Ailly can also argue (p. 154) that "il estoit plus expedient que l'Eglise fust reformée par les Conseaux Generaux que par la puissance Laicorum."

2. *Tractatus de materia concilii generalis;* below, Appendix III, pp. 338 ff. He also included this passage in his *Tractatus super reformatione ecclesiae* which he read to the Fathers at Constance (see below, p. 250).

3. *Epistola I ad Joannem XXIII,* Dupin, 2, 881–82: "Ad te [i.e., Regem Romanorum] inquam, caeterosque Principes terrae confugio, pro consolationis

on the papal and imperial powers are basically a reworking of the old analogy between the twin luminaries of the skies, the sun and the moon, and the twin luminaries of mankind, the Pope and the Emperor.[4] It is true that he gives this ancient conceit a new astrological twist, and extends it to embrace the stars, inferior luminaries which are to be understood as "a variety of diverse estates subordinate to the greater ones." But this mutation may have been the result of his desire to stress the position of the churchmen currently assembled at the Council of Constance, or perhaps merely the outcome, in the case of one of the sermons, of the exigencies of the Gospel of the day, and in the other of the lucky coincidence of an impending solar eclipse, which enabled him to re-use, in a new and portentous setting, the greater part of his earlier discourse.[5] Whatever the explana-

---

auxilio, et executionis subsidio: nam propter hoc a Deo recepistis gladium, ut sitis Ecclesiae pugiles, ad vindictam malefactorum." The allegory of the swords was derived ultimately from Luke 22:38, and by d'Ailly's time had become a cliché common to both papalist and antipapalist polemics. The elucidation of this theme has been one of the central endeavors of A. M. Stickler. His results are presented in the articles which he himself lists in *Traditio*, 7 (1949–51), 462, n. 20. To these should be added "Il 'gladius' negli atti dei concilii e dei R. R. Pontefici sino a Graziano e Bernardo di Clairvaux," *Salesianum*, *13* (1951), 414–45. Brian Tierney, "Some Recent Works on the Political Theories of the Medieval Canonists," *Traditio*, *10* (1954), 610–12, gives a brief summary of Stickler's findings.

4. *Sermo in die omnium sanctorum*, Tschackert, *Ailli*, Appendix XIII, pp. [41]–[50]. Much of this d'Ailly had taken from his *Oratio de officio imperatoris*, Dupin, 2, 917–24, where he says (918) "in praesenti Ecclesia . . . ordinatissimus Rex, omnium dispositor, diversa luminaria disposuit, de quibus in principio Libri Genesis scriptum est: 'Fecit Dominus duo magna luminaria, luminare majus, ut praeesset diei, et luminare minus, ut praeesset nocti, et stellas.' . . . Habet igitur Ecclesia duo luminaria magna, Solem et Lunam habet et Stellas varias. In Sole, Papalis Majestas, quae praeest diei, id est, spiritualibus; in Luna, Imperialis Potestas, quae praeest nocti, id est, temporalibus. In Stellis vero diversorum statuum Ecclesiasticorum varietas, quae suis subest majoribus, congrue designatur." Cf. Tschackert, *Ailli*, p. [45]. The analogy itself had enjoyed an extraordinary popularity (especially among the canonists) ever since Innocent III had employed it in some of his letters. The texts are cited in Carlyle, *History*, 5, 158, n. 4; also 2, 147, n. 4 and 215, n. 1.

5. In the case of the *Oratio de officio*, he was preaching on the text "Erunt signa in sole, luna et stellis" (Luke 21:25) which was drawn from the Gospel of the day—see V. Martin, *Les origines du Gallicanisme* (Paris, 1939), 2, 102, n. 5. For d'Ailly's remarks about the impending eclipse, see Tschackert, *Ailli*, p. [49].

tion, it did not prevent his repeating the traditional implications explicit in the analogy. It was the Pope who was to be equated with the sun, the greater light which presides over the day, and the Emperor who was to be equated with the moon, a lesser luminary casting a borrowed light upon the darkness of temporal affairs.[6] He drew, however, no specific conclusions from this priority in dignity.

If these vague and rhetorical remarks were all that d'Ailly had to say on the question of the proper relations between the regnum and sacerdotium, it would be impossible to ascribe to him any definite position at all. In a passage, however, in one of the works already mentioned, there are indications of a more positive stand.[7] The context is a discussion of whether or not France, in restoring obedience to the Popes, should also restore the administration of such temporalities as the administration of ecclesiastical benefices. In the course of this discussion d'Ailly asserts not only that the Apostolic Church did not possess "the civil and judicial exercise or administration of temporal things of this sort," but also that Christ, by deed and word, seems rather to have forbidden than permitted the exercise of such civil jurisdiction. He refuses, however, to hold rigidly to this latter statement, and goes on to admit that, since the time of Constantine the Great, it has pleased God to permit the Church to receive and to use such temporal possessions. These comments concern a comparatively narrow issue and, by themselves, do not give us much of an indication of d'Ailly's position—the less so, indeed, in that he had taken them (as he acknowledged later on) from one of the works of his former pupil, Jean Gerson.[8] But they do not stand alone. If d'Ailly was willing to appropriate Gerson's words it was because he agreed with them, and they do in fact consort very well with the position which he himself had

---

6. See above, n. 4, p. 43.

7. *Tractatus de materia;* see below, pp. 259 ff.

8. Gerson, *De concilio generali unius obedientiae,* Dupin, 2, 24–32. The arguments of cols. 24–29 reappear with added material in d'Ailly's *Tractatus de materia* (below, pp. 253–56), and the passage in question is taken from col. 27. For the attribution of the *De concilio* see below, pp. 246–47.

adopted in a more comprehensive discussion of the Church in relation to temporal power and possessions, when, over twenty years before, he had fulfilled the last scholastic requirement for the Doctorate in Theology by discoursing on the question: *Utrum Petri ecclesia rege gubernetur, lege reguletur, fide confirmetur, jure dominetur.*[9]

As the title suggests, it is the first part of this work which is relevant to the issue in question, and although it contains no verbatim borrowings from John of Paris, it witnesses to the pervasive influence of his teaching upon the evolution of the doctrine of the royalty of Christ. Leclercq has pointed out that although political thinkers had always considered the person of Christ under the aspect of his kingship, the doctrine of the royalty of Christ had never been set forth fully and precisely before the time of James of Viterbo and John of Paris.[10] During the course of the thirteenth century it had attracted growing attention, not only as a result of the internecine struggle between the Papacy and the Empire, but also, later on, as a result of the controversy raging among and around the Franciscans on the question of the poverty of Christ and the Apostles;[11] James of Viterbo, writing at the start of the fourteenth century, had seen fit to put it at "the center of his doctrine of the Church."[12] It was John of Paris, however, who made the crucial contribution to the clarification and development of the doctrine; he

9. The reason for this agreement between the fragmentary remarks taken from Gerson and the position adopted earlier by d'Ailly is to be sought in the further indebtedness of both men to the doctrines of John of Paris. This is manifest in the case of d'Ailly and at least probable in that of Gerson. Compare the passage from Gerson cited above and John's *Tract. de pot.*, Proemium; Leclercq, pp. 173–75. For further suggestions concerning the probability of John's influence on Gerson see Leclercq, p. 155, n. 2, and also Leclercq's article: "L'Idée de la Royauté du Christ pendant le grand schisme et la crise conciliaire," *Arch. d'hist. doct. et litt. du M.A.,* 24 (1949), 265; reprinted in his *L'Idée de la Royauté du Christ au Moyen Age* (Paris, 1959), pp. 212–13.

10. Leclercq has presented the results of his lengthy researches on this topic, not only in the book and article cited above but also in a series of further articles, all now reprinted with some additional material in his *L'Idée de la Royauté du Christ au Moyen Age.*

11. For a brief discussion of this controversy, see below, Ch. 3, pp. 73 ff.

12. Leclercq, p. 105.

emphasized a simple but decisive distinction between that which pertained to Christ by reason of His divinity and that which pertained to Him by reason of His humanity.[13] And although the uneasy years of schism generated something of a reaction to more extreme positions, they also witnessed a reaffirmation of John's central teaching on the royalty of Christ.[14]

Such a contention is certainly borne out by the disputation to which we must now address ourselves. On this point, as on many others, d'Ailly reveals his familiarity with the teaching of the *Tractatus de potestate regia et papali* and also his substantial agreement with it.[15] Claiming the support of some of the papal decretals issued on the subject of the Rule of St. Francis, he declares that it is clear from the Scriptures that Christ embraced the most severe poverty in all human things, even in the food He ate and the clothes He wore, for of these things he had, strictly speaking, merely the use and not lordship (*dominium*), either personally or in common with others.[16] This assertion is, in turn, only an argument in support of the more general proposition that Christ did not wield a temporal or *regal* monarchy while on earth.[17] And among the other arguments in support of this posi-

13. *Tract. de pot.*, cap. 8; Leclercq. pp. 190–91.

14. Leclercq, "L'Idée de la Royauté du Christ pendant le grand schisme," pp. 264–65; cf. *L'Idée de la Royauté du Christ au Moyen Age*, pp. 212–13.

15. In this tract it is a matter of doctrinal assent rather than of any direct borrowing, although in one passage d'Ailly comes very close to the language of John; see below, n. 19, p. 47.

16. Dupin, *1*, 680: "Tamen hoc certum est, quod in istis [i. e. food, clothing, etc.], seu in aliis quibuscumque rebus temporalibus, Christus ultra usum, non habuit proprie dictum dominium, sive in proprio, sive in communi; et quod sua arctissima paupertas quam docuit et servavit, tale dominium excludit. Nam ubi dat consilium perfectionis, dicens: 'Si vis perfectus esse' etc Matth., xix, 21, nihil excipit; sed dicit Omnia, 'quaecunque habes da pauperibus' Marc. x, 21, nec addit proprium, vel commune, sed universaliter, hoc intelligit . . . . Igitur tale dominium non habuit vel habere voluit, quod Scriptura plerisque locis possessionem nominat . . . . Ad hoc possem inducere Decretales factas super declaratione regulae Beati Francisci; sed transeo causa brevitatis." For the exact meaning of *dominium*, see below, Ch. 3.

17. Dupin, *1*, 679: "Christus tenuit arctissimum paupertatem: igitur non habuit Monarchiam temporalem seu Regalem. Consequentia tenet: quia arctissima paupertas excludit tam in proprio quam in communi, omne dominium temporalium rerum, et per consequens Regale dominium"; cf. *De legitimo dominio*, Dupin, *1*, 645–46.

tion was the inevitable quotation of Christ's reply to Pilate that his kingdom was not of this world,[18] and also the positing of two important distinctions.

The first of these is that between the kingship of Christ as God and of Christ as man. D'Ailly admits that *secundum divinitatem* Christ—just as God the Father—is King and Lord of all things, but notes that this lordship over an eternal kingdom is clearly not the temporal lordship which is in question. Concerning Christ's human lordship, however, it is important to draw a further distinction—between spiritual or priestly and temporal or secular lordship—and to realize that the Scriptures cannot be interpreted to imply that Christ had in any sense wielded temporal lordship.[19] For the temporal affairs which are the province of the prince, lord, or civil judge, are not "ordained to

18. Dupin, *1*, 676: "Quod Christus, secundum humanitatem, habuerit totius Orbis Monarchiam Regalem, non convincitur ex Scriptura sacra . . . . Nam Christus interrogatus utrum Rex esset, respondit Pilato: 'Regnum meum non est de hoc mundo.' Joan., xviii, 36. Per hoc dans intelligere quod ipse secundum humanitatem, quantum ad temporalia, quae mundana vocabat, non habebat totius Orbis Monarchiam Regalem."

19. Dupin, *1*, 677: "Pono istam distinctionem, quod Regnum Christi, sive ejus Regale dominium, potest imaginari triplex. Unum scilicet divinum, per quod, secundum divinitatem, est Rex et Dominus Omnium, sicut Deus Pater—et de isto dominio potest illa intelligi auctoritas Apoc. 'Rex regum et Dominus dominantium.' . . . Nec etiam loquitur ibi de tali dominio de quo loquimur, scilicet temporali, sed de dominio Regni aeterni . . . . Aliud est Christi dominium, scilicet humanum, et illud potest subdistingui; et intelligi duplex. Unum spirituale, seu Sacerdotale; aliud temporale sive saeculare. . . . De temporali ergo, et corruptibile Regno non intelliguntur Scripturae, nec tale Regale dominium dicunt Christo convenire—et maxime, loquendo de generali Regno totius mundi." This teaching is very close to that of Ockham, who draws the same distinction between Christ's lordship as God and as man—*Breviloquium de Potestate Papae*, Lib. 2. cap. 9, ed. L. Baudry (Paris, 1937), pp. 32–33. The distinction, however, had first been stressed by John of Paris (see above, n. 13, p. 46), and these pages may be added to the others which Leclercq (p. 153, n. 5) cites in support of his suggestion that Ockham, too, may have made use of the *Tractatus de potestate regia et papali* when writing the *Breviloquium*. But for Ockham's teaching on the Royalty of Christ, see now Georges de Lagarde, *La Naissance de l'esprit laïque au déclin du moyen age*, new ed. *4 Guillaume d'Ockham défense de l'Empire* (Louvain and Paris, 1962), 160–76. D'Ailly himself is clearly drawing his material directly from John's tract. A comparison of the whole passage in question (Dupin, *1*, 677–78) with the *Tractatus*, cap. 8 and 9 (Leclercq, pp. 190–94) reveals that on this point d'Ailly approximates very closely to John's language as well as to his teaching.

spiritual things, [and] indeed, rather hinder them." [20] Neither
the words of the Apostles nor the tradition of the Church lead
us to believe that Christ, Peter, the other Apostles, or their successors behaved like temporal kings and princes, but suggest
rather that they remained subject to the laws and judgments of
such rulers. Thus Christ accepted judgment at the hands of
Pilate, and, indeed, said to him: "You would have no power
against me, were it not given to you from above." Similarly
Peter, far from claiming that the whole world was subject to him
in temporal matters, told men to obey their secular rulers, while
Paul, of course, ordered that every one without exception should
be subject to these higher powers.[21]

According to d'Ailly, then, the conclusion to be drawn is that
although Christ (and Peter his Vicar insofar as he was head of
the Church) possessed a spiritual monarchy, he did not possess
a temporal kingship.[22] The difference between these two types of
kingship is that the spiritual or sacerdotal is ordained to spiritual
ends and the temporal to temporal ends. Thus, while it pertains
to temporal rulers, *principally and essentially* to rule their
subjects through civil laws and by the moral virtues to guide
them to the political end of this life, it also pertains *principally*

20. Dupin, *1*, 674–675: "quod temporalia, id est negotia rerum temporalium et
saecularium, sicut Principatus, Dominium, vel Judicium coactivum litium, aut
contentiosorum actuum civilium, non disponunt, nec ordinantur ad spiritualia,
immo magis ea impediunt."

21. Dupin, *1*, 675–76: "cum sit clarum quod nec ex doctrina vocali Apostolorum,
aut Traditione Ecclesiae, habetur quod Christus aut Petrus et alii Apostoli, et
eorum successores, gesserint se tanquam Reges, aut Principes temporales; nec
quod eis imposuerunt Leges, aut Regulas judiciales; nec quod circa eos Judicia
saecularia exercuerunt, sed suis Legibus et Judiciis se humiliter subjicere volu-
erunt. Nam Christus per Pilatum, Vicarium Romani Imperatoris, sustinuit judicari. . . . Immo per hoc quod dixit ei: 'Non haberes potestatem ullam adversus
me, nisi tibi datum esset desuper' . . . innuere videbatur quod haberet potestatem ipsum judicandi, et hanc desuper . . . Petrus etiam non dicebat totum
mundum in temporalibus sibi esse subjectum, sed loquens de Principibus saecularibus, dicebat: 'Obedite Dominis vestris, etiam dyscolis.' . . . Et Paulus: 'Omnis
anima potestatibus sublimioribus subdita sit.' . . . et dicit 'omnis anima'—id est,
omnis homo nullum excipiendo."

22. Dupin, *1*, 673: "Quod licet tam Christus quam ejus Vicarius Petrus, in
quantum caput Ecclesiae, habuerit Monarchiam spiritualem, non tamen Regiam
temporalem."

48

and essentially to priests to rule their flocks through divine laws, and by the heroic virtues to guide them to the ultimate end of the future life and eternal salvation.[23]

D'Ailly is clearly committed, therefore, to a dualistic solution to the problem of Church-State relations. The civil and spiritual powers are distinguished not only by their respective and discrete functions, but also by the difference in quality of the ends to which they are ordained. But it should be noted that he does not explicitly append the obvious corollary that the spiritual power is superior in kind to the temporal because of the superiority of the values which it serves, and as a result it would be very easy to represent him as saying more than he actually does. It should not be forgotten, however, that he has already indicated his belief that the spiritual power is superior *in dignity* by his employment of the old papalist sun-moon analogy. Nor should the remarks which he makes in one of his last works, the *Tractatus de ecclesiastica potestate*,[24] be overlooked—even though they are limited to the question of lordship over ecclesiastical and temporal property—for they are relevant to this very issue.

In this tract d'Ailly, though he nowhere admits it, speaks directly with the voice of John of Paris. In the preface to his work John had distinguished two errors, that of the "Waldenses," which denied to the Pope and clergy any temporal possessions or anything to do with temporal things, and that of the "Herodians," which attributed to the Pope, inasmuch as he is in the place of Christ, lordship and jurisdiction of the possessions of princes and barons. He had gone on to conclude that the truth

23. Dupin, *1*, 678: "differentia inter istos Principatus est: quia Principatus temporalis ordinatur ad temporalia Sacerdotalia ad spiritualia. Et ad Reges temporales pertinet principaliter et de per se, et proprie subjectos regere per Leges studiosas, non quascumque, sed per Leges humanas, civiles, seu politicas, et per virtutes morales eos ordinare ad finem politicum hujus vitae. Ad Sacerdotes, principaliter et de per se pertinet eos regere per Leges divinas, et per virtutes heroïcas eos ordinare ad finem ultimum vitae futurae, et salutis aeternae. Et hoc fecit Christus, per hoc ostendens se esse Sacerdotem et non Regem temporalem."

24. This is the title which d'Ailly himself normally used, but the work is printed in Dupin, 2, 925–60 under the title: *Tractatus de Ecclesiae Concilii Generalis, Romani Pontificis, et Cardinalium Auctoritate.*

lay between these two extremes and that the Pope and clergy do have lordship in temporal things, not as Vicars of Christ and successors of the Apostles, but through the donations made by princes out of piety.[25] This argument is echoed in an abbreviated form by d'Ailly, not only in substance, but also almost word for word, although he inflates John's statement, "I think that the truth lies in the mean . . . between these contrary opinions," to "Catholic truth teaches," and "Catholic truth holds the mean between these two errors." Similarly, he is again repeating John's arguments verbatim when he goes on to argue that the Pope has no proprietary right over any Church possessions—which belong, rather, to the whole ecclesiastical community—but is merely universal administrator and dispenser of them.[26] And it is natural that he should go on then and follow John in asserting that the Pope is not even administrator or dispenser of the goods of laymen. The reason is that lay possessions, unlike ecclesiastical, belong to the individuals who have acquired them, and that therefore neither the Prince nor the Pope has lordship over or administration of such possessions.[27] Nevertheless the Prince, as a judge set over men, may interfere in these things if necessity or the common good demands it, and it follows there-

25. *Tract. de pot.*, Proemium; Leclercq, pp. 173–76; the relevant text is printed side by side with that of d'Ailly in Appendix I; see below, pp. 241–42.

26. Dupin, 2, 943: "Quod Papa habet plenariam dispensationem omnium bonorum et Beneficiorum, et non Dominium . . . ;" ibid., 942: "quod bona Ecclesiastica, ut Ecclesiastica sunt, fuerunt collata Communitatibus, et non solum personae singulari. Unde Fundatores Ecclesiarum intenderunt Dominium et proprietatem bonorum quae dabant, transferre primo et directe in communitatem Collegii, scilicet talis Ecclesiae, ad usum Deo servientium, et non in aliquam personam singularem"; cf. *Tract. de pot.*, cap. 6; Leclercq, pp. 187–88. It should be noted, too, that John of Paris himself had taken the greater part of the following chapter—equally without acknowledgment—from one of the *Quodlibets* of Godfrey of Fontaines (d. 1306). See Leclercq, p. 35 and J. Hoffmans ed., *Les Quodlibets treize et quatorze de Godefroid de Fontaines* (Louvain, 1935), pp. 224–29.

27. Dupin, 2, 944: "Exteriora bona laïcorum, non sunt collata Communitati, sicut bona Ecclesiastica, sed sunt acquisita singulis personis, arte, vel labore, vel industria propria; et ideo personae singulares, ut singulares sunt, habent in ipsis Jus et potestatem, ac verum Dominium . . . . Unde sequitur, quod nec Princeps nec Papa habet proprie Dominium vel dispensationem in talibus." Cf. *Tract. de pot.*, cap. 7; Leclercq, p. 189.

fore that the Pope, who is head not only of the clergy but of all the faithful, may, by the divine law and "as Pastor and general instructor in faith and morals," dispose of the external goods of all the faithful in cases of the supreme necessity of the Church— as, for example, during the onslaughts of the heathen. The qualification is appended, however, that in so acting, the Pope is not, properly speaking, *administering* these goods; he is, rather, declaring what the law is.[28]

From these remarks it is clear that d'Ailly does attribute some priority to the spiritual power, as indeed did John of Paris. But John had had a great deal more to say on the subject, and it must be admitted that what d'Ailly has left unsaid is of greater importance than what he has said. From this silence a host of inferences might possibly be drawn (and the existing texts rearranged accordingly), but it would be impossible to assess their validity.[29] In conclusion, then, it must suffice to say that d'Ailly's statements, though they express no fully elaborated position, serve adequately to locate his solution to the Church-State problem among those dualistic solutions of the type most usually associated with Aquinas, John of Paris, and the chastened papalists of the fifteenth and sixteenth centuries.

---

28. Ibid.: "Quia vero propter talis bona exteriora, contingit interdum pacem, hominemque turbari, dum aliquis quod est alterius usurpat; quia etiam interdum homines quae sua sunt nimis amantes, ea non communicant, prout necessitati vel utilitati publicae convenit, ideo positus est Princeps cum populo qui talibus praeest, ut Judex discernens justum et injustum . . . . Ex quo sequitur, quod Papa, qui est quasi supremum caput, non solum Clericorum, sed generaliter omnium fidelium . . . tanquam generalis omnium pastor, et informator fidei ac morum, in casu summae necessitatis Ecclesiae . . . habet, Jure divino, bona exteriora omnium fidelium dispensare, et ut exponenda sunt discernere, prout expedit communi necessitati Fidei: utpote, quia alias subverteretur Fides, propter impugnationem infidelium . . . . Et talis ordinatio Papae non esset nisi Juris declaratio" (or, as earlier in col. 944: "in qua etiam necessitate, non est proprie dispensator, sed magis potest dici [juris?] declarator"). Cf. *Tract. de pot.*, cap. 7; Leclercq, pp. 189–90.

29. It might, for example, be argued that d'Ailly's extensive borrowings from John of Paris indicate an acceptance of his complete position on the matter. On the other hand, the echoes of more traditional formulas in other of his works might be taken as arguing against his complete acceptance of John's position. And so on.

III

D'Ailly's patent lack of concern with the old problem of the relations between the ecclesiastical and temporal powers will be the occasion of no disappointment if it is remembered that it was more than counterbalanced by a renewed preoccupation with what were to be in modern times the central issues of political theory. J. N. Figgis has suggested, indeed, that it was precisely this lack of concern with the Church-State question that gives the speculations of the Conciliarists their peculiar value.[1] For the Conciliarists, he goes on to say, seem "to have discovered that arguments applicable to government in general could not be inapplicable to the Church," and "speculation on the possible power of the Council as the true depositary of sovereignty within the Church, drove the thinkers to treat the Church definitely as one of a class, political societies." Figgis's implication that the Conciliar theory sprang from the conscious application to the Church of constitutional principles already applied in the secular kingdoms has not gone unchallenged,[2] but this issue is not relevant to the present discussion because all parties are agreed that the Church was being conceived as a political community similar to other political communities. This is the fact that is crucial to our discussion because upon it depends the validity of treating many of d'Ailly's arguments as the expression of a consciously *political* theory. Although he does elaborate a philosophy of law, and although he does examine problems relating to dominium in general, his other political ideas have to be drawn from arguments which, for the most part, are concerned not with the secular state, but rather with "the ecclesiastical polity."

It is not difficult to justify the validity of this procedure. In both of the principal works of his mature years—the *Tractatus*

1. Figgis, *Studies*, pp. 44–45; and following, in order of quotation, pp. 36, 42.
2. Tierney, *Foundations*, has rejected Figgis's contentions, stressing that it had long been the practice of the canon lawyers to apply to the constitutions of the individual collegiate churches and of the Universal Church itself, the terms and concepts applicable to all corporations.

de materia concilii generalis (1402–03) and the *Tractatus de ecclesiastica potestate* (1416)—he dismisses the argument that because the greater cannot be judged by the lesser—the Pope cannot be judged by a General Council—by pointing out that the King of France, "who is greater than and superior to [anybody] in the whole kingdom, often and in many cases is judged in his Parlement, and against him is brought sentence." [3] Again, in the latter of these two works he follows John of Paris in applying Aristotle's analysis of forms of government to the constitution of the Church, concluding therefore that a mixed monarchy of Pope and Cardinals is manifestly the best government for the Church.[4] It is significant that when, in the former tract, he finds it necessary to qualify the application to the Pope of the old dictum of the Roman law, *princeps legibus solutus,* he does so not in terms of the irrelevance of such secular maxims to the constitution of the Church, but rather in terms of the superior status of divine law to human.[5]

All this is by no means surprising. The habit of thinking of the Church as a political society, though it was to owe much to the Conciliar movement, was not started by it. One of the more prominent by-products of the protracted struggles between the Papacy and the temporal monarchs of Europe had been a marked secularization of the way in which men conceived of the Church. As the *De regimine christiano* of James of Viterbo so clearly indicates, already at the start of the fourteenth century, the Church could be consistently treated as a Kingdom presided over by its own king—the Pope.[6] Canon lawyers of the high-papalist school were quick to explore the consequences of this conception, and the application to the Pope of the maxim *princeps legibus solutus* was only the most notorious of these.[7] D'Ailly, it is true, disagreed with some of the arguments about

---

3. See below, p. 304; cf. Dupin, 2, 957.

4. Dupin, 2, 946. See below, Ch. 4, pp. 125–26, where the text is cited and discussed.

5. See below, p. 313.

6. Kantorowicz, *King's Two Bodies*, p. 202, n. 28, points out that the term *regnum ecclesiasticum* had already become very common in the thirteenth century.

7. Ullmann, *Papalism*, pp. 154 ff.

the papal power that were grounded upon this maxim, but his failure to question its very applicability reveals his own commitment to the conception of the Church which made it relevant. This commitment is underlined by the language he uses when speaking of the Church. His most usual definition of it is *congregatio fidelium,* but we also find him speaking of it as a kingdom,[8] or more characteristically as "the Christian commonwealth" (*respublica christiana*) or "the ecclesiastical commonwealth," and perhaps most frequently as "the Christian polity" or "the ecclesiastical polity"[9]—from which, in one place, he finds it necessary to distinguish the state as "the secular polity."[10] Thus because, according to Aristotle, excessive inequality among its citizens can corrupt a political society, he can conclude that the concentration of excessive power in the hands of a few members of the Church is a sign of its imminent dissolution.[11]

It is clear enough, then, that d'Ailly treats of the Church as "one of a class, political societies," but what does he do about its unique characteristics? Does he ignore or gloss over them? And, if he does, is it not a rash undertaking to attempt to elevate his views to the status of a truly *political* theory? The answer is, of course, that d'Ailly is well aware that the Church possesses

8. Hence the title of one of his early disputations: *Utrum indoctus in jure divino possit juste praeesse in Ecclesiae Regno;* Dupin, *1,* 646–62.

9. *Tract. de eccl. pot.,* in Dupin, 2, 948, 959, 960; *Sermo factus in concilio generali Constantiensis,* in *Sermones,* f. x3v; *Epistola I ad Joannem XXIII,* Dupin, *2,* 877; *Quaestio de resumpta,* Dupin, *1,* 672; *Sermo de quadruplicia adventu domini,* in *Sermones,* f. t3r.

10. *Tract. de mat.,* see below, pp. 307–12; *Tract. de eccl. pot.,* Dupin, 2, 959–60; *Propositiones Utiles,* Martène et Durand, 7, 910; *Ep. I ad Joannem XXIII,* Dupin, *2,* 878. The word "polity" may be said to mean a "politically organized community." Its decline to the status of an archaism in the English language has contributed to the difficulties attendant upon the translation not only of the medieval but also of the Greek vocabulary of politics. See Ernest Barker, *The Politics of Aristotle* (Oxford, 1946), pp. lxiii–lxviii.

11. *Ep. I ad Joannem XXIII,* Dupin, 2, 877–78: "Tertium signum sumitur ex proportione inaequalitatis nimiae Ecclesiasticorum membrorum, cur alius quidem esurit, alius vero ebrius est. Sicut enim ad bonam armoniam requiritur inaequalitas moderata, quae si nimis excedit, tollit melodiam: sic, secundum Philosophum, propter immoderatam disparitatem, scilicet civium, corrumpitur politia . . . . Sextum signum, est promotio indignorum, et vilipensio meliorum. Hoc enim, secundum Aristotelem, est malorum causa maxima, quam occasio dissolutionis politiae."

certain unique characteristics which distinguish it from any other political society, but these characteristics are not necessarily relevant to his central question, which concerns the unity and internal constitution of the Church and the respective authorities of the Pope and General Council. Having once said this, it becomes necessary to face those awkward and embarrassingly numerous texts in which d'Ailly links the ecclesiastical unity with the doctrine of the Church as the Mystical Body of Christ. It has recently been claimed that this doctrine did not play as prominent a rôle in d'Ailly's thinking as it did in that of his pupil, Gerson, and if this claim is a valid one, we should, indeed, be grateful.[12] But even if it is, the doctrine still plays a rôle prominent enough to place a serious obstacle in the way of treating d'Ailly's ecclesiological arguments as the expression of a political theory. For whether these arguments occur in his sermons and more pietistic works, or in his early disputations, or even in his later publicistic writings, one may find in them crucial references to the Church as the Mystical Body, and these references are too frequent to be ignored or to be dismissed as the irrelevant echoes of a senescent traditionalism.[13]

At first sight, the doctrine of the Mystical Body would scarcely seem compatible with any attempt to apply to the Church the profane categories of secular political thinking, and some scholars have seen fit to stress this incompatibility.[14] During the last few years, however, considerable attention has been paid to the history of the doctrine itself, and Henri de Lubac has drawn attention to an important change in terminology which occurred in the mid-twelfth century, a change crucial to the later development of the doctrine and most relevant to our current di-

12. John B. Morrall, *Gerson and the Great Schism* (Manchester, 1960), p. 119.

13. Thus in his last major work, the *Tractatus de ecclesiastica potestate,* there are no less than four references to the Church as a Mystical Body (Dupin, 2, 932, 942, 949, 953). Cf. e.g., his *Sermo do Sancto Trinitate, Sermo secundus factus in Synodo Cameracensis,* and *Verbum abbreviatum,* in *Sermones,* ff. z2r–z2v, B4r, d5v; *Utrum Petri ecclesia lege reguletur,* Dupin, *1,* 665; *Propositiones utiles,* Martène et Durand, 7, 910; *Epistola secunda ad Benedictum XIII,* Lettenhove, *1,* 140.

14. Leclercq, p. 110; Walter Ullmann, *The Growth of Papal Government in the Middle Ages* (London, 1955), p. 456 (but note his remarks on pp. 2–3).

lemma.[15] D'Ailly's own formulations, indeed, bear witness to this change. Whereas in some texts he speaks of the Church as *corpus Christi*,[16] in others he uses the expression *corpus mysticum Christi*,[17] and still elsewhere he speaks of it simply as *corpus mysticum*.[18] Lubac leaves us in no doubt as to the significance of these apparently innocuous variations. Of the three formulations only the first is Biblical. St. Paul had stressed again and again that the faithful are united with one another and with Christ because they are the members of a single body of which Christ is the head.[19] From the very start this idea was intimately connected with Eucharistic doctrine in that it is the sacramental Body of Christ which nourishes the faithful and fosters among them a true unity so that they remain one with Christ and members of His Body.[20]

In the Patristic period, then, it became customary (and remained so throughout the early Middle Ages) to speak of the Church as corpus Christi. The familiar expression corpus mysticum, though not unknown, is not prominent in the literature prior to the Carolingian period, and at that time was used not to describe the Church but rather to designate the Eucharist.[21] From the mid-twelfth century onwards, however, something of a reversal took place. Perhaps under the impact of the great controversy of the previous century concerning the nature of Christ's presence in the Eucharist, theologians became anxious to emphasize the real—as opposed to a mystical or merely spiritual—presence of Christ in the sacrament. As a result, it became

15. Henri de Lubac, *Corpus Mysticum: L'Eucharistie et l'église au Moyen Age* (Paris, 1944), esp. Ch. 5, pp. 117–37. See also Gerhart B. Ladner, "Aspects of Medieval Thought on Church and State," *Review of Politics, 9* (1947), 403–22, and Kantorowicz, *King's Two Bodies,* pp. 193 ff., where he notes the relevance of this change to secular political theorizing.

16. E.g. *Utrum Petri ecclesia lege reguletur,* Dupin, *1,* 665; cf. *Utrum Petri ecclesia rege gubernetur,* Dupin, *1,* 673.

17. E.g. *Verbum abbreviatum* and *Sermo de Sancto Trinitate,* in *Sermones,* f. d5v and z2r.

18. *Tract. de eccl. pot.,* Dupin, 2, 649; *Propositiones utiles,* Martène et Durand, 7, 910.

19. I Cor. 12:12–27; Col. 2:19; Eph. 4:4 ff., 5:29–30; cf. Lubac, pp. 89–97.

20. Lubac, p. 103.

21. Ibid., pp. 34–43.

common to designate the Eucharist as *verum corpus, ipsum proprium corpus,* or *verum et proprium corpus,* and the term corpus mysticum ceased to be used in this context.[22] But instead of being allowed to lapse into redundancy, it was gradually transferred to a new (and for us more familiar) context, and was applied to the Church itself. Thus the two expressions may be said to have exchanged places, and the term corpus mysticum, its original liturgical or sacramental affiliations having been severed, fell victim to a progressive secularization.

While transitional formulas such as corpus Christi mysticum were the usual ones, the original sacramental connotations which gave the doctrine its full meaning were not easily ignored, but Lubac has charted the gradual disappearance of these connotations. In St. Bonaventure, and more frequently in Aquinas, we may find the analogy of the Church as a mystical body being drawn, not from the sacramental body of Christ, but from natural bodies, or bodies in general, so that Aquinas who still speaks of "the Mystical Body of Christ" can also speak of "the mystical body of the Church" (*corpus ecclesiae mysticum*).[23] This is an expression almost devoid of sacramental associations and one already on the way to acquiring those juristic connotations which were to be fully exploited by canonists and publicists alike in the fourteenth century, when it had become normal to speak of the Mystical Body without any reference to the Eucharist.[24] Thus James of Viterbo bluntly asserts that it is by analogy to the natural body that the Kingdom of the Church is called a mystical body,[25] and Aegidius Romanus argues from the position

22. Ibid., pp. 106–07.

23. Lubac, pp. 129–30. Kantorowicz, *King's Two Bodies,* p. 201, comments that the Church thus became "a 'mystical body' in an almost juristic sense: a mystical corporation. The change in terminology . . . signified just another step in the direction of allowing the clerical corporational institution of the *corpus ecclesiae juridicum* to coincide with the *corpus ecclesiae mysticum* and thereby to 'secularize' the notion of 'mystical body.' "

24. Lubac, pp. 131 ff. For the way in which the canonists capitalized upon the juristic implications of the doctrine of the Mystical Body, see Tierney, *Foundations,* pp. 132–41.

25. *De regimine christiano,* Pt. I, cap. 3: "Quia et in corpore naturali, ad cujus similitudinem dicitur ecclesia corpus mysticum"; Arquillière, p. 109.

of the Pope as head of "the mystical body" to his lordship over temporals and his plenitude of power.[26]

The latter was certainly not alone in doing this. The doctrine was very frequently used "as a means to exalt the position of the emperor-like pope," who could now be regarded as head of "the mystical body," [27] but it should be noted that it was also at the disposal of those others who were anxious to stress the limits of the papal authority. John of Paris rejected the argument put forward by Aegidius Romanus and other papalists, and insisted that although the Church is "one mystical body" it is not to be concluded from this that all power in the Church is derived from the Pope as its head, for Christ alone is *proprie et maxime caput ecclesie*.[28] This line of reasoning was to recur in Conciliar polemics,[29] where one also encounters the characteristic argument that the mystical body of the Church, just as any natural body, has the power to prevent its own ruin and dissolution.[30]

Arguments such as these clearly reflect the degree to which the designation of the Church as a mystical body had, by the latter part of the fourteenth century, lost all sacramental connotations and begun to acquire political and corporational associations. Kantorowicz has convincingly illustrated the way in which *corpus mysticum* and *corpus morale et politicum* became in the later Middle Ages "almost interchangeable notions," [31] and it will suffice here to note that so distinguished a theologian as

26. *De ecclesiastica potestate*, Lib. II, cap. 4, Lib. III, cap. 2; Scholz, pp. 50 and 152.

27. Kantorowicz, *King's Two Bodies*, p. 203; cf. Lubac, pp. 131–32. See Kantorowicz, pp. 203–05 for related texts in Alvarus Pelagius, Panormitanus, and others.

28. *Tract. de pot.*, cap. 11 and 18; Leclercq, pp. 204 and 229.

29. See Henry of Langenstein, *Consilium pacis*, cap. 15, Dupin, 2, 832; Jean Gerson, *De unitate ecclesiastica*, ibid., 114; *Sermo ambulate dum lucem habetis*, ibid., 205; d'Ailly, *Propositiones utiles*, Martène et Durand, 7, 910, and *Tractatus de materia*, below, p. 307.

30. Gerson, *De unitate ecclesiastica*, Dupin, 2, 114; Dietrich of Niem, *De modi uniendi et reformandi ecclesiam*, ed. H. Heimpel, *Dietrich von Niem Dialog über Union und Reform der Kirche* (Leipzig and Berlin, 1933), pp. 74–76. Cf. the cognate arguments of William of Ockham, *Octo quaestiones de potestate Papae*, qu. 1, cap. 11; ed. J. G. Sikes, *Guilielmi de Ockham opera politica* (Manchester, 1940), *1*, 48–49.

31. Kantorowicz, *King's Two Bodies*, pp. 211 ff.

Gerson could speak "with some regularity" of the corpus mysticum of France,[32] and could argue that "the mystical body of the
Church, perfectly established by Christ, has, no less than any
civil, *mystical,* or truly natural body, the right and the power to
procure its own union." [33]

I know of no text in which d'Ailly definitely applies the term
corpus mysticum to any body other than the Church, but he does
speak of the General Council as being *velut corpus mysticum,*[34]
and he does argue that the mystical body of the Church has the
power of assembling itself in a General Council "by the common
natural law," for "any natural body naturally resists its own division and partition . . . and, in a like way, any civil body, or
civil community, or rightly-ordained polity." [35] Similarly, he
uses the term "the mystical body of the Christian Church" unambiguously as a synonym for "the ecclesiastical polity," [36] and
this identification, explicitly stated here, is implicit elsewhere
even when he uses transitional or traditional formulas. Thus in
the *Tractatus de materia* he speaks of Christ as "the true and
supreme Head of the Church and its most wise institutor," and
argues from this that the Church or ecclesiastical polity must be
perfectly ordained, and must therefore, like any perfectly-

32. Ibid., pp. 218–19.

33. *De unitate ecclesiastica,* Consid. 2; Dupin, 2, 114: "non enim habet corpus
Ecclesiae mysticum a Christo perfectissime stabilitum minus Jus et robur ad pro-
curationem suae unionis, quam corpus aliud civile, mysticum vel naturale verum."

34. *Tract. de eccl. pot.,* Dupin, 2, 953: "Quinto dico quod Concilium, praesente
Papa, a quo ipsum Concilium vocatum est, est velut corpus mysticum cujus Papa
est caput, et alii sunt membra."

35. *Propositiones utiles,* Martène et Durand, 7, 910: "Nam solum auctoritate
Christi, sed etiam communi jure naturali, praemissam auctoritatem sive potestatem habet corpus mysticum ecclesiae Dei. Patet quia quodlibet corpus naturale
naturaliter resistit suae divisioni et destructioni. . . . Similique modo quodlibet
corpus civile, seu civilis communitas, vel politia rite ordinata." Cf. *Epistola II ad
Benedictum XIII,* Lettenhove, *1,* 140, where he argues that the division created
by the Schism in the body of the Church is "contra legem Dei et naturae."

36. *Propositiones utiles,* Martène et Durand, 7, 910 (see above, n. 35), D'Ailly
continues as follows: "adeoque corpus spirituale seu mysticum ecclesiae Christianae, quod ordinatissime compositum est, propter quod ecclesiastica politia in
Canticis describitur 'velut castrorum acies ordinata,' simili modo uti poterit ad
suam unitatem conservandam" etc.

ordained community, be able to avert its own ruin.[37] Again, he cites St. Paul's teaching that "Christ is Head of the body of the Church and His Body is the Church," in one place, to distinguish the Universal Church, which is unique, from the multiple particular churches of Christendom,[38] and in another to prove that Christ Himself, and Peter, His Vicar (in so far as he was head of the Church), possessed a spiritual monarchy.[39] Finally, there occurs in his *Tractatus de ecclesiastica potestate* a statement to the effect that Church property is vested in "the community of the faithful, which is the Body of Christ," [40] a statement which despite the traditional formula is very close to an argument of Innocent IV recently adduced by Tierney to illustrate the juridification, at the hands of the canonists, of the doctrine of the Mystical Body.[41]

There is no reason, then, to regard d'Ailly's use of the image of the Mystical Body as incompatible with his conception of the Church as a political community similar to other political communities, for his own references to the Church as a mystical body may well serve to illustrate the truth of the contention that "to the extent . . . that the Church was interpreted as a polity like any other secular corporation, the notion *corpus mysticum* itself was charged with secular political contents." [42] When he and

37. See below, p. 310; cf. *Ep. I ad Joannem XXIII*, Dupin, 2, 877, where he employs the curious hybrid "in corpore reipublicae ecclesiasticae."

38. *Utrum Petri ecclesia lege reguletur*, Dupin, *1*, 665.

39. *Utrum Petri ecclesia rege gubernetur*, ibid., 673.

40. Dupin, 2, 942: "Unde Fundatores Ecclesiarum intenderunt Dominium et proprietatem bonorum quae dabant, transferre primo et directe in communitatem Collegii, scilicet talis Ecclesiae, ad usum deo servientium, et non in aliquam personam singularem ut 12 qu. 3 Can. *Pontifices*, et ita intelliguntur esse oblata Christo, id est Communitati Fidelium, quae est Corpus Christi, ut 12 qu. 2 Can. *Nulli*. Ex quo sequitur manifeste quod Communitas ipsa sola, habet immediatum et verum dominium in hujusmodi bonis, et non Praelatus aliquis, aut quaevis persona singularis."

41. Tierney, *Foundations*, pp. 140–41, where he cites Innocent's dictum: "aggregatio fidelium quae est corpus Christi capitis," and comments that "in assuming that the Church, defined as the *corpus Christi*, was an entity capable of the quite prosaic function of property ownership. Innocent was apparently regarding it not only as a *corpus mysticum* but as something closely akin to a legal corporation."

42. Kantorowicz, *King's Two Bodies*, p. 203.

his contemporaries, therefore, speak of the Church as a mystical body they are not pinpointing some feature distinguishing it from other communities, but are stressing, rather, the element which it has in common with all bodies, whether natural or civil.[43] And this is borne out by the way in which the notion of the mystical body was linked up with the ancient categorization of ecclesiastical power into power of a sacramental nature (*potestas ordinis*) and power of a jurisdictional or governmental nature (*potestas jurisdictionis*). Whereas the former was said to be power over "the true Body of Christ" in the Eucharist, the latter—the governmental power—was said to pertain to "the Mystical Body of Christ." [44]

D'Ailly himself does not make this explicit identification,[45] but there is no reason to suppose that he would have queried it. The distinction itself, moreover, plays a notable part in his thinking, in that it enables him to set aside that aspect of ecclesiastical power which could hardly be confined within the profane categories of corporational or political argumentation, and with which, therefore, he was not concerned. His preoccupation was with the internal constitution of the Church, with the respective authorities of the Pope and General Council. As a result, he was not interested in the potestas ordinis which was equal in all the

43. Only because of this does it make any sense to claim—as d'Ailly and other Conciliarists claimed—that to foment any schism or division in the mystical body is against the *natural* law. See above, notes 33 and 37, pp. 59–60.

44. See Lubac, p. 128, n. 48, where he quotes the Roman Catechism as saying: "Ordinis potestas ad verum Christi domini corpus in sacramento eucharistia refertur, jurisdictionis vero potestas tota in Christi corpore mystico versatur." He also cites Gerson (p. 128, n. 47), but Gerson's views do not quite coincide; see his *Tractatus de potestate ecclesiastica*, Consid. 2, 5, 6; Dupin, 2, 228, 232–35.

45. But see his *Tract. de eccl. pot.*, Dupin, 2, 932, where, following John of Paris, he says: "Sciendum est quod prima et secunda potestas, secundum aliquos, sunt una secundum essentiam, sed differentes secundum diversos actus *respectu corporis Christi veri, et mystici*" (italics mine). For the words of John, see Leclercq, pp. 208–09. D'Ailly is speaking here, however, not quite of governmental authority, but of the "potestas administrationis sacramentorum, et praecipue Sacramenti Poenitentiae, quae est potestas clavium vel spiritualis Jurisdictionis in Foro conscientiae" (Dupin, 2, 927). Tierney, *Foundations*, p. 33, n. 2, comments that by the thirteenth century the canonists were using the word *jurisdictio* to connote generally the powers of government possessed by prelates in the Church.

Apostles, but rather with that "power of regulating subjects and governing them to their salvation." This latter power—which he refers to both as the *potestas jurisdictionis* and as the *potestas regiminis*—was not that possessed to an equal extent by all the Apostles but was conferred in its fullness upon Peter alone, and the central problem confronting d'Ailly is that of deciding just what was entailed in the government of the Church by this plenitude of power.[46] The application of this familiar distinction to the power of the Papacy itself was by no means unprecedented,[47] but although it enables d'Ailly to dismiss from the discussion the features which, above all others, distinguish the Church from other political societies, it does not remove all his difficulties. The canonists had commonly argued that prelates derived their jurisdictional and administrative powers not from the sacerdotal superior who conferred upon them the potestas ordinis, but rather from election.[48] But such an argument could hardly apply to the Pope, the successor of Peter, who, as d'Ailly himself insisted, derived his primacy in the Church not from any election but from direct institution by Christ. Confronted, however, with but this one remaining obstacle to the univocal treatment of the ecclesiastical and civil polities, d'Ailly does not allow himself to be halted, but simply goes on to demolish it.

He does so largely by means of a salvo of distinctions. It is true, he says, that Peter and his legitimate successors have been Vicars of Christ, and, under Christ, heads of the Church. It is equally true, therefore, that their authority (as, indeed, that of the Roman Church and of the General Council) is principally

46. *Utrum Petri ecclesia lege reguletur*, Dupin, *1*, 667–68: "in Petro et ceteris Apostolis duplex fuit potestas: scilicet potestas ordinis et potestas Regiminis. Prima, fuit potestas consecrandi, ligandi, et solvendi. Secunda, fuit potestas ordinandi subjectos et ad eorum salutem gubernandi. Secunda propositio est, quod in Petro et ceteris Apostolis fuit aequalis potestas Ordinis, quia unus Ordo erat in singulis, scilicet Ordo Sacerdotalis. . . . Tertia est, quod in Petro et ceteris Apostolis non fuit aequalis potestas Regiminis, sed ex Christi institutione, in hac potestate Petrus fuit major et praefuit aliis." Cf. *Tract. de eccl. pot.*, Dupin, *2*, 950, where he calls the above-mentioned second power the *potestas jurisdictionis*.

47. See John of Paris, *Tract. de pot.*, cap. 25; Leclercq, pp. 258–60; cf. Tierney, *Foundations*, pp. 175–76.

48. Tierney, *Foundations*, pp. 126–29.

derived immediately from God. This is not to say, however, that it does not in any way come from men, for it depends *in a ministerial way* upon their agency.[49] When Christ placed Peter at the head of all Christians, giving him power legitimately to establish his episcopal seat where he wished, this in no way deprived his chosen flock of the natural right "which belongs to all those over whom *any authority, either secular or ecclesiastical, is placed"*—that is, the right to elect their ruler.[50] Similarly, although, strictly speaking, the plenitude of power resides in the Pope alone, because any power is said properly to pertain to the one who has the general exercise of it, it belongs to him, nevertheless, *in a ministerial way,* and is ordained to an end beyond him, which is the universal Church. It is said, therefore, to pertain to the Church *causally* or *finally,* and also, *in a representative way* to the General Council which represents the Church. Thus, despite his admission that Christ conferred the plenitude of power on Peter, d'Ailly is able to conclude that if the Pope abuses this power—that is to say, uses it to destroy rather than to preserve the Church—he can be subjected to correction by a General Council representing the whole Church.[51]

49. *Tract. de eccl. pot.,* Dupin, 2, 938: "Authoritas Papae, seu Romanae Ecclesiae et Concilii Generalis, immediate est a Deo *principaliter,* licet sit ab homine, seu dependeat ab humana potestate *ministerialiter:* nam Papa fit per Cardinalium electionem," etc. (italics mine).

50. *Tract. de eccl. pot.,* Dupin, 2, 936: "Quando Christus praefecit Beatum Petrum omnibus Christianis, dans sibi potestatem, ut ubi vellet sedere, Sedem eligeret, ita ut esset quodammodo proprius illorum Episcopus; non privavit illos Jure naturali, large sumpto, quod omnibus competit, quibus est aliqua praeficiendi potestas, *sive saecularis sive Ecclesiastica,* videlicet eligendi sibi rectorem" (italics mine).

51. *Tract. de eccl. pot.,* Dupin, 2, 950: "Dico quod haec plenitudo Jurisdictionis, proprie loquendo, solum residet in Romano seu Summo Pontifice, Petro succedenti: quia proprie, aliqua Potestas plene dicitur esse in aliquo, quia illam potest *generaliter* exercere, et *ministerialiter* in omnes dispensare." And 951: "Primo ergo modo, plenitudo Potestatis est in Papa, tanquam in subjecto ipsam recipiente, et ministerialiter exercente. Secundo, est in Universali Ecclesia, tanquam in objecto ipsam *causaliter* et finaliter continente. Tertio, est in Generali Concilio tanquam in exemplo ipsam repraesentante, et regulariter dirigente. . . . Patet quia plenitudo Potestatis non est *causaliter* propter Papam, sed Papa et ejus Potestas propter Ecclesiam, et ad eam ordinatur sicut ad finem, id est, ad ejus aedificationem. . . . Tertium, patet ex eodem verbo Apostoli, quia si

This is the conclusion at which he has been aiming all along, and which has inspired his careful distinctions. For if this is not true—which is, in effect, to say that the arguments concerning the source and purpose of political authority which are applicable to secular polities cannot be applied to the Church—then Christ, who instituted the Church, did not ordain it in a sufficiently perfect manner. But to assert this is heretical and against the Scriptures which tell us that "the works of God are perfect." [52] It might be asserted, therefore, that d'Ailly has proved on the basis of Scripture that the Church must, in certain crucial aspects, be regarded as a political society and viewed in terms of political categories. Such an assertion, however, would overlook the initial assumption essential to the validity of his scriptural argument, that is, that a "community is not sufficiently ordered, if it cannot resist its own ruin and open destruction." [53] It is this assumption that indicates the depth and extent of his commitment to the conception of the Church as a political society, for it never occurs to him that the Church might be excluded from its scope.[54]

Papa uteretur hac Potestate ad destructionem Ecclesiae, Generale Concilium est exemplum, vel speculum dictam Universalem Ecclesiam repraesentans, et ejus vice et nomine, abusus hujusmodi plenitudinis Potestas coercens, regulans, et dirigens" (italics mine).

52. *Tract. de eccl. pot.*, Dupin, 2, 959: "Ex omnibus praemissis concluditur . . . Papam posse ab Universali Ecclesia, vel a Generali Concilio eam repraesentante, in multis casibus judicari, et condemnari, et ab eo ad Concilium in multis casibus posse appelari, videlicet in casibus Ecclesiae destructionem tangentibus. . . . Quia aliter, sequeretur ipsum Christum, verum et supremum caput Ecclesiae et institutorem ejus sapientissimum eam non perfecte sufficienter ordinasse, quod est haereticum et contra illud Deuteronomii, xxxii, 4: 'Dei perfecta sunt opera.' "

53. Ibid.: "quia illa Communitas non est sufficienter ordinata, quae perditioni suae, et demolitioni publicae non potest occurrere. Sic esset de Ecclesiastica Politia, in casu quo Papa per haeresim manifestam et tyrannidem apertam, aut aliud notorium crimen, conaretur eam subvertere, et nemo ei dicere posset: 'Cur ita facis?' " Cf. *Propositiones Utiles*, Martène et Durand, 7, 910; cited above, notes 35 and 36, p. 59.

54. Put in this form d'Ailly's argument may seem to be a circular one. It should be noted, however, that commitment to the initial assumption does not necessarily entail commitment to the further belief that all political power is of the nature of a trust and is ultimately based upon the consent of the governed.

In the pages that follow, therefore, d'Ailly's political philosophy will be expounded and analyzed on the basis of arguments formulated as often with reference to the ecclesiastical as to the civil polity, the validity of such a method being assured by the fact that d'Ailly employed these arguments precisely because he himself believed that they could properly be applied to "any rightly ordained polity."

3.

Dominium

The type of discussion concerning the relation of the temporal
and ecclesiastical powers to which d'Ailly was spasmodically
prone, though not wholly irrelevant to modern political problems, is as alien to modern as it would have been to ancient
political theorizing. It is so because it was born of the travail of a
social order peculiar to the Middle Ages. The same is true of the
concept of *dominium*, which has already come to our attention
in examining d'Ailly's Church-State views. Although this concept, at least in its fully developed form, is the outcome of a
conscious attempt to specify the grounds on which a ruler may
rightfully claim to exercise authority over his subjects, it cannot
properly be said to reflect an approach to the problem of *political* obligation, for that presupposes some notion of political
community—some idea comparable, at least, to our modern idea
of the state.

The word dominium itself, if not impossible to translate into
English, at least defies transliteration, not because it was "created by medieval Latin to express the feudal conception of ownership," [1] but rather because its meaning underwent a significant

1. J. B. Morrall, *Political Thought in Medieval Times* (London, 1958), p. 87.
On the contrary the term appears in the *Corpus juris civilis* and elsewhere (see,
e.g., *C.* 2, 3, 20).

mutation during the medieval period. By dominium the Roman lawyers had meant property or right of ownership, and d'Ailly could still use the word in what is superficially, at least, the same way, when he spoke of the power of the Prince and the Pope over the goods of laymen.[2] But he could also speak of "principative" dominium as something distinct from "original" or "civil,"[3] as well as listing "regal," "imperial," and "apostolic" dominium, none of which seem to refer to merely proprietary rights.[4] The term clearly had a broader connotation than our word "property," but still retained shades of meaning that "dominion" does not possess and "lordship" would not satisfactorily convey.[5] It will be my policy, therefore, to retain the Latin term to indicate that the concept is now an archaism, a product of a uniquely medieval state of affairs, and therefore to underline the fact that d'Ailly's ideas on the subject, though not necessarily completely irrelevant to modern social and political conditions, form one of the more distinctively medieval strands in his thought.

I

The later medieval concept of dominium was produced by the coalescence of two main traditions of thought, the first medieval in origin, and the second a blending of Patristic and Aristotelian ideas.

In Roman private law ownership had been unique and indivisible, entailing an exclusive right on the part of the owner against anyone else, and involving as its "essential attribute" the legal right of *abusus*—that of disposing of the property in question.[1] Rights in the property of another (*jura in re aliena*) were

2. See above, p. 50.

3. *Utrum indoctus in jure divino*, Dupin, *1*, 650: "Et hoc intendit probare tam de originali dominio, quam de civili et principativo dominio."

4. See below, p. 76.

5. Whereas "lordship" has lost much and "dominion" has lost all of its former proprietary connotations, the medieval *dominium* had "to stand now for *ownership* and now for *lordship*."—F. Pollock and F. W. Maitland, *The History of English Law before the Time of Edward I* (2nd ed., Cambridge, 1911), *1*, 230.

1. "Le vrai symbole de la propriété romaine c'est *l'abusus*, la faculté de détruire la chose, puisqu'elle suppose, pour être reconnue, qu'il n'existe aucun autre

recognized, but such rights—as, for example, those of a tenant—
were clearly distinguished from ownership, extending only to
the power of using the object and of enjoying its fruits (*usus et
fructus*). This position underwent a certain modification towards
the end of the imperial period, but this modification affected
only those who had tenancies of indefinite duration, and such
tenancies continued to be exceptional.[2] It is this view of property that substantially re-established itself in the early modern
period and that continues to dominate modern laws on the
subject. It could not, however, fully comprehend medieval
views, fashioned as they were by the development and proliferation of feudal institutions.

Early Germanic landholding remains a subject dogged by controversy, but it has been suggested that it was the source of the
characteristically medieval view of property, so different from
that of the Roman lawyers. This view involved no exclusive
right of ownership, and what the law protected was rather
"seisin," or actual possession "rendered venerable by duration."
And possession—for example, of a piece of land—was merely
one right which by no means excluded others.[3] To own a thing
meant simply to be able to enjoy its use and fruits, so that there
was no "essential difference" between usufruct and property and
no barrier, therefore, to multiple ownership. For "nothing is
more varied, less absolute and more divisible than the enjoy-
ment of a thing." [4] With the growth of feudalism and the con-

---

droit parallèle ou complémentaire, qui mette obstacle à cet *abusus* et que le
propriétaire ait le devoir de respecter."—E. Meynial, "Notes sur la formation
de la théorie du domaine divise du xiiie au xive siècle dans les Romanistes,"
Mélanges Fitting (Montpellier, 1908), 2, 412. This whole paper (pp. 411–61),
though it limits itself to the evidence to be found in Civilian writings and does
not explore the canonistic literature or the cartularies, still seems to be the best
study of the problem of divided dominium. Short but useful accounts are to be
found in McIlwain, *Growth*, pp. 176–82; Lewis, *Ideas*, *1*, 88–92; F. L. Ganshof,
Feudalism, trans. P. Grierson (London, 1952), pp. 117–18.

2. And up to the time of Justinian, they concerned only the lands of the
public domain (see Meynial, p. 417).

3. Marc Bloch, *La Société féodale: La formation des liens de dépendance* (Paris,
1939), pp. 182–84.

4. Meynial, p. 415.

comitant proliferation of tenancies of indefinite duration, divided ownership became increasingly common, although at first the lord tended to be regarded as the owner in the sense envisaged by Roman law, and the vassal as possessing rights akin to the Roman usufruct. But the fact that the vassal had the effective possession of the fief enabled him to consolidate his real right and to extend it at the expense of the lord's, so that "already in the eleventh century the rights of a vassal over his fief had extended far beyond those allowed by the Roman conception of usufruct." [5] After the revival in the twelfth century of the study of Roman law in the West, the Civilians tried to reconcile these rights with Roman legal ideas, and finally succeeded in doing so (if at the expense of a somewhat forced interpretation of Roman private law) by means of the doctrine of divided dominium. According to this, the vassal was conceded to possess more than a mere *jus in re aliena*. He had a real right in his fief, for he possessed the *dominium utile* or useful ownership of it. This did not mean, however, that the lord had forfeited his ownership for he was said to possess the *dominium directum,* often known in more modern times as "the eminent domain." [6] Thus the Roman conception of ownership as unique and indivisible finally collapsed under the sustained and stubborn pressure of feudal social conditions, and divided ownership was enshrined at the very heart of the law. There can certainly be no doubt about the value of this doctrine in rationalizing the feudal hierarchy of landholding, for it permitted the original possessor to retain his legal right over the land even after it had passed,

5. Ganshof, p. 117.

6. Meynial, pp. 420 ff., where he traces the development of the doctrine. It found clear expression in the *glossa ordinaria* of Accursius in 1228, but only in the work of Bartolus in the early 14th century were the full ramifications of the theory worked out and the earlier hesitancies and inconsistencies removed. Ganshof, p. 118, comments that "it began to be applied in France before the end of the 13th century, and was further developed and became general only in the fourteenth." Cf. A. Esmein, *Cours élémentaire d'histoire du droit français* (2nd ed., Paris, 1895), pp. 216–17; R. Huebner, *A History of Germanic Private Law*, trans. F. S. Philbrick (Boston, 1918), pp. 227–34. It does not, however, seem to have penetrated into English law, which solved the problem in its own characteristic way (see Pollock and Maitland, *History of English Law*, 2, 4–6).

in accordance with the feudal contract, out of his hands and into those of a vassal or even of a vassal's vassal. Even if the passage of time had strengthened the rights of the immediate holders of the land, and gradually extended to them the protection of the law, the rights of the overlord to stipulate payments in money or kind continued to be recognized.

A society arose, therefore, in which divided dominium was the norm, and in which a multiplicity of rights could exist in any one piece of land, each protected by the appropriate legal remedy. But the feudal contract was concerned with more than the land or the payments arising from the use of land, and feudalism entailed more than divided ownership. Of its very nature it involved from the start a personal element of protection offered in return for service pledged, and later on, with the collapse of central government, there accrued to it further elements which were judicial and administrative in nature. In this way the Roman distinction between public and private law and between "ideas of proprietary right and governmental authority" [7] was broken down, and to the term dominium acceded the jurisdictional and political connotations which were to be so apparent when Richard Fitzralph came, in the fourteenth century, to discuss its meaning.[8] But while Fitzralph's conception of dominium could hardly have been formulated against an institutional background other than that of a feudal society, it derived much of its hierarchial coherence from Christian and Aristotelian ideas.

The most relevant of these Christian ideas were the overriding belief in the divine origin of all power, temporal as well as spiritual, with its concomitant stress on duty rather than right, and the Stoic-Patristic idea of private property as merely a useful

7. McIlwain, Growth, p. 177; cf. Pollock and Maitland, *1*, 230–31.

8. Richard Fitzralph, an influential Oxford theologian, Vice-Chancellor of the University ca. 1333, and Archbishop of Armagh from 1347 until his death in 1360. His analysis of the nature of dominium is contained in his *De pauperie salvatoris* (see esp. Lib. I, caps. 1–2), a complex analysis of the problem of Apostolic poverty written in 1350. An edition of the first four books of this treatise is included as an appendix to R. L. Poole, ed., *Johannis Wycliffe: De dominio divino libri tres* (London, 1890), pp. 257–476. D'Ailly was well acquainted with this work.

remedy for evil, a result of the Fall before which all things had been held in common. These beliefs blended with feudal theories, and, with the recovery of the *corpus Aristotelicum,* there was added to the compound the idea that there is, throughout nature in general, a principle of rule and subordination. This idea was given full expression in the fifth chapter of the first book of the *Politics,* which McIlwain has described as "one of the main sources of the medieval theory of 'dominium.' " [9] The amalgam thus produced was a complex one in which the relationships between the different elements were by no means fixed. Two contingencies served to bring these elements into the ultimate equilibrium that characterized the fully developed doctrine of dominium by grace. The first of these was the impressive synthesis achieved by the papalist, Aegidius Romanus, in his *De potestate ecclesiastica,* with the publication of which, in 1302, the theory of dominium might be said to have come of age, if not to have reached maturity.[10] The second was the prolonged controversy that raged within the Franciscan Order concerning the observance of the Rule, and the doctrine of Apostolic poverty.

Citing St. Augustine's denial of true justice to the commonwealth that is not Christian,[11] Aegidius Romanus placed his fundamental stress on the derivation from God of all authority —whether over people or over things—dominium being for him, as it was to be for Fitzralph and Wyclif, the divinely ordained relation of superior being to inferior. The de facto exer-

9. McIlwain, *Growth,* p. 70, n. 1. Our sketch of the evolution of the various conceptions which went to make up the theory of dominium is necessarily extremely schematic. In any full outline, the ideas contributed by Aquinas and Ptolemy of Lucca would, of course, merit consideration. See McIlwain, *Growth,* p. 259, n. 2.

10. McIlwain, *Growth,* p. 259, comments that "the theory of *dominium* in its complete form implies a combination of ideas which could not have occurred much before his time and he [i.e., Aegidius] seems to have been the first of whom we have any knowledge to see and to take full advantage of all its implications as an argument for papal claims."

11. *De. eccl. pot.,* Lib. II, cap. 7; Scholz, p. 73. Chapters 7–12 of the second book (Scholz, pp. 70–111) contain the central statement of Aegidius's teaching on dominium; cf. McIlwain's useful analysis (*Growth,* pp. 250–57).

cise of authority, either proprietary or governmental, even when it serves the ends of social utility and is in accordance with human laws of inheritance, can give merely a presumptive title to dominium, which is truly possessed only if the person claiming to exercise it is in proper subordination to God and has received it through the grace of God. Because the sacraments of the Church are the channels of God's grace, pagans and those excommunicated can have no just dominium, not even a mere dominium utile.[12] Nor, indeed, can there be any true dominium whatsoever except that subject to the Church, which has, therefore, a general dominium over all persons and things.[13]

The value of such a conception of dominium as a basis for papal claims is evident, and it was not without its influence on other papalists such as James of Viterbo and Alvarus Pelagius.[14] The doctrine was reiterated in its full rigor about the year 1326 by William of Cremona who, like Aegidius, was an Augustinian friar, and from whom, Gwynn has conjectured,[15] it was inherited by Fitzralph. In the latter's hands, however, it underwent a modification which left it, at least potentially, of less exclusively papalist value. Although Fitzralph agreed with Aegidius that rightful dominium was contingent upon grace, he did not follow him in attributing, therefore, a universal dominium to the Church, but asserted instead that men held such authority directly from God.[16] This is the theory which, with Wyclif, provided an argument in favor of secular appropriation of ecclesiastical property—the clergy having, by their unrighteousness,

12. Aegidius defines *dominium utile* as "illud quod est fructiferum," and contrasts it with *dominium potestativum* which is "illud quod est jurisdiccionale, ad quod spectat justiciam exercere" (Scholz, p. 87; cf. p. 71). The distinction is very close to the juristic distinction between *dominium utile* and *dominium directum*, but dates back before the latter was commonly employed, for Aegidius took it, in essence if not in the same words, from the *De sacramentis christianae fidei* of Hugh of St. Victor (1096–1141), Lib. II, secunda pars, cap. 7; PL *176*, 420 B–C. In Hugh's work, the word dominium does not appear.

13. Scholz, pp. 70 and 111.

14. See Lewis, *Ideas, 1*, 340, n. 27.

15. Aubrey Gwynn, *The English Austin Friars in the Time of Wyclif* (Oxford, 1940), pp. 65–67. The whole of Ch. 4 is valuable for information concerning the history of the doctrine of lordship as contingent on grace.

16. *De paup. salv.*, Lib. 4, caps. 3–5; ed. Poole, pp. 440–43.

forfeited their dominium.[17] Such a position is comprehensible only against the background of another and independent development, that of the Franciscan controversy concerning Apostolic poverty.[18]

Early in the history of the Order difficulties had inevitably arisen concerning the interpretation of the Franciscan Rule which included, in imitation of the life of Christ and the Apostles, the obligation of individual and collective poverty. Gregory IX had sought to solve the problem by the bull *Quo elongati* which not only permitted the reception and employment of money on behalf of the friars by "spiritual friends," but also distinguished between the dominium and simple use (*usus facti*) of goods, and asserted that the friars, neither individually nor in common, possessed dominium over the goods which they used.[19] In 1245, Innocent IV went a stage further and definitely laid down the principle that the dominium of goods left for the use of the friars was vested in the Holy See,[20] and in 1279 and 1312, this interpretation was confirmed by the decretals *Exiit qui seminet* of Nicholas III and *Exivi de paradiso* of Clement V.[21]

Such a solution failed, admittedly, to satisfy the Spiritual wing of the Order, but under the firm rule of Michael of Cesena, the

17. Wyclif expressed his views on dominium primarily in his two works *De dominio divino* (see above, n. 8) and *De civili dominio*, ed. J. Loserth, R. L. Poole, and F. D. Matthew, 4 vols. (London, 1884–1904). D'Ailly may never have read any of Wyclif's writings. He took part at Constance in a commission which condemned some of Wyclif's propositions, but they seem to have been drawn at second hand from Huss's *De ecclesia*. See Salembier, *Schisme*, pp. 334–35; J. Loserth, ed., *Johannis Wyclif tractatus de ecclesia* (London, 1886) p. iii. The works in which he discusses the problem of dominium, moreover, were written ca. 1380, probably not much more than a decade after Wyclif had written his *De dominio divino*, which does not seem to have been known on the Continent before the opening years of the fifteenth century (see Poole, *Johannis Wycliffe de dominio divino*, pp. vii ff.). D'Ailly certainly seems, at least at this stage, to have been unacquainted even at secondhand with Wyclif's views, for he directs his attack solely against Fitzralph.

18. For a brief discussion of this see Ernst Benz, *Ecclesia Spiritualis, Kirchenidee und Geschichtsphilosophie der Franziskanischen Reformation* (Stuttgart, 1934), pp. 236–41, and for a lengthier treatment, Decima L. Douie, *The Nature and the Effect of the Heresy of the Fraticelli* (Manchester, 1932), esp. Ch. 6.

19. Douie, pp. 2–3.

20. Douie, p. 4.

21. Douie, pp. 10, 14–15.

opposition of the most extreme zealots had largely been crushed, and the Order was enjoying a period of comparative tranquillity when, after an inquiry instituted in 1321, John XXII adopted a stand that split the Order and drove Michael of Cesena into opposition and exile. For in the two bulls, *Ad conditorem canonum* (1322) and *Cum inter nonnullos* (1323), John not only denied the legal validity, when applied to goods which are consumed by use, of the distinction between dominium and usus facti, but also declared it heretical to assert that Christ and the Apostles owned no property either individually or collectively.[22]

The ensuing long and acrimonious controversy ranged against the Pope not only Michael of Cesena but also William of Ockham, both of whom found refuge at the court of the excommunicated Lewis of Bavaria. It also served to center a great deal of attention upon property and theories of property, and although the Spiritual Franciscans were finally defeated, the dispute left as its legacy (as the works of Wyclif reveal) a renewed sense of the evil and corruption entailed by ecclesiastical wealth. D'Ailly's discussion of dominium, however, largely revolves around the pre-Wyclifite doctrine set forth in Fitzralph's tract, which, while deeply influenced by the mendicant controversy, shows little sympathy either with the Spiritual Franciscans or with any branch of the Order. It was composed at the request of the Pope, Clement VI, and although the doctrine of dominium it contains is not predicated upon an extreme papalist position, it forms part of an elaborate attack upon the privileges of the mendicants and upon the idea of apostolic poverty, and involves the assertion of the dominium of Christ *as man* over all created things.[23]

Such are the developments that moulded the mature doctrine of dominium as contingent upon grace, and they help to throw

22. Douie, pp. 160–64. The texts of these two important bulls were included in the *Extravagantes Johannis XXII*, 14, c. 3 and 4.

23. *De paup. salv.*, Lib. II, cap. 10; Poole, pp. 350–52. Gwynn, *English Austin Friars*, p. 69, comments that Fitzralph's attacks upon the mendicants "have little apparent connection with his previous long disquisitions in abstract theory." The clarification of his position will probably have to await the appearance in print of the complete text of the *De pauperie salvatoris*. The last three books were edited as early as 1932 but have not been published (see Douie, p. ix).

some light on the meaning and significance of d'Ailly's own views on the subject, views that are neither extensively nor systematically elaborated. What we have been witnessing is in fact the emergence, perhaps for the first time, of a distinctively medieval but, at the same time, comprehensive political theory —a theory predicated upon the combination of certain Christian beliefs with a feudal view of society.[24] It reveals the characteristic medieval blurring of the distinction between public office and private property; it is dominated by the dichotomy between those who rule and those who are ruled; it lacks the idea of a political *community* organized as a body for the pursuit of goals common to those who constitute it. Such a point of view is, as we have suggested, alien both to ancient and modern political speculation, and the relevance of d'Ailly's political ideas to more modern developments must necessarily be in inverse proportion to the extent of his adherence to this doctrine of dominium.

II

In the last chapter we brushed against some of d'Ailly's remarks about dominium because they were relevant to his position upon matters of Church and State.[1] These remarks are to be found in his compendious *Tractatus de potestate ecclesiastica* (1416) and his early disputation *Utrum Petri ecclesia rege gubernetur* (1381), but they are fragmentary in nature and give no coherent picture of his views. A more complete treatment of the question is to be found in his other early disputations entitled *Quaestio de legitimo dominio* and *Utrum indoctus in jure divino possit juste praeesse in ecclesiae regno*,[2] the former written in 1381 and the latter at about the same time.[3]

24. H. J. Laski stressed the uniqueness of this theory of society constructed on feudal lines, but noted that because everyone, according to it, holds directly of God, it is an "eternal feudalism built upon the English and not upon the continental model" ("Political Theory in the Later Middle Ages," *C Med H, 8,* 633).

1. See above, Ch. 2, pp. 46 ff.

2. Dupin, *1,* 641–62.

3. Salembier, *Cardinal,* p. 369, says that the work was written at some time between 1372 and 1395, and d'Ailly himself indicates (col. 657) that at the time of

It takes no more than a quick glance at these early works to perceive that d'Ailly has to a considerable extent embraced the doctrine of dominium as formulated by Aegidius of Rome, reiterated by William of Cremona, and elaborated and modified by Fitzralph. In his *Quaestio de legitimo dominio,* his very first conclusion is that "just as by the gift of God, Christ-made-man is Lord-Creator of all things, so without the gift of Christ, no other man may wield just *dominium*," because "just as every secondary cause is contingent upon the first cause, so from the first and supreme *dominium* is derived every secondary *dominium*." [4] On the basis of this contention—which he repeats elsewhere, quoting St. Paul's dictum that there is no power unless from God [5]—he can go on to conclude that it is the "uncreated gift of divine approbation" which "principally constitutes any just *dominium*." [6] This might well be Fitzralph speaking, and the analogy becomes more compelling when d'Ailly reiterates without question Fitzralph's distinction between "original," "civil," and "principative" dominium.[7]

---

composition Clement VII (1378–94) was the Avignonese pontiff. The last paragraph, however, reads as follows: "Circa reliqua hanc materiam tangentia, principaliter tractavi in quibusdam cedulis variis temporibus per me scriptis. Secundo principaliter *in Concilio generali celebrato in civitate Pisana,* et in quibusdam Congregationibus antea Parisiis celebratis" (Dupin, *1,* 662; italics mine). This last sentence was added during the years 1410–13 when d'Ailly corrected and reworked several of his earlier tracts; see M. Liebermann, "Chronologie Gersonienne VIII: Gerson et d'Ailly," *Romania, 81* (1960), 80–81.

4. Dupin, *1,* 642: "Sicut Dei dono Christus homo factus est Dominus Creator omnium: sic absque Christi dono nullus homo alius gerit justum dominium . . . quia sicut a prima causa dependet omnis causa secunda; sic a primo et supremo dominio omne secundum dominium derivatur."

5. *Utrum indoctus in jure divino,* Dupin, *1,* 651: "Deus habet plenissimum omnium rerum dominium, primum ac supremum: sed omne secundum dominium a primo et supremo derivatur. Ideo dicit Apostolus: 'Non est potestas nisi a deo.'"

6. *De legitimo dominio,* Dupin, *1,* 642: "donum increatum divinae approbationis principaliter constituit aliquem justum dominium."

7. *Utrum indoctus in jure divino,* Dupin, *1,* 650; cf. *De legitimo dominio,* Dupin, *1,* 643, and 641–42 where he speaks of *regale dominium,* as he does also in *Utrum Petri ecclesia rege gubernetur,* Dupin, *1,* 677 and 679. Fitzralph had divided *dominium* into "natural or original" and "adventitious or political." The former was that enjoyed by man before the Fall (and by Christ as man from the very moment of his conception), and received back through grace by a repentant Adam. The latter is the creation of positive laws and is divided into domestic,

Closer inspection reveals some interesting idiosyncrasies in d'Ailly's version of the doctrine. It is true, he says, that *secundum divinitatem* Christ is King and Lord of all things, just as God the Father is, but this refers, not to temporal things, but to the dominium of the eternal kingdom. From this should be distinguished, he goes on to argue, Christ's human dominium, which itself can be taken to mean two things—spiritual or sacerdotal and secular or temporal dominium. It is the former and not the latter that the New Testament ascribes to Christ. For Christ adhered to the strictest poverty. Even in the food He ate and the clothes He wore, He had, strictly speaking, not dominium, either personally or in common with the other Apostles, but merely the use of them. Hence we cannot ascribe to Christ or to Peter (insofar as he succeeded Christ as head of the Church) any kind of temporal kingship.[8] To these refinements may be appended two related arguments. The first is d'Ailly's reiteration in the *Tractatus de ecclesiastica potestate* of John of Paris's denial that the Pope had, properly speaking, any dominium over ecclesiastical goods, and still less over the goods of the laity.[9] The second is his contention that even the spiritual or sacerdotal dominium which Christ possessed is not really dele-

---

civil, and regal dominium, this last category coinciding with what d'Ailly calls *principativum dominium*. See *De paup. salv.*, Lib. I, cap. 2, and Lib. II passim; Poole, pp. 280, 332–78. Note also d'Ailly's approving citation in the *Sentences* of Fitzralph's opening chapters, clearly revealing his own adherence to the idea of divided dominium (*Princ. in II Sent.*, N, f. 30v).

8. See above, p. 47. It is interesting to note that in support of this position d'Ailly gives a general reference to the decretals which had been issued to elucidate the Franciscan rule. Not even John XXII's denial (in the bull *Ad conditorem canonum*—see above, n. 22) of the validity of the distinction between dominium and usus, when applied to things the use of which involves their consumption, gives him pause, for, as he argues elsewhere: "illud dictum: 'In rebus quae usu consumuntur, non differt usus a dominio,' debet intelligi quod quando alicujus rei tale habetur dominium, unum non separatur ab altero etc" (*De legitimo dominio*, Dupin, *1*, 646).

9. *Tract. de eccl. pot.*, Dupin, *2*, 942–44; see above, pp. 49–51. The argument involves the parallel assertion that secular princes likewise lacked true dominium over the possessions of their subjects, and may serve to indicate the fact that later medieval publicists, despite the hesitancies in their thinking which the doctrine of dominium entailed, were able to distinguish between public and private law and to disentangle the notion of political authority from that of propriety right. See below, p. 102.

gated to ecclesiastics. They are in the position of the bailiffs of a
king, who possess, not the royal dominium, but only the power
to exercise it on the king's behalf. Thus the purely spiritual
power which they wield is not properly speaking dominium at
all, but merely *ministerium*.[10]

It is difficult to evaluate the exact significance of all these distinctions, but their context suggests that d'Ailly drew them
rather because he wished to exclude any extreme propapalist inferences that might be drawn from the doctrine of dominium
than because of any desire to modify Fitzralph's teaching that
just dominium was contingent upon grace. Indeed, from the
point of view of the history of the doctrine itself, the most interesting aspect of his discussion is that, unlike Aegidius, William
of Cremona, and (perhaps) Fitzralph, but like Wyclif, he extended the concept of dominium to cover ecclesiastical authority
in spiritual matters.[11] This provides at least a partial answer to
Gwynn's question as to whether this extension to spiritual claims
was uniquely the work of Wyclif or was to be "traced back to the
earlier controversy between Fitzralph and the friars." [12]

10. *De legitimo domino*, Dupin, *1*, 642: "aliud est dominari, sive esse Dominum,
aut habere dominium; et aliud exercere dominium, sive domini actum: nam
utrumque potest ab altero seperari . . . Rex est dominus in Regno, qui tamen
plures actus Regii dominii non exercet: contra vero Baillivus, authoritate Regis,
plures actus Regii dominii exercet, nec tamen est Dominus Regni, nec habet
Regale dominium . . . . Sed et consimiliter loquitur Apostolus de potestate Ecclesiastica pure spirituali, dicens: 'Quid est Paulus, quid est Apollo, nisi minister
ejus cui credidistis?' Unde ex hiis sequitur quod potestas Ecclesiastica pure spiritualis, non est proprie dominium, sed solum ministerium exercendi Domini
actum a Christo concessum." Cf. *Utrum indoctus in jure divino*, Dupin, *1*, 652.

11. It is true that d'Ailly said that ecclesiastics possess only *ministerium*, but
he did insist that no less than *dominium* itself, the exercise of ministerial power
was contingent upon the gift of God: "non stat aliquem juste exercere dominium, seu Domini actum, a Christo non habere collatum dominium, vel concessum
ministerium" (*De legitimo dominio*, Dupin, *1*, 642).

12. *English Austin Friars*, pp. 67–68. Speaking of Fitzralph's doctrine of dominium he says: "Twenty years later, when Wyclif uses this same doctrine as a
weapon of attack on the temporal power and spiritual jurisdiction of the Catholic Church, the Augustinian theory of lordship and grace has been extended to
include not merely temporal lordship and jurisdiction but also spiritual jurisdic-
tions . . . Is this extension of the Augustinian principle to spiritual claims the
work of Wyclif, or can it be traced back to the earlier controversies between Fitzralph and the friars?"

Whatever interest these aspects of d'Ailly's thought may possess, they do little to indicate the extent to which he has embraced the central thesis of the contingence of dominium upon grace. The importance of gauging this commitment has already been stressed, for it would be a commitment to a political theory credible only within the context of medieval religious belief. Furthermore, if d'Ailly is found to be wholly committed to such a thesis, what then is the relevance of his typically Conciliarist stress on consent as the source of authority, and indeed what peace can be found to grow between these two divergent principles? For if a ruler who lapses from grace no longer rightfully possesses dominium, then there is no need to appeal to a theory of consent in order to justify his expulsion; nor, conversely, can any wish or expressed consent of his subjects make his rule righteous. D'Ailly's doctrine of dominium must assume, therefore, in any examination of his political thought, a position of importance out of all proportion either with its intrinsic value, or with the space devoted to it in his writings. For it may indicate an early adherence to a position later abandoned, or, more likely and more important, the existence of a dangerous lack of consistency in his thinking. It is indeed fortunate that in two of the works already mentioned d'Ailly actually addresses himself to the precise question of the validity of Fitzralph's doctrine of "lordship founded in grace."

In one of these works[13] d'Ailly is discussing the proposition that the unjust can have a just title to the office of ruler, and to oppose the proposition he adduces the opinion of a "certain great Doctor"—Richard Fitzralph—and elaborates it at length. The essence of this position, he tells us, is that "no one who does not have the created grace of God is rightful lord of anything—indeed, if he loses his grace, he forfeits *dominium*."[14] Among

13. *Utrum indoctus in jure divino possit juste praeesse*, Dupin, *1*, 646–62.

14. Ibid., 649–50: "Injustus potest juste praeesse. Ita quod potest acquirere et habere jus et authoritatem, seu justum titulum praesidentiae . . . . Sciendum est autem quod contra quarta propositionem est opinio cujusdam magni Doctoris, scilicet Domini Richardi Armachani, qui in Libro suo, *De pauperie Christi*, tenet quod 'Nullus absque creata Dei gratia, est alicujus rei justus Dominus; immo perdens gratiam, perdit dominium." Cf. *De legitimo dominio*, Dupin, *1*, 643.

79

the supporting arguments he mentions is that to live an innocent life is merely to pay the homage due to God for His having conferred dominium upon us, and that just as the vassal who does no homage is deprived of his fief, so also he who is in mortal sin is unfaithful to the Lord, and is therefore unworthy to have dominium.[15] This "celestial feudalism," along with the whole of Fitzralph's position, d'Ailly rejects as "sophistical reasoning"—referring to the *Dialogus* of Ockham who, he says, "miraculously" proved from both the Old and New Testaments that even infidels, and therefore those who are in mortal sin, can possess true dominium.[16] And in his *Quaestio de legitimo dominio*, where he again attacks Fitzralph's doctrine, he elaborates this by saying that when St. Paul ordered that every soul be subject to the higher powers he was talking, not only of authorities persisting in a state of grace, but also of infidel rulers and even of those in a state of mortal sin.[17] Indeed, if this were not so, he adds, the situation would be absurd for no man would know when he had rightful dominium over the things he possessed.[18]

15. Ibid., 650: "Innocenter vivere, est homagium Deo debitum pro collato sibi dominio . . . . Sed qui non solvit homagium, privandus est Feudo: et per consequens, peccans mortaliter, est infidelis Dominio, et ingratus accepti dominii, igitur indignus dominio."

16. Ibid., "Sed hiis et aliis hujuscemodo sophisticis rationibus non obstantibus, teneo praedictam opinionem esse falsam et haereticam: et hoc idem tenet Venerabilis Doctor Guillielmus Ockam, in tertio Tractatu sui dialogi, Lib. 7, cap. 24, ubi mirabiliter probat ex Scriptura sacra, quod plures non Christiani fuerint veri Imperatores, et quod verum dominium, tam in veteri, quam in Novo Testamento potest competere infidelibus; et per consequens, in peccato mortali existentibus." The reference to Ockham is to *Dialogus*, III, II, I, cap. 25; Goldast, 2, 896–98. Cf. D'Ailly's *Appreviatio dialogi Okam*, Paris, Bibl. Nat. *Ms. Lat.*, 14,975, ff. 99r–99v, where he also numbers the chapter as 24. A. G. Little, *The Grey Friars in Oxford* (Oxford, 1892), p. 231, has drawn attention to the fact that d'Ailly's nomenclature differs from that used generally in the printed editions, so that his "Tertius tractatus" refers to "Pars III, Tract. ii," the only section of Part III known to him.

17. Dupin, *1*, 643: "'Omnis anima potestatibus sublimioribus subdita sit.' Ubi loquitur Apostolus non solum de potestatibus, vel Dominis existentibus in gratia, sed etiam de infidelibus, ac aliter existentibus in mortali culpa."

18. Ibid., "consequens est absurdum; quia sic nullus homo sciret quando esset justus Dominus rei quam possideret."

But this does not close the discussion for d'Ailly. If he has insisted that all rightful dominium or exercise of dominium is contingent upon divine concession, he has also denied that mortal sin can in any way revoke that concession or entail the forfeiture of dominium. Must it be said, therefore, that dominium in no way depends upon grace? His answer is a firm negative, but he does intimate that it is necessary to be a little more precise about what is meant by grace. Rightful dominium requires, he tells us, neither the created grace which justifies in this life (*gratia gratum faciens*), nor the [uncreated] grace of eternal predestination which leads to the final good; but it does require a certain *gratia gratis data,* in this case the free concession by God to the creature of dominium or ministerium under God. It also requires the grace of eternal predestination, not that which leads towards the ultimate end, but that which is directed towards some such temporal or created good as dominium or the possession and use of things.[19]

It is important to grasp the exact meaning of these highly technical distinctions, and in order to do so it is necessary to realize that some of the terms used do not possess the meaning which it became customary to give them in post-Tridentine theology.[20] It was usual to define grace in general as a supernatural gift (or the totality of supernatural gifts) of God to a rational creature with a view to its final salvation; by the time at which d'Ailly was writing, theologians had long agreed that grace was to be distinguished into the two main categories, "uncreated"

19. *Utrum indoctus in jure divino,* Dupin, *1,* 653: "Ex quibus omnibus patet quae gratia Dei requiratur ad juste dominari, et quae non. Non etiam requiritur gratia temporaliter gratum faciens, seu justificans; nec gratia aeternae praedestinationis finaliter consummans, et ad finale bonum deducens: sed requiritur [gratia] gratis data, scilicet gratuita communicatio dominii ipsi creaturae a Deo, vel gratuita concessio ministerii, sub Deo; gratia etiam aeternae praedestinationis, non tamen specialiter ad finem ultimum, sed ad tale creatum bonum, puta talis, aut talium rerum possessionem et usum." Cf. *De legitimo dominio,* ibid., 644–45.

20. See *Dictionnaire de théologie catholique,* s. v. "Grace." For a short but valuable discussion which indicates the points of difference between fourteenth-century and modern Roman Catholic usage, see Gordon Leff, *Bradwardine and the Pelagians* (Cambridge, 1957), esp. pp. 140–51, 267–68.

81

and "created." The former signified "God Himself acting directly through His will," and indicated, therefore, "less a distinct quality than an attribute of His nature . . . the source of all created grace, and the ultimate cause for dividing the saved from the damned." [21] It was to this category of uncreated grace that d'Ailly was referring when he spoke of "the gift" or "the grace of eternal predestination." [22] "Created grace," on the other hand, signified a supernatural gift of God which, although it derived from His will, remained distinct from it, and both Fitzralph and d'Ailly had this type of grace in mind when they discussed the connection between just dominium and the possession of grace.[23]

This is straightforward enough. But the theologians went further and dissected created grace in turn into several subordinate categories. They did so from the point of view of its causes, subjects and effects, its modalities and its ends, and it is fortunate that only the last need detain us here. From this point of view, created grace was divided into *gratia gratum faciens* and *gratia gratis data*. The former is that interior grace the presence of which is incompatible with mortal sin. It renders the soul pleasing to God and may, therefore, be called justifying grace. The latter is that grace directed not to the justification of the recipient but to the salvation of others through his agency. It is not given to all Christians and it may reside even in sinners.[24] Aquinas (and the theologians of the post-Tridentine era who usually followed him on this) attached to these terms the meanings given above, but, as Leff has pointed out, "the terms for the different kinds of supernatural aid differed with individual

21. Leff, p. 141.

22. See *De legitimo dominio,* in Dupin, *1*, 642; *Utrum indoctus in jure divino,* ibid., 653, where he actually makes the identification: "Decimaquarta propositio est, quod: Quamvis aliquando Deus *ex gratia increata aeternae praedestinationis* aliquem constituat Dominum" (italics mine).

23. It should be noted that when the scholastics used the word "grace" without any qualifying adjective, they usually intended to indicate created grace, and in particular that subspecies called sanctifying or habitual grace; see *Dict. de théol. cath., 6,* 1557.

24. The powers of the priest or confessor may be cited as an example.

thinkers," and other Scholastics were able to attach different meanings to the same terms.[25]

This is in part the case with d'Ailly and it will confront us with a certain difficulty. He gave to the term gratia gratum faciens, it is true, a meaning close to that given it by Aquinas, using it to signify divinely infused justifying grace.[26] As we have seen, he denied that such created grace is required for the possession of just dominium, and it may now be noted that in doing so he was dissociating himself specifically from Fitzralph's position. When Fitzralph had insisted that rightful dominium was contingent upon the possession of grace and that it was forfeited, therefore, if the claimant lapsed into mortal sin, he had made it clear that what he had in mind was justifying grace.[27] So far, so good. But we are on more difficult ground if we try to determine what d'Ailly meant by the gratia gratis data which he did believe was necessary for rightful dominium. The question is an important one if we are to know whether or not d'Ailly really maintained, in any meaningful fashion, the doctrine of "lordship" as founded on grace.

Unfortunately, the term seems to lack for him the technical precision which it possesses for the Thomists, since he can describe as a *donum gratis datum* the very justifying grace which he has insisted is not a requisite for just dominium and which elsewhere he has also called gratis gratum faciens.[28] All that can be said with any degree of certainty is that by the gratia gratis data that is required for just dominium d'Ailly does not mean any form of created grace, for he tells us that without created

25. Leff, pp. 141–42; cf. p. 267.
26. Thus he can say: "absque gratia justificante loquendo de gratia infusa gratum faciente" (*De legitimo dominio*, Dupin, *1*, 645); cf. *Sent.* I, qu. 9, art. 3, HH, f. 127r: "Charitas creata potest sumi dupliciter: scilicet pro charitate infusa quae proprie dicitur charitas creata, et pro charitate acquisita . . . . Prima charitas dicitur gratia gratum faciens."
27. *De paup. salv.*, Lib. II, caps. 6–8, Lib. IV. cap. 3; Poole, pp. 344–48 and 441. Note that he also called this type of created grace "gratia gratificans" (see pp. 347, 441).
28. *De legitimo dominio*, Dupin, *1*, 642: "Sicut donum aeternae praedestinationis non requiritur ad justum dominium, sic nec gratiae justificans donum gratis datum."

83

grace, God can and does confer just dominium—as, for example, in the case of Judas—and that it is principally "the uncreated gift of divine approbation which endows anyone with just dominium." [29]

The exact implications of this position remain to be seen; at this point one must admit that despite his careful distinctions d'Ailly still clings in the last analysis to a conception of dominium as contingent upon grace. And, qualified though it may be, it still survives as a formidable threat militating against any attempt to locate the source of authority outside the divine will, and therefore as a logical barrier to the elaboration of a political theory that could have much weight with, or influence upon, a later and more secularized world. This barrier, however, d'Ailly circumvents by means of two final qualifications.

He has maintained that it is "the uncreated gift of divine approbation" or a gratuitous concession by God which is needful for just dominium or ministerium. Now, however, he goes on to admit that God's "effectual will" still sustains that dominium or exercise of dominium which does not spring from what may properly be called His "approving will" and which, therefore, is lacking in a just title.[30] He admits, too, that we may not assume the unjust ruler necessarily to be lacking in a just title of divine origin. This is to say, not only that God may *permit* an unjust ruler to rule, but that He may even have conferred dominium upon him. Not, he hastens to add, that God is in any way impli-

---

29. *Utrum indoctus in jure divino,* Dupin, *1,* 653: "sine . . . creata gratia [deus] potest quemlibet constituere Dominum . . . et non solum potest, immo de facto fecit et facit . . . . Nam et Judas fuit ad dominium Apostolatus electus . . . nec tamen per quodlibet suum mortale peccatum perdidit hujusmodi dominium . . . immo forsan ex sola desperatione." *De legitimo dominio,* ibid., 642: "donum increatum divinae approbationis principaliter constituit aliquem justum Dominum."

30. *Utrum indoctus in jure divino,* Dupin, *1,* 652: "Quodlibet aliud dominari, vel exercitium dominii, quod non procedit ex gratis communicato dominio, vel concesso ministerio est injuste dominari . . . et tamen, non obstante quod tale dominium sit injuste dominari, tamen Deus ad illud concurrit per suum velle efficax." Cf. *De legitimo dominio,* ibid., 663–64, where he admits that although God may be said to approve unjust dominium, in that he permits it, such "permissive approval" is not what is meant by divine approval in the proper sense of the term.

cated in injustice, but that He sometimes uses the rule of the unjust as a punishment for sin, or for the correction of sins, and no
one can deny that this pertains to justice.[31] These admissions involve, no doubt, an extension of the doctrine of dominium, but
it is one that marks its downfall. For this doctrine, which in the
thought of Aegidius Romanus had been a powerful weapon for
the assertion of papal supremacy, which in the hands of Wyclif
was a means to the regeneration of the Church and in those of
some of his followers would be a justification for social revolution—this doctrine d'Ailly now seems bent on reducing to a
mere reiteration of the Pauline dictum that all authority is of
God. So transformed, it will lose its importance as a political
theory.[32]

That this is d'Ailly's intention would seem apparent from his
second qualification. Although he repeats his claim that every
secondary dominium is derived from God's first and supreme
dominium, citing St. Paul and claiming that the divine approbation is the "requisite, necessary and sufficient" cause of dominium, he nevertheless admits that God freely associates with His
approving will "many created circumstances or titles." Experience proves this, he says, because "among us parental succession
is required as a title to regal *dominium* and for Imperial and
Apostolic, the common choice of many." [33] Thus, even though

31. *Utrum indoctus in jure divino,* Dupin, *1,* 648: "Injustum praeesse facit
Deus, non quidem injuste, sed juste, cum nihil injuste facere possit. Unde patet
primo, quod non solum concedendum est, ut aliqui dicunt, quod Deus permittit
injustum praeesse, prout permissio praescindit a Dei actione vel factione; immo
proprie concedendum est quod Deus primaria actione facit injustum praeesse.
Secundo, patet quod referendo injustum praesidentem, ad Deum ipsum instituentem, injustus potest juste praeesse. Nam quidquid deus facit in punitionem
peccati, aut in emendationem peccatorum, hoc juste fit, quia sic fit in ordine ad
bonum justitiae. Sed Deus sic facit injustum praeesse quod utitur injusti praesidentia in punitione culpae; sicut sub tyrannide Pharaonis voluit filios Israël
affligi, in suorum poenam peccatorum, et sub Nabuchodonosor."

32. For the only political conclusion that might follow from its acceptance could
be an unquestioning obedience to the powers that be, and the political speculation of the preceding centuries had shown that even this was not a necessary
deduction.

33. *Utrum indoctus in jure divino,* Dupin, *1,* 651: "Nullus dominatur, absque
sibi a Deo gratis communicato dominio. Patet, quia Deus habet plenissimum

the approving will of God is cause sufficient to bestow just dominium, this bestowal is manifested to us only through the recipient's possession of the appropriate human title, for this is "the true sign of the divine approbation." [34]

Thus despite the recondite distinctions between God's effectual and approving will, between uncreated and created grace, between the eternal predestination which is directed towards eternal salvation and that which leads to the attainment of some purely temporal goal—despite all these distinctions, what d'Ailly is in fact telling us is simply that, if we are to assess the rightfulness of earthly dominium, we must look not to the inscrutable dispositions of the Almighty, but rather to the customary and familiar human criteria of legitimate inheritance or election. Such a conclusion certainly leaves the way clear for the elaboration of a political theory on rational rather than dogmatic grounds, and because of this it is a very important one. But those who have had the patience to follow d'Ailly faithfully through all the convolutions of his labyrinthine argumentation may be forgiven if they feel a little cheated and inclined to ask: "Is that all?" The question, indeed, is not only permissible, it is one that must be asked. For if d'Ailly merely wished to repudi-

---

omnium rerum dominium, primum ac supremum; sed omne secundum dominium a primo et supremo derivatur. Ideo dicit Apostolus: 'Non est potestas nisi a deo.'" Ibid., 652: "Nono propositio: Velle Dei approbativum est causa necessario requisita et sufficiens ad justum creaturae dominium, et ad juste dominari, seu dominii exercitium . . . . Decima propositio, quod hoc non obstante *de facto,* Deus cum tali velle approbativo libere associat sibi multas creatas circumstantias, seu titulos, ad hoc ut aliquem justum Dominum constituat, ac per consequens ad hoc ut quis juste dominetur. Patet per experientiam, nam in Regali dominio, *de facto* requiritur apud nos parentalis successio. In imperiali vero, ut Apostolico, multorum communis electio. Exemplum est etiam ad hoc de velle efficaci quo Deus universa producit, non tamen solus, sed cum causis secundis" (italics mine). Cf. *De legitimo dominio,* Dupin, *1,* 643–44.

34. *De legitimo dominio,* Dupin, *1,* 644: "Nullus a nobis censendus est habere dominium alicujus rei dominabilis; nisi habens ad hoc titulum creatum, qui [sic] sit verum signum divinae approbationis. Patet ex secunda parte conclusionis. Unde licet approbatio sit ad hoc sufficiens causa; tamen de illa non constat nobis, nisi per aliqua signa creata: nec sufficit quodcumque signum, sed signum verum."

86

ate Fitzralph's teaching and to concentrate attention on the purely human dispositions of authority, why then did he devote quite so much wearisome effort to ascertaining the precise rôle of God in the conferring of dominium? In order to answer this question it will be necessary not only to draw into the discussion some relevant but scattered remarks which d'Ailly made elsewhere, but also to glance back once again at those final qualifications which we have already examined—keeping in mind this time, however, not the threat posed by the doctrine of dominium to the elaboration of a purely rational political theory, but rather the incompatibility of his basic theological positions with any temptation to ascribe an absolute validity to any "created law," whether human or divine.

In his commentary on the *Sentences* of Lombard, d'Ailly was not, of course, concerned with political questions, but he did include a lengthy discussion on the nature of law. In the course of this he pointed out, by way of analogy, that although it is not common usage to speak of forms of dominium as being *de jure divino* simply because they enjoy the benediction of God's approving will, this is simply because common usage is concerned with the purely human roots of authority, and not in any way because God's rôle in the conferring of dominium is not important.[35] Elsewhere, moreover, he tells us that it is God and not man Who "first and principally confers authority";[36] and in other places, insisting on the literal truth of the Pauline dictum that all power is of God, he argues that the divine will alone is the first, independent cause in the hierarchy of efficient causation, and again that just as from the first cause depends every

35. *Princ. in II Sent.,* N, f. 30r–30v, and *Princ. in III Sent.,* L, f. 36v; see below, pp. 192 ff., where the whole discussion is analyzed.

36. *Utrum indoctus in jure divino,* Dupin, *1,* 647: "Distinguendum est quod cum Praelatus seu Praesidens injustus praesit ex susceptione authoritas quam ipse habet in subditos exercere. Juxta hoc possunt tria considerari seu ad tria comparari. Uno modo, ad illos a quibus authoritas sibi datur . . . . Iterum primo modo potest duplici comparari. Uno modo ad Deum, qui primo et principaliter dat authoritatem. Alio modo, ad homines, qui eam contrario et unius principaliter conferunt."

second cause, so also from the first and supreme dominium is derived every secondary dominium.[37] These last statements occur in those very disputations which contain his criticism of Fitzralph's teaching and which we have already examined; and, again, in another passage which we overlooked, we may read that no human law governing the bestowal of dominium is true or just unless it is understood to possess the divine approval.[38]

Such statements clearly reflect a profound conviction of the importance of the divine rôle in the constitution of human authority, but one may wonder to what extent they clarify d'Ailly's position. If he insists that human provisions concerning the bestowal of authority are contingent upon divine approval he also implies that they must be assumed to enjoy that approval, in that it is manifest to us only through such human devices as the laws governing inheritance and election.[39] But before dismissing the whole discussion as a piece of specious circularity, we should recall that when d'Ailly first argued that God associates "created circumstances or titles" with His approving will, and when he identified these circumstances or titles as primogeniture in kingdoms and election in the Empire and in the Church, he had in both cases qualified his assertions by saying that this was so *de facto*.[40] And by this phrase—so crucial, but so easy to overlook—he meant to indicate that there was nothing necessary or essential about such human provisions. God chooses to endow them with the concurrence of His approving will, but

37. *Princ. in II Sent.*, J, f. 29r: "Sicut attribuitur voluntati divinae esse primam causam efficientem, sic attribuendum est eidem esse primam legem obligantem . . . . Quia sicut nullus res creata habet ex se potestatem obligandi. Nam sicut dicit Apostolus ad Romanos 13: 'Non est potestas nisi a deo.' Igitur, sicut sola divina voluntas est prima causa independens in causando, sic ipsa est prima lex independens in obligando." Cf. *De legitimo dominio*, Dupin, *1*, 642; *Utrum indoctus in jure divino*, ibid., 651.

38. *De legitimo dominio*, Dupin, *1*, 644: "Nulla lex utiliter dictans alicui deberi dominium alicujus rei dominabilis, est vera aut justa, nisi intelligitur cum circumstantia divinae approbationis . . . . Lex dictans quod quilibet primogenitus debet succedere dominio paterno, non est justa, nisi intelligitur cum hac circumstantia, scilicet, si fuerit ad hoc a Deo approbatus."

39. See above, n. 34, p. 86.

40. See above, n. 33, p. 86.

88

he does so "freely." Indeed, "of His most free will," He could bestow dominium upon, or withdraw it from, anyone, even without or in spite of the coincidence of such human titles; just as, by His effectual will, He can do anything, even without the concurrence of secondary causes.[41]

Thus, although the actual terms are not used, we are back face to face with that basic distinction between the absolute and ordained powers of God which plays so great a rôle in d'Ailly's epistemology, in his ethics, and in his natural and legal philosophy.[42] Once its pervasive presence is detected, the reason for his manifest reluctance to dismiss Fitzralph's teaching out of hand, and for his tortuous attempts to specify the exact part played by God in the constitution of rightful authority becomes clear. This reluctance and these attempts are simply another (though perhaps unexpected) by-product of a fundamental theological preoccupation with the freedom and omnipotence of God. It is this preoccupation which made the distinction in question so useful to nominalist theologians in general. Nowhere in d'Ailly's thinking is its value more apparent than here, for it enables him to accord absolute validity to the proposition that all power is of God without having to neglect the merely human arrangements for its disposition. It is indeed true, he is telling us, that all rightful dominium is of God, and that by His absolute power God can dispose of it as He will. But the important thing for us here and now is that, of His ordained power, He chooses to associate with His bestowal of dominium the purely human signs of legal disposition. Once this has been said, the temptation is to reverse

41. *Utrum indoctus in jure divino,* Dupin, *1*, 652: "Deus absque talibus titulis creatis, per velle suum liberrimum, potest quemcumque constituere Dominum, cujuscunque rei dominabilis, et, quibuscunque talibus positis destituere. Patet ex praemissis, ex quo tale velle est causa sufficiens; patet etiam per simili de velle efficaci, quo agere posset quodlibet sine causa secunda."

42. See above, pp. 27 ff. See *De legitimo dominio,* Dupin, *1*, 645, where the use of the qualification *secundum statum praesentis justitiae* again reveals the presence of this distinction between the *potentia dei absoluta et ordinata*—which, indeed, d'Ailly cites quite frequently in his early disputations. See *Utrum Petri ecclesia rege gubernetur,* Dupin, *1*, 680, 687, 689, 690, 692; *Utrum Petri ecclesia lege reguletur,* ibid., 671; *De conscientia erronea,* ibid., 637; *De libertate creaturae rationalis,* ibid., 632; *De Trinitate,* ibid., 619.

the proposition, and with a somewhat profane temerity to assume that God will always associate with the merely human disposition of dominium the divine approval which guarantees its rightfulness.

The fact that we shall hear little of the *potentia dei absoluta* in d'Ailly's Conciliar writings may perhaps give rise to the suspicion that not even he himself was able to resist this temptation, and that, in the bulk at least of his political thinking, he paid only lip service to the qualifications imposed by the absolute power. Such a suspicion, however, would be ill-founded.[43] It was suggested at the outset that the lowly status which is accorded, in d'Ailly's hierarchy of knowledge, to propositions such as those concerning the world of politics, is the outcome of the pressure exerted upon his theory of knowledge by the dialectic of omnipotence. Here again, in the discussion of the legal criteria by which the possession or nonpossession of rightful dominium is assessed, d'Ailly is constrained to admit that we cannot know whether a prelate or prince possesses a just title to authority in any *evident* sort of way, but merely with a degree of probability.[44] The reason for this becomes manifest when he comments that God could elevate someone to the Papacy even in opposition to the laws or decrees of the Church, and actually canvasses the possibility that at some point in the dark period of schism during which he was writing, such a miraculous inter-

43. Note the following characteristic conclusion. *Utrum Petri ecclesia rege gubernetur,* Dupin, *1,* 690; "et licet temerarium esset asserere talem casum *de facto* aliquando evenire, tamen esset etiam temerarium hujus casus potestatem negare, quia hoc esset de futuris temere divinare, et *contra articulum de dei omnipotentia impudenter impingere,* quod est absurdum" (italics mine).

44. *De legitimo dominio,* Dupin, *1,* 644: "Contra ultimum corollarium tertiae conclusionis arguitur sic: Ex illo sequitur quod de Papali, Imperiali et Regio dominio . . . a nobis, et a quolibet viatore non super hoc specialiter illustrato, esset verisimiliter dubitandum vel potius illos esse Dominos negandum. . . . Quia nullus talis princeps habet titulum creatum quem sciamus esse verum; ergo nec habet forte, licet sit verus, quem intrusus et invasor non aeque videantur habere." To this d'Ailly replies: "Ad primum. Nego quod illud sequatur, et ad probationem dico quod assumptum est verum de scientia proprie dicta, quae est scientia evidentiae. Sed illa in proposito non exigitur; sed sufficit scientia probabilis conjecturae, et illa hic habetur, et sic antecedens non est verum."

position might well take place.[45] In the meantime, however, and given these qualifications, he clearly feels that it is the duty of men of good will to explore the more proximate and mundane possibilities, and to attempt by whatever human devices as are both legitimate and appropriate, to put an end to the enduring scandal of a divided Christendom. This is the task to which d'Ailly applies himself in his Conciliar tracts, and if the arguments are almost wholly confined within the established frontiers of the presently-ordained economy, it is in no way because d'Ailly has forgotten that God, of His absolute power, could intervene and cross these frontiers or suspend the working of that economy.

In this chapter we have again heard in d'Ailly's teaching the echoes of political speculations which may seem remote from more modern methods of reasoning and alien to them. We have seen him articulate with his own theological principles the Patristic views of political authority as a punishment and remedy for sin, or as an authority legitimized only by divine approval. We have also seen him cope, as he had to cope, with the peculiar theory of dominium built upon this view by theological minds accustomed to the conditions of feudal society—to the assimilation of public powers to proprietary rights and the eclipse of the notion of political community. These are the more exclusively medieval elements in his political thought, and although his philosophical position denies to him the synthesizing potenti-

45. *De legitimo dominio*, Dupin, *1*, 644: "Nullus a nobis censendus est habere dominium alicujus rei dominabilis; nisi habens ad hoc titulum creatum, qui sit verum signum divinae approbationis. Patet ex secunda parte conclusionis. Unde licet approbatio sit ad hoc sufficiens causa; tamen de illa non constat nobis, nisi per aliqua signa creata: nec sufficit quodcunque signum, sed signum verum." It should be noted, nevertheless, that he makes the following topical reservations: "Patet quod Deus posset contra, vel praeter Leges seu Decreta Ecclesiae, aliquem in Papatum assumere, seu constituere. Et utrum hiis temporibus novissimis, et pessimis, nostris exigentibus demeritis, hoc fecerit, vel forte facturus sit, incertum est" (*Utrum indoctus in jure divino*, ibid., 653). This is no random speculation since d'Ailly was inclined to think that the Schism itself was a sign that the end of the world was nigh. See, for example, his *Sermo de quadruplici adventu domini*, in *Sermones*, f. 16r.

91

ality of an Aquinas, it does not prevent his according these elements the respect which it is courteous to show towards the members of an older generation. He is far, however, from allowing them to dominate his political thought, concerned, as it has to be, with the disposition of authority in the presently-ordained divine economy. His careful distinctions leave them venerable but in the present dispensation powerless, and open the way for an analysis of the source and purpose of political authority more closely related to the problems of his day and to the thought of the ages which followed.

4.

The Purpose and Form
of Government

The most striking fact of political life is the subjection to their ruler of those who are ruled, and political philosophy is the outcome of the perennial urge to find rational grounds for this subjection. Such a quest may fall short of its goal and terminate with an appeal to divine or prescriptive right; but if it goes beyond this, its first move must be the ascription to political authority of some necessary function which men will accept as justifying its existence. Such a move is prior, even in the most democratic of theories, to any appeal to popular consent, for were there no clear need for political subordination it would be irrelevant to attempt to make it rationally defensible by grounding it, in one sense or another, upon the wishes of the governed. Even theories appealing to prescriptive or divine right rarely neglect entirely to ascribe some justifying purpose to the state, though such a purpose, as we have seen in our discussion of the doctrine of dominium,[1] may tend to be assumed until the problem arises of the evils endured by those subjected to a tyrant. This tendency, it must be admitted, is not limited to advocates of the fully developed doctrine of dominium. Medieval formu-

1. See above, Ch. 3.

lations of the purpose of governmental authority—perhaps because of the wide measure of general agreement on the matter
—are rarely notable for their precision, and d'Ailly's efforts constitute no exception. No apologies can be required for examining these efforts, nevertheless, for it is precisely the purpose
ascribed to political authority that lies at the heart of any political theory, bearing the imprint of its basic philosophical principles, explicit or assumed, and of its nature pointing forward to
more specific conclusions concerning the respective rights of
governments and individuals.

I

The history of the development of the doctrine of dominium
should suffice to convince us that we would be ill-advised to assume that a thinker in the earlier medieval period would find
much meaning in the question: What is the purpose of *the
state?* [2] He would probably, however, be willing to agree that the
kingship had a purpose, and the answer he would give would be
conditioned by the political fact of feudal institutions and modified by a combination of traditional Germanic and ecclesiastical
conceptions.

The nature and date of the evidence available makes specula-
tive any discussion of the social structure of the Germanic races
in the period before the development of feudalism. It does seem
to be a matter of general agreement that the chief or king was
regarded as being limited in the exercise of his power by the law
of the community, and that his function was one of service to the
nation or tribe which he, in a sense, represented. The precise
nature of this service is harder to establish, but it is clear that it
involved leadership in war and the doing of justice in peace—
the latter involving, above all, the declaration and interpretation
of the customary law, that "good old law" which was at once the
embodiment of justice, the basis of the king's authority, and the
bulwark of the private rights and privileges of his subjects.[3]

2. See above, Ch. 3, esp. pp. 66 ff.
3. See e.g. Carlyle, *History, 1,* 219–52; *3,* 11–12, 181–85; Kern, *Kingship,* esp.
pp. 70–79.

Feudalism did much to transform these ideas. It tended to reduce the king to the status of lord of lords at the apex of the feudal hierarchy, and to transmute his public powers into private proprietary rights, not annexed to his office as king, but belonging to him simply as a private person.[4] At the same time, however, it did contribute to the specification of the types of service required of him and to the actual insistence upon his subjection to the law, since it confirmed the ultimate right of his subjects to resist his commands if he ignored the law or failed to perform his duties.[5]

It was the belief of Gierke that these ideas—to him basically Germanic but deriving "new profundity" from Christianity—formed the "genuinely" medieval idea of kingship,[6] and, without debating what claim such a conception may have to be more genuinely medieval than, for instance, later views bearing the imprint of the civil and canon law, it may well be conceded that it dominated the earlier medieval period. The rôle of Christian ideas and of the Stoic conceptions to which they were wedded in the writings of the Fathers deserves, however, greater emphasis than Gierke seemed willing to give it. Speaking of the famous passage of St. Paul in Romans 13:1–6, d'Entrèves has remarked that "the whole history of Christian political theory can well be said to be nothing else than an uninterrupted commentary upon this text." [7] If his exaggeration is real it is also pardonable, for it is true that the principal ideas which the passage expresses—that all political power is of divine origin and that obedience is,

---

4. Thus, during the Investiture Contest, Peter Crassus, one of the pro-imperial publicists, was able to use as an argument against Gregory VII's deposition of Henry IV the fact that Henry held his kingdom by hereditary right, which could no more be brought into question by the Pope than the right of any man to possession of inherited property—*Defensio Heinrici IV Regis*, in *Monumenta Germaniae Historica: Libelli de Lite Imperatorum et Pontificum* (Hanover, 1891–97), *I*, 432–53.

5. Kern, *Kingship*, pp. 87–88, 121–22; Marc Bloch, *La Sociéte Féodale: Les classes et le gouvernement des hommes* (Paris, 1940), pp. 258–59.

6. Gierke–Maitland, p. 33.

7. A. Passerin d'Entrèves, *The Medieval Contribution to Political Thought* (Oxford, 1939), p. 9.

therefore, a religious duty, along with the implication that, for the ruler, power is a source rather of duties than of rights—were of immense influence during and after the Middle Ages. Christians and Stoics had agreed in their acceptance of the contrast between nature and convention, and merging this with the doctrine of the Fall, the Fathers had argued that coercive political authority was not natural to man but became necessary only because of the human sinfulness and corruption which followed Adam's expulsion from Paradise. Political authority, or at least coercive political authority, was therefore a divinely appointed "punishment and remedy for sin." [8] Viewed in this light its purpose was both negative and positive. Medieval views continued to oscillate between these two "polar" positions. The negative was most usually stressed in times of political chaos or of persecution and tyrannical oppression, and found ready support in St. Paul's statement that the ruler is "an avenger for wrath to him that doeth evil." But St. Paul had also spoken of the ruler as "a minister of God . . . for good" and, under happier political conditions, the stress tended to be placed on the positive aspects of the king's function, usually conceived as the preservation of order and justice.

In the context of such ideas, and despite the proprietary notion of royal authority characteristic of feudalism, kingship was normally conceived during the early medieval centuries as an office of divine origin, and the task of the king as that of furthering "the commonweal, peace and justice." [9] This conception was reflected in the ecclesiastical coronation ceremonies which spread throughout the kingdoms of western Europe between the seventh and tenth centuries, ceremonies at which the king swore faithfully to guard the law of the community which was the touchstone of justice.[10] With the recovery of Europe from

8. This was the view, for instance, of SS. Irenaeus, Ambrose, Augustine, Gregory the Great, and Isidore; see Carlyle, *History, I*, 126–31.

9. Gierke–Maitland, p. 34; cf. p. 142, n. 124.

10. For a valuable discussion of the English and continental coronation ceremonies, see P. E. Schramm, *A History of the English Coronation*, trans. L. G. Wickham Legg (Oxford, 1937), esp. pp. 179 ff.

the comparative chaos which followed the recurrent barbarian incursions and with the growth of more settled and prosperous living conditions, this more positive view became increasingly dominant. And in the whole medieval period before the reception of Aristotelian learning it found perhaps its most extreme expression in the *Policraticus* of John of Salisbury,[11] in which he speaks of the ruler as bearing the responsibility for the whole community, and as being "the minister of the public utility and the servant of equity." He does not, it is true, delineate these governmental functions very precisely, but he does define equity as the justice of God. He also tells us that "the interpreter" of equity is law, and concludes, therefore, that the ruler who is not a tyrant will rule his people by law.[12]

Such a point of view is no longer wholly dominated by the dichotomy between ruler and ruled, and reaches out to comprehend the notion of a political community organized for the achievement of common ends. Moreover, it reflects the Germanic belief in the supremacy of a nation's law and also a more potent belief which often (but not always) blended with it an assumption fundamental to the greater part of medieval political theorizing—the Stoic-Christian doctrine of an eternal natural law possessing universal validity and accessible to the reason of all men.[13] The importance of this doctrine cannot be overestimated, for it was precisely this "belief that an objective common standard existed in nature" which not only "freed medieval dispute from the sterility of appeals to custom and precedent," as Ewart Lewis rightly says,[14] but also, by prescribing rationally accessible norms of conduct, set limits to the power which a ruler might justly exercise. It provided at least a negative definition of the purpose of political authority. And this, it should be noted, is relevant not only to the earlier medieval theories at which we have glanced, but also to those formulated after the philosophi-

11. John of Salisbury (ca. 1115–78) completed the *Policraticus* in 1159.
12. *Policraticus*, Lib. IV, cap. 2, ed. C. C. J. Webb (Oxford, 1909); first and second quotations, in order, pp. 515b, 514d; conclusion, cap. 1, p. 513b.
13. Kern, *Kingship*, pp. 70–75; see below, Ch. 6.
14. Lewis, *Political Ideas, 1,* 16; Kern, *Kingship*, pp. 71–72.

cal upheaval entailed in the thirteenth century by the recovery of the *corpus Aristotelicum,* and after the parallel but more far-reaching revolution which the prior revival of the Roman law had wrought in European legal and political thinking.

As we have seen, the earlier theories had echoed the Stoic-Christian view that political organization was an artificial thing made necessary only by the Fall and the *sinfulness* of man. The works of Aristotle presented a more ancient and radically different conception of the state as a natural thing, rooted in the deepest requirements of human nature and necessary to man for the attainment of that rational and virtuous life which is his true end. Such a view constituted, of course, something of a challenge to the Christian belief in suprapolitical values attainable only by supernatural means, but Aquinas found it possible to harmonize it with the Christian tradition. He did so by placing the Aristotelian conception within the larger setting of the natural law theory, and also by drawing several careful distinctions. We have already seen in the context of another problem the value of his principle that "grace does not destroy nature but perfects it," [15] and here it may be said to have permitted and, indeed, to have implied "the recognition of the existence and dignity of a purely 'natural' sphere of rational and ethical values," [16] which had neither been superceded by the revelation of supernatural justice nor obliterated by sin, although sin had adversely affected the possibility of man's attaining to their practice. It was unnecessary, therefore, to look to a previous change in the condition of man to explain the state. It was rooted in the very nature of man and its historical origins were irrelevant to its rational justification. Aquinas was able, however, to accommodate older views about the consequences of sin by distinguishing between slavery, which could not have existed in the state of innocence and is clearly a result of sin, and that political subjection which is natural to man because it is necessary for the attainment of the common good.[17]

15. See above, p. 39.
16. D'Entrèves, *Aquinas,* p. xiii.
17. *ST,* 1a pars. qu. 96, art. 4, d'Entrèves, *Aquinas,* pp. 134–37.

If, then, we were to question Aquinas about the purpose of the state he would tell us that it existed for the common good. It may be felt, however, that this expression is dangerously obscure, especially when he can speak of the common good as being greater and more divine than that of the individual,[18] and assert that "all men being part of the city, they cannot be truly good unless they adapt themselves to the common good." [19] But fears that this may have a totalitarian import seem to be groundless, for the place of the individual is not denied, the end of the state —which is the achievement of the virtuous life by its members— is judged by the same standards as the end of the individual,[20] and it is admitted that, in a sense, the "final end of a human multitude must be the same as that of the individual man." [21]

In the context of so positive a view of political organization, even questions concerning the purpose of the state become partly redundant.[22] But influential though this view may have been—and its influence is apparent especially in the works of James of Viterbo, John of Paris, Dante, and Marsilius of Padua —it remains true to say that no medieval thinker went as far as Aquinas in subjecting so completely to Aristotelian ideas the older feudal and patristic notions and in attributing, therefore, so positive a rôle to the state. The actual conditions of

18. *ST*, 2a 2ae, qu. 39, art. 2. These expressions are based upon Aristotle's *Ethics*, I, 1094b 7, and recur at least sixty-seven times in Aquinas's works: see I. Th. Eschmann, "A Thomistic Glossary on the Principle of the Pre-Eminence of a Common Good," *Mediaeval Studies, 5* (1943), 146–52, where he cites the relevant texts.

19. *ST*. 1a 2ae, qu. 92, art. 1; d'Entrèves, *Aquinas*, p. 119.

20. Namely, the natural and divine law. An important point for "the assumption of a fixed common end independent of human will and knowable with certainty by human reason simplified the problem and avoided the worst of the modern liberal dilemma" (Lewis, *Political Ideas, 1,* 211).

21. *De regimine principum*, I, cap. 14; d'Entrèves, *Aquinas*, p. 75; he notes (p. xix): "The integration of the individual in the whole must be conceived as an enlargement and an enrichment of his personality, not as a degradation to the mere function of a part without a value of its own"; cf. Ewart Lewis, "Organic Tendencies in Medieval Political Thought," *Am. Pol. Sci. Rev., 32* (1938), 852–55.

22. Thus d'Entrèves, *Aquinas*, p. xvii: "political obligation is inherent in man's nature. Man is unthinkable without the State, because it is only in the State and through the State that he can achieve perfection."

medieval political life militated against the popularity of such ideas. Aristotelian conceptions, predicated as they were upon the all-embracing political life of the Greek *polis,* were fully at home with no medieval political institution—not even the Italian commune—and always retained an academic flavor.[23] The categories of feudal law, moreover, continued to exercise a persuasive influence even after the decay of feudal institutions, making it difficult even for later medieval thinkers to distinguish, in any consistent fashion, public authority from private right, and easy for them to go on thinking of political life primarily in terms of the personal relationship of ruler to ruled.[24] It is this which helps to explain the stubborn persistence of the feudal-patristic tradition which, as we have seen,[25] burst into autumnal flower in the doctrine of dominium espoused primarily by Aegidius Romanus, Fitzralph, and Wyclif, but reflected in the thought of many others. This is not to suggest that late medieval thinkers wholly failed to distinguish between public and private law, or that they were, in general, unacquainted with something approximating to our modern notion of the state. It is rather to insist that they owed such ideas less to the influence of philosophical doctrines than to their own growing experience of corporate organization for the achievement of common goals, and from the twelfth century onwards to the teaching of the revived Roman law which provided them with the legal conceptions necessary to the full development of these nonfeudal forms of social and political collaboration. As a result of these developments, church as well as state came gradually to be conceived in corporative terms,[26] and Tierney has clearly shown the influence of the corporative ideas

23. A fact which helps to explain the confusion entailed by the attempt to render the Greek political vocabulary into Latin terminology; see Ernest Barker, *The Politics of Aristotle* (Oxford, 1948), pp. lxiii–lxxvi.

24. Thus Lagarde, *Naissance, 4,* 170–74, accuses St. Bonaventure, Duns Scotus, Aegidius Romanus, John of Paris, Henry of Ghent, and William of Ockham of failing to distinguish between these notions of property and that of authority, and comments that Aquinas alone seems to have been able to avoid this confusion.

25. Above, Ch. 3.

26. Lewis, *Political Ideas, 1,* 201, comments that "the central political problem of the later Middle Ages was the thrashing out of all the implications involved in conceiving the kingdom and the Church as corporate communities."

elaborated by the canon lawyers, not only upon the leading Conciliarists at the time of the Great Schism, but also upon the earlier ecclesiastico-political thinking of John of Paris and William of Ockham.[27] Thus if from the thirteenth century onwards we quite frequently hear echoes of the Aristotelian-Thomistic idea that the purpose of the state is to lead men to virtue,[28] we constantly find (sometimes in the same writers) the idea that political organization is an *instrument* for the pursuit by joint action of the common interests of the citizens. These common interests are accepted simply as facts rather than predicated upon any philosophical view of the nature of man, and are taken in a somewhat collective fashion more at home with nominalist than with Thomistic views.[29]

The manner in which the purpose of the state was conceived by later medieval political thinkers tended, then, to be the outcome of a blending of Aristotelian concepts and of ideas drawn from the Roman law and elaborated by civil and canon lawyers alike.[30] Despite the persistence of Germanic and feudal conceptions, it was less and less the common or customary law guaran-

27. *Foundations,* esp. pp. 157–78; see also his "Ockham, the Conciliar Theory and the canonists," *Journal of the History of Ideas, 15* (1954), 40–70.

28. See, e. g., John of Paris, *Tract. de pot.,* cap. 18; Leclercq, p. 229; James of Viterbo, *De regimine christiano,* II, cap. 6; Arquillière, pp. 223–24.

29. Thus the Aristotelian idea that the state *"was* a common end of man tended to be narrowed to the idea that in its own special way, it *served* the common ends of man" (Lewis, *Political Ideas, 1,* 214–15). Whereas Aquinas had been able to ascribe to the state or to the Church a *formal* unity and to speak of the common good as being, therefore, *formally* distinct from the good of the individual (see *ST,* 1a 2ae, qu. 96, art. 1), the nominalists were forced by their own fundamental assumptions to conceive of political bodies, and therefore of the common good, only in collective terms. Thus Ockham could argue against Pope John XXII that social and political groups in general and the Order of Friars Minor in particular are nothing more than the aggregate of the individuals composing them; see Lagarde, *Naissance, 5,* 79.

30. This is true to a certain extent even of Aquinas himself. I. Th. Eschmann, "A Thomistic Glossary," *Mediaeval Studies, 5* (1943), 124, claims that "historically speaking, the principle of the superiority of a common good and related doctrines are a legacy to scholasticism from a Roman and patristic heritage," the Aristotelian authority being but "an addition to a pre-established doctrine whose main lines and significations had been fixed quite apart from Aristotelian philosophy." He lists (pp. 142–46) no less than forty-two Thomistic texts in which the expression of the principle is derived from the Roman-patristic tradition.

teeing the private rights and privileges of his subjects that was invoked as the touchstone of the legitimacy of a king's rule, and more and more the notion of the common good, the "common utility," or the "public welfare" or "utility." The term *status regni* [31] was often substituted for these expressions by the lawyers; from the thirteenth century onwards, civil and canon lawyers claimed (and kings increasingly enforced the claim) that the preservation of the status regni in cases of emergency or evident necessity justified resort to extraordinary measures even if they ran counter to the common law and infringed private rights, for necessity knows no law.[32]

This development is immediately relevant to our present concern, for canonists and publicists had also applied these ideas to the Church and to the Pope's constitutional position vis-à-vis lay and ecclesiastical property, the common law of the Church, and even the temporal authority.[33] Although some of the conclusions which they deduced from these ideas were analogous to those deduced by civil lawyers and secular rulers,[34] others were not,

31. See Gaines Post, "The Theory of Public Law and the State in the 13th Century," *Seminar, 6* (1948), 57–58: "Although normally *status* means the condition or standing of individuals, classes or regimes, in connection with the public law it means the common welfare or public utility of the whole community of the kingdom." Cf. Kantorowicz, *King's Two Bodies*, p. 386, n. 182.

32. See J. R. Strayer, "The Laicization of French and English Society in the Thirteenth Century, *Speculum, 15* (1940), 80–83, and the admirable series of articles by Gaines Post, notably that cited above in n. 30 and "The Two Laws and the Statute of York," *Speculum, 29* (1954), esp. 422–27. Private rights were not infringed without the consent of those concerned, but, as Post says ("The Theory of Public Law," pp. 56–57), "in the late 13th century the defense of the kingdom and all the members was a superior right of the *status regni;* and that if 'what touched all must be approved of all,' the King had the right to *compel* all . . . to consent to measures taken to meet the danger." See also his "A Romano-Canonical Maxim, 'Quod Omnes Tangit,' in Bracton," *Traditio, 4* (1946), 197–99, 245–51; cf. below, Ch. 5. Strayer and Post draw their evidence mainly from the writings of the lawyers, but similar arguments are to be found in the publicist literature; see, e. g., Ockham, *Dialogus,* III, II, II, caps. 20 and 23; Goldast, *2,* 917–18, 920–21; *Somnium Viridarii,* Lib. I, cap. 141, ed. Gilles d'Aurigny (Paris: Jacques Pouchin, 1516), f. xliir.

33. Post, "Plena Potestas and Consent in Medieval Assemblies," *Traditio, 1* (1943), 381–83, 398–400.

34. This is true of nonpapalist writers. See, e. g., John of Paris, *Tract. de pot.,* caps. 6 and 7; Leclercq, pp. 185–90; Ockham, *De imperatorum et pontificum potestate,* caps. 8 and 10, ed. C. K. Brampton (Oxford, 1931), pp. 20–23.

and in the works of Conciliarists like d'Ailly it was these latter conclusions which came to the fore.

II

Of the earlier medieval political views Germanic and feudal ideas do produce some attenuated echoes in d'Ailly's thought,[1] but on the present issue they are completely lost in views of ecclesiastical origin. Thus, even after having distinguished from the dominium possessed by a temporal ruler the ministerium which is ecclesiastical authority, he admits, in reply to an objection, that the temporal prince is also, as St. Paul tells us, a "minister of God." [2] We have already seen some of the specific conclusions which he draws from this, at least about the duties of kings who are Christians, for they must rule their people, he tells us, not on their own behalf, but on behalf of Christ, punishing malefactors, suppressing heresy, defending the Church, and setting above all a good moral and religious example.[3] Nor does he ignore the more negative view of the purpose of government which the Fathers had deduced from this conception of kingship as an office under God. Referring to St. Augustine he argues that it is possible for the unjust ruler to hold his office justly from God because "whatsoever God does for the punishing of sin or the correction of sins—that is just," since it is ordained to the end of justice. Thus God makes the unjust to rule in order that he may use their tyranny to effect the punishment of the guilty, as in the case of the affliction of the Israelites under Pharoah and Nebuchadnezzar.[4]

1. See above, Ch. 3.

2. *De legitimo dominio*, Dupin, *1*, 645; the objection is: "Nulla est ratio quare Regnum dicitur plus dominium quam Sacerdotium, quia etiam Princeps temporalis *Dei minister est* (Rom., xiii, 4). Et ita praelatus potest vendere Sacramenta sicut rex temporalia." And his reply (col. 646): "ad . . . confirmationem nego assumptum et ad probationem concedo primam partem, sed nego secundam."

3. *Tractatus de materia*; see below, p. 339; cf. *Oratio de officio imperatoris*, Dupin, 2, 920; *Epistola I ad Joannem XXIII*, ibid., col. 883.

4. *Utrum indoctus in jure divino*, Dupin, *1*, 648: "Patet quod referendo injustum praesidentem, ad Deum ipsum instituentem, injustus potest juste praeesse. Nam quidquid Deus facit in punitionem peccati, aut in emendationem peccatorum, hoc juste fit, quia sic sit in ordine ad bonum justitiae. Sed Deus sic facit

Ideas such as these revolve wholly around the bilateral relationship between king and subjects rather than around the more
complex notion of a political community corporately organized
for the pursuit of common interests. Despite this it is the latter
conception that dominates d'Ailly's political thinking. This fact
is underlined in the later Conciliar tracts in which, for the first
time, and in an ecclesiastical context, he addressed himself systematically to constitutional problems, but it is also manifest in
one of his earlier writings.

This work was written as early as 1385 and was occasioned by
a squabble within the University of Paris itself.[5] The Chancellor of the University, Jean Blanchard, contrary to traditional
practice and to the decretals relating to matters academic, had
begun to exact payments from those who applied for the *licentia
docendi,* and in January 1385 the University appealed to the
Pope. D'Ailly was named as proctor to represent the Faculty of
Theology in the case and wrote two tracts designed to refute the
arguments with which the Chancellor strove to defend his practices. The second tract is the one relevant to our problem. In it,
in the course of lengthy and prolix argumentation, he contrasts
the authority of the Chancellor with that of the Rector of the
University and the Rectors of the various Faculties, a move
necessitated by his previous admission that the latter had the
right to exact payments from their students. The authority of
the Rectors is in fact, he tells us, of a political nature, whereas
that of the Chancellor is not. For these Rectors possess "a certain
political rank [*ordo*]" with respect to those subjected to them
and by virtue of this they may receive and exact from them those
things that are useful to "the preservation and defense of their
own political community," just as "any rightly ordained and
approved community" can, in accordance with its needs, impose

---

injustum praeesse quod utitur injusti praesidentia, in punitionem culpae: sicut
sub tyrannide Pharaonis voluit filios Israël affligi, in suorum poenam peccatorum;
et sub Nabuchodonosor. Quandoque etiam hoc Deus convertit in emendationem
peccatoris . . . . Et quantum ad hoc dicit Augustinus: Lib. 4, *De Civitate Dei,*
Cap. 3."

5. For a discussion of the controversy and of d'Ailly's part in it, see Salembier,
Cardinal, pp. 69 ff.; cf. H. Denifle, *Chartularium Universitatis Parisiensis* (Paris,
1891), *3,* 340, 485–86.

reasonable exactions upon those whom it is admitting to membership.[6] When, therefore, the University or Faculty exacts payments from its Bachelors or Masters it does so, not for the Baccalaureate or *magisterium* itself, but for its own preservation.[7] It may with justice be claimed that whatever d'Ailly is doing here he is certainly not viewing political organization in corporative terms, but rather vice versa, since it is clear that a university (in fact and by definition a corporation) [8] is for him a political community, the government of which is ordained to the end of its maintenance and preservation. But his mental assimilation to one another of corporative and political organizations is unquestionable, and this fact proved to be of immense importance when later on he turned his attention to the ecclesiastical polity.

The purpose of political authority, then, must be to secure the common interest of the political community as a whole, and d'Ailly construes the common interest in a somewhat factual and collective fashion.[9] Sometimes, it is true, tones clearly of Aristotelian inspiration are to be heard in his works, but only in those

6. *Tractatus II adversus cancellarium Parisiensis,* Dupin, *1,* 769–70: "Rector Universitatis, et Facultas quaelibet, respectu Baccalaureorum, et generaliter respectu omnium suorum suppositorum, habet quemdam politicum ordinem, et ordinatam superioritatem, ratione cujus potest recipere, et exigere a suis suppositis illa quae sunt utilia, et expedentia ad conservationem et tuitionem suae politicae Communitatis. Nam quaelibet rite ordinata, et approbata Communitas, ab illis quos in suum consortium admittit, potest, secundum sui status exigentiam, onera rationabilia, sive pecuniarum, sive juramentorum, sicut suis subjectis imponere, recipere et exigere . . . . Cancellarius vero, respectu Universitatis, seu ejus suppositorum, non habet talem politicum ordinem, seu superioritatem." It should, perhaps, be noted that the Chancellor of the University of Paris was, at least in origin, an official of the Bishop of Paris, and as Chancellor was not even a member of the University—as, indeed, the University did not fail to point out in 1368; H. Rashdall, *The Universities of Europe in the Middle Ages,* ed. F. M. Powicke and A. B. Emden (Oxford, 1936), *1,* 304–12, 398–402.

7. *Tractatus* II, Dupin, *1,* 769: "Et in propositio, exigit Universitas vel Facultas quaelibet a suis Baccalaureis, non pro ipso Baccalaureatu vel Magisterio, sed pro ipsius conservatione et tuitione."

8. See Rashdall, *1,* 2–4. In the case of the University of Paris in particular, Gaines Post has argued that the University of Masters was a "legal corporation, fully recognized by the highest ecclesiastical authorities, by 1215 at the latest"— "Parisian Masters as a Corporation 1200–1246," *Speculum, 9* (1934), 444.

9. His tendency to think of political organization in corporative terms would incline him to this point of view, as also would his nominalism; see above, p. 24.

few, fragmentary discussions of secular political society not wholly taken up with the doctrine of dominium as contingent on grace. Thus he can define a tyrant as a ruler who seeks his own interest and not the common good of his subjects.[10] Again, having stated that the temporal authority is principally and essentially ordained to temporal things, he makes it clear that this involves, not only ruling subjects through "human, civil, or political laws," but also guiding them by the moral virtues to the political end of this life.[11] Despite such echoes of Aristotelian views, the chief influence upon his thinking concerning the function of political authority is clearly that Roman-patristic tradition which found its most influential medieval expression in the canon law and in the numerous canonistic commentaries.

If one looks closely, the workings of this influence can be detected even in the most general statement that d'Ailly makes about the common good. It occurs in his *Sentences*, where he denies that the common good is always to be preferred to a particular good since "this is not universally true except in cases where the particular good is included in the common good." [12] He makes no reference here to the canon law but the reason he gives for his position is a religious one and reflects, as does his very formulation of the issue, the lengthy discussions of canonists and theologians alike concerning the superiority of the contemplative to the active life, as well as the canonistic conclusion that "the Christian's inner life of obedience to the Holy Spirit is his own affair and holds pre-eminence over the public or the

10. *Epistola I ad Joannem Papam*, Dupin, 2, 878: "Tyranni proprietas est quaerere non commune bonum subditorum, sed utile Principum." Cf. Aristotle, *Politics*, iii, 1279a, trans. Barker, pp. 113–14; Aquinas, *ST*, 1a 2ae, qu. 42, art. 2.

11. These "moral virtues" appropriate to the political life being contrasted with the "heroic virtues" necessary for the attainment of eternal salvation. See *Utrum Petri ecclesia rege gubernetur*, Dupin, *1*, 678; cited above, Ch. 2, n. 23, p. 49.

12. *Sent.*, I, qu. 2, art. 2, f. 65v: "Non est nobis evidens quod bonum commune semper sit magis diligendum quam bonum particulare. Immo, hoc non est verum universaliter nisi quando bonum particulare includitur in bono communi. Aliter sequitur quod homo magis deberet eligere salutem unius communitatis quam suiipsius, et se damnari quam unam communitatem cujus non esset pars, quod est falsum."

common good." [13] But canonistic principles and indeed the legacy of the whole Roman-patristic tradition is more clearly reflected in the numerous works in which d'Ailly addresses himself to the problems of the *ecclesiastical* polity, and it is upon these texts that any analysis of his conception of the purpose of political organization must primarily depend.

He has told us that it is the duty of secular rulers to guide their subjects "by the moral virtues to the political end of this life," or, again, that it is the duty of priests to rule their flocks in accordance with the divine laws and by the heroic virtues to lead them to the ultimate goal—the future life and eternal salvation.[14] Moreover, in speaking of the priestly power he has been careful to distinguish, in the traditional fashion, between power of a sacramental nature (*potestas ordinis*) and power of a jurisdictional or governmental nature (*potestas jurisdictionis seu regiminis*). Now it is the latter with which he is concerned, and he defines it as "the power of regulating subjects and guiding them to their salvation." [15] This is the end he has in mind when he refers, as he constantly does, to the common good or common utility of the Church,[16] for a tyrant is one who seeks his own good rather than the common good of those subjected to him, and those pastors must be called tyrants who feed themselves but

13. Eschmann, "A Thomistic Glossary," *Mediaeval Studies*, 5 (1943), 136; for citation and discussion of the relevant canonistic texts, see pp. 137–39. Note that here, too, the exception is relevant only in those cases in which the private good is not contained in the public. When it is, as in the case of the incumbent of a public office such as a bishop, the common good is always to be preferred to his own private interests. Aquinas, too, addressed himself to the same dilemma, though he resolved the matter in a different way than did the canonists—see Eschmann, "Bonum commune melius est quam bonum unius: Eine Studie ueber der Wertvorrang des Personalen bei Thomas von Aquin," *Mediaeval Studies, 6* (1944), 62–120, esp. 100–15.

14. See above, n. 11.

15. *Utrum Petri ecclesia lege reguletur,* Dupin, *1,* 667–68; see above, p. 62, where the text is cited and discussed.

16. In the *Tractatus de ecclesiastica potestate* alone, he appeals to the "public utility," "the common utility," "the common good," or to the "common," "ultimate" or "supreme necessity," on about twenty occasions (see Dupin, 2, 931, 932, 935, 943, 944, 945, and 946), not to mention the *status ecclesiae* (947), the *bonum regimen ecclesiae* and the *utile regimen ecclesiae* (935).

not the Lord's flock.[17] This is that common good for which the jurisdictional authority within the Church is established. This, too, is the criterion by which we must judge the worth of all types of ecclesiastical policy and of every form of ecclesiastical government. Thus, when a General Council is assembled, it is with the object of securing the welfare of all; if ecclesiastical reform is envisaged, it must be directed to the utility and integrity of the whole Christian republic, and not simply to that of the particular Church at Rome. Similarly, it is only because of the public utility that the Roman people have received their right of electing the popes, and they must exercise the right in accordance with this. Above all, popes, if they are to rule well, must pursue policies conducive to the common welfare.[18]

There is nothing very striking about all this. It is parallel to what was generally assumed at the time about the function of political authority in *secular* society, and to what d'Ailly himself has said or implied on that matter. This is true of his general principle, and it is true at least of some of the conclusions which he draws from it. This is the case in one passage of the *De ecclesiastica potestate*—his last major work—where he reiterates the theory of property espoused by John of Paris. In this passage, part of which we have already had occasion to examine,[19] he asserts that the temporal ruler has no proprietary rights over the property of his subjects and may interfere with it only as judge and only for reason of necessity, if the public welfare or the common good demands it. He asserts similarly that a fortiori the Pope has no power at all over possessions belonging to the laity

17. *Epistola I ad Joannem XXIII*, Dupin, 2, 878: "Tyranni proprietas est quaerere non commune bonum subditorum, sed utile Principum. Tales sunt Pastores qui non pascunt gregem Domini sed semetipsos." Cf. *Sermo in die Pentecostes factus in Concilio Generali*, in *Sermones*, f. y3r, where he says to the assembled prelates: "Attendite vos positos ad regendum hanc ecclesiam *non modo tyrannico sed more apostolico*" (italics mine).

18. *Oratio de officio imperatori*, Dupin, 2, 917; *Tract. de pot.*, ibid., 948 and 931; *Epistola secunda ad Benedictum XIII*, in *Chronique de Jean Brandon*, Lettenhove, *1*, 142; *Sermo in die omnium sanctorum*, in Tschackert, *Ailli*, App. XIII, p. [45]; *Octo conclusiones*, Dupin, 2, 111.

19. Above, pp. 49 ff.

except at times when "the supreme necessity of the Church" requires it, and even then only in a way proportioned to "the common necessity of the faith." [20]

More important, however, is his analysis of the authority of the Pope over ecclesiastical possessions. For here, again following John of Paris, d'Ailly applies to the Universal Church the rules of corporation law which the canonists had applied to the individual collegiate churches. It was the wish of the founders of such churches, he tells us, to transfer directly to the collegiate community and not to any single person the dominium of the goods which they were donating. Thus the prelate who is the head of such a community merely has the administration and general dispensation of such goods "for the common good of the College." This, he says, is "by the earliest common law" the position of the bishop in any cathedral church. For, as Hostiensis points out, the bishop is merely the proctor and not the proprietor of the goods of his church.[21] But just as each ecclesiastical congregation has its own special unity, so also all these congregations together share a general unity "in so far as they are one Church under one head—namely the Pope." And just as the dominium of its possessions rests, in a collegiate church, with the whole community, so also in the case of the Universal Church. Thus the Pope as its head is merely *minister et dispensator* or *universalis dispensator*. He himself does not own these possessions; nor can he dispose of them at will. What power he does

20. *Tract. de eccl. pot.*, Dupin, 2, 944: the text is cited and discussed above, p. 51; cf. John of Paris, *Tract. de pot.*, caps. 6 and 7; Leclercq, pp. 185 ff.

21. *Tract. de eccl. pot.*, Dupin, 2, 942–43: "Fundatores Ecclesiarum intenderunt Dominium et proprietatem bonorum quae dabant, transferre primo et directe in communitatem Collegii, scilicet talis Ecclesiae, ad usum Deo servientium, et non in aliquam personam singularem . . . . Principale et caput communitatis . . . habet administrationem et dispensationem generalem omnium bonorum Communitatis approprians cuilibet quod ei debetur secundum debitam justitiae portionem, dispensans etiam pro communi bono Collegii bona fide, ut sibi videtur, expedire, et ita est Episcopus in qualibet Ecclesia Cathedrali, de communi Jure primitivo. . . . Secundum Ostiensem: 'Dicuntur Episcopi procuratores hujusmodi bonorum, et non Domini sed proprietarii,' ut De dona. cap. 2 et De praebend, cap. 3." For the meaning which d'Ailly attached to *jus commune*, see below, pp. 173–75. Cf. John of Paris, *Tract. de pot.*, cap. 6; Leclercq p. 186.

have over them is "for the necessity or common utility of the Church." [22]

With one difference, this is parallel to what civil lawyers in the later Middle Ages were saying about the power of monarchs over the property of their subjects.[23] The difference, however, is a big one. For whereas kings and civil lawyers used the appeal to the common utility and public necessity as a lever for extending the governmental powers of the king at the expense of private rights and privileges,[24] the same appeal is intended in the theory of papal property rights put forward by John of Paris and d'Ailly

22. Ibid., "Quia vero non solum quaelibet congregatio Ecclesiasticorum est una, speciali unitate, imo Ecclesiasticae congregationes habent quandam generalem unitatem, in quantum sunt una Ecclesia, sub uno capite, videlicet Papa, cui incumbit cura Ecclesiae generalis; ideo ipse est universalis dispensator, tanquam supremum membrum Ecclesiae, omnium generaliter Ecclesiasticorum bonorum spiritualium et temporalium: non quidem quod sit eorum Dominus; sed sola Communitas Ecclesiae Universalis Domina est, et proprietaria illorum bonorum generaliter . . . . Papa non potest ad libitum detrahere bona Ecclesiarum ita quod quicquid ordinet de ipsis, teneat: hoc enim haberet si esset Dominus. Sed cum sit minister et dispensator bonorum Communitatis . . . non habet collatam sibi potestatem super bonis ipsis, nisi ad necessitatem, vel communem Ecclesiae utilitatem." Cf. John of Paris, *Tract. de pot.*, cap. 6; Leclercq, pp. 186–87. D'Ailly and John were not alone in applying such corporative concepts to the Universal Church. Otto von Gierke, *Das Deutsche Genossenschaftsrecht* (Berlin, 1868 ff.), *3*, 254–55, and esp. n. 33, noted years ago that the views of John of Paris corresponded very closely with canonistic views. More recently, Tierney has shown that they are, by and large, a reiteration and extension of the corporative ideas of such canonists as Huguccio, Innocent IV, and Hostiensis, given "a new and surprising significance simply because John of Paris consistently assumed that the structure of the whole Church was subject to the same rules that the canonists had evolved in considering the affairs of lesser groups within it" (Tierney, *Foundations*, p. 166).

23. See above, pp. 101–02. The parallel is strengthened by d'Ailly's justification of papal taxation of the Church on the grounds that the Pope has "care of the common *status* of the multitude." *Tract. de eccl. pot.*, Dupin, 2, 947: "Unde nunc eadem ratione, tenentur Clerici Summo Pontifici dare decimam partem decimae, si exigeret. Naturalis enim ratio dictat, ut illi qui habet curam de communi statu multitudinis, provideatur unde possit exequi ea quae pertinent ad communem salutem."

24. Thus Post, "The Theory of Public Law," *Seminar*, *6*, (1948), 53: "When for the common welfare or the defense of the realm a king asks for an extraordinary tax to meet the necessity, special privileges, immunities, and liberties, such as exemptions . . . from taxation, all of which amount to private contracts between King and individuals and corporations, are not valid."

to limit the despotic power over ecclesiastical property which some of the canonists, less hampered than their civilian colleagues by theories of divided dominium, had claimed for the Papacy. It is only on the grounds of public or common necessity, d'Ailly tells us, that the Pope can dispose of ecclesiastical property, and "from this is evident the error of those who say that the Pope . . . is not only the administrator and steward of the Church but true lord and owner of its goods." [25]

This restrictive use of the principle of the common welfare is characteristic both of the thinking of the Conciliarists in general and of d'Ailly in particular, and stems from the glosses of the Decretists, who, like their civilian colleagues, were quite clear that the maintenance of the common welfare or *status ecclesiae* "was an overriding consideration in all matters of ecclesiastical policy," but who drew from this premise "constitutional implications . . . very different from those deduced later by the secular kings, and, indeed, by the popes themselves." For them the status ecclesiae "was not a vague indefinable concept which might be used to justify any extraordinary action of the Church's ruler," but was something quite precise and closely associated with the venerable laws laid down by the General Councils.[26]

D'Ailly, then, is echoing a well-established Decretist position when he argues that the dictum, *princeps legibus solutus,* is true

25. *Tract. de eccl. pot.*, Dupin, 2, 943: "Ex his apparet error eorum qui dicunt, quod . . . Papa . . . non solum est administrator vel dispensator Ecclesiae universalis sed bonorum ejus verus Dominus et proprietarius"; cf. John of Paris, *Tract. de pot.*, cap. 6; Leclercq, pp. 186–88. For an account of the more high papalist position on this matter, expressed in embryonic form by Innocent IV, and developed by Aegidius Romanus and the canonist Petrus Bertrandi, see Ullmann, *Papalism*, pp. 133–37, and Tierney, *Foundations*, pp. 140–42.

26. Tierney, *Foundations*, p. 51, where he adds that "in the Decretist writings (as in the Conciliarist works of two centuries later) the necessity to preserve the *status ecclesiae* was always presented as imposing a limit on papal authority rather than as a ground for extending it," and that "the question of the *status ecclesiae* was most commonly considered in discussions on the limitation of papal authority by a General Council." For the position of a Conciliar thinker other than d'Ailly, see, e.g., Gerson's sermon of 1415, *Prosperum iter faciat*, Dupin, 2, 274, and his *De potestate ecclesiastica, consid.* 12; Dupin, 2, 248. Cf. John B. Morrall, *Gerson and the Great Schism* (Manchester, 1960), Ch. 5, pp. 95–111.

of the Pope only in the case of those laws of his own promulgation, but not in the case of "divine laws or of those laws promulgated with the divine authority by the Universal Church . . . above all in those matters which affect the whole body and *status* of the Universal Church." [27] Nor has he left the teaching of the Decretists completely behind him when he goes on to apply the principle of the status ecclesiae or common welfare of the Church to the problems posed by the Great Schism. For he concludes that "that community is not sufficiently ordered if it cannot resist its own ruin and open destruction"; that the ecclesiastical polity would be a badly organized community if it were not possible to resist a pope who, by manifest heresy, open tyranny, or other notorious crime, is trying to subvert it; that this would be to concede that the Pope has his authority "not for edification but in destruction"; [28] and finally, that in such "a case of urgent necessity or evident utility" a General Council can be assembled without the authority of the Pope and can even proceed to judge and condemn him if he is incorrigible.[29] And

27. *Tract. de mat.*, below, p. 313; cf. ibid., pp. 261 and 320; Tierney, *Foundations*, p. 52. The same holds for his citation of the Romano-canonical principle "Quod omnes tangit" in relation to definitions of matters of faith (below, pp. 253 and 320), but, like Guilielmus Durantis before him, he seems "to have overstepped the bounds of Decretist thought" in requiring the consent of a General Council for changes in ecclesiastical law affecting the whole Church (ibid., p. 255). Cf. Tierney, *Foundations*, pp. 191–95. Ullmann, *Papalism*, pp. 42–43, notes that some of the canonists equated ecclesiastical law with divine law, but this was not d'Ailly's opinion—see below, p. 175, n. 9.

28. *Tract. de eccl. pot.*, Dupin, 2, 959: "illa Communitas non est sufficienter ordinata, quae perditioni suae, et demolitioni publicae non potest occurrere. Sic esset de Ecclesiastica Politia in casu quo Papa per haeresim manifestam, et tyrannidem apertam, aut aliud notorium crimen, conaretur eam subvertere, et nemo ei dicere posset: Cur ita facis? per viam Juris eidem resistendo, *id est ab eo appellando, eum accusando et per Concilium judicando:* hoc esset Papae concedere Potestatem non in aedificationem, sed in destructionem, quod est contra praemissam sententiam Apostoli" (italics mine). Cf. *Tract. de mat.*, below, p. 310; also *Propositiones utiles*, Martène et Durand, 7, 910–11.

29. *Tract. de eccl. pot.*, Dupin, 2, 935, 959–60; *Tract. de mat.*, below, pp. 300–13; *Propositiones utiles*, Martène et Durand, 7, 911. As was true of the theories of the civil lawyers, this whole line of argument concerning the status ecclesiae is intimately connected with a theory of consent. For d'Ailly's views on representation and consent, see below, pp. 139 ff.; cf. above, n. 32, p. 102.

when d'Ailly insists that the faithful ought to obey the Pope as head of the Church in those things that pertain to its edification and not to its destruction, the phraseology may, indeed, be Pauline, but the inspiration, it seems, is at least in part the ideas of the Decretists and the corporative thinking of the Decretalists.[30]

These, then, are some of the constitutional implications which d'Ailly drew from the principle that governmental authority exists to promote the common welfare when he applied it to the ecclesiastical polity. We shall have to examine them again in another connection, but for the moment, and in the first place, they may serve to underline the fact that his dominant conception of the purpose of political authority represents, in its admixture of Aristotelian and corporative elements, no startling departure from the main stream of later medieval political thought. They may also serve to indicate that when d'Ailly spoke of the common interest or common good as the end which ecclesiastical authorities must strive to realize, what he had in mind was not necessarily something imprecise and indefinable, but rather a goal which the canon law itself went some way towards defining.[31] The same, it is true, cannot be said when he asserts the common good to be likewise the purpose of secular political organization, for here he fails to proffer any but the vaguest indications of what should be taken to constitute the common good or public utility, and no indication at all of the procedures by which the nature of the common good might be ascertained. In this he is again no exception, and it would be anachronistic to view it as a serious failing in any medieval political thinker, for the theories of the vast majority of them were predicated on the fundamental assumption that there exist, in the principles of the

30. See below, pp. 207 ff.

31. Indicative of this is the fact that "in discussions of the Pope's authority to dispense from the decrees of Councils the terms *generalis status ecclesiae* and *generale statutum ecclesiae* were used indifferently to express the same idea" (Tierney, *Foundations*, p. 52); cf. J. Brys, *De dispensatione in jure canonico* (Brugis, 1925), pp. 195–97. The identification is not explicit in d'Ailly but he would clearly sympathize with it—see above, n. 27, p. 112.

natural law, universal objective norms which are accessible to the reason of all men—rulers and subjects alike—and in terms of which the justice of governmental activities can be gauged.[32]

III

If the natural law provided some rational criterion whereby the relevance of governmental action to the common good might be ascertained, it did little to indicate the best *institutional* means for ensuring the achievement of that common good. In a sense, indeed, it even militated against any institutional approach to the problem; as Lewis has said, "when natural law was conceived as a doctrine of ultimate ends, the whole structure of institutional rights became a secondary structure, not immediately inherent in the nature of man, but deriving its validity from its demonstrable usefulness to his ends." [1] Given the political conditions of the times, it is hardly surprising that monarchy was generally assumed during the Middle Ages to be the most suitable form of government both in the secular and ecclesiastical polities. This seemed so obvious a fact that it was scarcely thought necessary to elaborate arguments in support of it, until the translation of Aristotle's *Politics* in the latter half of the thirteenth century confronted men with arguments in favor of other forms of government. Not that such arguments succeeded in weaning medieval men from their devotion to monarchy, for

32. Thus John Dickenson, *The Statesman's Book of John of Salisbury* (New York, 1927), p. lxxviii: "Kings and governments and organized communities had no peculiar prerogative to know and enforce that law; it was binding upon them no less than upon private individuals, [and] . . . its precepts were as accessible to private persons as to officials." Marsilius of Padua is, in this respect, an exceptional figure; see *Defensor pacis*, I, caps. 10, 11, and 12, ed. C. W. Previté-Orton (Cambridge, 1928), pp. 36–54; cf. Alan Gewirth, *Marsilius of Padua* (New York, 1956), *1*, 60, 141–43, 203 ff.

1. *Political Ideas*, *1*, 221, where she adds: "Thus the way was clear for the application of the test of utility to all political institutions; and if one thought that an organically constructed and monarchically integrated society would best serve the ends of man, such a conclusion would be in logical harmony with an individualistic conception of those ends."

114

"almost with one voice," Gierke tells us, "the medieval publicists declared a monarchical to be the best form of government," [2] and the notable exceptions—Tholommeo of Lucca [3] and Marsilius of Padua—reflected, in their attitude towards forms of government, not so much the influence of Aristotelian arguments, as that of the political experience of the Italian communes. [4]

It should not be thought that this loyalty to the monarchical form of government precluded discussion of its nature and of the proper extent of its power in relation to private rights and privileges, nor that it in any way implied an abandonment of the idea that all human government is subject to very real limitations. The general medieval conception of the purpose of political authority and the widespread belief in the objective standards of the natural law ruled out this possibility in relation both to the temporal kingship and to the papal monarchy over the *regnum ecclesiasticum*. Nor were more concrete limitations lacking. We have already noted that some of the canonists regarded the Pope as bound by the laws of the General Councils, [5] and McIlwain has insisted that when a medieval lawyer like Bracton speaks of the king, on the one hand as being under the law and limited by it, and on the other as being subject to no human agency, as having "no peer much less a superior" in his kingdom, he is not simply putting forward a confused statement of monarchical absolutism. On the contrary, his remarks presuppose an important distinction between the area of "government" (*gubernaculum*), over which the king "has *plenam potestatem et*

2. Gierke–Maitland, p. 31.

3. The probable compiler of the *De regimine principum* which contains the *De regno* of Aquinas, and which throughout the Middle Ages was attributed in toto to Aquinas. For a discussion of the relationship between the two works see the introduction by I. Th. Eschmann to *St. Thomas Aquinas: On Kingship, to the King of Cyprus*, trans. G. B. Phelan (Toronto, 1949), pp. xi–xiv.

4. McIlwain, it is true, dismisses the influence upon Marsilius of the Italian political experience and asserts, instead, the impact of Aristotelian ideas and of French monarchical institutions (*Growth*, pp. 299 ff.). But see Gewirth, *Marsilius of Padua, 1*, 117 ff.

5. Above, p. 111 and n. 26.

liberum regimen[6] . . . and, on the other hand, those prescriptive rights of tenants and subjects which are wholly outside and beyond the legitimate bounds of royal administration and fall properly under *jurisdictio* not *gubernaculum*." [7]

McIlwain's interpretation of Bracton has not gone unquestioned, but nobody would claim that theoretical limitations on the power of monarchs were lacking in the Middle Ages, or deny that they were grounded in positive as well as in natural and divine law. What were lacking were those institutional forms which alone can provide "effective sanctions short of force" for the protection of the "legal rights of the subject against the arbitrary will of the prince." [8] If the prince spurned the suggestion of Bracton and refused to put on "the bridle of temperance and the reins of moderation," [9] the remedies which remained—the feudal *diffidatio*, the resort to revolutionary opposition, or tyrannicide [10]—these were scarcely institutional, but were essentially dependent upon the verdict of the individual outraged conscience. In this context the views of the Conciliar thinkers take on an added significance. For the prolonged crisis of the Schism

6. The phrase is the of St. Louis in his "Award" or decision against the Provisions of Oxford, in William Stubbs, *Select Charters* (9th ed. Oxford, 1913), p. 396; cf. F. M. Powicke, *King Henry III and the Lord Edward* (Oxford, 1947), *1*, 411–55.

7. C. H. McIlwain, *Constitutionalism Ancient and Modern* (Ithaca, N. Y., 1958), p. 81. Note that McIlwain (pp. 77–78) regards Bracton's position not as something specifically English but as "a commonplace of late–thirteenth century European political theory." The whole of Ch. 4 (pp. 67–92) is important for this. See esp. p. 85, where he adds "In *jurisdictio*, unlike *gubernaculum*, the law . . . is not merely the *vis directiva* of St. Thomas, or the moral inhibition implied in the *Digna vox* . . . . The king may legitimately disregard them, for they are only self-imposed, and, if he refuses to be so guided, he is within his undoubted legal rights in so doing . . . . [But] in *jurisdictio*, as contrasted with *gubernaculum*, there are bounds to the King's discretion established by a law that is positive and coercive, and a royal act beyond these bounds is *ultra vires*." Cf. McIlwain, *Growth*, pp. 364 ff.; Kantorowicz, *King's Two Bodies*, pp. 148 ff.; Brian Tierney, "Bracton on Government," *Speculum, 38* (1963), 295–317 (criticizes McIlwain's interpretation).

8. McIlwain, *Constitutionalism*, p. 93.

9. *De legibus et consuetudinibus Angliae*, f. 107v, ed. George E. Woodbine, (New Haven, 1915 ff.), 2, 305; cited in Lewis, *Political Ideas, 1*, 247.

10. See below, p. 155.

stimulated these men to reexamine "the basic principles of all political organization and brought into comparatively explicit statement ideas that in the realm of secular theory remained vague suggestions." [11] It is, accordingly, in its faltering moves toward the institutionalization of what had been essentially personal rights to enforce the limitation of government to its proper goals that the interest and value of d'Ailly's position concerning forms of government is to be found.

Little agreement has been reached about which form of government Aquinas regarded as the best,[12] but among the various relevant passages broadcast throughout his works perhaps the most "constitutional" is one that occurs in the *Summa theologica* in which he advocates, with arguments drawn from Aristotle and the Old Testament, a "mixed" form of government.[13] This passage was echoed by John of Paris, who went on to apply Aquinas's arguments to the constitution of the Church; [14] d'Ailly's clearest statement of his views on forms of government is substantially a reiteration, with significant modifications, of John's point of view.[15] Pure monarchical rule, he tells us, is best in itself, if it is not corrupted, but because of the concentration of so much power in the hands of the king, such a form of rule easily degenerates into tyranny, for kings of perfect virtue are indeed rare. The most practicable form of government is therefore that form of kingship which contains an admixture of aristocracy and democracy as well; such a regimen is best because all elements of the community have some part in it.[16] Such was the form of

11. Lewis, *Political Ideas*, 2, 357.

12. For a recent defence of the consistency of Aquinas's varying dicta on the subject see Morrall, *Political Thought in Medieval Times*, pp. 77–79.

13. *ST*, 1a, 2ae, qu. 105, art. 1; d'Entrèves, *Aquinas*, pp. 149–51.

14. *Tract. de pot.*, cap. 19; Leclercq, pp. 236–37.

15. *Tract. de eccl. pot.*, Dupin, 2, 946–47.

16. *Tract. de eccl. pot.*, Dupin, 2, 946: "Sciendum est, quod licet regimen Regium, in quo unus singulariter principatur multitudini, secundum virtutem sit melius quolibet alio regimen simplici ut ostendit Philosophus, 3. *Politicorum:* tamen si fiat mixtum cum Aristocratia, in qua plures dominantur secundum virtutem; et cum Democratia, in qua populus principatur, tale regimen melius est, in quantum in regimine mixto omnes aliquam partem habent in Principatu: et etiam quia licet regimen Regale sit optimum in se, si non corrumpatur; tamen

government instituted by God for His people of Israel: monarchical, in that one man such as Moses or Joshua was preeminent over all; aristocratic, in that under him were elected seventy-two Elders; democratic, in that these seventy-two were "chosen from all the people and by all the people." [17]

Thus far, d'Ailly's description of the mixed constitution is substantially only a repetition of what both Aquinas and John of Paris had said, and it is certain that it does not necessarily imply any institutional limitation of monarchical power. The formulation is very vague, and d'Ailly adds to its vagueness by assuring us that when he speaks of democracy he is not taking it in its strictest sense, but in a more general way, simply to mean "the reign of the people" (*principatus populi*).[18] It is tempting, therefore, to dismiss his argument—just as J. B. Morrall dismisses that of Aquinas—as "no more incompatible with support of an absolute monarchy than are the theories of popular sovereignty embodied in the Roman law in the days of the absolute Empire." [19]

To do so would be to overlook the fact that both d'Ailly and John of Paris go beyond Aquinas when they apply this mixed constitution to the Church. Indeed, the very passage in which d'Ailly treats of the whole issue is to be found in a discussion concerning the limitation of the papal *plenitudo potestatis*. "It seems manifest," he tells us, using John's words, "that it would be the best regimen for the Church if, under one Pope, many men were elected by and from every province," and—going one step beyond John—that "such men should be Cardinals, who, with the Pope and under him, might rule the Church and

---

propter magnam Potestatem quae Regi conceditur, de facili regimen degenerat in tyrannidem, nisi sit in Rege perfecta virtus, quae raro et in paucis reperitur."

17. Ibid.: "In cujus rei signum, in populo Israël, cui succedit populus Christianus, Deus instituit quodammodo Regem, licet non cum plena Potestate, ut patet in Moïse, et Josue, et eorum successoribus, qui toti illi populo praeerant . . . . Licet autem in eis esset regimen Regale, in quantum unus principaliter praeerat omnibus; erat tamen aliquid de Aristocratia, in quantum sub illo uno, septuaginta duo seniores eligebantur . . . . Erat etiam aliquid de Democratia, in quantum septuaginta duo eligebantur de omni populo, et ab omni populo."

18. Ibid.: "et capitur hic Democratia generaliter, pro Principatu populi, et non stricte."

19. *Political Thought in Medieval Times*, p. 79.

118

temper the use of the *plenitudo potestatis.*" [20] This statement is
not in itself precise, but it is significant because it provides the
link between d'Ailly's central statement of his views on the matter of forms of government, and his other complex but illuminating statements about the constitution of the Church.

The most important of these statements occurs towards the
end of this same treatise, where d'Ailly addresses himself to the
vital question: *Utrum videlicet plenitudo potestatis ecclesiasticae resideat in solo Romano Pontifice.*[21] For his answer is that it
does not, but rather pertains *separably* to the Pope, *inseparably*
to the *universitas* of the Church, and *representatively* to the
General Council.[22] Later on, nevertheless, having made it clear
that he is speaking of the *potestas jurisdictionis* and not the
potestas ordinis, he qualifies his position by saying that "properly speaking" this plenitude of power belongs to the Pope
alone, for he is the one who generally exercises it, and as a result
it is possessed by the Church and the General Council representing it merely "figuratively and in some equivocal way." [23] The

20. *Tract. de eccl. pot.,* Dupin, 2, 946: "manifeste videtur, quod esset optimum
regimen Ecclesiae, si sub uno Papa eligerentur plures de omni, et ab omni Provincia, et tales deberent esse Cardinales, qui cum Papa et sub eo Ecclesiam
regerent, et usum plenitudinis Potestatis temperarent"; cf. John of Paris, *Tract.
de pot.,* cap. 19; Leclercq, p. 237. This statement reflects d'Ailly's increasing stress
on the importance of the Cardinalate in the years after 1411 when he himself
became Cardinal, a change of attitude which is made explicit by the contrast
between certain passages in the *Tractatus de materia* (1402–3) and the revised
version included in the *Tractatus super reformatione* which was written in 1416.
See below, Appendix III, p. 251 and Appendix V.

21. Dupin, 2, 949–51.

22. Ibid., 950: "Prima est, quod plenitudo Potestatis Ecclesiae, *seperabiliter*
residet in Romano Pontifice. Secunda, quod plenitudo Potestatis Ecclesiasticae,
inseperabiliter residet in Universitate Ecclesiae Catholicae. Tertia, quod plenitudo Potestatis Ecclesiasticae, *repraesentative* residet in Generali Concilio." The
application to the Church of the term *universitas* is not, in this context, without
significance. D'Ailly goes on to attribute this formulation to the theologian
Maurice of Prague who, he says, put it forward at Constance but was prevented
by adversaries from explaining and defending it. Hence "quia ergo dictus Magister sic impeditus fuit ad hac responsione, ego hujus conclusionis nodum breviter
explicabo." For the rôle of Maurice at Constance, see J. A. Fabricius, *Bibliotheca
Latina Mediae et Infimae Aetatis* (Hamburg, 1734 ff.), 5, 175.

23. Dupin, 2, 950: "Dico quod haec plenitudo Jurisdictionis, proprie loquendo,
solum residet in Romano, seu Summo Pontifice Petro succedenti; quia proprie,

meaning of this is not at all clear; it may well be felt that for d'Ailly the authority inherent in the Church exhausts itself in the mere election of a Pope, for he does insist that although the election of the Pope in his capacity as Roman Pontiff belongs, by natural and divine law, to the *universitas* of the Romans, his election as Supreme Pontiff of the Universal Church belongs, equally by natural and divine law, to the *universitas fidelium* or the General Council representing it,[24] and that if this election is left in the hands of the Romans, it is only "in the place and name of the Universal Church," and for practical reasons of expediency.[25]

Such an interpretation is, however, ruled out by d'Ailly's further explication of his position concerning the plenitude of ecclesiastical power. This power, he tells us, resides in the Pope "as if in the subject receiving it and as a minister exercising it," in the Universal Church as in the object, that is to say, the final end to which it is ordained, and in the General Council "as it were in the image representing it, and as a matter of course (*regulariter*) ordering it." [26] This again is vague enough to ad-

aliqua Potestas plene dicitur esse in aliquo, quia illam potest *generaliter* exercere, et *ministerialiter* in omnes dispensare: hoc autem est in solo Papa, et non proprie in aliqua Communitate . . . . Tertio, dico quod hujusmodi plenitudo Potestatis, tropice et alio modo equivoce, est in Universali Ecclesiae, et in Concilio Generali ipsam repraesentante."

24. Dupin, 2, 936: "sicut ad universitatem Romanorum pertinet Jure naturali vel divino electio Papae, tanquam Romani Pontificis; sic ad universitatem fidelium, simili Jure naturali et divino, pertinet electio Papae, tanquam Summi Pontificis Universalis Ecclesiae, vel ad Generale Concilium ipsam repraesentans; quia Ecclesia Universalis, vel congregatio eam repraesentans originaliter et principaliter, habet Jus eligendi sibi caput seu rectorem."

25. Ibid.: "ex qua sequitur, quod si universitas Romanorum, naturali aut divino Jure habeat potestatem in electione Summi Pontificis, hoc est vice et nomine Universalis Ecclesiae, cujus Summus Pontifex est particularis Romanae Ecclesiae Episcopus, et quia universitas Romanorum, vel aliqui, ejus authoritate, facilius et commodius possunt congregari, quam tota Ecclesia, vel Concilium Generale."

26. Dupin, 2, 951: "Prima ergo modo, plenitudo Potestatis est in Papa, tanquam in subjecto ipsam recipiente, et ministerialiter exercente. Secundo, est in Universali Ecclesia, tanquam in objecto ipsam causaliter et finaliter continente. Tertio, est in Generali Concilio tanquam in exemplo ipsam repraesentante, et regulariter dirigente."

mit, without protest, diverse interpretation, and if we relate it to the statement with which d'Ailly opened his treatise, we may well be disposed to dismiss all these distinctions simply as part of a dialectical smokescreen behind which he is withdrawing to the safety of a more traditional and less exposed position.

He had begun in a seemingly conservative fashion, distinguishing six ecclesiastical powers which Christ conferred upon the Apostles, and insisting that although most of these were conferred equally upon all, the fifth—that of regulating ministers and delimiting their jurisdiction—was conferred upon Peter and his successors in a special way, with the object of avoiding confusion among the laity and dissension among the clergy.[27] Thus Peter or his successor, as Vicar of Christ chief among ministers, may be said, after Christ, to be head of the Church. Indeed, it is heretical to deny either that the Pope is head of the Church, or that the Roman Church is head of all churches.[28]

This is an unambiguous statement both of the jurisdictional primacy of the Pope and of the divine origin of this primacy, but it should be noted that it is not original with d'Ailly. It is drawn almost verbatim not from any high papalist but from John of Paris, and we should not allow it, therefore, to obscure the significance of d'Ailly's more radical statements.[29] For though he

27. *Tract. de eccl. pot.*, Dupin, 2, 928: "Quinta potestas est dispositionis ministrorum, quoad determinationem Jurisdictionis Ecclesiasticae, ut evitetur confusio, et dissensionis materia in populo et inter ministros, si ipsi aequaliter, et indistincte de omni populo curam haberent: et haec potestas collata est Petro, et successoribus ejus, ubi ei specialiter dictum est: 'Pasce oves meas' etc. . . . Conclusio est, quod sex praedictae potestates a principio communes fuerunt, et quasi pares omnibus Apostolis, praeter quintam quae Petro specialiter collata est."

28. Ibid.: "Sequitur ex praedictis: quod sicut Apostoli et Discipuli, sic Episcopi et Praesbyteri Ecclesiae, ministri a Christo immediate potestatem Ecclesiasticam susceperunt, tanquam ab eo, qui solus est proprie et maxime caput Ecclesiae: tamen nihilominus Petrus, et quilibet ejus Vicarius Pontifex Summus, potuit dici caput Ecclesiae inquantum principalis est inter ministros, a quo tamen, tanquam a principali hierarcha et architecto, aliquo modo dependet totus ministrorum Ecclesiasticus ordo. Unde [col. 929] . . . negare Romanam Ecclesiam esse caput omnium Ecclesiarum, est haereticum, sicut etiam negare Summum Pontificem esse caput ecclesiae."

29. John, *Tract. de pot.*, caps. 12 and 18; Leclercq, pp. 207–10, 230; cf. Tierney, *Foundations,* pp. 165–66.

does not develop the idea with the consistency and vigor of John of Paris, he does assume with John that the relationship to the Universal Church of the Pope as its head is "the same as that of any other prelate to his ecclesiastical corporation." [30] He also follows him in concluding from this that just as a monastery can depose its abbot, or a particular church its bishop, for misappropriating ecclesiastical property to his own rather than to the common good, so also can the Universal Church depose the Pope if he has been admonished and remains incorrigible.[31] This clearly rules out the possibility that the authority inherent in the Church exhausts itself in the mere act of electing a pope. It also suggests that d'Ailly posed his complex and obscure distinctions concerning the plenitude of power with the object of proving the existence of some more enduring limitation of papal power. The two corollaries which he appends to his distinctions may serve to support this contention for they are refreshingly concrete.

The first is perhaps the more important, and runs as follows: Since the plenitude of power is not causally ordained to the Pope himself, but to the Church—or rather to the edification of the Church—as to its final end, then if the Pope abuses this power in such a way as to encompass the destruction of the Church, the General Council is "the image or mirror of the same Universal Church, and in its place and name" restrains and limits this abuse of the plenitude of power.[32] For the precise details concerning this function he refers us to the last chapter of

30. Tierney, *Foundations*, p. 167.

31. *Tract. de eccl. pot.*, Dupin, 2, 943–44: "sicut Monasterium posset agere ad depositionem Abbatis, vel particularis Ecclesia, ad depositionem episcopi, si constaret quod dissiparet bona Monasterii, vel Ecclesiae, et quod infideliter, non pro bono communi, sed privato ea detraheret; sic et de Papa, si admonitus non corrigeretur"; cf. John of Paris, *Tract. de pot.*, cap. 6; Leclercq, p. 188.

32. Dupin, 2, 951: "plenitudo potestatis non est causaliter propter Papam, sed Papa et ejus Potestas propter Ecclesiam, et ad eam ordinatur sicut ad finem, id est, ad ejus aedificationem." Citing St. Paul, he continues: "Patet ex eodem verbo Apostoli, quia si Papa uteretur hac Potestate ad destructionem Ecclesiae, Generale Concilium est exemplum, vel speculum dictam Universalem Ecclesiam repraesentans, et ejus vice et nomine, abusus hujusmodi plenitudinis Potestatis coërcens, regulans, et dirigens."

the tract, where he defends the subjection of the Pope to the correction of the General Council and, if the Pope is obdurate, to its judgment, deposition, and punishment.[33] The importance of this lies in the fact that here, in the context of a discussion concerning the plenitude of power, d'Ailly reaffirms his conviction that the authority inherent in the Church is not exclusively concentrated—by the mere act of election—in the hands of its papal monarch, but remains latent in the body of the whole Church, and can in cases of necessity be called into play to put a stop to the Pope's exercise of his power illegally in a way not conducive to the common good. Nor should his support of this position with misleading analogies drawn from French governmental practice [34] obscure, as it does for Ewart Lewis, [35] the genuine constitutional advance entailed by such a position. For d'Ailly not only asserts the existence of actual institutional machinery for restraining, on extraordinary occasions, monarchical abuses of power, but also envisages—as his belief in the mixed constitution indicates [36]—some more continuously operating institutional restraints. This is reflected in his suggestion that General Councils should in the future assemble automatically every thirty or fifty years, with or without special mandate from the

33. *Tract. de eccl. pot.*, Tertia pars, cap. 3; Dupin, 2, 956–60. The material in this section is drawn almost wholly from his *Tract. de mat.*, Secunda pars; see below, pp. 300–11. Behind this, of course, lies the whole theory of consent and representation which is discussed below, Ch. 5, esp. pp. 134–54. For he is careful to tell us that "auctoritas Papae seu Romanae Ecclesiae et Concilii Generalis immediate est a Deo principaliter" but is "ab homine, seu dependeat ab humana potestate ministerialiter: nam Papa sit per Cardinalium electionem" etc. (*Tract. de eccl. pot.*, Dupin, 2, 938).

34. Dupin, 2, 957: "Nam Rex Franciae qui est major et Superior in toto regno, saepe in aliquibus casibus judicatur, et contra eum fertur Sententia, in suo Parlamento; similiter Papa in Foro conscientiae, a simplici Sacerdote judicatur, etiam in Foro exteriori potest judicari ab inferiori suo, si se et sponte subjiciat." Cf. *Tract. de mat.*, below, p. 304. D'Ailly is referring presumably, to the frequent condemnation by the *Parlement* of royal officers, or to clashes with the King over alienations of the royal domain. It should be remembered, however, that in both cases the *Parlement* was working in the real interest of the King—see E. Lavisse, *Histoire de France*, (Paris, 1901), *3*², 235; F. Aubert, *Histoire du Parlement de Paris* (Paris, 1894), *1*, 263.

35. *Political Ideas*, *1*, 273–74.

36. See above, n. 20, p. 119.

Pope,[37] and in his assertion that in order to prevent the abuse of the papal plenitude of power, the General Council can restrict its use.[38] It is indicated much more clearly, however, by the second conclusion which he draws from his examination of the location of the plenitudo potestatis, the aristocratic implications of which distinguish his position from that of most of the other Conciliarists,[39] and also serve to underline his own change of attitude after he himself had become a member of the Sacred College.[40]

The heart of this conclusion is the assertion that "just as the plenitude of power is *repraesentative* in the General Council, so also is it, in some way, though not equally, in the Roman Church, since it represents the Universal Church itself, and in the creation of ecclesiastical laws or canons, acts in its place." The reason that the Roman Church is endowed with this power is that its head is the Pope, who is specially preeminent in the Universal Church.[41] It is clear, moreover, that the Pope in some sense shares his rule of the Roman Church with the Cardinals (whom d'Ailly describes elsewhere as *pars corporis papae*),[42] for

37. *Tract. de mat.*, below, p. 317.

38. *Tract. de eccl. pot.*, Dupin, 2, 945–46: "Sciendum est quod licet Papalis dignitas a Deo sit, unde ab homine nec major nec minor fieri potest; tamen, usus plenitudinis Potestatis ad excludendum abusum potest Concilii Generalis authoritati restringi: ideo antiquo Jure institutum est quod Papa professionem faceret"; and he goes on to appeal to the alleged *professio fidei* of Boniface VIII, on which see Stephanus Baluzius et Joannes Dominici Mansi, *Miscellanea* (Lucae, 1761 ff.), *3*, 418.

39. Cardinal Zabarella (1360–1417) is a notable, and, it seems, a lucid exception to this generalization; see Walter Ullmann, *The Origins of the Great Schism* (London, 1948), pp. 191–231; Tierney, *Foundations*, pp. 220–37.

40. See above, n. 20, p. 119.

41. Dupin, 2, 951: "sicut plenitudo Potestatis est in Generali Concilio repraesentative, ita aliquo modo, licet non aequaliter, est in Romana Ecclesia, quia ipsam Universalem Ecclesiam repraesentat, et in condendis Ecclesiasticis Juribus seu Canonibus, ipsius vices gerit, et hoc sibi competit, ratione sui capitis, scilicet Papae, qui huic Ecclesiae specialiter praeest."

42. *Tract. de eccl. pot.*, Dupin, 2, 946: "ad idem facit quod Cardinales sunt *pars corporis Papae*, et ejus Coadjutores" (italics mine). The expression is an ancient one. The former senators of the Roman Senate had been called "pars corporis imperatoris," and as early as the eleventh century it became customary to regard the cardinals as forming an ecclesiastical senate, a corporate body with senatorial functions. Hence they became the "pars corporis papae" (St. Peter

124

before his consecration he has to promise that Church that he will wield his ministerium "with the advice, consent, love and remembrance of the Cardinals." [43] D'Ailly flatly asserts that the College of Cardinals inherited this task from the "Sacred College or Senate of the Apostles," which it had replaced in the hierarchical order [44] but which had exercised the *"ministerium* of the Cardinalate." [45] But Peter was head of the Universal Church before he became Bishop of Rome, and the Apostles were Cardinals of the world before they became Cardinals of that city. It follows, therefore, that the Cardinals are co-assistants and, "as it were, special collaborators" of the Pope "in the place and name of the Universal Church as well as of the Roman Church." And it is their duty to assist the Pope as his principal

Damiani being the first to use the expression). See Walter Ullmann, *The Growth of Papal Government in the Middle Ages* (London, 1955), pp. 319 ff.; cf. J. B. Sägmuller, *Die Thätigkeit und Stellung der Cardinäle* (Freiburg im Breisgau, 1896), pp. 225–26; Stephan Kuttner, "Cardinalis: The History of a Canonical Concept," *Traditio, 3,* (1945), 172–77.

43. Dupin, 2, 929–30: "Papa ante suam consecrationem, profiteri debet sanctae Romanae Ecclesiae. Cardinalium consilio, consensu, dilectione [sic], et rememoratione, ministerium suum gerere et peragerere, ut patet in Professione quam fecit Bonifacius Octavus." The alleged *professio* in fact reads: "Cum quorum [i.e., the cardinals] consilio, consensu, *directione* et rememoratione ministerium meum geram et peragam," etc. (Baluzius-Mansi, 2, 418).

44. Dupin, 2, 930: "sacro Collegio, vel Senatui Apostolorum, succedit in Ordine hierarchico Collegium sacrum Cardinalium, videlicet, quantum ad illum statum, quo Apostoli coassistebant Petro, antequam . . . fierent particularium Ecclesiarum Episcopi." Thus, as he insists later on (p. 934): "sicut status Papae, sic et post eum, status Cardinalium ad ordinem hierarchium Ecclesiae ex Christi institutione pertinet. Nam ipsi, quantum ad hunc statum, statui Apostolico immediate succedunt." Tierney, *Foundations,* pp. 176–77, comments that Innocent IV "had revived the description of the Sacred College as Senate of the Church and the definition was widely repeated among canonists contemporary with John of Paris." He adds that "the term was not used merely as a vague title of honour, for various technicalities of Roman law relating to the Senate were used to define the authority of the Cardinals, and technically, according to the texts of Roman law, the senators acted on behalf of the whole Roman people." The implication is certainly clearly drawn by d'Ailly.

45. Dupin, 2, 929: "sciendum est quod . . . ante divisionem Apostolorum, per quam ad diversas mundi partes dispersi sunt Apostoli, Petro tanquam Papale officium gerenti assistebant, tanquam Cardinalatus ministerium exercentes." For the very similar views of Aegidius Romanus, see Sägmuller, p. 214, but see also Tierney's criticisms of Sägmuller, *Foundations,* pp. 185–86.

assistants, counsellors and co-operators in the rule of the Universal Church.[46]

It is fitting, therefore, that the election of the Pope should pertain to the Cardinals, for in this, he says, they succed the Apostles. Nevertheless, this power "principally and originally pertains to the Universal Church or the General Council representing it," [47] and as he says elsewhere, the Cardinals in exercising it are not merely enjoying some inherent prescriptive right but are acting as vicegerents of the Universal Church.[48] Indeed, they act as vicegerents of the Church not only in electing the Pope, but in anything which they legitimately do with the object of promoting the union of the Church.[49] Thus, when— for the conservation of the faith or the well-being of the Church —necessity or utility demands the convocation of a General Council and the Pope fails to act, then the authority to convoke the council devolves upon the Cardinals, "not so much by human as by divine institution, in the place and name of the whole Universal Church." [50]

46. Dupin, 2, 929: "Papae assistunt Cardinales, tanquam ejus principales Assessores, et Consiliarii, atque Cooperatores, in regimine Universalis Ecclesiae. Nam sicut Petrus prius fuit Papa Orbis, id est Universalis Ecclesiae, antequam Episcopus Ecclesiae Romanae, ut dictum est; sic et Apostoli, prius fuerunt Cardinales Orbis, quam aliqui fierent Cardinales Romanae Urbis. . . . In utroque vero, tam urbis quam orbis praesidentia, coassistunt Papae Cardinales, tanquam speciales ipsius coadjutores, vice et nomine tam Romanae quam Universali ecclesiae."

47. Dupin, 2, 935–36: "Valde magna congruentia est, ut ad eos [cardinales] pertinet electio Papae Christi Vicarii, quia videlicet in hoc succedunt Apostolis Christi: hoc tamen Jus, principaliter et originaliter pertinet ad Unversalem Ecclesiam, seu Generale Concilium ipsam repraesentans."

48. *Octo conclusiones*, Dupin, 2, 110–11: "Veri Cardinales in electione Papae vices gerunt Universalis Ecclesiae Christianae." Note that d'Ailly himself urged not only that the Cardinals should be representative of all the provinces of the Church, but that they should also be chosen by them—see above, notes 17 and 20, pp. 118 ff.; cf. his *Consultationes Cardinalium*, Hardt, 2, 584–85.

49. Dupin, 2, 111: "Veri Cardinales hujusmodi vices Ecclesiae gerunt, non solum in Papae electione; sed etiam in his quae circa eam rite et legitime fiunt pro Ecclesiastica unione."

50. *Tract. de eccl. pot.*, Dupin, 2, 935: "sequitur quod ubi necessitas, aut utilitas imminet, pro conservanda Fide, vel bono regimine Ecclesiae, ad Papam, vel, in ejus defectu, ad Cardinales pertinet Generale Concilium convocare, et hoc eis convenit, non tam humana quam divina institutione, vice et nomine totius Universalis Ecclesiae."

It can therefore be said that d'Ailly viewed the ecclesiastical constitution as a mixed one embodying monarchical, aristocratic, and "democratic"elements.[51] The stress on papal monarchy was common to well-nigh all medieval thinkers, the stress on the democratic he shared in common with all the Conciliarists, and even his final predilection for aristocracy was not unique. For in this he betrays the influence of an old curialist tradition which predated the Conciliar movement and which had its origin in the de facto share increasingly taken by the Cardinals, from the Investiture struggle onwards, in the day-to-day government of the Church, strengthened by the wide measure of financial autonomy which they enjoyed from 1289 onwards.[52] This tradition received what seems to have been its first theoretical formulation [53] in the anonymous apparatus on Gratian's *Decretum* which bears the name *Ecce vicit Leo* and which was written early in the thirteenth century.[54] This formulation was given more explicit expression by the later decretalists Hostiensis and Johannes Monachus [55]—who maintained that the Cardinals shared with the Pope the exercise of the plenitudo potestatis—but all these men took as their premiss the idea that "Pope and Cardinals together formed a single corporate body subject to the normal rules of corporation law" so that "the Pope stood in exactly the same relationship to the Cardinals as any other Bishop to his cathedral chapter." [56] In its origin such a

51. When we speak of "democracy" in this context we should not forget that medieval thinkers did not necessarily link the idea of representation with that of election—see below, Ch. 5.

52. In this year Nicholas IV, by the bull *Coelestis altitudo,* apportioned to the Cardinals half of the revenues which the Roman Church possessed at the time; see W. E. Lunt, *Papal Revenues in the Middle Ages* (New York, 1934), *1,* 26-27. On the whole issue, see Sägmuller, pp. 170 ff., 215 ff.

53. See Tierney, *Foundations,* pp. 74–75.

54. For a description of this gloss see Stephen Kuttner, *Repertorium der Kanonistik (1140–1234)* (Città del Vaticano, 1937), *1,* 59–66.

55. Monachus, as Bishop of Meaux, was an adviser to Philip the Fair. He became a cardinal in 1294 and died in 1313. For his views, which were shared in part by Guido de Baysio (d. 1313) as well as by Hostiensis, see Ullmann, *Origins of the Great Schism,* pp. 204–08. D'Ailly cites all three of them in support of his claims for the rôle of the Sacred College; see *Tract. de eccl. pot.,* Dupin, 2, 933.

56. Tierney, *Foundations,* p. 184; cf. R. Scholz, *Die Publizistik zur Zeit Philipps des Schönen und Bonifaz' VIII* (Stuttgart, 1903), pp. 194–98.

view was not, of course, necessarily related to Conciliar ideas and might even seem to be incompatible with them. Nevertheless, these curialist arguments eventually came to be synthesized with the more "democratic" views of the Conciliarists to produce, in Cardinal Zabarella's Commentary on the Decretals, a coherently articulated view of the corporative structure of the Church.[57] The *De potestate regia et papali* of John of Paris marks a milestone on the tortuous route to this synthesis and it is fitting that d'Ailly, who was so strongly influenced by this tract, should have advanced the process a stage further. His arguments on the subject, though they go some way beyond the position of John of Paris, admittedly do not have the precision of Zabarella's, nor are they stated in so comprehensive a way, but they are very close to them in intention, unmistakably draw their inspiration from the same sources, and have had, it seems, much greater influence.[58]

In itself this forms an illuminating chapter in the neglected history of late medieval ecclesiology, but what is more important for our purpose is that, set in the context of such an analysis of ecclesiastical government, d'Ailly's advocacy of a mixed constitution as the best form of government clearly entails far more than that of Aquinas, and will certainly resist any attempt to whittle it away to an affirmation of practical absolutism. It may be felt that his conception of limited government was the outcome of conditions peculiar to the Church, but there is no reason to doubt that he thought of it as in principle applicable to any "rightly-ordained polity." The claims made on behalf of the

57. Tierney, *Foundations,* pp. 220–37.

58. See esp. Tierney, *Foundations,* pp. 236–37. Both d'Ailly and Zabarella speak of the cardinals as being *partes corporis papae,* and both cite in support of their oligarchic theories the glosses of Guido de Baysio and Joannes Monachus. For d'Ailly, see above, n. 55, p. 127; for Zabarella, *Tractatus de schismate,* in S. Schardius, *De jurisdictione authoritate et praeeminentia imperiale ac potestate ecclesiastica* (Basel, 1516), pp. 698–702. D'Ailly, however, does not cite, though he may have known it, the important gloss of Monachus on X, 5, 2, c.4 *in v. fratrum nostrorum* on which Zabarella leans so heavily. Nevertheless, Hostiensis had in many ways anticipated the views of Monachus, and d'Ailly does refer to his glosses, e.g. that on X, 5, 33, c.23; cf. Ullmann, *Origins of the Great Schism,* pp. 204–09; Tierney, *Foundations,* pp. 149–52, 183–90.

Cardinalate and the Council could, after all, be paralleled by similar (if less coherently developed) claims made on behalf of the *curia regis* and the estates, and d'Ailly himself, as we have seen, appealed to secular analogies to bolster his contentions. His considered verdict seems to have been, therefore, that the form of government most likely to fulfill the purpose for which political authority exists is a government that actually embodies institutional checks against the abuse of power.[59] And it was precisely in his attempts to justify these checks that he was led to examine the sources of political authority.

59. It is perhaps significant that this institutionalization of resistance to the abuse of authority is paralleled in d'Ailly's thought by a complete rejection of the time-honored individual right of tyrannicide—see below, pp. 156–58.

5.

The Source of Authority: Consent—Its Expression and Its Consequences

Even when it has taken the form of a search for historical origins, curiosity about the source or sources of political authority has rarely been quite disinterested.[1] It has rather been the product of the constant search for grounds upon which obedience or disobedience to constituted political authority can be justified. It is understandable that such a quest has not concerned those who, following Aristotle, have viewed political association as grounded in the very nature of man, and political relationships as reflecting (ideally, at least) the natural differences in the intellectual capacities of men. Nor has it troubled the minds of those who, even though they have admitted the conventional character of political association, have either found

1. Medieval writers in general were not concerned about questions of historical origins but rather with questions concerning the basis of political authority. D'Ailly is no exception to the rule. Note, however, that from the thirteenth century onwards, some fragmentary accounts of the alleged historical origin of government are to be found in the publicistic literature. See, e.g., John of Paris, *Tract. de pot.*, cap. 1; Leclercq, pp. 176–78.

enduring tradition a sufficient justification for current arrangements, or have deemed it unwise to question, even in theory, the
persuasive fact of organized force. It may be urged—and with
some cogency—that in one or other of these excluded categories
will, in most ages, be found the majority of men. If this is true
then our concern will be with the minority—a most important
and influential minority.

The thinkers who form this minority have located the source
of political authority either in God, or in the people, or in both.
The choice of any one of these alternatives has by no means,
however, ensured agreement upon the consequences which may
legitimately be derived from it. Those who have conceived of
political authority as a divine delegation have been able to use
this conception in support of any one of three main positions.
They argue, in the first place, that the ruler's power being of
God, he is responsible for its exercise to God alone and in no
way to his subjects, whose sole duty it is to obey. Secondly, that
the ruler, precisely because his authority is of God, is therefore
merely a minister of God, an office-holder who must exercise his
power for the good of the people in accordance with God's laws;
if he does not do so, his people need not and indeed should not
obey. In the third place—a medieval variant on this—that all
political authority being a divine concession, it is automatically
forfeited if a ruler so much as falls out of grace through mortal
sin—in much the same way as a vassal who has broken faith with
his lord forfeits his fief.

Similarly, three principal positions have been open to those
who have regarded the people as the source of authority. The
first position is that this popular derivation of power is essentially an historical one, by virtue of some occurrence in the past
when power was once and for all handed over to the ruler, perhaps by some irrevocable *lex regia*. The second is that although
the people have conferred authority upon their rulers, this concession is neither absolute nor irrevocable. According to this
second position, a residual power remains with the people by
virtue of which they may judge their rulers, and limit or even
recall their power if it is not being exercised in the common

interest. The third—a more modern variant—is that political authority is legitimate—and political enactments are valid— only when they express the desires of all the people or of a majority, for these desires must be taken to indicate what the common good actually is.

Such an analysis is schematic rather than descriptive. The "positions" described are the discrete elements of points of view which, in the actual course of history, have usually been more or less stable compounds of one sort or another. Of these positions the two third alternatives have, it should be noted, enjoyed a much more limited vogue than the others. The third alternative open to those who viewed God as the source of political authority is almost wholly limited to those few thinkers who adhered wholeheartedly to the mature doctrine of dominium as contingent upon grace, advocated, as we have seen,[2] by Fitzralph and Wyclif. It is therefore more characteristically a medieval position. The other third alternative, that political authority is legitimate only when it reflects the wishes of the majority (although earlier qualified approaches to it are to be found), did not really come into its own until after the publication of Rousseau's *Du contrat social;* it is therefore primarily a modern position. The reason is that while a general belief in the natural law persisted, men possessed objective criteria in terms of which the common good might be assessed; popular consent remained, as a result, very much a secondary consideration. In the pages which follow, therefore, we will be less concerned with these latter alternatives than with the more characteristic expressions and combinations of the other four positions.

I

The belief that political authority is not natural but artificial or conventional was prominent among some of the post-Aristotelian philosophers; blending easily with the Christian doctrine of man's original innocence and his subsequent fall, it found its way into medieval thought by two main routes, the works of the

2. Above, pp. 71 ff.

Christian Fathers, and the *Corpus juris civilis*.[3] Behind the many formulations in these writings lay the common belief that "only a great and momentous change could account for the contrast between the present political and social institutions of man and his original freedom and equality."[4] Patristic literature stressed that the source of all authority was divine, and wavered between viewing the ruler as "a punishment and remedy for sin" and as a minister to men for a somewhat narrowly defined good. Roman law, on the other hand, ascribed to political institutions a voluntary origin, and suggested that the people were certainly the original and perhaps the continuing source of political authority, for by the lex regia they had conceded to the prince (or conferred upon him) all their *imperium* and *potestas*.[5] Such ideas jostled side by side with the more vaguely defined Germanic view that kings were subordinate to the customary law and held their authority, in part at least, by virtue of some form of popular election,[6] and these ideas derived added strength from the ubiquity of feudal institutions. For the relationship between lord and vassal was truly contractual; as Bloch points out, in a society in which the chief subjects of the king were at the same time his vassals, this inevitably exercised a profound influence on political ideas.[7] Such conventionalist conceptions, therefore,

---

3. See Carlyle, *History*, *3*, 4 ff., *5*, Ch. 2. By a "natural" was meant first of all the primitive, but it was also understood to refer to what was permanent, essential, and rooted in the deepest requirements of human nature.

4. D'Entrèves, *The Medieval Contribution to Political Thought*, p. 14.

5. *Digest*, 1, 4, 1, where the word "conferat" is used; in *Inst.*, 1, 2, 6, "concessit" replaces "conferat." C. 1, 17, 1, 7, has "translata sunt". Cf. C. H. McIlwain, *Constitutionalism Ancient and Modern* (Ithaca, N.Y., 1958), pp. 45–46, 156 n. 5; Kantorowicz, *King's Two Bodies*, pp. 103–06.

6. Kern, *Kingship*, pp. 12–13: "The part played by the people or their representatives in the elevation of the monarch fluctuated between genuine election and mere recognition (or acceptance) of a king already designated. But at least the community gave legal assent to the prince's accession to the throne."

7. Marc Bloch, *La Société Féodale: Les classes et le gouvernment des hommes* (Paris, 1940), p. 259; speaking of Manegold of Lautenbach, the supporter of Gregory VII, Bloch comments: "Ces doctrinaires du clergé eux-mêmes ne manquaient pas d'invoquer, parmi les justifications de la déchéance à laquelle ils condamnaient le mauvais prince, le droit universellement reconnu au vassal d'abandonner le mauvais seigneur."

had the field to themselves until the recovery of Aristotle in the thirteenth century; they found expression, for example, in the introduction to a constitution (dated 1239) of the Emperor Frederick II, and even in the *Summa theologica* of Albertus Magnus, written, as it was, on the eve of the translation of Aristotle's *Politics*.[8] Nor did they yield upon the arrival of Aristotle, for by this time the notion that the community is the ultimate source of political authority and of positive law had become common intellectual coinage, qualified only by the Christian idea of the divine origin of such authority. Although Aristotle himself understandably showed little interest in the sources of authority,[9] Aquinas's acceptance of the natural character of the state did not entail his complete rejection of these conventionalist ideas. Indeed, it was by means of Aristotelian modes of thought that he was able to reconcile the beliefs in the divine and in the popular sources of authority, for he argued that "the ultimate divine source of all authority (its *causa formalis*) does not exclude, but on the contrary requires (as its *causa materialis*) an intervention on the side of man in the setting up of a particular form of government." [10]

Later medieval thinkers, therefore—though they might, with Aegidius Romanus or John of Paris, follow Aristotle in grounding political association in the nature of man—continued to regard the community as in some sense the source of authority. The political and territorial consolidation of the medieval kingdoms and its corollary, the displacement of the personal loyalties of feudalism by the richer notion of political community,

8. Carlyle, *History*, 5, 9 cites these examples.

9. His stress on "the principle of ensuring that the number of those who wish a constitution to continue shall be greater than the number of those who do not" can hardly be construed as a theory of the source of authority. *Politics*, V, ix, § 5; *The Politics of Aristotle*, ed. Ernest Barker (Oxford, 1948), pp. 231–32.

10. D'Entrèves, *Aquinas*, p. xxvi, explicating *Sent. II*, dist. 44, qu. 2, art. 2. Lewis, *Political Ideas*, *1*, 157, comments: "Philosophical publicists of the later Middle Ages commonly reconciled these two views through the principle . . . suggested by Aquinas, that God worked through the mediation of human reason; and this principle was increasingly associated with the further idea that human reason issued in the popular consent which was the immediate basis of valid authority."

helps to explain this. So too does reference to the name of John of Paris, for it points to what was perhaps the principal factor militating for the survival and contributing to the development of this idea, namely, the spread of a wide variety of corporate forms of organization both in ecclesiastical and in secular life. We have already had occasion to refer to this phenomenon,[11] it must suffice here to note that the application of corporative ideas to political society as a whole involved the belief that the will of the people does not simply explain the historical origin of political authority, but is in some sense the continuing source of that authority. The very conception of political society as a corporate community which has vested authority in its ruler as in an officer was facilitated by the interpretation of the lex regia both as a constitutional principle of universal validity, and as one indicative rather of the enduring authority of the people than of the absolute power of the monarch.[12] It was facilitated also by the popularity of the dictum Quod omnes tangit, ab omnibus approbetur," a maxim drawn from Roman private law but sufficiently general in expression to be extended to the larger world of politics.[13] The logical summation of this general development is

11. Above, Ch. 4.

12. The *lex regia* was interpreted in different ways during the Middle Ages; for French absolutist interpretations see A. Esmein, "La Maxime *Princeps Legibus Solutus est* dans l'ancien droit public français," *Essays in Legal History*, ed. Paul Vinogradoff (Oxford, 1913), pp. 201 ff.; for Bracton's "constitutionalist" reading, see McIlwain, *Constitutionalism Ancient and Modern*, pp. 70 ff. On this point see also Fritz Schulz, "Bracton on Kingship," *The English Historical Review, 60* (1945), 153–56. Ullmann, *Papalism*, p. 165, claims that whereas the civilian argued that by the lex regia "the people had transferred all power to the emperor and that this transfer was irrevocable," the canonists usually regarded the transfer merely as a revocable concession. At the same time, some of the Decretists also applied the idea of the lex regia to the Pope, but apparently with the object of enhancing rather than diminishing his authority; see Tierney, *Foundations*, pp. 55–56.

13. *Cod.* 5, 59, 5 § 2. For an older discussion of this, see P. S. Leicht, "Un principio politico medievale," *Rendiconti della Academia dei Lincei: Scienze Morale, 29* (Rome, 1920), 232–46; more recently, Gaines Post, "A Romano-canonical Maxim 'Quod Omnes Tangit' in Bracton," *Traditio, 4* (1946), 197–251. Post admits that in the case of England, Edward I did, broadly speaking, transform *Quod omnes tangit* into a "constitutional principle" but argues that, strictly speaking, what he did "was to complete the transition from private to public

perhaps to be found in the *Defensor pacis* of Marsilius of Padua; this, despite the denials of McIlwain,[14] does seem to reflect the political experience of the corporately organized Italian communes,[15] and has been referred to as "the first systematic statement of the popular basis of authority." [16]

By the fifteenth century, therefore, the idea that the whole community was the source of political authority had become something of a cliché, not only among secular political thinkers, but also among the canon lawyers; this is indicated by the ease with which the Conciliar thinkers were able to apply it to the ecclesiastical polity as well. Such a view differs from post-Lockeian forms of the consent theory insofar as it was in no way the outcome of egalitarian individualism. It was from the community as a whole that political authority was regarded as deriving,[17] and whereas modern thinkers, assuming the equality of the individuals composing the community, have regarded the will of the numerical majority as the will of the whole, this was not usually the case with medieval thinkers, living, as they did, in a sharply hierarchical society, accepting without question the inequality of men.

Medieval theories of representation did not necessarily involve the idea of delegation, and when they did it was often that of absolute rather than of popularly controlled delegation. Representation thus conceived is hardly distinguishable from trusteeship, and in the earlier medieval period at least no contradic-

---

law in so far as private and public were distinguished in his time" (p. 251). But he also insists (p. 199) that the consent involved "was not so much political as conciliar, administrative and judicial; and it was subordinate to the royal prerogative exercised for the public welfare." For the rôle of the principle in ecclesiology, see Yves M. J. Congar, "Quod omnes tangit, ab omnibus tractari et approbari debet," *Rev. d'hist. de droit français et étranger*, *4me sér.*, *36* (1958), 210–59, esp. 243 ff.

14. McIlwain, *Growth*, pp. 299 ff.

15. See Alan Gewirth, *Marsilius of Padua* (New York, 1956), *1*, 23–31.

16. Lewis, *Political Ideas*, *2*, 159.

17. Thus Lagarde, *Naissance*, *6*, 184, even while stressing Ockham's "individualism," notes that when Ockham insisted that men have the liberty to choose their own ruler, he was thinking not of a liberty attached to the individual person but rather to the community.

tion was felt in regarding kings or popes as representing the communities which they governed, for they in some sense "personified" and embodied in themselves all the authority of these communities. In the thirteenth century, however, the "dawning conception of public right and state sovereignty," and the concomitant determination on the part of rulers to elicit from their subjects a greater measure of cooperation and support, led first popes and then kings to adapt to political ends the procedures (Romano-canonical) of proctorial representation. During the previous half-century or more, these procedures had been used in the representation of corporate bodies in law suits.[18] They did involve the issuing of mandates by the communities to their representatives, but in order that the latter should be free to consent to what was ordained for the common good, it was usual to insist that the delegation of power to them should be absolute and without reservation. This, as Gaines Post has pointed out, is the meaning of the reiterated and ultimately successful insistence that such representatives should come armed, not with limited mandates or powers qualified by an obligation to refer back to their communities, but with *plena et sufficiens potestas* to commit these communities to whatever was decided for the common good and public safety.[19] It is clear that none of these views of representation involved any assertion of precocious constitutionalism; the insistence on full powers, indeed, was bound up with the dawning conception of *raison d'état,* and was

18. The Church seems to have been the first to revive these procedures for judicial matters and the first to transfer them to the larger world of politics. Innocent III played a big rôle in the latter development. In 1215 he became the first pope to summon proctors to represent cathedral chapters at a general council. On this whole issue, see Congar, "Quod omnes tangit," pp. 210–59, and the notable series of articles by Gaines Post: "Roman Law and Early Representation in Spain and Italy: 1150–1250," *Speculum, 18* (1943), 211–32; "Plena Potestas and Consent in Medieval Assemblies," *Traditio, 1* (1943), 355–408 (the words cited above will be found on p. 372); and his article cited above in n. 13. For a useful and recent report on work concerning both the political theory of representation and the development of representative assemblies, see H. M. Cam, A. Marongiu, G. Stökl, "Recent Work and Present Views on the Origins and Development of Representative Assemblies," *Relazioni del X Congresso Internazionale di Scienze Storiche* (Florence, 1955), *1*, 1–101.

19. Post, "Plena Potestas and Consent," pp. 355 ff.

fundamentally a device employed by monarchs eager to promote the cause of efficient government.[20]

Nevertheless, neither the old idea that the ruler represented his community in the sense that he personified it nor the newer procedures of representation involving actual delegation were necessarily at the disposal solely of the supporters of royal or papal absolutism. Tierney has stressed the constitutional ambiguities latent in the idea of personification and has pointed out that these ambiguities became explicit in the Church when the Decretalists elaborated the idea of the prelate or proctor as true representative of his corporate Church, receiving his power by delegation from the corporation and stringently limited in the exercise of it by the exigencies of the common utility.[21] Similarly, while claiming that plena potestas "stood not for political, sovereign consent, but for judicial-conciliar consent to the decisions of the prince," Post has admitted that "absolutism was made impossible by the very theory of judicial consent and by the procedure of obtaining that consent through the full power of representatives." [22] In the fourteenth and fifteenth centuries, at least in Spain and England, representative procedures were less exclusively at the service of the monarchy; this is indicated by the powers wielded in the fourteenth century by the *Cortes* of Aragon and Catalonia and by the rôle Parliament played in the deposition of Richard II.[23]

It must be admitted that in the secular polities the importance of this development lay in the future. In the ecclesiastical polity, however, this was not the case. As early as 1225, at the Council of Bourges, the proctors of the cathedral chapters successfully re-

20. Thus when in 1200 Innocent III summoned to his curia proctors with plena potestas from six cities they "obviously come provided with full powers to submit to the Pope's orders, not to refuse obedience and limit the papal authority" (Post, "Plena Potestas and Consent," p. 369).

21. *Foundations*, pp. 4–5, 35–36, 125–27. He notes (p. 126): "It may be that in this refinement of the proctorial concept is to be found an important link between the earlier medieval concept of representation as mere personification and the later idea, growing ever more explicit in the fourteenth century, that a true representative needed an actual delegation of authority from his community."

22. Post, "Plena Potestas and Consent," p. 408.

23. Ibid., p. 403; cf. C. H. McIlwain, "Medieval Estates," *C Med H*, 7, 702–04.

fused consent to a papal request for prebends (presumably because it was not clear that it would benefit the *status universalis
ecclesiae*); later on in the thirteenth and fourteenth centuries
there are similar instances of proctorial opposition at provincial
councils to papal fiscal demands.[24] But it took the crisis engendered by the Great Schism to give rise in the years after 1378
to a bold assertion of the continuing authority of the community
of the faithful over its elected ruler, and of the power of its representatives to wield this authority for the common good of the
Universal Church and the restoration of its unity.

It is this development that brings us back to our starting
point, for, as was then suggested, views concerning the source of
political authority derive their interest primarily from the theoretical or practical consequences. In deference, however, to what
may be but a logical priority, an examination of these consequences should be postponed until d'Ailly's own conception of
the source of political authority has been analyzed.

II

The protracted scandal of the Schism and the ultimate conviction that a General Council representing the whole Church was
the only agent that could end it lent a particular force and clarity
to d'Ailly's views on this subject, in particular to his location of
the source of authority in the consent of the community. There
was nothing new about such a position, but the fact that so much
now depended on it militated against his relegating it, as he so
often relegated the idea of the common good, to the rôle of a
tacit assumption, and led him to state it repeatedly and unequivocally. In his adherence to this position and in the use to which
he put it, d'Ailly illustrates excellently the "constitutionalism"
of the Conciliar thinkers.

In order, however, to be a Conciliarist he had first to be a
Christian; as a Christian, though he might attempt to accommo-

---

24. Post, "Plena Potestas and Consent," p. 381; cf. Lagarde, *Naissance*, *4*, 152–
55; Albert Hauck, *Kirchengeschichte Deutschlands* (Leipzig, 1911 ff.), *5*, 634 ff.;
Congar, "Quod omnes tangit," p. 220.

date to his consent theory the thirteenth chapter of St. Paul's Epistle to the Romans, he could never ignore it. Aquinas, it is true, had already faced this difficulty and had surmounted it with the help of a simple distinction between *formal* and *material* causality. But convincing though this distinction might have been to the more thoroughgoing Aristotelian, it could hardly seem at home in the reduced dimensions of a nominalist world of efficient causality. D'Ailly was forced to propound a solution more in keeping with his basic philosophical and theological presuppositions.

The nature of this solution has already been analyzed,[1] but it will be useful to glance again at its broad outlines. Appropriately enough, it ultimately depends upon his distinction between the *absolute* and *ordained* powers of God. All authority is of God, Who of His absolute power can dispose of it as He will. But just as God, as first cause of all things, freely chooses, of His ordained power, to operate through the agency of secondary causes, so also He similarly chooses to associate with His bestowal of authority the purely human signs of legal disposition, so that the possession of legitimate authority is manifest to us de facto only through the possession of some "created title" or "sign." Thus, to quote a particular example, the authority of the Pope, the Roman Church, or the General Council "immediately is *principally* from God, although it is from man, or depends on human power *in a ministerial way,*" for the Pope attains to his position by means of the election of the cardinals, and the cardinals to theirs by the authority of the Pope.[2] This reference to the cardinals serves to indicate, however, that d'Ailly does not necessarily regard election as the sole valid "created title," and he does in fact admit, in the case of kingdoms other than the Empire, the validity of "parental succession."[3] As we have seen, such an admission does not, in a medi-

1. Above, pp. 88 ff.

2. *Tract. de eccl. pot.*, Dupin, 2, 938: "auctoritas Papae seu Romanae Ecclesiae . . . immediate est a Deo principaliter, licet sit ab homine, seu dependeat ab humana potestate ministerialiter: nam Papa sit per Cardinalium electionem; et Cardinales per Papae authoritatem."

3. *De legitimo dominio*, Dupin, *1*, 644; *Utrum indoctus in jure divino*, ibid., 652; see above, p. 85. On the appointment of cardinals, see below, n. 25, p. 147.

eval thinker, necessarily entail the abandonment of a belief in the popular origin of royal authority, and the comprehensive remarks which d'Ailly makes in his *De ecclesiastica potestate* serve to establish that it does not in his case.

These remarks, which are taken almost word for word from the *Dialogus* of William of Ockham,[4] are specifically about the right of the Romans to elect the Pope, but they are couched in the most general terms. The Romans have this right, d'Ailly tells us, because when Christ gave Peter authority to establish his episcopal sect where he wished, this in no way deprived his chosen flock of the natural right "which belongs to all those over whom any authority, either secular or ecclesiastical, is placed— that is the right to elect their ruler." This would, no doubt, settle the matter, were it not for the fact that d'Ailly appends a brief qualification. It is a very awkward one. All people have this right, he tells us, "unless the contrary is ordained by themselves . . . or by their superior." [5] Nor does reference to a parallel text help, for there too a similar qualification is to be found; we are told that a community has the right to elect its head, whether prelate or prince, "unless the contrary is ordained by the person or person whose affair it is." [6] Indeed, this makes the position somewhat worse. For when d'Ailly implied that the community might confer the right of choosing its ruler upon someone else, he was not, as a medieval thinker, denying that the community was still to be regarded as the ultimate source of authority; all that has to be explained is his strange reference to some "su-

4. *Dialogus*, III, II, III, cap. 6; Goldast, 2, 933–35. Some of d'Ailly's text is printed in parallel with that of Ockham in Roberts, "Pierre d'Ailly," pp. 140–42.

5. *Tract. de eccl. pot.*, Dupin, 2, 936: "quando Christus praefecit Beatum Petrum omnibus Christianis, dans sibi potestatem, ut ubi vellet sedere, Sedem eligeret, ita ut esset quodammodo proprius illorum Episcopus: non privavit illos Jure illo naturali large sumpto, quod omnibus competit, quibus est aliqua praeficiendi potestas, sive saecularis sive Ecclesiastica, videlicet eligendi sibi rectorem, *nisi per illos quibus praeficienda hujusmodi potestas, vel per eorum Superiorem contrarium ordinetur*" (italics mine).

6. Dupin, 2, 930: "Ex hac namque suppositione, quod aliquibus sit aliquis Praelatus, vel Princeps, vel Rector praeficiendus, naturali ratione evidenter colligitur, quod (*nisi per illum vel illos, cujus vel quorum interest, ordinetur contrarium*) illi quibus est praeficiendus; habent Jus eligendi praeficiendum eis" (italics mine).

perior." Now we are faced with the further admission that the right of popular election of a ruler may be subordinate to the right of some other unspecified persons "whose affair it is." And d'Ailly in no place explains what exactly he means.

These qualifications should not be taken to contradict his reiterated assertions that the community is the source of political authority. This belief, as we have seen, was by no means necessarily connected in the minds of medieval thinkers with the fact of election. If we consult the passage in Ockham that d'Ailly is following so closely, we can see how little such qualifications entail [7] in that Ockham himself gives two specific justifications for introducing them. The qualifications are made, in the first place, because the people can "in many cases at least" transfer their elective rights to some other person or persons—such as, for example, the Emperor—who can in turn transfer the right to still other persons. In the second place, he says, they are made because "in matters of this type" the people may be subject to a superior who has the power of ordaining that they should not have the right of election, but lest any case be built on this, it should be noted that the superior whom Ockham has in mind is, in this case of the Romans, Christ Himself.[8] D'Ailly does not, it is true, reproduce this particular passage, but it would be unwise to infer from this that he in any way disagreed with it, for it is assumed in his later reiteration of Ockham's examples of rulers who had wielded the conceded right of choosing the Pope; [9] in any case, his *Abbreviatio* notes that it is Christ and not the Pope Who has the power to deprive the Romans of their elective powers and that Christ has not done so.[10]

It may well be concluded, therefore, that when d'Ailly speaks of certain "created titles or signs" as being invariably associated

7. *Dialogus*, III, II, III, cap. 6; Goldast, 2, 934.

8. It would seem justifiable to conjecture that this is the only case to which the qualification would be relevant.

9. Dupin, 2, 932; *Dial.*, III, II, III, cap. 6; Goldast, 2, 935. Both passages are printed in Roberts, "Pierre d'Ailly," pp. 141–42. Note, too, that d'Ailly also assumed in his *Abbreviatio* Ockham's tripartite classification of natural law though he did not reproduce it; see below, p. 243.

10. See below, p. 243.

with the divine delegation of authority, he is referring either to
the election of the community, or to some other title the validity
of which is derived from popular concession at some point in
the past. His main concern, however, is to work out the implications of this belief in the popular source of authority for the
ecclesiastical rather than the civil polity and the first implication
he draws from it is that the Pope is to be elected by those subject
to him. He now goes on to discuss at length what precisely is
meant by this, and the discussion is a revealing one. We have
seen that he considers that the universitas Romanorum possesses
the natural right of electing its ruler, the Pope,[11] but what about
the rôle of the Cardinals, and even more important, what about
the rights of the universitas fidelium which is equally subject to
the Pope? His answer to this is complex but clear. By natural
and divine law, he says, it does "in a sense" pertain to the cardinals to elect the Pope, but only "in a sense," because they
possess the *monopoly* of this right not by natural and divine but
by merely positive law.[12] It may perhaps more properly be said
that, by natural and divine law, it is the Romans who have the
right to elect the Pope, since as they have no other bishop he
is in a special sense their ruler, and that in this right the cardinals, as leading members of the Roman clergy, participate, unless the Romans or a superior who possesses authority in this
matter were to ordain to the contrary.[13] But although the Pope,
as Roman Pontiff, is especially the head of the Roman Church,
he is also the Supreme Pontiff of the Universal Church; as such,

11. Above, p. 120.

12. *Tract. de eccl. pot.*, Dupin, 2, 930: "ad sanctae Romanae Ecclesiae Cardinales, de jure naturali et divino, aliquo modo pertinet Romani Pontificis electio:
et dixi aliquo modo hoc pertinere ad eos, quia ad eos solos de Jure naturali et
divino, non pertinet hujusmodi electio: sed quod ad eos totaliter pertineat, hoc
est de Jure positivo, in quo, ex causa rationabili, cadere potest justa dispensatio."

13. Ibid., 931: "Cum ergo Romanus Pontifex quodam modo specialiter praeferendus est Romanis, quia non habent alium Episcopum; sequitur quod ipsi Jure
praedicto ex suppositione facta, scilicet quod debent ipsum habere episcopum,
habent jus eligendi ipsum; in quo Jure participant Romanae Ecclesiae Cardinales,
cum ipsi, ratione suorum Titulorum, sint principaliores in Clero Romano: et hoc
verum est, nisi per ipsos Romanos, vel alium superiorem Romanis, qui habeat in
hoc potestatem, contrarium ordinetur vel statuatur."

the right of electing him pertains—equally by natural and divine law—to the *universitas fidelium* or the General Council representing it. D'Ailly clearly regards this right as prior, by virtue of its origin, to that of the Romans, for it belongs to the Universal Church "originally and principally"; and although the Roman Church may wield its elective authority by natural and divine law, it does so *vice et nomine universalis ecclesiae,* and because of considerations of practical expediency such as the difficulty of assembling so great a multitude.[14] Similarly, although strictly speaking all the clergy and laity have the right to elect their prelates, this right was conceded in ancient times to the clergy alone, since they were regarded as "more wise and holy." In accordance with this practice, the Romans themselves transferred the right of electing the Pope to a small group drawn from their own ranks or, more precisely, from the ranks of the Roman clergy.[15]

The fact that d'Ailly devotes so much attention to the matter of papal election should not be taken to indicate that he views the election of a ruler as the sole exercise of the authority inherent in the community. It is worthy of note that in the passage of the *Dialogus* from which d'Ailly draws so much of his argument about the question, Ockham justifies election by the community partly on the ground that it touches all, and therefore according to the well-known legal maxim should be approved by all.[16] D'Ailly does not repeat this justification, but there is ample ground for believing that he too would agree that the right of election is but a particular application of a more general right. Speaking in 1396 at a national assembly summoned by the

14. Dupin, 2, 936; the text is cited above, Ch. 4, notes 24 and 25. Cf. ibid., 931.

15. *Tract. de eccl. pot.,* Dupin, 2, 931: "Romani, ad evitandum confusionem multitudinis, rationabiliter potuerunt et debuerunt transferre praeductum Jus suum eligendi Summum Pontificem, in aliquos paucos ex Romanis, vel in Clerum Romanum, aut aliquos ex ipsis. Sic enim ab antiquo Electiones Praelatorum concesse fuerunt Clericis; quia licet omnes Clerici et laïci habuerunt Jus eligendi, de consensu tamen laïcorum (quia Clerici erant sapientiores et sanctiores, respectu multitudinis) concessum fuit et ordinatum, quod ipsi soli eligerent."

16. *Dialogus,* III, II, III, cap. 6; Goldast, 2, 934: "Quod omnes tangit debet tractari per omnes; quod autem debet aliquis praefici aliis omnes tangit; igitur per omnes tractari debet."

French king to discuss ways and means to end the Schism,[17] he can be heard to urge that the Avignonese Pontiff should summon a common council of the Avignonese obedience in order to decide upon a way to end the Schism, for since such a matter "touches all the prelates of this obedience in no small way, it seems that it should be approved by all," [18] a sentiment which he echoes again in somewhat different words two years later.[19] What applies to a single obedience applies equally, of course, to the whole Church. It follows therefore that it would be the occasion of "great scandal and peril" for an Avignonese Council to treat "in a determinative way" of matters of faith "which touch all and should be approved by all." [20] Such matters cannot be treated, nor can the addition of new statutes and canons or the withdrawal of old ones justly be made for the whole Church without common consent, for the Pope cannot be said to be *legibus solutus* in the case of those laws "which affect the whole body and *status* of the Universal Church." [21]

This use of the quod omnes tangit principle is clearly political rather than "judicial" or "conciliar," [22] and it clearly involves the imposition by the ecclesiastical community as a whole of limits upon the absolutism of the papal monarch. The authority inherent in the community finds expression, then, not only in the election of its ruler but also in the promulgation

17. *Secunda schedula pro secundo concilio regis;* for the text and its historical setting, see Ehrle, pp. 475–80; cf. Salembier, *Cardinal,* pp. 154–56.

18. *Secunda schedula,* Ehrle, p. 480: "Videtur expediens pro modo precedendi in hac materia unanimiter concludendo, quod dominus papa exhortetur per regem et praelatos regni sui de convocando omnium prelatorum hujus obediencie commune concilium. . . . Cum enim via cedacionis scismatis et modus prosecucionis *omnes hujus obediencie prelatos non mediocriter tangat, videtur quod ab omnibus debeat approbari"* (italics mine). There can be little doubt that this is clearly a political use of the Quod omnes tangit principle; cf. above, n. 13, p. 135.

19. *Declaratio opinionis;* text and comment in Ehrle, p. 493: "utile et expediens videretur congregari generale concilium hujus obediencie, ubi *quod commune est, communi consensu ageretur, et decerneretur,* que via esset tenenda ad unionem ecclesie sancte Dei" (italics mine); cf. Salembier, *Cardinal,* p. 159.

20. *Tract. de mat.,* below, p. 253; cf. p. 320.

21. Ibid., pp. 313 and 261; cf. pp. 320–21. For a discussion of these texts and of their canonistic background, see above, pp. 111–13 and esp. notes 26 and 27.

22. See above, n. 13, p. 136.

or repeal of such laws as affect the welfare of the whole Church. We shall see later on that such functions themselves do not necessarily exhaust this enduring authority.

The question we must face first concerns the means by which this consent is to find expression. It is already apparent that d'Ailly does not think it has to be expressed directly by the whole community, but believes that it can more conveniently be expressed via the representatives of the community. This is a normal medieval position and one which is clearly reflected in d'Ailly's frequent allusions to the representative function of the General Council. But it remains to be seen what precisely he means when he speaks of "representation." It takes little effort to perceive that he does not necessarily have in mind the modern notion of popularly controlled delegation, for he speaks more than once of the Pope as a *persona publica* who represents the Universal Church, and in so doing is merely reiterating the earlier medieval idea of representation as personification, an idea which in the works of the high papalists had been taken to imply that the Pope embodied in his own person the whole authority of the Church.[23] Similarly, he tells us that the cardinals, too, in electing the Pope and in acting as his assistants, represent the Universal Church; here there can be no question even of absolute delegation, for the cardinals are not elected but, as he admits, are appointed by the Pope.[24] Finally, though he can speak of the cardinals as possessing, in certain emergencies, and "in the place and name of the whole Universal Church," the authority to convoke a General Council, he adds

23. *Tract. de eccl. pot.*, Dupin, 2, 945: "Papa . . . in pluribus casibus habet Jus et Potestatem circa bona, et Jura Ecclesiastica Clericorum . . . in quantum est persona publica repraesentans ecclesiam et generalis pastor" etc.; cf. ibid., col. 936, and *Utrum Petri ecclesia rege gubernetur*, Dupin, *1*, 689: "Quia Papa est persona publica, gerens vices totius ecclesiae." In this last example, though he does not acknowledge it, d'Ailly's words are taken from Ockham, *Dialogus*, I, V, cap. 25; Goldast, 2, 494. Cf. J. Haller, *Pappstum und Kirchenreform* (Berlin, 1903), *1*, 343–44, notes 6 and 7.

24. *Octo Conclusiones*, Dupin, 2, 110: "Veri Cardinales in electione Papae vices gerunt Universalis Ecclesiae Christianae." *Tract. de eccl. pot.*, ibid., col. 929: "In utroque vero, tam Urbis quam Orbis praesidentia, coassistunt Papae Cardinales, tanquam speciales ipsius coadjutores, vice et nomine tam Romanae quam Universalis Ecclesiae." For the manner of their appointment see the next note.

that this is so because the cardinals themselves are successors of the Apostles,[25] or as he puts it elsewhere because "they represent the Apostles in that they assist the Pope who is the Vicar of Christ and the successor of Peter." [26]

It would be unwise, however, to allow the occurrence of these scattered traditional or transitional formulations to convince us that the more modern idea of representation as delegation was unknown to d'Ailly or was dismissed by him. His descriptions of the Pope as a persona publica representing the Church would seem to indicate that by representation he meant simply personification; but even if we were not already aware of his ideas concerning forms of government, the context in which one of these descriptions occurs would make it quite clear that he was far from regarding the Pope as embodying in his own person the whole authority of the Church. For it occurs in that lengthy discussion of the Pope's power over ecclesiastical property most of which is taken from John of Paris, and the whole of which is predicated upon the assumption that the relationship of the Pope as its head to the Universal Church is "the same as that of any other prelate to his ecclesiastical corporation." As the same discussion indicates, the prelate is related to his particular Church as a proctor to his corporation, deriving his administrative authority from his election by that corporation, and forfeiting it to the corporation if he presumes to abuse it.[27]

25. *Tract. de eccl. pot.*, Dupin, 2, 935: "sequitur, quod ubi necessitas, aut utilitas imminet, pro conservanda Fide, vel bono regimine Ecclesiae; ad Papam, vel in ejus defectu, ad Cardinales pertinet Generale Concilium convocare, et hoc eis convenit, non tam humana quam divina institutione, vice et nomine totius Universalis Ecclesiae; quia ipsi Cardinales succedentes Apostolis in ministerio generali verbi Dei . . . licet in hoc officio sint instituti a Papa, vice tamen Christi, veritates necessarias Orbi docere tenentur." Cf. ibid., col. 935–36.

26. Dupin, 2, 936: "Cardinales repraesentant Apostolos, in hoc quod assistunt Papae qui est Christi Vicarius et Petri successor." Georges de Lagarde thinks formulations such as these indicative of a fundamentally theological approach to representation and as alien to the jurists, "L'Idée de représentation dans les oeuvres de Guillaume d'Ockham," *Bulletin of the International Committee of Historical Sciences*, 9 (1937), 430. He also notes that the high papalist, Augustinus Triumphus, makes use of them.

27. *Tract. de eccl. pot.*, Dupin, 2, 943–45; John of Paris, *Tract. de pot.*, cap. 6; Leclercq, pp. 185–89. See above, p. 122.

It has been claimed that such a point of view is "an important link" between the older idea of representation as personification and the later idea "that a true representative needed an actual delegation of authority from his community." [28] D'Ailly's sympathy with this later idea is manifest in most of his writings and is revealed, oddly enough, even in what he has to say about the cardinals. Though he can speak of them as representing the Apostles or succeeding in their place, he can also recommend that they should be chosen from all the provinces of the Church, and, more important, chosen by the provinces themselves.[29] Moreover, even as things stand, though the cardinals may be successors to the Apostles, they derive their most important power—that of electing the Pope—from the Universal Church or from the General Council.[30] It is above all the General Council that, in d'Ailly's opinion, can be said to represent the Church; and by the Church he means, not just the clergy, but the whole Church militant.[31] This opinion is perhaps most characteristically expressed when, having stated that the plenitude of power resides *separably* in the Pope, but *inseparably* in the Church,[32] he goes on to say that it resides representatively in the General Council and "in some way, *though not equally*," in the Roman Church, in that it too represents the Universal Church, and in the creation of ecclesiastical laws or canons acts in its place.[33] His criterion of the adequacy of representation

28. See above, n. 21, p. 138.

29. *Tract. de eccl. pot.*, Dupin, 2, 946; cited above, Ch. 4, notes 17 and 20, pp. 118–19; cf. *Consultationes Cardinalium*, Hardt, 2, 584–85.

30. *Tract. de eccl. pot.*, Dupin, 2, 935–36: "valde magna congruentia est, ut ad eos pertinent electio Papae Christi Vicarii, quia videlicet in hoc succedunt Apostolis Christi; hoc tamen Jus, principaliter et originaliter pertinet ad Universalem Ecclesiam seu Generale Concilium ipsam repraesentans"; cf. *Tract. de mat.*, below, pp. 322–23; *Tertia schedula*, Ehrle, p. 482.

31. *Tract. de mat.*, below, p. 307; cf. *Utrum Petri ecclesia lege reguletur*, Dupin, *1*, 666, where he defines the Church thus: "Ecclesia est omnis homo fidelis, vel omnes homines fideles, in mortali corpore naturaliter viventes." Lewis, *Political Ideas*, 2, 378, is incorrect in claiming that d'Ailly defined the Church as the clerical hierarchy.

32. See above, p. 119.

33. Dupin, 2, 951: "Sicut plenitudo Potestatis est in Generali Concilio repraesentative, ita aliquo modo, licet non aequaliter, est in Romana Ecclesia, quia

would seem to be the proximity of the representative body to the whole community. Thus, although both the Pope and the Roman Church can claim to represent the Universal Church, in that they act in its place and name, it is nevertheless the General Council which has the strongest claim to be representative.[34]

It remains to be seen in what way a General Council can claim to be representative. This is a matter that d'Ailly never fully elucidates, though he does tell us that General Councils derive their authority from "the consent of all the faithful" as well as from the authority of Christ.[35] It had been the practice since the Fourth Lateran Council of 1215 for the Pope to summon not only the prelates of the Church but also proctors from the cathedral chapters and collegiate churches; these proctors would come as delegates furnished with precise mandates by the corporations which they represented.[36] D'Ailly makes only indirect and fleeting mention of this procedure,[37] probably because he simply took it for granted, since as we have seen he does regard prelates very much as ex officio proctors of their particular churches, and as bearers therefore of what was in essence merely a delegated authority. He does, however, address himself on more than one occasion to problems concerning the composition of the Council and its voting procedures, and his remarks on these matters are of some value in the present context.

The first of these remarks are to be found in a sermon which he delivered at Constance in 1416. He states that no Catholic,

ipsam Universalem Ecclesiam repraesentat, et in condendis Ecclesiasticis Juribus seu Canonibus; ipsius vices gerit."

34. See above, p. 124.

35. *Epistola ad regem Carolum directa*, Denifle, *3*, 621: "Sed jam iterum aliud ab emulis audimus obstrepi. Quis, inquiunt, dabit authoritatem Concilio? In promptu responsio est: Dabit consensus omnium fidelium, dabit Christus, in Evangelio dicens: 'Ubicunque duo vel tres in nomine meo congregati' etc."

36. See above, n. 18, p. 137.

37. In *Tract. de eccl. pot.*, Dupin, *2*, 942, where, speaking of the practice of deliberating by nations at Constance, he says: "referendo deliberationem unius Nationis, notandae sunt personae, ut eorum status, ut, quot sunt majori Praelati, quot Abbates, quot Doctores, quot Ambassiatores, quot Procuratores."

even if schismatic, may be excluded from the Council, but adds, significantly enough, that unlearned people and those of the lowest ranks are not specifically summoned "but those especially, who in nobility of a triple nature should justly be compared with the stars—that is, in the sublimity of their excellent eminence, in the clarity of their shining wisdom, in the power of their surpassing influence." [38] Such a statement, rhetorical though it may be, is sufficient to indicate that d'Ailly's view of representation was by no means democratic in spirit. It would have been strange if it were, in view not only of his own advocacy of the ideal of the mixed constitution [39] but also of the general attitudes of his age, to which, elsewhere, he gives an excellent formulation when he says (also speaking of the Council) that "what touches all, should be approved by all, or, at least, by many and by the more notable ones." [40] This affects not only the composition of the Council but also the weight to be given to its various deliberations, and even to the deliberations of the individual "nations" which compose it, for in such deliberations, he says, attention should be paid not only to the number of the people involved but also to their "dignity" or status.[41]

Such statements certainly reflect the influence of the canonis-

38. *Oratio de officio Imperatoris*, Dupin, 2, 921: "Licet enim nullae personae Catholicae, etiamsi sint schismaticae, ab hac congregatione sint exclusae: non tamen specialiter sunt vocatae infimae, aut ignorantes personae; sed illae praecipue, quae in triplicis conditionis nobilitate Stellis coeli sunt merito comparandae, videlicet, in sublimitate excellentis eminentiae, in claritate refulgentis sapientiae, in potestate praecellentis influentiae."

39. See above, pp. 117 ff.

40. *Additio circa tertiam viam supratactam*, in Ehrle, p. 506: "quod omnes tangit, ab omnibus vel saltem a pluribus et notabilioribus debet approbari"; cf. the passage from the statutes of the Benedictine order in England dated 1249: "Moreover it has been provided that if any business shall arise in the realm which touches all the prelates of monasteries, when this comes to the notice of the heads they shall call the prelates together if it can be done; but if not, they shall call those who, on account of the character of the business, they think ought to be called, so that what touches all should be done by all or by their *senior pars*" (cited in McIlwain, *Growth*, p. 303).

41. *Tract. de eccl. pot.*, Dupin, 2, 642: "multis videtur Juri esse consonum, quod in tali deliberatione Nationum, non solum attendendum est ad personarum deliberantium numerum, sed etiam ad dignitatem."

tic principle that the whole power of a corporation could be wielded by its *major et sanior pars*,[42] and the reference to the practice at Constance of voting by "nations" suggests, perhaps, that they also reflect d'Ailly's long personal experience of the working of that famous corporation, the University of Paris.[43] For, by 1379, it had become an established principle there that a resolution passed by the major et sanior pars of the nations and faculties was binding upon the whole university.[44] In the tract entitled *Disputatio de jure suffragii quibus competat*, which he wrote in 1415,[45] d'Ailly not only betrays another sign of his academic affiliations,[46] but also gives us a clear indication

42. See X, 3, 11, c. 6; X, 3, 10, c. 6; X, 1, 6, c. 6; X, 3, 11, c. 1. The civilians took over from the revived Roman corporation law the idea of the binding power of a numerical majority, but the canonists evolved this more characteristic principle and the author of the *glossa ordinaria* to the Decretals was of the opinion that "piety" as well as "reason" was relevant to the assessing of the "greater and wiser part"; see gloss to X, 3, 11, c. 1. See Pierre Gillet, *La personnalité juridique en droit ecclésiastique* (Malines, 1927), pp. 137–40; Otto von Gierke, Über die Geschichte des Majoritätsprinzips," *Essays in Legal History*, ed. Paul Vinogradoff (Oxford, 1913), pp. 312–35; E. Ruffini Avondo, *Il Principio Maggioritario: Profilo Storico* (Turin, 1927) includes material on post-medieval developments; L. Moulin, "Sanior et maior pars. Note sur l'evolution des techniques electorales dans les Ordres religieux du VIe au XIIIe siècle," *Revue historique de droit français et étranger*, 4th ser., *36* (1958), 368–97 and 491–530; the last gives a long and exhaustive bibliography on the subject (pp. 521–30) and underlines the numerous problems outstanding.

43. Hastings Rashdall, *The Universities of Europe in the Middle Ages*, ed. F. M. Powicke and A. B. Emden (Oxford, 1936), *1*, 576, suggests that the practice of deliberating and voting by nations at the Council reflected the influence of Parisian practice, and it is certain that the University of Paris supported, later on, the continuance of this practice at Constance. See Valois, *France, 4*, 271. Not only Cardinal Fillastre, however, but also d'Ailly disagreed with it on this point; see below, Appendix VI.

44. Rashdall, *1*, 415: Denifle, 2, 593, n. 1129.

45. Hardt, 2, 224–27.

46. For example, in his argument that the vote should be extended to doctors of theology and of law. In this he followed a pronouncement of the University (see Valois, *France, 4*, 270).

The background to this, as also to the adoption of the procedure of voting by nations, is the fact that, especially at the opening of the Council, the Italian bishops, compatriots of John XXIII, vastly outnumbered the rest, and that it was therefore in the interest of John to admit to the vote only bishops and abbots, and to retain the practice of voting by head rather than by nation (Valois, *France, 4*, 264–72). Salembier, *Cardinal*, pp. 268–69. D'Ailly himself certainly

of what precisely he means. This tract is particularly valuable in the context of political thought because he makes it quite clear that his remarks do not concern deliberations about purely spiritual things, such as the faith and the sacraments, but rather those things that pertain to the ending of the Schism and the reestablishment of union and peace in the Church,[47] in short, to matters concerning the Church in its political aspect. The question he is answering is this: Who should have a definite say or a vote in the Council on these political matters? The answer he gives to it is interesting because it indicates, at the same time, both the stress he places on the representative rôle of the members of the Council and also the gulf that divides such a notion of representation from more modern and more democratic concepts.

He begins by attempting to explain away the position he had adopted in 1403 when he wrote the *Tractatus de materia concilii generalis.*[48] In that work he had clearly stated that the definitive authority of the Council, and not only in matters of faith, should rest with the bishops alone, not with the princes or any others. As we have seen, he makes it clear that he is discussing Councils such as that assembled at Constance and met to deal, not with matters of faith, but with an abnormal situation, concerning which, he says, there is no definitively established procedure.[49] He goes on to explain that when, in General

---

feared the power of the Italian bishops at the Council, as is clear from his *Tractatus de reformatione* (see Appendix VI), and in this context his advocacy of the extension of the vote may be seen purely as a tactical move in the realm of practical politics. It retains its theoretical value, however, because the principle consistently invoked is that of the better representation of the whole Church.

47. *Disputatio,* Hardt, 2, 224: "Primo distinguendum est de agendis in Concilio. Quia vel illa essent, quae solum pertinerent ad fidem catholicam, sacramenta, et pure spiritualia Ecclesiastica, de quibus antiquitus, inter Sanctos Patres in Conciliis generalibus agebatur. In quo casu saepe loquuntur jura canonica, et de iis de praesenti nihil scribitur. Vel illa essent pertinentia ad exterminationem praesentis schismatis, et unionis ac pacis integrae procurandae. In quo casu maxime habent locum sequentia."

48. See below, pp. 268 ff.

49. Hardt, 2, 224: "Item, sciendum etiam, quod sicut a tempore nascentis Ecclesiae, schismatis circa electionem Summo Pontificis, varii fuerunt modi observati, sicut patet per jura et antiquas historias, sic in modo congregationis et deliberationis Conciliorum generalium."

Councils in the past, bishops alone used to have a definitive voice, this was because "they were responsible for the administration of the people, were holy and learned men, and were elected by the others in the Christian Church." [50] And, later on, when abbots were included, it was for the same reasons. It follows, therefore, that rather than useless titular bishops and abbots who do not meet these requisite conditions, there should be added the priors and superiors (*majores*) of any congregation.[51] For it is unjust that such possessors of titular ecclesiastical dignities, men who have few or no suffragans and "little or nothing subject to them," should have as much say in the Council as leading prelates and others who have subject to them many parochial churches in which there are more people than in many of these titular archbishoprics and bishoprics.[52] Nor is it "just, equitable or consonant with reason" that on this matter of terminating the Schism, even kings, princes, or their ambassadors should be denied a voice, even a conclusive voice, for the end of the Schism and the restoration of peace concerns their subjects very deeply, and it will be impossible, without their counsel, help, and favor, to execute the decisions of the Council.[53] Finally, those who should have a vote in the Council in-

50. Hardt, 2, 225: "Sciendum est, quod quando in Conciliis generalibus soli Episcopi habebant vocem definitivam, hoc fuit, quia habebant administrationem populi, et erant viri sancti et docti et electi prae ceteris in Ecclesia Christiana."

51. Ibid.: "Postea fuerunt additi Abbates eadem de causa, et quia habebant administrationem subjectorum. Et eadem ratione addi deberent Priores aut Majores quarumcunque congregationum, plus quam Episcopi, vel Abbates inutiles, solum titulares, in quibus deficiunt conditiones supradictae."

52. Ibid.: "Et mirabile videretur, quod unus talis Archi-Episcopus, aut Episcopus, vel Abbas, paucos aut nullos suffragentes habens, et parvum aut nullum sibi subjectum, haberet vocem in Concilio, sicut Archi-Episcopus Moguntinus, ac alii magni Praelati, et Principes Imperii, et multi particulares Archi-Episcopi, in Francia, et Anglia et aliis regnis, qui plures habent parochiales Ecclesias in quibus est major populus, quam in pluribus Archi-Episcopatibus et Episcopatibus praedictis."

53. Hardt, 2, 227: "Item quantum ad materiam terminandi praesens schisma, et dandi pacem Ecclesiae, velle excludere Reges, Principes, aut Ambasiatores eorum, maxime cum magnam et honorabilem partem faciant hujus Concilii, a voce seu determinatione etiam conclusiva, non videtur justum, aequum, aut rationi consonum. Cum hujusmodi pacis Conclusio ad eos, et populos eis subjectos valde pertineat, et sine eorum consilio, auxilio et favore non possint ea quae in hoc Concilio concludentur executioni mandari."

clude Doctors of Canon and Civil Law, and especially Doctors of Theology, for to them is given "the authority to preach and teach anywhere on earth, which is no little authority among a Christian people, but much greater than that of a single, ignorant, and merely titular, bishop or abbot." [54]

D'Ailly believes, therefore, that the right to represent the Universal Church belongs especially to those who are preeminent in wisdom and influence. These are the notable people who can be expected to discern the policy most clearly consonant with the common good and also to be able to enforce it. This is a doctrine clearly alien to any age inclined to view the common good as definable in terms not of the mandates of the natural law but of the consensus of individual desires. It is fundamentally a doctrine of trusteeship, but one in process of transition towards a more modern view of representation, for it should not be forgotten that he believes that no Catholic, however ignorant, should be excluded from the Council, or that he grounds the original right of the bishops and abbots to a definitive say at least in part upon the fact of their election by their congregations. D'Ailly's views on the subject are dominated by his general belief that the community is the actual source of authority; he is forced to conclude, therefore, that those who speak for the community, even if not necessarily chosen by it, must at least be responsible for parts of it.[55] The more aristocratic aspects of his concept of representation should not serve to blind us, then, to his unswerving belief that all political authority not only originally derives from the community, but also continues ultimately to reside with it. It now remains only to determine what practical constitutional consequences will follow from this belief.

54. Hardt, 2, 225–26: "Item eadem ratione, qua supra, non sunt excludendi a voce definitiva Sacrae Theologiae Doctores, ac Juris Canonici et Civilis. Quibus, et maxime Theologis, datur autoritas praedicandi aut docendi ubique terrarum, quae non est parva auctoritas in populo Christiano, sed multo major quam unius Episcopi vel Abbatis, ignorantis, et solum titulati."

55. Even his argument for the extension of the vote to the Doctors of Theology and of Canon and Civil law is based not on their superior wisdom but on their authority over large numbers of the faithful, and presumably their responsibility for them.

III

The consequences to be discussed concern the duty of subjects to obey their rulers or their right to disobey; attention has already been called to the connection between arguments concerning such rights and duties and ideas about the source of political authority. It will be remembered that agreement on the source did not necessarily entail agreement on the consequences, and it was possible therefore to construe the Christian belief in the divine origin of authority as entailing consequences that were diametrically opposed to one another. St. Augustine and Isidore of Seville had attributed a sacred authority to the tyrannical ruler in that he might be a divinely appointed punishment for the sins of men, and had therefore inclined to a belief in the sinfulness of resistance.[1] This view was stated very clearly and without compromise by Gregory the Great, of whom Carlyle has said that "even the 17th century apologists of the Divine Right hardly go further in preaching the necessity of obedience and the wickedness of resistance." [2]

Such a point of view, though never forgotten, did not dominate medieval thinking. The command to obey God rather than man entailed the duty of disobedience to the unlawful commands of an evil ruler and opened the way for the acceptance of the idea that men had a right to resist tyrannical oppression. This interpretation consorted well with the familiar theory of the feudal *diffidatio* and its frequent practice by outraged vassals.[3] It also harmonized with the older Germanic belief in the right of the people to resist and even to depose a king who had betrayed his trust, on the ground that his authority was ultimately based upon their consent. Whether authority was conceived as deriving from God or from the community it was generally agreed that men had a right to disobey a tyrannical ruler, and even to resist him by force. John of Salisbury's de-

1. Carlyle, *History, I,* 151–53.
2. Ibid., p. 153, n. 1.
3. See F. L. Ganshof, *Feudalism,* trans. P. Grierson (London, 1952), pp. 89–90.

fense of tyrannicide [4] and Aquinas's recognition of the right to revolt against a tyrant [5] are merely the best known of countless expressions of the same sort of position. The selection of tyrannicide as a rightful sanction against an evil ruler suggests, however, that such a right of resistance was conceived very much as an individual thing; this conception was true of most medieval thinkers, including Aquinas. The person who resisted did so not because he possessed special public powers to do so but because his own conscience told him that, as the ruler was not fulfilling or was exceeding the terms of his office, it was his right and his duty so to resist. He was "justified, not by a superior authority in himself, but by a deficiency of authority in the ruler." [6] Even the old Germanic right of resistance, which was much more intimately connected with the derivation of the ruler's authority from the people, was characterized by a "lack of fixed legal forms and method" and occupied a position "midway between force and right." [7]

It was only in the later Middle Ages, with the increasing acceptance of the idea of the continuing authority of the community, that a tendency appeared to institutionalize this right of resistance to the abuse of power. This tendency was by no means limited to the Church, but it did find perhaps its most coherent and influential expression in the writings of the Conciliarists and in the events of the Council of Constance. Herein lies the interest of d'Ailly's views on the subject. He does not, as we have seen,[8] reject the Patristic idea that God might sanction the rule of a tyrant for the punishment of human sins, but he does forebear to erect this into an argument for passive obedience. In one of his early academic works is to be found a twofold assessment of the justice of a ruler's authority in terms both of the legitimacy of the title by which it is held and of the equity of the manner in which it is exercised; [9] this reflects

4. *Policraticus*, Lib. III, cap. 15, ed. C. C. J. Webb, pp. 512 b–d.
5. *ST*, 2a 2ae, qu. 42, art. 2; d'Entrèves, *Aquinas*, pp. 160–61.
6. Lewis, *Political Ideas, 1*, 249.
7. Kern, *Kingship*, p. 96; cf. p. 86.
8. Above, Ch. 4, p. 103.
9. *Utrum indoctus in jure divino*, Dupin, 2, 649: "Cum quaeritur utrum indoctus potest juste praeesse, hoc dupliciter potest intelligi: Uno modo ut ver-

that distinction between tyranny *ex titulo* and tyranny *ex exerciitu* so clearly drawn by Aquinas.[10] Unlike Aquinas, d'Ailly does not use it to preface remarks about either obedience or disobedience. That he did reject tyrannicide comes out very clearly, however, in his cooperation with Gerson to secure the condemnation by the Council of Constance of the argument in favor of tyrannicide which had been proffered by the Dominican, Jean Petit, in an attempt to justify the assassination in 1407 of the Duke of Orleans.[11] Moreover, d'Ailly argues that Petit's central thesis is even more to be condemned than the already censured argument of Wyclif to the effect that "the multitude (*populares*) can, of its own choice, correct a delinquent lord." [12]

This should not be taken to indicate that he rejects all forms of resistance to tyranny. The condemnation of Petit's thesis, as repeated by d'Ailly, specifically concerns the killing of a tyrant "without having waited for the sentence or order of any judge whatsoever," [13] and the villainy of Wyclif's proposition lies in the fact that it advocates action not by the community but by the *populares* and *ad eorum arbitrium*. In condemning such forms of resistance d'Ailly is emphasizing their arbitrary and

---

bum 'juste' determinet jus seu authoritatem praesidendi, sic quod juste habeat praesidentiam id est juste titulo, et non furtive, seu violenter. Alio modo, ut verbum 'juste' determinet actum seu usum officiandi sic quod juste exerceat officium praesidendi, ita quod careat culpa, officium praesidentiae exercendo."

10. *Sent.* II, dist. 44, qu. 2, art. 2; d'Entrèves, *Aquinas,* pp. 182–85.

11. D'Ailly offered, for instance, publicly to defend the condemnation by the Council (see *Conclusiones Cardinalis Cameracensis,* Dupin, 5, 671). For a full discussion of the whole affair, see A. Coville, *Jean Petit: la question du tyrannicide au commencement du XVe siècle* (Paris, 1932), esp. pp. 504–61.

12. *Additio Cardinalis Cameracensis pro sua opinione,* Dupin, 5, 475: "dicta doctrina multo magis est condemnanda, quia multo pejus circumstantionata est, quam illa damnata Propositio Johannis Wicleff, quae ponit quod populares possunt ad eorum arbitrium Dominos deliquentes corrigere." And d'Ailly had already taken part in the condemnation of Wyclif's ideas (see Salembier, *Schisme,* pp. 334–35).

13. *Declaratio circa propositiones Joannis Parvi,* in Dupin, 5, 474: " 'Quilibet tyrannus. Potest et debet licite et meritorie occidi per quemcunque vassalum suum, sive subditum, etiam per insidias, et blanditias, vel adulationem, non obstante quocunque juramento, seu Confoederatione factis cum eo, *non expectata Sententia, vel Mandato cujuscunque Judicis.*' Quae condemnatio in una Sessione hujus sacri Concilii facta est."

illegal status; he does not close the door upon the possibility of legal action against an ill-behaved ruler—as, indeed, is indicated by his very choice of words. He hopes, it is true, that a mixed form of constitution would help to prevent the degeneration of monarchy into tyranny,[14] but in the unhappy event of its failure to do so he does not think that the community is legally powerless to do anything. On the contrary, many of his writings on the Schism are specifically designed to prove that the community, by virtue of its being the original and continuing source of all political authority, has the power to judge, reform, and even depose a tyrannical ruler, and this means for him, it should be remembered, a ruler who pursues his own interests rather than the common good or public utility.

This position finds its best expression in his later works, and, indeed, in the story of his strenuous activity at the Council of Constance,[15] but it was certainly no newly developed theoretical justification for what he was actually doing. As early as 1381 he had defended the resort to a General Council as the best means for ending the Schism, not only before the French Court, but also in his *Epistola diaboli leviathan*.[16] Later on, it is true, he felt at times that although the way of the Council might be "more in conformity with the common law," it nevertheless entailed greater difficulties than the other possible ways of cession or compromise.[17] The behavior of the rival pontiffs finally disabused him of any belief that these alternatives were actually realizable. Most of his polemics on the Schism are devoted therefore to urging the convocation of a General Council, and to stating that such a Council, because it represents the Universal Church, is possessed of the necessary authority to re-

14. See above, pp. 117–18.

15. Salembier perhaps exaggerates the general importance of d'Ailly's rôle at the Council, but Valois, *France, 4,* 256–313, confirms the preponderance of his influence during its opening stages.

16. See above, p. 10; cf. Salembier, *Cardinal,* pp. 57–58; the *Epistola* is printed in Tschackert, *Ailli,* App. V, pp. [15]–[21].

17. *Prima schedula in primo regis concilio,* in Ehrle, p. 472: "Secundo dico quod, licet via concilii generalis videretur aliquibus juri communi conformior, tamen ipsa est difficilior et ad prosequendum prolixior." Cf. John P. McGowan, *Pierre D'Ailly and the Council of Constance* (Washington, 1935), pp. 13–14.

store unity, even if this entails the judgment and deposition of the several popes.

Examples of this point of view are broadcast throughout d'Ailly's writings, and the most complete statement is that contained in the second part of his *Tractatus de materia concilii generalis,* a statement the bulk of which he transferred, almost verbatim, to his later *Tractatus de ecclesiastica potestate.*[18] Perhaps the most valuable and revealing exposé, however, is that to be found in the several "useful propositions" which he appended to a letter sent in 1409 to the Cardinals assembling for the Council of Pisa; [19] it is valuable because of its combination of brevity and comprehensiveness, revealing because of its clear enunciation of the theoretical assumptions involved. The unity of the Church, he tells us, does not necessarily originate in the unity of the Pope, for the Church always remains one, even if it has no Pope.[20] It has within it not only by the authority of Christ but also by the natural law the means of preserving its own unity, for just as natural and animate bodies naturally resist their division and destruction, so also does "any civil body, or civil community, or rightly ordained polity." [21] The ecclesi-

18. See, e.g., his *Responsio ad alias Johanni Papae,* Hardt, 2, 220–27, or his *Conclusiones in civitate Tarraconensi,* in Martène et Durand, 7, 916–18; *Tract. de eccl. pot.,* Dupin, 2, 956–60; *Tract. de mat.,* below, pp. 300–11. For an earlier and more tentative statement, see *Utrum indoctus in jure divino,* Dupin, 1, 660–61.

19. Printed in Martène et Durand, 7, 909–11. For a further discussion of this tract, see Salembier, *Cardinal,* pp. 243–44. Dupin incorrectly ascribed it to Gerson and included it, in a version that omitted its closing sentence, in his edition of Gerson's works (2, 112–13). This attribution has recently been endorsed by John B. Morrall, *Gerson and the Great Schism* (Manchester, 1960), pp. 86–87, though he seems at another point to ascribe the work to d'Ailly as well (see p. 112, n. 2). But there can be no doubt that it was d'Ailly who wrote it. The version printed in Martène et Durand ends "in civitate Aquensi prima Januarii anno MCCCCIX per episcopum Cameracensem," and d'Ailly cites it as his own in one of his later works, the *Apologia concilii Pisani;* Tschackert, *Ailli,* App. X, p. [34].

20. *Propositiones Utiles,* Martène et Durand, 7, 909–10: "Licet Papa in quantum Christi Vicarius quodammodo dici possit caput Ecclesiae, tamen Ecclesiae unitas non necessario dependet aut originatur ab unitate Papae . . . quia nullo existente Papa, semper Ecclesia remanet una."

21. Ibid., 910: "Non solum auctoritate Christi sed etiam communi jure naturali praemissam auctoritatem habet corpus mysticum Ecclesiae Dei. Patet, quia quodlibet corpus naturale *naturaliter* resistit suae divisioni et destructioni; et

astical polity is such a rightly ordained polity, and the history of the primitive Church indicates that the General Council is the means by which it preserves its unity. It is true that in the course of time the authority to convoke a Council was, to avoid Schism or heresy, restricted to the Pope, as is laid down in the canon law. Despite this restriction, that "authoritative power always and absolutely remains in the Universal Church itself," for "positive laws cannot absolutely take away from the Church that power which belongs to it by natural and divine law." [22] Positive laws which dictate that no rightful General Council can be held without the authority of the Pope should be interpreted *civilly,* in accordance with Aristotle's teaching on the virtue of *epikeia,* as applying rather to normal times when such an arrangement is clearly useful and suitable.[23] In certain circumstances it would be to the detriment of the Church to observe these positive laws, and it is evident that in such a case (and the present Schism is such a case) the Church can assemble in General Council without the authority of the Pope, and even

---

si sit corpus animatum, naturaliter congregat omnia membra omnesque vires suas ad conservandum suam unitatem, et repellendum suam divisionem. Similique modo, quodlibet corpus civile, seu civilis communitas, vel politia rite ordinata"; cf. *Tract. de mat.,* below, p. 310.

22. Ibid.: "adeoque corpus spirituale seu mysticum Ecclesiae Christianae, quod ordinatissime compositum est . . . simili modo uti poterit ad suam unitatem conservandam . . . . Praemissa auctoritate et auctoritativa potestate usa fuit Ecclesia primitiva. Patet, quia in Actibus Apostolorum quatuor leguntur Concilia generalia congregata, et non habetur quod auctoritate Petri fuerint convocata, sed communi consensu Ecclesiae . . . . Post incrementa nascentis Ecclesiae primitivae, praemissa auctoritas et potestas congregandi generalia concilia rationabiliter limitata fuit et restricta, sic scilicet quod sine auctoritate Papae nulli liceret Concilia hujusmodi congregare . . . . Et ratio fuit, ut honoraretur Sedes Apostolica, et obviaretur haereticis et schismaticis . . . . Praemissa limitatio seu restrictio non tollit, quin praedicta auctoritativa potestas semper absolute remaneat in ipsa Universali Ecclesia. Patet, quia jura positiva non possunt ab Ecclesia absolute tollere illam potestatem quae ei competit divino et naturali jure."

23. Ibid., 911: "Jura positiva, quae communiter dicunt quod absque auctoritate papae non est fas generale concilium congregari, debent civiliter intelligi; scilicet quando est unicus Papa concorditer ab Ecclesia receptus, et ad congregandum hujusmodi Concilium, evidenti utilitate, idoneus et paratus. Patet ex praedictis, et ex doctrina Aristotelis in Ethicis ubi loquitur de epicheia." D'Ailly is speaking here of the interpretation of the law in what is, broadly speaking, an equitable manner. For the history of the concept, see below, Ch. 6, n. 4, p. 164.

against his wishes.[24] And it can be convoked, not only by the cardinals, but also by any of the faithful.[25]

What d'Ailly has said so far, therefore, is this: that the authority inherent in the Church is not exhausted by the mere act of electing its ruler. Just as any other community, it retains by natural law the power to prevent its own destruction, and it can exercise this power, if necessary, against the command of its ruler. This can entail, he tells us elsewhere, the summoning of a General Council as well as the necessary action to be taken by such a Council. For if the Pope, whose power is ordained to the "edification" and not to the "destruction" of the Church, tries to subvert it by manifest heresy, open tyranny, or other notorious crime, it must be possible to chastise him, since otherwise the Church would not be a perfectly ordained community. It follows therefore that in such cases "which touch the destruction of the Church," the Pope can be judged and condemned by the Universal Church or by the General Council representing it.[26] And as he points out later on in the *Tractatus de ecclesiastica potestate,* "this conclusion has been acted upon in the condemnation and deposition of Pope John XXIII by the General Council, the decision of which it is forbidden to gainsay." [27]

D'Ailly's rejection of any arbitrary, individual right to kill a tyrannical ruler or to revolt against him should, therefore, be seen in the context of his other conclusion that the whole com-

24. Martène et Durand, 7, 911: "in certis casibus Ecclesia sine auctoritate Papae potest Concilium generale celebrare. Patet . . . quia illud quod est in favorem Ecclesiae introductum, non est in ejus damnum et grave periculum observandum. Sed praedicta limitatio seu restrictio, quae in favorem Ecclesiae jure positivo legitur introducta . . . posset in certis casibus eidem gravissime praejudicare . . . [e.g.] si plures essent contendentes de Papatu ita quod nulli eorum tota obediret Ecclesia, nec ad alicujus eorum aut amborum simul vocationem compareret, sicut esse videtur in praesenti schismate."

25. Ibid.: "Pro sedando praesentis schismate absque papae auctoritate immo ipso contradicente, potest auctoritate Universalis Ecclesiae generale concilium congregari: et non solum per dominos cardinales convocari, sed etiam, in casu, per quoscumque fideles."

26. *Tract. de mat.,* below, pp. 309 ff.; *Tract. de eccl. pot.,* Dupin, 2, 959.

27. Dupin, 2, 951: "Haec autem conclusio in condemnatione et depositione Joannis Papae XXIII practica est per hoc Concilium Generale, cujus determinationi contradicere non licet."

munity possessed the right to protect itself by legal, institutional means, against the depredations of such a ruler. It is his belief that political authority exists for the common good of the community that necessitates this conclusion, and it is his further belief that the community is the source of political authority that makes its practicable. These two beliefs, which together form the heart of his political philosophy, are contingent upon the further assumption of the existence of the natural law in terms of which they are formulated. D'Ailly's political philosophy, like that of Aquinas, draws its strength from an underlying philosophy of law, which, as we shall see in the next chapter, forms a coherently articulated link between his social and political ideas and his basic philosophical and theological assumptions.

6.
Law—Natural and Divine

A recurring motif in d'Ailly's writings is the blunt expression of his contempt for lawyers and for the study of law. He dismissed as "jurists" those thinkers who alleged that the omnipotent God was bound by "created laws," and the title was clearly intended to be derogatory.[1] In his *Epistola diaboli leviathan*, it is in the mouth of the devil that he puts the exhortation to follow "the laws of Justinian and the decrees of Gratian," [2] and he frequently asserts that one of the "common errors" of the times is the belief that the knowledge of human laws, whether civil or ecclesiastical, pertains more to the office of the prelate than does theological wisdom.[3] In view of this attitude, we can

1. See above, p. 21.
2. In Tschackert, *Ailli*, App. V, p. [19].
3. E.g.: *Utrum indoctus in jure divino*, Dupin, *1*, 654: "est hodie communis error quorundam, dicentium quod ad praelatorum officium magis pertinet doctrina Juris humani Civilis scilicet et canonici, quam Theologica sapientia seu doctrina Juris divini." This work—d'Ailly's most extensive attack upon the "juristic" temper of his day—contains a bitter rejection of the high claims made by Hostiensis for the study of canon law; see 655: *"Negatur plane, et sine ulla reverentia, dictum Hostienum, tanquam falsum et haereticum:* si intelligat generaliter, quod Juris scientia sit dicenda scientia scientiarum, et omnibus aliis anteponenda: excipienda enim est Theologia" (italics mine). For the attitude of Hostiensis, see Ullmann, *Papalism*, pp. 27 ff. Further expressions of d'Ailly's

hardly expect to learn anything from d'Ailly about the customary law which governed so much of the lives of medieval
men, or even much concerning the civil and canon laws, the
study of which flourished at the universities and exerted pressure under which the feudal lawyers attempted to systematize
their own law. Thus the title of this chapter is chosen advisedly.
The extent of d'Ailly's canonistic citations tends to belie his
own antijuristic protestations, but his interest does not extend
beyond the canon law and he is no legal scholar. His philosophy
does, however, embrace a philosophy of law which it will be the
purpose of this chapter to examine.

It is this philosophy, indeed, that lies behind d'Ailly's attacks
on the jurists. His position is not purely a negative one. In his
thought, as in that of the other Conciliarists, the Aristotelian
idea of *epikeia* plays a notable part. What upsets him about the
legalistic spirit of the times is that it is encouraging men to
forget this notion, to forget the rôle of equity in the interpretation of positive laws and to prefer, therefore, the letter of the
law to its spirit.[4] Echoing St. Bernard, he says that the clerics
and prelates are paying too much attention to the laws of this

distaste for the jurists may be found in his *Tractatus de materia*, below, p. 330;
Sermo de Beato Bernardo, Tschackert, *Ailli*, App. VI, p. [22]; *Invectiva Ezechielis
contra Pseudopastores*, ibid., App. IV, pp. [14] and [15]; *Principium in cursum
Bibliae*, Dupin, *1*, 615; *Sermo factus in concilio generali Constantiensi*, in *Sermones*, f. x3v.

4. *Tractatus Brevis*, Ehrle, p. 502: "et ideo in ejus provisione recurrendum est
ad jus divinum et rationem moralem et etiam ad illam virtutem et juris aequita-
tem, quae ab Aristotele in quinto Ethicorum dicitur Epykeia. Quare bonus jurista
in hac materia magis debet sequi juris racionem quam sensum juris litteralem,
juxta illud Apostoli: 'Littera occidet' etc." Cf. *Propositiones Utiles*, Martène et
Durand, 7, 911; *Oratio de officio Imperatoris*, Dupin, 2, 921. For Gerson's use of
the idea, see John B. Morrall, *Gerson and the Great Schism* (Manchester, 1960),
pp. 121–22. Aristotle examines the notion in his *Nichomachean Ethics*, V, 10;
cf. also *Rhetoric*, I, 13. Brief discussions of his position may be found in Ernest
Barker, *The Politics of Aristotle* (Oxford, 1946), pp. 367–72, and Sir Paul Vinogradoff, *Outlines of Historical Jurisprudence* (Oxford, 1922), 2, 68–71. For an
outline of the changing meanings of the concept during the course of its long
history, see L. J. Riley, *The History, Nature and Use of Epikeia in Moral Theology*
(Washington, 1948), pp. 1–67; also Guido Kisch, *Erasmus und die Jurisprudenz
seiner Zeit* (Basel, 1960), pp. 1–54. The scholastic theologians seemed to have
used *epikeia* with some consistency as a synonym for "equity."

world—civil or canonistic—and too little to the laws of God,[5] that they are obeying the edicts of Caesar rather than "the laws of the celestial emperor." [6] D'Ailly is clearly a believer in the supremacy of a law higher than the merely positive; in more modern terms, an advocate of the subordination of law to ethics. As with the vast majority of medieval thinkers, his belief rests upon a firm adherence to the natural law theory, or rather to *a* natural law theory. It is necessary to make this emendation because the conceptions of natural law held by the Roman lawyers, canonists, and theologians were by no means uniform. Passerin d'Entrèves has correctly insisted that "the different meanings of natural law are but the consequences of the different meanings of nature," [7] and even the medieval theologians differed in their concepts of nature.

I

The words "nature" and "law" are both susceptible of the most varied definition and it is hardly surprising that their union has been blessed with equivocal issue. Even today, when the expression "natural law" is suffering an eclipse in popularity, surviving usage manifests a certain ambiguity in that the expression is used both with a juristic and moral and with a scientific connotation. For purposes of clarity I shall employ the term "natural law" to refer to the juristic concept, and the term "law of nature" to indicate the scientific usage.

5. *Sermo de Beato Bernardo*, Tschackert, *Ailli*, p. [22]: "Nostri clerici et ecclesiarum praelati non legem dei, sed legem mundi studiose scrutantur, nec in lege Christi, sed magis in lege Justiniani nocte ac die meditantur"; also *Invective Ezechielis contra Pseudopastores*, Tschackert, *Ailli*, pp. [14]–[15]. Cf. St. Bernard, *De Consideratione libri tres ad Eugenium tertium*, I, cap. 4; PL *182*, 732–33.

6. *Principium in cursum Bibliae*, Dupin, *1*, 614: "Venio ad scholam Jurisperitorum . . . . In primo vero hujus scholae ingressu civilis Juris Doctores invenio, qui Imperatorum Leges, Caesaris Edicta tanta veneratione suscipiunt, tanto honore praeferunt, ut pro ipsis venerandis, aliqui plerumque coelestis Imperatoris Leges contemnant; pro ipsis defendendis, Edictis summi Caesaris contradicant." A little ironic in that some of the canonists had not hesitated to speak of the Pope as "the celestial emperor" (see above, Ch. 2, I, n. 6, p. 37).

7. A. P. d'Entrèves, *Natural Law: An Introduction to Legal Philosophy* (London, 1951), p. 11.

The twin concepts of the natural law and the laws of nature have their roots deep in classical and Semitic antiquity. They have influenced the formation of western thought, however, primarily through the pages of three documents of immense importance during the Middle Ages—the *Corpus juris civilis,* the Bible, and Gratian's *Decretum.*[1]

Behind the utterances about natural law which are to be found in the introductory sections of two of Justinian's law-books, the *Digest* and the *Institutes,* stretches a long and ancient tradition which had been at its richest during the Hellenistic period. The strand of this tradition most relevant to the statements of the jurists was the pantheistic Stoic view which conceived of natural law as an expression of the divine reason immanent in the universe. It was regarded as embracing the universal practice of men, in all times and in every country, and as analogous to the principle of harmony or cohesion which governed the movements of the heavenly bodies and the habits of animals. Accordingly, the *Corpus juris civilis* can contrast natural law with decreed laws as being universal, immutable, and founded on reason, and can illustrate these qualities by referring to moral obligations such as obedience to parents or veneration of God.[2] Accordingly, Ulpian can speak (or be made to speak) of natural law as "that which nature has taught all the animals." [3] In such a view, then, the natural law and the laws of nature are conceived as being at least in essence one, a body of rational principles inherent in the fabric of nature and possessing divine or cosmic sanction.[4]

1. This is in no way to deny the pervasive influence of Patristic views on natural law, for these were incorporated, in the form given to them by Isidore of Seville, in the *Decretum.* See Carlyle, *History, 1,* Ch. 9, esp. 106–10.

2. *Inst.,* 1, 2, 11; *Dig.,* 1, 1, 2.

3. *Dig.,* 1, 1, 1 § 3; *Inst.,* 1, 2 *pr.* To be exact, the definition attributed to Ulpian may not fully accord with Stoic views; see Sir Frederick Pollock, "The History of the Law of Nature," *Essays in the Law* (London, 1922), pp. 36–37, and Fritz Schulz, *History of Roman Legal Science* (Oxford, 1946), pp. 136–37.

4. The various statements in the *Corpus juris civilis* about the natural law are not, of course, fully consistent one with another; despite attempts to explain the discrepancies, some doubt has arisen about the authenticity of their attribution to the classical jurists; see H. F. Jolowicz, *Historical Introduction to the Study of*

When we turn to the Old Testament, we find no clear reference to natural law, but instead a few crucial and historically influential references to what may be described as laws of nature, or more precisely as divine laws regulating nature. One of the ideas central to Judaism was that of the divine lawgiver, and He was conceived as imposing His laws upon nature as well as upon men. Thus, for instance, He "placed the sand for a bound of the sea by a perpetual decree, that it cannot pass it," [5] or as Job said, "made a law for the rain and a way for the lightning and thunder." [6] The Old Testament laws which were given by God to man may well appear to have little in common with the Stoic idea of natural law, for they were the direct mandates of a transcendent and sovereign Deity, but by the end of the pre-Christian era, a hellenizing Jew such as Philo, already deeply imbued with the Pythagorean concept of the king as a *lex animata,* found it possible to regard Moses as an embodiment of the unwritten natural law, and to view the Decalogue as merely the overt statement of a law already implanted in the minds of men.[7] Similarly, as time went on, natural law tended to be identified with the essence of scriptural morality; the basis for such an identification was found in St. Paul's Epistle to the Romans, where he speaks of the law as being written in the hearts of the Gentiles, to whom it has not been explicitly revealed, but "who do by nature the things contained in the law." [8] This identification is to be found complete in Gratian's

---

Roman Law (Cambridge, 1939), pp. 100–05; d'Entrèves, *Natural Law,* pp. 17–29. The problem of attribution is of little importance in the present context.

5. Jeremiah 5:22.

6. Job 28:26. Edgar Zilsel, "The Genesis of the Concept of Physical Law," *The Philosophical Review, 51* (1942), 247, comments that "the Hebrew text uses the word *chok* . . . derived from the verb *chokak* meaning to engrave, and it is the same term which is used for moral and ritual laws in the Old Testament."

7. Erwin R. Goodenough, *The Politics of Philo Judaeus: Practice and Theory* (New Haven, 1938), pp. 111, 44–45; H. A. Wolfson, *Philo: Foundations of Religious Philosophy in Judaism, Christianity and Islam* (Cambridge, Mass., 1947), 2, 189–94. For a general discussion of the notion of the king as a *lex animata* see Goodenough, "The Political Philosophy of Hellenistic Kingship," *Yale Classical Studies, 1* (1928), 55–102.

8. Rom. 2:14–15. This identification is typically Patristic (see Carlyle, *History, 1,*

Decretum [9] and was constantly reiterated by subsequent canonists.

The concepts, therefore, of the natural law and the laws of nature found expression in, and were publicized by, three most influential authorities—the Bible, the civil law, and the canon law. The last of these deserves special emphasis. The canonists of the twelfth century, commenting on the relevant texts of Gratian, laid the foundations for the great scholastic discussions of the problem later on, and d'Entrèves speaks of them as giving the natural law an "unprecedented coherence, clearness and force." [10] It is certainly true that whereas the *Corpus juris civilis* in no place clearly subordinates positive to natural law, the *Decretum* leaves no doubt about the fact that natural law, being divine in character, is unequivocally superior in force to all other laws, and if conflicts occur completely overrules them.[11] Nevertheless, along with the more coherent version of the canon law survived the discrete Judaic concept, as well as the ambiguous and uncoordinated ideas enshrined in the civil law; by the mid-thirteenth century, when Aquinas wrote his *Summa theologica,* they had become common intellectual coinage. What Aquinas did was to secure their survival, for he took these concepts, systematized them, and fitted them, in an ordered fashion, into the framework of a Christianized Aristotelian metaphysic.

---

105). D'Entrèves (*Natural Law,* p. 35), pointing out that such a view involves the restriction of natural law to essentially human concerns, as against the general instinct of all animals and beings, remarks that "however different their conception of man, Christian writers like St. Ambrose or St. Augustine had developed the notion of a *lex naturalis in corde scripta* and of an *innata vis* to attain to the knowledge of it."

9. D. *1, proemium, dictum Gratiani:* "Jus naturae est, quod in lege et evangelio continetur." For the attitude of the canonists to the natural law, see Ullmann, *Papalism,* pp. 38–75. Also useful, though not solely concerned with *medieval* canon law, is Stephan Kuttner, "The Natural Law and Canon Law," *University of Notre Dame Natural Law Proceedings* (Notre Dame, Ind., 1950), *3,* 95–116.

10. *Natural Law,* p. 33; see also O. Lottin, *Le droit naturel chez St. Thomas d'Aquin et ses prédécesseurs* (2nd ed. Bruges, 1931), pp. 13–23. Nevertheless in this the canonists clearly fell far short of the coherence attained by the theologians later on, for Ullmann, *Papalism,* Ch. 2, and esp. pp. 45–66, stresses the vagueness of their terminology and the eclecticism of their teaching.

11. *ST,* 1a 2ae, qu. 90, art. 1.

Law, according to Aquinas, is not founded on will but is "something pertaining to reason" *(aliquid rationis)*.[12] It is "a rule and measure of action in virtue of which one is led to perform certain actions and restrained from the performance of others," and "the rule and measure" or "first principle" of human action is reason.[13] As the law is "nothing else but a certain dictate of practical reason 'in the prince' who rules a perfect community," it follows, if it is granted that the world is ruled by divine providence, that

> The whole community of the Universe is governed by the divine reason. Thus the rational guidance of created things on the part of God, as the Prince of the universe, has the quality of law . . . . This we can call the eternal law.[14]

Or again, God is related to the world of which He is the creator and ruler as an artist is related to his work. As in the mind of every artist there pre-exists the idea of the work he produces, so also in every ruler there pre-exists the idea of the order to be followed by those being governed. Hence "the ideal of the divine reason, considered as moving all things to their appropriate end, has the quality of law," and "the eternal law is nothing other than the ideal of the divine wisdom considered as directing all actions and movements." [15] Moreover,

> Since all things which are subject to divine providence are measured and regulated by the Eternal Law . . . it is clear that all things participate to some degree in the eternal law; in so far as they derive from it certain inclinations to those actions and aims which are proper to them. But, of all others, rational creatures are subject to divine providence in a very special way; being themselves made participators in providence itself, in that they control their own actions and the actions of others. So they have a certain share in

12. *ST*, ibid., in d'Entrèves, *Aquinas*, pp. 108–09.
13. *ST*, 1a 2ae, qu. 91, art. 1; d'Entrèves, *Aquinas*, pp. 112–13.
14. *ST*, 1a 2ae, qu. 93, art. 1; d'Entrèves, *Aquinas*, pp. 120–21.
15. *ST*, 1a 2ae, qu. 93, art. 1; d'Entrèves, *Aquinas*, pp. 120–21.

the divine reason itself, deriving therefrom a natural inclination to such actions and ends as are fitting. This participation in the eternal law by rational creatures is called the natural law.[16]

Aquinas's position, therefore, amounts basically to this: that there is an eternal law which orders to their appointed ends all created things, irrational as well as rational. Insofar as it concerns man and is apprehended by his reason the eternal law is called natural law.[17] To these two categories he adds two further ones—*divine positive law,* the decrees of God, which supplement the natural law and which are made known to man by revelation rather than reason,[18] and *human positive law,* the laws enacted by rulers for their subjects.[19] Finally, he maintains, every human positive law "bears the nature of law only in so far as it is derived from natural law." For if it contravenes that natural law at any point "it is no longer legal, but rather a corruption of law." [20] In this synthesis, therefore, natural law, laws of nature, Stoic, and Biblical ideas are welded into an Aristotelian mode of thought, and the notion of an eternal law emerges which is completely teleological in conception. In the centuries after the death of Aquinas, this view persisted, in its broad outlines, among the realist philosophers who followed the *via antiqua.*[21]

We have already had occasion to trace the origin and rise of a nominalist, or rather a voluntarist reaction against the rationalistic conception of God, Nature, and the world which lies behind this realist view of law, and have already suggested that

16. *ST,* 1a 2ae, qu. 91, art. 2; d'Entrèves, *Aquinas,* pp. 112–15.

17. But it should be noted that Aquinas is able to comprehend within the natural law all those instincts which, in Ulpian's troublesome phrase, "nature has taught all the animals." It is the further "inclinatio ad bonum secundum naturam rationis" which is the part of natural law proper to man alone (*ST,* 1a 2ae, qu. 94, art. 2, in d'Entrèves, *Aquinas,* pp. 122–23).

18. *ST,* 1a 2ae, qu. 91, art. 4; in d'Entrèves, *Aquinas,* pp. 114–17.

19. *ST,* 1a 2ae, qu. 95, art. 1; ibid., pp. 126–29.

20. *ST,* 1a 2ae, qu. 95, art. 2; ibid., pp. 128–29.

21. But Ullmann (*Papalism,* p. 47), claims that it "made no impression upon contemporary or later canonists."

such a reaction necessarily entailed a thoroughgoing revolution in ethical and legal thinking.[22] The validity of this contention can best be illustrated by glancing at the position of William of Ockham.

What Ockham did was to ground the natural law, and indeed all ethical values, on the will of God. Natural laws ceased, therefore, to be a "dictate of reason as to what is right, grounded in the being of God but unalterable even by Him," and became "a divine command . . . right and binding merely because God was the lawgiver." [23] Thus "evil is nothing other than the doing of something opposite to that which one is obliged to do." [24] Hate of God, adultery, robbery—and all such vices— could be stripped of their evil and rendered meritorious if they were to agree with the divine precept, just as now de facto their opposites agree with the divine precept.[25] For "God is obliged to the causing of no act." [26] It is true that, of His ordained power (*potentia ordinata*) God condescends to work within the framework of the moral law which He has actually established, and to which right reason is the infallible guide.[27] It is true also that, given the endurance of this moral order, the natural law can be regarded as absolute, immutable, and admitting of no dispensation.[28] But it must never be forgotten that, of His absolute power (*potentia absoluta*), God could suspend the working of that order.[29] The dictates of natural law, the infallibility of right reason, the very fact that it is virtuous to act in accordance with right reason—all of these amount to nothing more than the inscrutable manifestations of divine omnipotence.[30]

22. See above, pp. 21 ff.

23. Gierke-Maitland, p. 173, n. 256.

24. Ockham, *Sent.* II, qu. 5, H.

25. Ibid., qu. 19, O.

26. Ibid., qu. 19, P.

27. Ockham, *Sent.* I, dist. xli, qu. 1, K.

28. *Dialogus*, III, II, I, cap. 10; Goldast, 2, 878, lines 27–31; *Dialogus*, III, II, III, cap. 6; ibid., p. 932, line 65.

29. *Opus nonaginta dierum* (Lyons, Jean Trechsel, 1495), cap. 95, see esp. § *Nota de duplici potentia dei.* Also *Quodlibeta septem una cum tractatu de sacramento altaris* (Strasbourg, Jordanus de Quedlinburg, 1491), Quodl. VI, qu. 1.

30. Ockham, *Sent.* I, dist. xli, qu. 1, I; cf. my article, "Medieval Theories of

This approach, with its dependence upon the distinction between the absolute and ordained powers of God, has a very familiar ring, and not without reason, for Ockham gave the clearest and most coherent expression to that much-neglected tradition of natural law thinking to which d'Ailly, by virtue of his philosophical assumptions, had logically to belong. We may perhaps be excused, therefore, if we turn peremptorily to an examination of d'Ailly's own views. While the ambiguities and uncertainties consequent upon the reception of natural law thinking persisted—especially among the lawyers—nevertheless, among the philosophers and theologians of the later Middle Ages, natural law theorizing was almost wholly trapped within the field of attraction exercised by the two influential poles of the realist and nominalist or rationalist and voluntarist positions.[31]

II

D'Ailly, no less than Ockham, laid his basic stress on the unity, freedom, and omnipotence of God, rejecting any distinction in God, even between His will and intellect, and any limitation of His power, even that supposedly entailed by the traditional doctrine of the divine ideas.[1] Given such basic assumptions, it seems reasonable to expect that d'Ailly must, like Ockham, ground natural law and ethical values on the divine fiat, though

Natural Law: William of Ockham and the Significance of the Voluntarist Tradition," *Natural Law Forum, 6* (1961), 68–72. In his lengthiest and best-known statement on natural law, Ockham actually distinguishes three varieties, but the analysis and the article above concern only his first variety, natural law in what is for him its primary and fundamental sense. For the statement, see *Dialogus*, III, II, III, cap. 6; Goldast, *2*, 933. Lagarde, *Naissance, 6*, Ch. 6 and 7, gives a valuable and detailed analysis of Ockham's whole theory of natural law and natural rights.

31. This generalization cannot be extended to cover the views on law expressed by Marsilius of Padua. It may be that Marsilius altogether abandoned the natural law tradition, but there is some disagreement about his position. He has, for example, been regarded as a "voluntarist" and a positivist of the Austinian type; see Lagarde, *Naissance, 2*, 164–74 and A. P. d'Entrèves, *The Medieval Contribution to Political Thought* (Oxford, 1939), pp. 61–64. But for a different view, see Alan Gewirth, *Marsilius of Padua* (New York, 1956), *1*, pp. 134–35.

1. See above, pp. 22 ff.

it may, perhaps, be excusable to wonder whether natural law can have any real place in a universe so radically contingent upon the will of its creator. Only d'Ailly, however, can answer these questions, and the problem becomes one of knowing where to look for his reply. Like most medieval theologians, he wrote no specific treatise on law as such, and his references to it are scattered throughout his works. I propose, therefore, to begin by casting a very wide net with a view to discovering, at the outset, what signs (if any) of a general philosophy of law are evident even in his most concrete references to law.[2]

The tract edited below may well serve as our point of departure, for despite d'Ailly's frequent attacks upon the jurists, the *Tractatus de materia*[3] reveals an extraordinary wealth of legal citations, drawn primarily though not exclusively from the canon law. In several places, following contemporary usage, he uses the expression "the common law" or "the common laws" to indicate the canon law. Thus, speaking of the General Council, he argues that it should be held "in the form of the common law instituted by the holy fathers in the sacred canons,"[4] or again, elsewhere, he speaks of certain common laws as "either established by General Councils or by their authority included in the body of the law."[5] In another work, however, the ex-

2. It should be noted at the outset that d'Ailly seems to employ interchangeably the two words *jus* and *lex* to mean law. It is true that he usually uses lex to indicate the laws governing nature itself (perhaps because jus has incongruous connotations of right and justice), but even this rule is not rigid. See *Tractatus II de falsis prophetis,* Dupin, *1,* 558, where he is speaking of the type of knowledge possessed by demons: "In daemonibus non est proportionaliter tanta obscuratio intellectivae; quanta est depravatio volitivae, nisi scilicet ad praedictum intellectum, et loquendo naturaliter. Ita quod quanto sunt pejores, tanto circa eamdem rem sunt magis ignorantes spiritualiter, idest minus cognoscentes incommoda spiritualia inde provenientia. Et sic ipse princeps malignorum spirituum, *jure et ordine naturae,* sicut in voluntate magis depravatus est, sic in intellectu tenebrosior et obscurior, et maxime circa illam rem circa quam depravata est ejus voluntas, scilicet circa Deum" (italics mine). For an analysis of the different meanings of jus, law and right see J. W. Salmond, *Jurisprudence* (7th ed., London, 1924), App. I, "The Names of Law," pp. 513–23.

3. See below, Appendix III, pp. 252–342.

4. Below, p. 266; cf. *Tract. de eccl. pot.,* Dupin, 2, 941.

5. *Secunda schedula pro secundo concilio regis,* Ehrle, p. 478: "Item consideranda essent et discutienda jura communia tangencia potestatem pape in

pression is given a wider meaning and is to be taken, it seems, to include all laws generally applicable to men (divine law is specifically mentioned), for it is placed in opposition to private laws such as the privilege, *Parens scientiarum,* granted to the University of Paris.[6] This formula is clarified in another passage where he argues that insofar as this privilege concerns the license in theology, it is not properly speaking a private law, "but is a common law, not only human, but natural and divine." [7]

This initial inconsistency is discouraging, the more so in that no reconciliation seems possible. All that can be said is that the extension of the term "common law" to embrace the natural and divine law is limited to this one work—his first tract against the Chancellor of Paris—and is perhaps explicable in terms of his desire to stress the contrast between a private law, a mere privilege limited to the University, and the laws common to all men.[8] More usually, however, it is only the canons which are referred to as "common laws," and they are also called "positive" and "human" laws.[9] These terms are nowhere defined, but

collationibus beneficiorum . . . que jura vel in consiliis generalibus condita vel ipsorum auctoritate in corpore juris redacta sunt. . . ." Cf. *Propositiones utiles,* Martène et Durand, 7, 910: "Patet ex juribus communibus, quae habentur in decretis et decretalibus"; *Prima schedula,* Ehrle, p. 472; *Tertia schedula,* Ehrle, p. 482.

6. *Tractatus II adversus Cancellarium Parisiensem,* in Dupin, *1,* 760: "Credo tamen quod ipsi, vel saltem multi ipsorum, agnoverunt hoc Privilegium. Ideo non intelligitur contumaciter fecisse contra ipsum, quia licet ignorantia Juris communis, et maxime Juris divini non excuset: ignorantia tamen Juris privati, sicut talis Privilegii bene excusat . . ." The privilege in question is *Parens Scientiarum,* granted to the University in 1231 by Gregory IX; cf. Hastings Rashdall, *The Universities of Europe in the Middle Ages* (ed. F. M. Powicke and A. B. Emden, Oxford, 1936), *1,* 338–39.

7. *Tract. I adversus Cancellarium Parisiensem,* Dupin, *1,* 731: "in quantum respicit licentiam in Theologia, non est proprie Privilegium, quasi privans Legem, vel quasi privata Lex; sed est Jus commune, non solum humanum, sed naturale, et divinum."

8. A suggestion borne out by his comment that privileges lie outside the "general" law (*Tract. II adversus Canc. Paris.,* Dupin, *1,* 770): "Universitas ultra Jus generale, habet speciale privilegium."

9. *Tract. I adversus Canc. Paris.,* Dupin, *1,* 737: "Hoc idem principaliter ex Jure humano, scilicet per Jura canonica. *Extra. De Magistris*" etc. *Tract. de eccl. pot.,* Dupin, *2,* 934, where, having cited canonistic texts, he says: "Sed

from the context it is at least clear that by them he means not merely customary norms but laws which have actually been promulgated by a law-making authority. This point is worth noting for d'Ailly betrays elsewhere a marked reluctance to regard custom as truly worthy of the name of law. He admits, it is true, the traditional medieval doctrine that the lack of all memory of any rule or practice to the contrary gives custom "the force of law," but while doing so he feels it necessary to cite in support of his admission the authority of one of the canons.[10] Similarly, he insists that custom has no place except in the absence of law, for it is inferior to merely human enactments as well as to natural and divine law.[11] Moreover, as becomes apparent elsewhere, he inclines to the belief that such human laws should properly be enacted only by the common consent of those who are to be affected by them.[12]

In the absence (in his publicist works) of any more definitive statement, it would seem fair to conclude that d'Ailly regarded

---

ultra Jura praemissa, humana et positiva, restat in Jure divino fundare statum hierarchicum cardinalium." In this assumption that the canon law is not to be regarded as divine law (although the canonists themselves often regarded it as such (see Ullmann, *Papalism*, p. 42), d'Ailly is following in the footsteps of Ockham (see Lagarde, *Naissance, 6,* 133).

10. *Tract. de eccl. pot.,* Dupin, 2, 933: "Et dato quod nullo Jure probaretur, sufficit quod sic est receptum a tempore, de cujus contrario non est memoria. Nam tale tempus habet vim Legis: De praescriptionibus, cap. 1, lib. 6."

11. *Tract. II adversus Canc. Paris.,* Dupin, *1,* 773. The Chancellor had argued that he possessed, by custom, the right of exacting payment for the *licentia docendi.* This d'Ailly rejects, saying: "Primo. Quia talis modus exigendi est contra Jus divinum. . . . Sed contra Jus divinum consuetudo non habet locum, nec praescriptio. . . . Secundo. Quia, esto quia sic exigere non esset contra Jus divinum, quod tamen omnino falsum est; tamen per Jus Canonicum exactio quaelibet in proposito, expresse prohibetur Cancellario, in Capitulo, *Quanto. De Magistris,* et ibi damnatur consuetudo, tanquam prava et inhonesta, praetextu Cancellarius Parisiensis volebat exigere. Si ergo hujusmodi consuetudo ante Jus conditum erat prava, et damnetur tanquam corruptela multo magis post Jus conditum ipsa est damnabilis et repudianda: maxime quia ex quo aliqua consuetudo est a Jure expresse prohibita, supposito quod prius fuisset justa, vel licita; tamen post nunquam fiet consuetudo justa, aliter esset frustra Jure damnata." Cf. *Tract. I adversus Canc. Paris.,* Dupin, *1,* 732.

12. This belief is expressed with reference to the making of new and the abrogation of old canon laws (*Tract. de mat.,* below, pp. 253 ff.); cf. *Secunda schedula pro secundo concilio regis,* Ehrle, p. 478.

the expressed will of a properly constituted law-making authority as of the essence of "positive" or "human" law. In addition,
it seems safe to assume that d'Ailly would not limit the application of these latter terms to ecclesiastical laws alone, for the
distinction which dictates their use is not that between the
ecclesiastical polity and any other but rather that which exists
between the laws of *any* human organization and the laws of
God. Thus, speaking of the restriction to the Pope alone of the
authority to convoke a General Council, he says that this restriction is clear "from the common laws which are to be found in
the *Decretum* and *Decretals*," but nevertheless that despite it
this authority remains in the Universal Church itself, "since
positive laws cannot absolutely take away from the Church that
power which belongs to it by natural and divine law." [13] The
implication is that natural and divine law are superior to positive law, and it is in accordance with this that we are told elsewhere that "man can endow no obligation with force, unless by
virtue of divine authority"; [14] or again that the Pope, like everyone else, is subject to natural and divine law, but as head of the
Church, is not subject to merely human law. [15]

A reading of his publicist works alone suffices to indicate,
therefore, that the distinction which dominates d'Ailly's conception of law is that between natural and divine law, on the

13. *Propositiones utiles*, Martène et Durand, 7, 910: "Post incrementa nascentis
ecclesiae primitivae, praemissa auctoritas et potestas congregandi generalia concilia, rationabiliter limitata fuit et restricta, sic scilicet quod sine auctoritate papae
nulli liceret concilia hujusmodi congregare. Patet ex juribus communibus, quae
habentur in decretis et decretalibus . . . . Praemissa limitatio seu restrictio non
tollit, quin praedicta auctoritativa potestas semper absolute remaneat in ipse
universali ecclesia. Patet, quia jura positiva non possunt ab ecclesia absolute
tollere illam potestatem quae ei competit divino et naturali jure." This leads
d'Ailly to plead that the law be understood *civiliter*, in accordance with the
virtue of *epikeia*—cf. above, n. 4, p. 164.

14. *Tractatus pro Carthusiensibus*, Tschackert, *Ailii*, App. VII, p. [26]: "nulla
obligatio ab homine habet vigorem, nisi virtute autoritas divinae."

15. *Tract. II adversus Canc. Paris.*, Dupin, *1*, 752–53: "Papa non potest licite
facere contra Jus naturale et divinum, cum non sit a tali jure exceptus, plusquam
quicumque alius,"—but "cum sit caput Ecclesiae, non est subjectus Juri humano;
scilicet Ordinationi, seu Constitutioni ab Ecclesia institutae." But he may have
wavered on this point later on. See above, Ch. 4, n. 27, p. 112.

one hand, and positive or human, on the other—the latter being subordinate to the former. Phrases such as *tam jure naturali et divino quam etiam humano,* or *non tam jure positivo quam jure divino et naturali,*[16] which are to be found throughout these works, serve to underline this distinction. It is perhaps significant that the appeal—very rarely—is to natural law alone, but more frequently to divine law. Thus in the *Tractatus de materia* there are over a dozen appeals to divine but none to natural law, and in the *Tractatus de ecclesiastica potestate,* though there are frequent appeals to divine law, and to divine and natural law, there are only two such appeals to natural law alone.[17] It might be permissible to doubt whether d'Ailly drew any clear distinction between divine and natural law were it not that the appeals to natural law in this latter tract indicate by their nature the existence of such a distinction. For he argues that it is probable that the Romans have the right of electing the Pope by natural and divine law, taking it in its broad sense to mean everything which is "in accordance with natural reason and explicitly or implicitly contained in the divine Scriptures."[18] Later on, referring to this definition, he says that the Romans have this right "from natural law, taken in a wide sense . . . and, as a result, from divine law—divine law being extended to cover all types of natural law, since such law comes from God, the founder of nature."[19]

Both of these statements are taken almost verbatim from the well-known discussion of natural law which is to be found in the third part of Ockham's *Dialogus,* but in the course of the transfer much of their significance has regrettably been lost. In the text in question, Ockham distinguishes three senses that the

16. Both phrases cited from *Tract. de eccl. pot.,* Dupin, 2, 947.

17. Lagarde, *Naissance,* 6, 134 and n. 26, has noted in Ockham a similar tendency to lump together divine and natural law.

18. *Tract. de eccl. pot.,* Dupin, 2, 930: "large sumendo Jus naturale et divinum, pro omni illo quod ex suppositione est naturali rationi consonum, et in divinis Scripturis explicite vel implicite comprehensum; sic Romani" etc.

19. *Tract. de eccl. pot.,* Dupin, 2, 936: "ex Jure naturali large sumpto, ut supra tactum est, et per consequens, ex Jure divino, extendendo Jus divinum ad quodcunque Jus naturale, ex eo scilicet, quia tale Jus est a Deo conditore naturae."

term "natural law" conveys. In its primary and fundamental sense it indicates the infallible dictates of natural reason. In its second sense it refers to that law observed by those who direct their actions by natural equity alone and without reference to human customs or constitutions. In the third sense it is that law "which is deduced by evident reason from the law of peoples or from some human fact, unless by the consent of those whose concern it is the contrary is decreed." It is, he says, in this last sense, and not in the first or second, that the Romans can be said to have from the natural law the right of electing the Pope.[20] D'Ailly was certainly aware of this classification of the varieties of natural law, for some years earlier, in his *Abbreviatio dyalogi Okam*, he had noted that according to Ockham the right in question pertained to the Romans "by the natural law *tertio modo dicto*," and had also ventured to commend the classification itself as *valde bonam*.[21] Nevertheless, in the *Tractatus de ecclesiastica potestate* he makes no mention of it, and his statements, torn out of context and highly condensed, are not even fully intelligible.[22] But it does seem legitimate at least to conclude from them that d'Ailly regards natural law, in the first place, as a broader category than divine law, and in the second place, as stemming from God and explicitly or implicitly contained in the teaching of the scriptures. The former conclusion finds partial confirmation elsewhere when he tells us that the sin of simony is forbidden by the natural as well as by the divine law (the former denoting that law which is naturally impressed upon the hearts of all men and the latter comprehending the Old as well as the New Law), and that the sin is named after Simon merely because Christ gives in the New Testament a clear formulation of its nature.[23] If, in this discussion of his

20. *Dialogus*, III, II, III, cap. 6; Goldast, 2, 933.

21. Paris, Bibl. Nat., *Ms. Lat.* 14,579 f. 101r. See below, p. 243, for a transcription of the relevant passage.

22. See above, pp. 141–42; below, p. 202.

23. *Tract. I adversus Canc. Paris.*, Dupin, *1*, 730–31: "Simonia est contra Jus naturale et divinum . . . . Et quod ipsa sit contra Jus divinum satis notum est; sed quod sit contra Jus naturale specialiter probari potest; quia Numerorum XXII, quod reprobatus est a Domino, et damnabilis judicatus Balaam, qui de

publicist works, the evidence of one of his earlier scholastic disputations be admitted, the latter assertion of the dependence of the natural law upon God is strikingly confirmed by d'Ailly's sweeping assertion that every law, to be valid, must be in conformity with the first law, which is the will of God.[24]

It follows that, even if we were to restrict our attention almost entirely to d'Ailly's publicist works, we would be able to extract a theory of law in which all human laws, civil or ecclesiastical (themselves, it seems, the expressed will of some lawmaking authority), are subordinated to divine and natural law —divine law being probably that law explicitly revealed in the scriptures, and natural law that wider category of law which is accessible to reason, but both of them deriving from the divine will. There is nothing extraordinary about such a theory, though it is far from being precisely defined or fully elaborated. It is only the stress upon the rôle of will that distinguishes it from the more realist view of law widely accepted during the Middle Ages. It would, however, be strange if a fully developed philosophy of law were set forth in publicist treatises of the type we have been citing. In a host of casual references made at different times and in widely differing contexts, d'Ailly has betrayed only one obvious inconsistency, and that on a matter of terminology.[25] But two difficulties arise. The first is this: d'Ailly maintains an internal consistency in these works, but how can a view of law as ultimately dependent for its validity upon the will of God

---

Balath rege Moabitarum pretium suae prophetationis accepit . . . et tamen ipse, nec Legem Dei novam, nec antequam receperat: et per consequens, istud vitium ex Lege naturae reprehensibile erat. Unde et hoc vitium ab ipso Balaam, ejus primo authore, Balaamina posset congrue nominari. Nominantur tamen a Simone, quia rationem hujus criminis, Christus in Novo Testamento clarius expressit, quando dixit: 'Gratis accepistis, gratis date.' Ideo magis peccant contra hoc venientes in nova Lege: tamen et sub Lege Moysi et sub Lege naturae: ratio, quia ut Christus hic innuit, omnium hominum cordibus naturaliter debebat esse impressa."

24. *De conscientia erronea*, Dupin, *1*, 638: "impossibile est quod aliqua res creata sit Lex vel regula, nisi a Lege prima, quae est voluntas divina."

25. I.e., that concerning the use of the term "common law." It should be noted that the tracts cited were written at different times over a period of thirty-one years (1385–1416), and cover subjects ranging from the right to vote at General Councils to an attack upon "false" prophets.

be reconciled with his philosophical rejection of any distinction between the will and intellect of God? The second: that even this internal consistency is not complete, for we have overlooked one obstinate text in which he equates natural law—at least analogically—with the natural powers or instincts of biological organisms.[26] The solution to difficulties of this sort is hardly to be found in works written with polemical objectives, and it is now necessary to turn our attention to his early theological writings.

III

Among these earlier theological works of d'Ailly only two devote much attention to questions concerning the nature of law—his disputation: *Utrum Petri ecclesia lege reguletur* [1] and his Commentary on the *Sentences* of Lombard [2]—but what they have to say is clear, comprehensive, and consistent. We find, in the first of these two works, a general analysis of the term law. This term is, he says, "common to all forms of law, but it is sometimes restricted to one prescribed type." [3] Sometimes it is taken to mean "the first law which is the uncreated law," defined by Augustine as the divine mind or will commanding that the natural order be followed and forbidding that it be disturbed. For it is clear that "just as the divine will is simply the first cause in the genus of efficient causes, so also is it simply the first law in the genus of obligating laws," and all laws depend

26. *Propositiones utiles,* Martène et Durand, 7, 910: d'Ailly argues that the Church has the authority to preserve its own unity, not only from Christ, "sed etiam communi jure naturali . . . . Patet, quia quodlibet corpus naturale naturaliter resistit suae divisioni et destructioni; et si sit corpus animatum, naturaliter congregat omnia membra omnesque vires suas ad conservandum suam unitatem, et repellendum suam divisionem: similique modo et quodlibet corpus civile, seu civilis communitas, vel politia rite ordinata."

1. In Dupin, *1,* 662–71.

2. The *principia* to the four books of the Sentences amount, if taken together, to a single and lengthy essay on law, and d'Ailly returns to the subject again in the fourteenth question of the first book.

3. Dupin, *1,* 663: "Et sic quamvis iste terminus *Lex* sit generalis ad omne Legem; tamen quandoque restringitur ad unam determinatam speciem."

for their validity upon it. Sometimes, on the other hand, law means merely the sign of the first law and is thus taken to mean created law. Even created law, however, can be divided into natural, human, and divine law, written and unwritten. D'Ailly restricts his comments on natural law to the reiteration of Cicero's statement that it is "the reason implanted by nature which orders that which is to be done, and forbids the contrary," [4] but he has more to say on the subject of divine law. This is taken to mean that law which is divinely inspired, such as the laws of Moses and Christ. And this, in turn, can be taken to mean either some one rule given by God which orders or forbids something, or a collection containing many such rules; thus Christ's whole doctrine can be spoken of as the law of Christ. But even if we take the divine law in this latter sense, it can still be understood in two different ways. In the first place, it can be taken to refer to such a collection containing only precepts and prohibitions; this is its more proper connotation, for "strictly speaking, these two alone pertain to law." More broadly, it can refer to a collection containing not only precepts and prohibitions, but also advice, permissions, historical testimony, parables, examples, and so on; and although these are not properly speaking of the essence of law "since they neither oblige nor bind," they do nevertheless play an ancillary rôle in that they help to sustain the divine law, and because of this are commonly regarded as being part of it.[5] Finally, having made

4. Ibid.: "Quandoque sumitur pro prima Lege quae est Lex increata. Et sic definit Augustinus Legem, Libro I, *De libero arbitrio*: 'Lex aeterna est summa ratio, cui semper obtemperandum est' etc, et XXII contra Faustum: 'Lex aeterna est divina mens seu voluntas, ordinem naturalem servari jubens, turbari vetans.' Unde patet quod sicut voluntas divina, est simpliciter prima causa in genere causae efficientis; sic ipse est Lex simpliciter prima in genere Legis obligantis. Quare, sicut nulla secunda causa potest agere, ipsa non agente; sic nulla Lex potest obligare, ipsa non obligante. . . . Quandoque vero sumitur Lex pro signo primae Legis, quod ex Lex creata. . . . Sed sic capiendo Legem pro Lege creata, adhuc quandoque sumitur generaliter pro qualibet tali Lege naturali humana vel divina; scripta vel non scripta. . . . Et sic definit Tullius, Libro *De Legibus*, quod 'Lex est ratio insita a natura, quae jubet quae sunt facienda, prohibetque contraria.' "

5. *Utrum Petri Ecclesia*, Dupin, *1*, 663: "Lex divina sumitur pro lege divinitus inspirata: qualis est Lex Moysis, vel Christi. Uno modo, potest sumi pro aliqua

some further precisions concerning the law of Christ—the most perfect of all created laws—and having insisted that the written or spoken word itself is not strictly law, d'Ailly admits, though grumbling that this is its "least proper" connotation, that law is sometimes taken to mean written law alone, as is the case, he adds, with Gratian and other jurists.[6]

This analysis, in the first place, posits a basic distinction between the first "uncreated law," which is the will of God, and all those "created laws," whether natural, divine, or human, which we have already encountered in d'Ailly's publicist works. In the second place, it gives us a clear indication of the hierarchical ordering of these laws. It will now be our object to examine the several stages of this hierarchy, from the first law down to the merely human, in the light of what d'Ailly says about them in the *Sentences,* where the above analysis is repeated word for word and serves as the pivot of a lengthy and more thorough discussion of the several categories of law.

Unfortunately, mention of the first law itself raises one of the difficulties already encountered, for how can d'Ailly equate this first and uncreated law with the will of God [7] when he has already rejected any distinction in God, including that between

---

una regula data a Deo aliquid praecipiente, vel prohibente. Alio modo, pro aliqua una congregatione plures tales regulas continente: qualiter tota doctrina Christi dicitur Lex Christi . . . . Sed sic capiendo, adhuc potest sumi stricte, pro aliqua tali congregatione solum continente Praecepta et prohibitiones; quia haec duo solum pertinent ad legem proprie dictam. Alio modo, potest sumi large pro aliqua tali congregatione non solum continente Praecepta et prohibitiones, sed etiam consilia et permissiones, testimonia historialia [etc.] . . . quae licet non sint de substantia Legis propriae, quia nec ligant, nec obligant eo quod his nihil imperatur, aut prohibetur: ipsa tamen sunt fortissima adjutoria ad Legem sustinendum."

6. Ibid., col. 663–65; his concluding remarks are: "Quod sicut vox audibilis non est Lex proprie, sic nec scriptura legibilis; sed solum aequivoce. Patet, quia vox, vel scriptura, Lex non dicitur, aut regula; nisi ea figura, vel tropo qua nomen rei et veritatis imagini imponitur, vel signo; sicut imago Regis, Rex dicitur. Patet: quia Juristae definientes Legem, definiunt eam secundum ejus minus propriam acceptationem: quia . . . Gratianus, et alii, solum definiunt Legem scriptam."

7. Or, as he calls it elsewhere, the eternal law (*Sent.* I, qu. 14, art. 2, M. f. 171v): "Licet voluntas divina sit lex aeterna" etc.

the divine will and intellect? The problem is not a new one for d'Ailly. We have already seen him cope with it in a different form when he hastened to assure us that the distinction between the absolute and ordained powers of God does not entail the existence in God of two powers, but is rather merely a way of speaking about God's modes of action.[8] Similarly in the present case, despite his reiterated insistence that "in God it is the same to will and to understand"[9] and that the divine will and intellect can be distinguished neither really nor formally, he does admit that to say that the divine will and intellect are distinguishable by reason, though not literally true, can be regarded as the abbreviated expression of something true. For "these terms [will and intellect], standing for the same thing, have diverse and distinct ideas [*rationes*] corresponding to them in the mind."[10] And if very properly we persist and go on to ask him why, then, he himself so consistently speaks of the divine *will* as being the first obligatory law, his reply is that to do so is most in accord with "the way of speaking of the saints and doctors." Because, according to this way of speaking, it is more correct to regard the divine will than the divine intellect as obligating law, since the divine will is the effective cause of things whereas the divine intellect is not, in that whatever that will decrees actually comes to pass, but not whatever that intellect comprehends.[11]

8. See above, p. 27.

9. *Princ. in I Sent.*, R. f. 26r: "cum in deo sit idem esse velle et intelligere."

10. *Sent.* I, qu. 6, art. 2, L, f. 97r: "Sicut deitas et divinus intellectus seu voluntas non distinguuntur realiter inter se. Sic nec proprie loquendo distinguntur ratione . . . . Tamen, licet de virtute sermonis non sit verum bene tamen quandoque gratia brevis locutionis conceditur ad bonum sensum quod intellectus divinus et voluntas distinguntur ratione—id est, isti termini supponentes pro eadem re habent diversae et distinctas rationes eis correspondentes in mente, et sic intelligunt doctores talem locutionem."

11. *Princ. in II Sent.*, G, f. 28 [B]v: "Tertia propositio est quod sit intellectus divinus est lex seu regula obligatoria etiam voluntas divina et e contra . . . . Quarta propositio non obstantibus praedictis est ista: quod secundum modum loquendi sanctorum et doctorum, magis proprie appropriatur voluntati divinae esse legem obligantem quam intellectui divino . . . quia . . . voluntas divina est causa effectiva rerum et non intellectus, ex eo quia quicquid voluntas vult est vel sit, et non quicquid intellectus intelligit."

D'Ailly is not being inconsistent, therefore, when he speaks of the divine will as being the first, eternal, uncreated law. As in all his discussions of the divine will, he goes on to distinguish between God's absolute and ordained powers. Moreover, although he is predominantly interested in the impact of this distinction upon the sphere of morality and of "obligating law," he does not ignore its implications for the world of nature—and indeed how could he? For it will be remembered that when we speak of God's power as absolute, we are considering it, according to d'Ailly, without keeping in mind either the indications apparent in the order of nature, or the details made known to us by divine revelation, and that, considered in this way, God can clearly do anything that does not imply contradiction.[12] It follows that although experience teaches us that no creature can create something else, or make something else *ex nihilo*, nevertheless of the absolute power of God this would be possible for it would involve no contradiction.[13] Similarly, although we normally assume that it is good to love God and bad to hate Him, nevertheless God could of His absolute power make it meritorious to hate Him, since He can ordain anything that does not imply contradiction,[14] and since acts are good and just or bad and unjust not of their own nature or essence, but simply because God has enjoined or forbidden them.[15] Therefore, although it is evidently impossible for God to hold a rational

12. See above, p. 27.

13. *Sent.* IV, qu. 1, art. 2, N, f. 188r: "Sciendum est quod sicut dicit quod deus aliquid potest de potentia absoluta, quod non potest de potentia ordinata, ita dico quod creatura. Ideo concedo probabiliter quod licet creatura de potentia naturali seu naturaliter ordinata non possit creare vel annihilare, ut dictum est, tamen ista potest de potentia simpliciter absoluta—scilicet supernaturaliter seu miraculose."

14. *Sent.* I, qu. 14, art. 3, T-U, f. 174v: (quoting with approval the argument of Ockham): "Ipse enim concedit nec reputat inconveniens quin voluntas creata possit meritorie deum odire, quia deus posset illud praecipere cum possit quicquid fieri non implicat contradictionem."

15. *Sent.* I, qu. 9, art. 2, R, f. 121v: "Dico quod nullum est bonum vel malum quod deus de necessitate sive ex nature rei diligat vel odiat . . . . Nec aliqua qualitas est ex natura rei justicia sed ex mera acceptione divina . . . [S, f. 122r] Nullus actus est meritorius vel demeritorius essentialiter et intrinsice, sed solum ex divina acceptatione vel deacceptatione"; cf. *Sent.*, I, qu. 14, art. 1, B, f. 167v, and also *Princ. in I Sent.*, E, f. 21v.

creature to disobey Him, it is not impossible for Him to order the same creature to hate Him, for whereas the former involves an evident contradiction, the latter does not.[16]

It has been necessary to introduce these somewhat remote considerations because the rigor of d'Ailly's position, with its emphasis on the transcendent omnipotence of God, demands them. It is, however, the ordained power of God which is more immediately relevant to questions concerning the existing divine and natural law. As we have seen,[17] when we speak of God's ordained power we can mean two things, His natural or His supernatural ordained power, the implication of the former being that as long as God refrains from suspending the presently-ordained world order, He will do only those things which by His ordination should be done. It is of this natural ordained power that d'Ailly most usually speaks, as indeed is indicated by his reiterated phrases equating the natural course of events with the divine ordination (*naturaliter vel de lege ordinata,* or *de communi lege et naturaliter,* or *de potentia naturali seu naturaliter ordinata* or *naturaliter . . . stante divina ordinatione*).[18] It is this natural mode of divine action which is the basis of that created law called the natural law—the term being used here to comprehend the scientific as well as the juridical concept. For when he is discussing the problem of whether any creature can create another, d'Ailly admits that God has ordained in things "such a natural law that one angel does not produce another."[19] It is important to note this interesting

---

16. *Princ. in I, Sent.,* H, f. 22v: "Evidenter enim est impossibile deum velle rationalem creaturam teneri ad non obediendum sibi: sed non sic est evidenter impossibile deum velle ipsam teneri ad odium sui, quia ad primum evidenter sequitur contradictio et non ad secundam . . . . Nam licet sit articulus Parisiensis quod aliquis posset mereri odiendo deum, error; tamen ex opposito non sequitur evidenter contradictio. Unde multi illum articulum restringunt ad potentiam dei ordinatam."

17. Above, pp. 27–28.

18. *De Trinitate,* Dupin, *1,* 619; *Sent.* I, qu. 1, art. 2, JJ, f. 96r; *Sent.* IV, qu. 1, art. 2, N, f. 188r; ibid., qu. 5, art. 3, QQ, f. 272r.

19. *Sent.* IV, qu. 1, art. 2, N, f. 188r: "Licet deus talem legem naturalem rebus ordinaverit quod unus angelus non producit alium angelum, tamen non apparet aliquae contradictio cur hoc non possit absolute, sicut ignis potest producere

185

statement, because it serves to underline the fact that he conceives the natural law to be that law which, so long as the present economy endures, runs throughout animate and inanimate, rational and nonrational creation, and because it helps to solve our second difficulty, which was raised by the seemingly inconsistent text in which d'Ailly clearly regarded the natural powers of a biological organism as relevant to the juridical natural law.[20]

His main preoccupation nevertheless is with the juridical concept of the natural law, and although this is closely analogous to the scientific concept,[21] its elucidation involves further distinctions. The divine will is of course the first law which obligates rational creatures, but the divine will can mean more than one thing. Properly speaking, he says, it signifies "the divine good pleasure which is nothing other than God himself willing." But it can be taken "improperly and metaphorically" —as is often the case in the scriptures—to refer not to the good pleasure or will of God, but to other things that are the signs of that will, such as the five listed in Lombard: precept, prohibition, counsel, permission, and fulfillment (*operatio*).[22] Not every-

---

ignem, cum sit perfectionis posse producere sibi simile, et angelus sit multo perfectioris speciei quam ignis." Cf. *Princ. in II Sent.*, A, f. 27r–27v, a somewhat rhetorical opening passage in which he speaks of "the laws of the heavens" and other laws which the Creator had imposed upon the world of nature.

20. Above, n. 26, p. 180.

21. A fact underlined again by the constant comparisons he makes between God's will as the first efficient cause and as the first obligating law. See, e.g., *Princ. in I Sent.*, D, f. 21r, and J, f. 23r: *Princ. in II Sent.*, J, f. 29r: *Princ. in IV Sent.*, L, f. 41v; *Sent.* I, qu. 14, art. 3, Q, f. 173r; *De conscientia erronea*, Dupin, *1*, 638.

22. *Sent.* I, qu. 14, art. 1, B, f. 167v: "Hoc nomen voluntas dei vel hoc totum voluntas dei quandoque sumitur proprie, et tunc signat divinum beneplacitum, quod non est aliud quam ipse deus volens. Quandoque vero sumitur improprie et metaphorice, et tunc supponit non pro beneplacito vel voluntate dei, sed pro aliquo alio quod est ejus signum . . . . Sic . . . aliqua quibus nobis voluntas quae deus est signatur vocantur in Scripturis divina voluntas. Et hujusmodi signa sunt praeceptum, consilium, prohibitio, operatio vel impletio, et permissio." Cf. *Princ. in I Sent.*, K, f. 23v. Cf. also Lombard, *Sent.* I, dist. 45, where he lists these five signs; PL, *142*, 643–44. They are also referred to in the *glossa ordinaria* to the *Decretals* (X, 1, 2, c. 1 in v. *Statuta*), and clearly enjoyed a long history, for the Puritan theologian William Ames (d. 1633) cites them in his *The Marrow of Sacred Divinity* (London, 1642), Bk. I, Ch. 7, § 54, p. 31.

thing that the divine will wishes is a law obliging the rational creature, but only "whatever the divine will wishes to be law." [23] Thus for example it can will the heavens to be moved, the sun to rise, and many other things to come to pass and yet clearly give rise to no obligation. For to be obliged is to be held bound either to behave or avoid behaving in a certain fashion or to possess or lack a certain disposition; this necessarily involves having from one's superior a precept or prohibition concerning some matter within the area of one's freedom of action.[24] As, therefore, obligation constitutes the distinguishing mark of law, and as, of the above-mentioned signs of the divine will, only the first two—precept and prohibition—are obligatory,[25] it must be concluded that only that which the divine will indicates by precept and prohibition is law. D'Ailly hastens to assure us that of His absolute power God could obligate a rational creature without the intermediary of any such created law, just as He can produce something without the intermediary of a secondary cause, but of His ordained power He can do so only by means of a created law, or in other words only by means of some signs which make known His obligatory will.[26]

As might be expected, these obligatory signs differ in kind;

23. *Sent.* I, qu. 14, art. 2, M, f. 172v: "Licet voluntas divina sit lex aeterna, et quicquid vult esse legem sit lex obligans creaturam rationalem ita quod creatura rationalis teneatur nihil velle contra voluntatem divinam, in quantum est lex, tamen non quicquid vult est lex."

24. *Princ. in I Sent.*, F, f. 21v: "divina voluntas aliquid vult esse vel fieri ad quod non sequitur aliquid obligari . . . quia vult coelum moveri, solem oriri . . . et sic de aliis multis ad quae non sequitur aliquid obligari"; and f. 22r: "Dico igitur quod obligari est teneri ad aliqualiter esse vel non esse; sive ad aliquam dispositionem habendum vel aliqua dispositione carendum. Sed teneri est habere a suo superiori prohibitionem vel praeceptum de aliquo existente in inferioris libera potestate. Istae autem descriptiones sunt terminorum declarationes, ideo non possunt probari, sed apparent rationabiles cuilibet recte intuente." These important definitions are reiterated later on in *Princ. in II Sent.*, O, f. 30v–31r.

25. See above, n. 5, p. 181.

26. *Princ. in I Sent.*, K, f. 23v: "Notandum est quod sicut voluntas divina quicquid potest producere, mediante causa secunda, potest producere se sola, sic ipsa de potentia absoluta posset rationalem creaturam obligare se sola . . . . Sed tamen ipsa de potentia ordinata non posset rationalem creaturam obligare nisi mediante aliqua lege creata. Hoc est per aliqua signa ex quibus sibi potest innotescere ipsa dei voluntas obligatoria."

the differences between them correspond to the differences between those created laws which are called natural and those which are called divine. For the natural law consists of those obligatory signs which are natural things, or naturally possessed.[27] Some of these natural signs, he tells us, spring immediately from nature "just as the first principles of morality which are known only by conscience [*sinderesim*] and the light of natural reason," that is to say, those moral principles such as "Render to each his own" to which anyone of sound mind naturally assents without recourse to the instruction of the learned. Other signs, such as the moral conclusions drawn from these axioms solely by means of a process of natural reasoning, come from nature only in a mediate way; these would include, for instance, the moral doctrines of the Gentile philosophers. It is of these latter signs that St. Paul is thinking when he speaks of the Gentiles who do not have the law but "who do by nature the things contained in the law." [28]

Statements as unblushingly rationalistic as these might well incline us to question the impact of d'Ailly's fundamental voluntarism on his natural-law thinking, just as others have felt impelled to query the extent to which Ockham before him "carried his metaphysics over into his theory of law." [29] But d'Ailly himself fully realized the danger of misunderstanding on this point and moved swiftly to avert it. He did so by repeating for our benefit an argument which had already been raised against his reiterated insistence on the primacy of the divine will in the sphere of obligating law.

27. *Princ. in I Sent.*, L, f. 23v: "Prima differentia est quod signorum divinae voluntatis quaedam sunt naturalia seu naturaliter habita, alia sunt supernaturalia et supernaturaliter data."

28. *Princ. in I Sent.*, L, ff. 23v–24r: "Signorum vero naturalium quaedam sunt a natura immediate: sicut prima principia moralia solum per sinderesim et lumen naturalis rationis habita. Alia sunt a natura mediate; sicut conclusiones morales mediantibus dictis principiis sola naturali ratiocinatione dictate. Sub primo membro continentur illa principia moralia quibus unusquisque compos mentis naturaliter assentit absque eruditione doctorum, ut quod cuilibet reddendum est quod suum est . . . . Sed sub secundo membro continentur doctrinae morales gentilium philosophorum . . . et de hujusmodi signis dicit Apostolus, Rom. II, quod gentes quae legem non habent, naturaliter quae legis sunt faciunt."

29. Thus George H. Sabine, *A History of Political Theory* (2nd ed., New York, 1959), p. 306.

The argument—bolstered, significantly enough, with an appeal to the authority of Aquinas—is a lengthy one, but its gist may be summarized as follows: Every rational creature possesses (in the natural law or law of reason indelibly stamped on his heart) a knowledge of the immutable principles of morality, so that it is impossible to sin mortally or to commit any offense against the divine will and not at the same time offend against the dictates of the natural law and of right reason.[30] And d'Ailly's reply is a revealing one. He comments that although much might be said about such a way of reasoning, he will limit himself to the remark that it in no way clashes with his own position so long as one keeps in mind the fundamental distinction between the absolute and ordained powers of God. The argument in question proves nothing more than that a rational creature de potentia ordinata cannot sin either by deed or omission against the will of God and not at the same time against the dictate of reason or the law of nature or of some other created law; this, he says, he is perfectly willing to concede. At the same time, such a view must not be taken to deny that de potentia absoluta it is quite possible for a rational creature to sin against the divine will and yet in no way to contravene the dictate of any created law whatsoever.[31]

Thus despite all the talk about the rule of reason in morality we must not get the idea that there is anything final about right reason. The ultimate priority lies with the divine will and though d'Ailly himself never put it quite so bluntly he would have had no difficulty in agreeing with Ockham's statement that it is only "by the very fact that the divine will wishes it that right reason dictates what is to be willed"; [32] the implication is that if de potentia absoluta God were to will otherwise, right

30. *Princ. in II Sent.*, P, f. 31r.

31. Ibid., f. 31v: "sed licet circa haec multa possent dici, tamen breviter dico quod ista nullo modo sunt contra me. Unde primo concedo quod de potentia ordinata non stat creaturam rationalem peccare, vel committere aut omittere, contra divinum velle et non contra dictamen rationis seu legis naturae, aut alterius legis creatae. Et nihil plus probant rationes praedictae . . . . Secundo, non obstantibus istis, concedo quod de potentia absoluta stat creaturam rationalem peccare et committere vel omittere contra divinum velle et non contra dictamen alicujus legis creatae."

32. Ockham, *Sent.* I, dist. xli, qu. 1, K.

reason could lose it proud rôle as the natural and infallible sign of His obligating law. It should not surprise us, then, if d'Ailly can conclude that since in the presently-ordained economy *morally* correct action is nothing other than action in conformity with the dictate of reason, then correct action of this type is possible through purely natural means and without the help of grace.[33] Nor should we be surprised when he goes on to say that in this same economy no man can act correctly *in a simple and absolute sense* unless, possessing grace, he acts in conformity with the divine law.[34] For with this statement d'Ailly has moved on from the naturally ordained order to a consideration of the supernatural.

When we speak of God as acting according to His ordained power in this sense, we mean that God may do anything that His absolute power permits Him to do, provided only that it does not contradict the truth of the divine law or scripture.[35] In accordance with this, d'Ailly tells us that in addition to the natural there are also supernatural signs of the divine will.[36] These are of two kinds: some of them are immediately from God, that is to say given by God alone, such as the doctrine that Christ Himself personally taught; others are only in a mediate way from God, that is to say divinely revealed by means of an angel or of a faultless man, such as, for instance, the Mosaic law, or the doctrine of Christ in the sense of those things that the apostles and disciples taught on His authority.[37] It is these

33. *Sent.* I, qu. 2, art. 2, M, f. 62v: "aliquis potest stante lege per pura naturalia sine gratia moraliter recte agere. Patet quia per recte agere moraliter nihil aliud intelligo nisi agere conformiter dictamini rationis."

34. Ibid.: "nullus homo potest stante lege [i.e. *de potentia ordinata*] per pura naturalia sine gratia recte agere simpliciter et absolute . . . nisi quod agit conformiter legi divinae. Sed nullus sic agit nisi sit in gratia *secundum legem statutam*" (italics mine).

35. See above, p. 27.

36. See above, n. 27, p. 188.

37. *Princ. in I Sent.*, L, f. 24r: "Signorum autem supernaturalium quaedem sunt a deo immediate: scilicet a solo deo data sicut doctrina Christi quoad illa quae ipsa docuit in propria persona . . . . Alia sunt deo mediate, scilicet mediante angelo vel homine puro divinitus revelata, sicut lex Moisi, doctrina Christi quoad illa quae docuerunt apostoli et discipuli ejus auctoritate sua; et similiter determinatio ecclesiae dei a spiritu sancto inspirata."

supernatural signs which constitute the divine law, and of them, it is the law or doctrine of Christ that constitutes the most perfect sign of the divine will "which itself is the most perfect law of the rational creature." [38]

A great amount of attention has been paid in our discussion to the divine will and to its signs, those created laws which are called natural and divine. It should be emphasized that this reflects d'Ailly's own preoccupation with these superior signs of the divine will, rather than with the nature of those other created signs, the positive laws he cites so often in his publicist works. This is—one must insist—an understandable preoccupation for a man whose main concern is with the establishment of the existence of a higher law to which all human laws are subject. His further remarks, which concern the lower stages of the legal hierarchy, are therefore much more limited in scope and much less coherently developed; but their significance far outweighs their bulk. They serve to give us a precious indication of the extent to which his theological voluntarism found its counterpart in a form of legal positivism, and also to reveal the importance of his philosophy of law as one of the routes via which purely theological considerations were able to make deep inroads upon his political thinking.

In his publicist works d'Ailly gave the impression (in the absence of any definitive statement on the issue) that he regarded the will of a properly constituted law-making authority as of the essence of positive or human law.[39] Unfortunately, the much-needed definitive statement is not to be found in his theological works either, for his attention is focussed there on other issues. But these writings do betray some evidence which may serve to strengthen the impression already conveyed. In discussing the divine law, d'Ailly told us that obligation is the distinguishing mark of law; he felt it necessary, therefore, to state what he meant by obligation. His definition is an interesting one. To be

38. *Princ. in I Sent.*, K, f. 23v: "Sicut divina voluntas est lex perfectissima rationalis creaturae, sic lex Christi vel doctrina est signum perfectissimum voluntatis divinae."

39. See above, p. 176.

obliged is to be held to do something or not to do it, and "to be held is to have *a precept or prohibition from one's superior*" concerning some matter on which one is free to act.[40] This definition certainly reflects an unambiguously voluntarist or positivist approach to the natural and divine laws, which as we have already seen are merely signs of the divine will; it would also seem to entail a similar approach to purely human enactments. It is impossible to be absolutely certain on this point, for d'Ailly nowhere pauses to deal with it specifically, but if we take this definition together with the statements he made in his publicist works it seems legitimate to conclude that he regarded the will of a superior, expressed in the form of a command to do something or not to do it, as the constitutive moment of positive law, since it is this expressed will that creates obligation.

Such a conclusion is based on the assumption that d'Ailly regarded his definition of obligation as valid generally of all forms of law, and this assumption is clearly a sound one, for it is also made by one of the opponents whose arguments he cites in the *Sentences;* d'Ailly himself, in replying, does not reject it. But he does reject the corollary argued by his opponent, and in so doing reveals very clearly the extent to which theological considerations dominate his whole thinking on law, and the precise manner in which they do so. The opponent's whole argument pivots upon d'Ailly's definition of obligation. From this definition, the opponent maintains, it follows that even in the absence of any divine command, the command of a human authority can by itself give rise to obligation. For if it were otherwise, we would be forced to say that all obligation stems from God, and this would be false.[41] He supports this contention with several reasons, two of which deserve our attention. The first is that just as there are forms of civil dominium which cannot be said to spring from the divine law, so also are there similar forms of

40. See above, n. 24, p. 187.

41. *Princ. in II Sent.,* N. f. 30r–30v: Here d'Ailly describes his opponent's argument and replies, "Primo, quia stat aliquid a creatura potente obligare praecipi, et illud non praecipi a deo. Igitur etc. Consequentia tenet, ut dicit per descriptionem meam de obligari, et antecedens probat, quia aliter omnis obligatio esset de jure divino, quod est falsum." Cf. *Princ. in III Sent.,* K, f. 36r.

obligation which are of purely human provenance. Second, that forms of obligation proceeding from divine sources on the one hand and human sources on the other simply do not coincide, for since an obligation emanating from the divine will is fully and perfectly obligatory, no merely human obligation can confirm it or add anything to it, and would therefore be superfluous.[42]

D'Ailly is unconvinced, if not unmoved, by this line of reasoning and replies that it is impossible to be obligated to do something by the just command of a created authority and not to have from God a similar command to do the same thing. But this, he quickly adds, is not to imply that all forms of obligation any more than all forms of dominium spring from the divine law alone. It is not normally accepted usage to speak of forms of obligation or of dominium as being *de jure divino* simply because they are sustained by God's approving will—since, otherwise, anything could be said to be *de jure divino*—and we normally stress instead their purely human roots.[43] Nor would it be proper for us to dismiss as superfluous a human form of obligation which coincides with the divine, since if we were to do so we would also have to dismiss as superfluous a second cause which cooperates with the divine causality.[44]

42. *Princ. in II Sent.*, N. f. 30v: "Secundo, aliquid est civile dominium quod non est de jure divino. Igitur etiam et obligatio etc. . . . Quinto, ad invicem non concurrunt humana obligatio et divina. Igitur etc. Antecedens patet, quia perfecte ad aliquid obligatus, scilicet obligatione divina, amplius ad illud obligari non potest . . . . Unde, si divinae obligationi potest succedere alia obligatio, cum illa primam non confirmaret nec intenderet, videtur quod superflueret." For the meaning of *dominium*, see Ch. 3.

43. Note that elsewhere (*Princ. in II Sent.*, K, f. 30v) d'Ailly speaks of the divine will as "radix obligationis."

44. Ibid.: "Dico quod ex hoc non sequitur quod omnis obligatio sit de jure divino, et concedo quod sicut est aliquid civile dominium quod non solum dici de jure divino, ita etiam de aliqua obligatione. Quia secundum modum loquendi communem, aliqua obligatio vel aliquid dominium, non dicitur de jure divino, quia sit a deo approbante, nam sic quodlibet esset de jure divino, sed ex alia radice hoc dicitur. . . . Nec valet quod dicit: scilicet quod si divinae obligationi posset succedere alia obligatio cum illam, primam non confirmaret nec intenderet, quod ergo superflueret. Nam consimili modo probaretur quod si divinae causalitati coageret aliqua causa secunda, quod illa causa superflueret." Cf. *Princ. in III Sent.*, L, f. 36v, where he repeats the argument.

The complexity of this difficult argumentation should not blind us to its true import, nor should we overlook the significance of these brief allusions to dominium and to secondary causality. Throughout his whole discussion of "created" law —of whatever variety—d'Ailly has been concerned to emphasize its total subordination to the will of God, for the divine will is "the first law from which every created law is derived," [45] and it is impossible "for any created thing to be a law or rule unless it is consonant with the divine will." [46] Or again, as "the divine will is the most perfect law obliging the rational creature, so also among created laws that one is more perfect which is more perfectly the sign of the divine will." [47] So that when it comes down to that variety of created law which is purely human, it must perforce be concluded that "no edict of a prince, precept of a prelate, political statute or ecclesiastical decree is just, or justly obligatory, unless it is in conformity with the divine will." [48]

Such statements constitute a forceful reiteration of the voluntarism that is fundamental to so much of d'Ailly's thinking, but it is only in the light of the exchange of views at which we have just glanced that their precise import becomes apparent.

When, in his discussion of dominium, d'Ailly had admitted that parental succession or popular election are regarded here on earth as the proper credentials for civil dominium, he had added that the value of such "created titles" is wholly contingent upon the concurrence of the divine will. This was no merely

45. *Sent.* I, qu. 14, art, 3, Q, f. 173r: "voluntas divina sit prima lex a qua derivatur omnis lex creata."

46. *Princ. in I Sent.*, D, f. 21r: "impossibile est quod aliqua res creata sit lex vel regula nisi sit divinae voluntati consona . . . ."; cf. *Sent.* I, qu. 14, art. 3, Q, f. 173r where d'Ailly comments that any law not derived from the divine will "non est proprie lex sive regula nisi forte secundum quid et non simpliciter sicut lex injusta" etc.

47. *Sent.* I, qu. 14, art. 3, Q, f. 173r: "sicut voluntas divina est lex perfectissima obligatoria rationalis creaturae, sic inter leges creatas illa est perfectior quae est perfectius signum voluntatis divinae."

48. *Princ. in I Sent.*, E, f. 21v: "Ex quo sequitur quod nullum principis edictum, praelati praeceptum, politice statutum aut Ecclesiae decretum est justum vel juste obligatorium, nisi sit divinae legi consonum."

routine bow in the general direction of St. Paul, for he had gone on to say that the approving will of God, even without the coincidence of such titles, is cause sufficient to confer dominium upon anyone.[49] This is directly analogous to what he has had to say about obligation; in that realm also, although we can be obligated by purely human laws, that, too, presupposes the sustaining concurrence of the divine will, so much so that it is possible for God to obligate us directly and without the intermediary of any created law whatsoever.[50] In both cases d'Ailly invoked the further analogy of natural causality. God, the First Cause, is Lord-Creator of all things, and "just as every secondary cause is contingent upon the First Cause, so from the First and Supreme dominium is derived every secondary dominium." [51] Similarly, "just as the divine will is the first efficient cause in the genus of efficient causality, so also is it the first obligatory rule or law in the genus of obligating law." [52]

These arguments are revealing—the more so in that d'Ailly himself points to the analogies which exist among them—for beneath the surface of them all, and even projecting on occasion beyond the surface, is that familiar nominalist distinction between the absolute and ordained powers of God which is fundamental to the whole of his theology and to much of his philosophy. What he is in fact insisting, in the course of these complex and convoluted arguments, is, once again, that de potentia absoluta God can do anything that does not involve contradiction. Within that unconditioned realm created titles, created laws, created causes—all of these are dissolved into nothing in the blaze of the divine omnipotence. Within that realm dominium is conferred and withdrawn, creatures are obligated

49. See above, pp. 85–86, and notes 33 and 34, where the texts are cited.

50. See above, n. 26, p. 187.

51. See *De legitimo dominio*, Dupin *1*, 642.

52. *Sent.* I, qu. 14, art. 3, Q. f. 173r: "sicut voluntas divina in genere efficientis est prima efficiens causa, sic ipsa in genere legis obligantis est prima lex seu regula obligatoria." Cf. *Princ. in II Sent.*, J, f. 29r: "sicut nulla res creata habet ex se potentia causandi, sic nulla lex creata habet ex se potestatem obligandi. Nam sicut dicit Apostolus ad Romanos, 13: 'Non est potestas nisi a deo.' Igitur, sicut sola divina voluntas est prima causa independens in causando, sic ipsa est prima lex independens in obligando." Cf. also, above, n. 21, p. 186.

and released from obligation, physical effects are produced and suspended, and all these things are done by simple fiat, without any recourse to human titles, human laws, or secondary causes. But this is not to say that such created titles, laws, or causes are wholly superfluous. Once we turn back across the frontier into the realm in which the ordained power holds sway, we find that God condescends to work through them, and by His approbation to endow them with efficacy. Thus, by the ordained laws God freely associates de facto with His approving will "many created circumstances or titles" which we rightly take, therefore, to be the criteria of just dominium.[53] Or similarly, He limits Himself in such a way that He cannot oblige a rational creature except by means of a created law.[54] Or again, He limits Himself to the producing of a natural effect not directly but only by means of a secondary cause, and this is to say that "He not only produces that effect, but also makes the second cause to be the cause of that effect," so that it is even possible to assert that such a second cause produces such an effect *ex natura rei!* [55]

The worlds of law and politics, then, are impregnated with the divine will just as much as is the physical world of nature. Command lies at the heart of law at every stage of the legal hierarchy, but the validity of the command of any human law-making authority is completely dependent upon its conformity with the will of God. It follows that d'Ailly's philosophy of law is a logical consequence of his basic theological assumptions. This philosophy finds its full expression in two of his earlier theological works, but as we have seen it is echoed throughout his publicist writings. It serves, even more than his teaching on dominium, to link his political views—the product, as they must

53. See above, p. 86, n. 33.
54. See above, n. 26, p. 187.
55. *Sent.* IV, qu. 1, art. 1, E, f. 185r: "Prima [propositio] est quod quandocumque deus facit aliquem effectum mediante causa secunda, ipse non solum facit illum effectum, sed etiam facit causam secundam esse causam illius effectus"; ibid., F, f. 185v: "Sequitur octava propositio quod licet omnis causa secunda proprie dicta causet effectum ex natura rei, tamen quod ipsa sit causa proprie dicta non est ex natura rei quia solum ex voluntate dei."

be, of the exercise of natural reason in a radically contingent world [56]—with his general theological position. And like his teaching on dominium, his theory of law belongs to that stream of voluntarist thinking, the legal implications of which have to so great an extent escaped the notice of historians of political thought, which found perhaps its clearest expression in the writings of Ockham, and which made its way, with profound effect, into the realms of ethics, law, and even of natural science.[57]

56. See above, p. 33.
57. For an attempt to prove this last point see Oakley, "Laws of Nature."

7.

Sources and Influence

Questions concerning the source or sources of an author's ideas or the influence which his ideas have themselves exerted upon the thinking of others are rarely easy to handle, but they take on added complexity if the author happens to be a medieval one. Pride will not prevent his borrowing from earlier authors— freely, without change, and perhaps at length. Nor will any craven scruple necessarily betray him into indicating the source of his plunder. He may, of course, cite authors very freely, but if he does so, as often as not he is relying less upon their ideas than upon the reassuring support of their names,[1] the surface froth of citation and quotation perhaps having the added dis- advantage of concealing the true source of his own ideas or even of obscuring their originality. The discussion which follows can make no claim to have answered all or even most of the ques- tions that might be raised about the sources of d'Ailly's ideas or about the historical fate of those ideas. I have confined myself, instead, to the modest task of establishing the main lines of d'Ailly's indebtedness and influence, and in doing so I have restricted attention almost wholly to instances of dependence

---

1. It was not without reason that authority was said to have a nose of wax.

clearly identifiable by conscious citation and commendation or by verbatim copying.

I

D'Ailly's works contain a wealth of citation. The authors whom he presses into service range from Justinian to Gratian, from Virgil and Ovid to Augustine and Jerome, from Plato, Aristotle, Cicero, and Boethius to Grosseteste, Aquinas, Scotus, and Ockham.[2] His citation of the classical authors and of the Fathers may well represent nothing more than the plunderings of *florilegia,* but the use he makes of canonistic sources, ecclesiastical histories, medieval pastoral and publicistic writings, and the scholastic theologians indicates a first-hand knowledge of a considerable number of such works. Few of them, however, are cited in more than one or two of his many writings.[3] These are Aristotle, Aquinas, the *Corpus juris canonici,* and the Latin Fathers (especially St. Augustine). And it is necessary to distinguish even among these. Although their names bulk so large in his writing, d'Ailly owes very little directly to Aquinas, Aristotle, or Augustine, whereas he is heavily indebted to Ockham, whose name he rarely mentions, and to John of Paris, whose name he never mentions at all. Similarly, although in the last analysis he rejects Richard Fitzralph's doctrine of dominium as

2. In one of his earliest works, the *Principium in cursum Bibliae* (1374), d'Ailly cites, among others, Aristotle, Augustine, Avicenna, Boethius, Cassiodorus, Cicero, Juvenal, Livy, Orosius, Ovid, Quintilian, Seneca, Virgil, the *Corpus Juris Civilis,* the *Corpus Juris Canonici* and, of course, the Bible; in Dupin, *1,* 610–17. A comparable diversity occurs in his last major work, the *Tractatus de ecclesiastica potestate,* Dupin, 2, 925–60, where he refers, among others, to Alexander of Hales, Aquinas, Aristotle, Augustine, Eusebius, Isidore of Seville, Maurice of Prague, the *Corpus Juris Canonici,* several of its glossators, and the Bible. Here, as in so many of his polemical works, the canonistic citations bulk far larger than any other—over one hundred and fifty in comparison with roughly fifty Biblical references.

3. Thus his references to the *Verbum abbreviatum* of the Parisian theologian Peter Cantor (d. 1197) are confined almost wholly to the *Tractatus de materia,* below, pp. 255 ff. For a discussion of the work, see E. M. Sanford, "The *Verbum abbreviatum* of Petrus Cantor," *Transactions and Proceedings of the American Philological Association, 74* (1943), 33–48.

contingent upon grace, his whole approach to the subject is colored by that doctrine.[4] But the very bulk of his citations of particular sources is not always misleading, and if the main lines of his indebtedness run straight to William of Ockham and to John of Paris, they also run—through these writers as well as independently—to the canonists

There is no doubt that d'Ailly's general theological position approximates very closely the views of Ockham, and his dependence on the English philosopher, which has often been noted,[5] is underlined by his laudatory references and quotations. He speaks, for example, of Ockham as having handled "very nicely" the question of the divine ideas,[6] and though his philosophy of law is in some ways more fully elaborated than that of Ockham, its broad dependence on Ockhamist views is indisputable and is well illustrated by his approving citation of the notorious argument that God could make it meritorious even for men to hate Him.[7] With this in mind, and taking into account also d'Ailly's citation of the *Dialogus* in his refutation of Fitzralph's doctrine of dominium,[8] it is natural to assume that d'Ailly's indebtedness to Ockham extends into the realm of those ecclesiastico-political views which have been our primary concern.

The question of the source of these views, however, can hardly be discussed in isolation from the larger question of the

4. Fitzralph, who was himself heir to a tradition of thinking going back to Aegidius of Rome, is cited in four of d'Ailly's works and plays a large rôle in his *De legitimo dominio* (Dupin, *1*, 641–46), and his *Utrum doctus in jure divino* (ibid., col. 646–62). See above, Ch. 3.

5. Tschackert, *Ailli*, p. 304; Salembier, *Cardinal*, pp. 291–98; Maurice de Wulf, *Histoire de la Philosophie Médiévale* (Paris, 1947), *3*, 150–51; C. Michalski, "Les courants philosophiques à Oxford et a Paris pendant le XIVe siècle," *Bulletin de l'Académie polonaise des Sciences et des Lettres*, 1920, printed separately (Cracow, 1921), p. 24, and "Le criticisme et le scepticisme dans la philosophie du XIVe siècle," ibid., 1925, printed separately (Cracow, 1926), p. 72.

6. *Sent.* I, qu. 6, art. 3, T, f. 99v.

7. *Sent.* I, qu. 14, art. 3, T-U, f. 174v. In the lengthy table of contents to this edition of the *Sentences*, the remark *Recitatur opinio Ockham et commendatur* occurs more than once.

8. *Utrum indoctus in jure divino* (Dupin, *1*, 650 and 653), where he cites *Dialogus*, III, II, I, caps. 25 and 27; Goldast, *2*, 896–98, 899–900. Cf. above, Ch. 3, n. 16, p. 80.

source of Conciliar theory in general. Early writers on this problem—such as Kneer and Bliemetzrieder [9]—concentrated almost exclusively on the task of relating the ideas of the Conciliarists to the immediate problems involved by the outbreak of the Schism, and if this approach were the only one, it would be our task simply to ascertain the extent to which d'Ailly's views are actually his own solutions to the problems facing the Church, and not merely the reiteration of the views of Conrad of Gelnhausen and Henry of Langenstein, who expressed their Conciliar theories first. We would not find it difficult to detect d'Ailly's individual reactions to events, for they are evident in his vacillations concerning the respective practical merits as a means for ending the Schism of the "ways" of compromise and of a General Council,[10] and in his shifts of opinion on more minor points such as the proper position of the Cardinalate in the Church,[11] or the right to vote and the manner of voting at the Council.[12] We would also discover that d'Ailly's general reaction was remarkably similar to that of Conrad of Gelnhausen and of Henry of Langenstein. It would, however, be unsatisfactory to stop at this point and to explain this similarity simply in terms of d'Ailly's dependence upon these earlier writers, for there is little indication that he borrowed anything from them.[13] Moreover,

9. A. Kneer, *Die Entstehung der Konziliaren Theorie*, Römische Quartalschrift, Erstes Supplementheft (Rome, 1893); F. Bliemetzrieder, *Das General Konzil im Grossen Abendländischen Schisma* (Paderborn, 1904); for a useful collection of early Conciliar texts and a discussion of their interconnections, see also his *Literarische Polemik zu Beginn des Grossen Abendländischen Schismas* (Wien und Leipzig, 1909); H. X. Arquillière, "L'appel au concile sons Philippe le Bel et la genèse des théories conciliares," *Revue des questions historiques, 45* (1911), 23–24.

10. See Salembier, *Cardinal*, pp. 108–12, 157 ff.

11. See above, p. 124.

12. See above, p. 152.

13. M. Spinka, *Advocates of Reform* (London, 1953), pp. 95 and 103, has alleged that the *Tractatus super reformatione*, d'Ailly's redaction of the third part of his *Tractatus de materia* (see below, pp. 314 ff.) is "wholly dependent upon the last part of Langenstein's *Epistola Concilii Pacis*." In this, Spinka has the support of Kneer, p. 82, and also of Tschackert, *Ailli*, p. 273. A comparison of the two works, however, reveals no apparent borrowings. It is true that d'Ailly mentions most of the ecclesiastical evils and potential remedies listed by Langenstein, but then there was nothing new about such abuses as clerical pluralism, nonresidence, and irresponsibility, which were enduring weaknesses in the medieval Church.

when we push the inquiry somewhat further, we find that many
of the positions to which all three Conciliarists inclined had, as
Hirsch pointed out, been adopted long before by Marsilius of
Padua and William of Ockham, and that at least some of the
similarities in their works are explicable in terms of their common dependence upon Ockham.[14]

D'Ailly's Conciliar sympathies, as well as his philosophical
predilections, would seem then to point to Ockham as an important source of his ecclesiastico-political ideas. In fact, the dependence of these ideas upon Ockham, which is very striking, has
often been remarked.[15] We ourselves have already had occasion
to note several instances of his borrowings from Ockham's *Dialogus*,[16] and his interest in this tract is further attested by the
fact that early in his career he went to the trouble of drawing
up an *Abbreviatio dialogi Okam*—a somewhat sparse synopsis of
Ockham's work, garnished with scattered comments of his own,
and serving no doubt as a useful index to that long and complex
discourse.[17] In his early scholastic disputations it is upon the fifth
book of the *Dialogus* that d'Ailly draws most heavily, sometimes

---

D'Ailly did not need Langenstein to point them out to him, any more than the
Tridentine Fathers needed to have read d'Ailly's own tract in order to discern
the importance of correcting the same evils. The extent to which d'Ailly anticipated the reforming decrees of the Council of Trent can be gauged by a glance
at the footnotes to Part III of the *Tract. de mat.*, where the parallels are noted
(see below, pp. 325–35).

14. K. Hirsch, *Die Ausbildung der Konziliaren Theorie im XIV Jahrhundert*
(Vienna, 1903), pp. 20–33, 41–54, 73 ff. The borrowings of Conrad and Henry from
Ockham are clearly discernible and have been noted not only by Hirsch, but also
by Kneer, p. 56, K. Wenck, "Konrad von Gelnhausen und die Quellen der Konziliaren Theorie," *Historische Zeitschrift*, 76 (1896), 32–35, and J. Haller, *Papsttum
und Kirchenreform* (Berlin, 1903), pp. 342–43.

15. Tschackert, *Ailli*, p. 43; Wenck, pp. 34–35; Hirsch, p. 84; Haller, pp. 342–43;
Salembier, *Alliaco*, passim; V. Martin, *Les origines du Gallicanisme* (Paris, 1939),
I, 347, and his "Comment c'est formée la doctrine de la supériorité du concile
sur le pape," *Revue des sciences religieuses*, 17 (1937), 288.

16. Above, Ch. 3, p. 80; Ch. 5, pp. 141 ff.; Ch. 6, pp. 177–79; this chapter, n. 8,
p. 200.

17. Unprinted. Paris, Bibl. Nat., *Ms. Lat.* 14,579, ff. 88v–101v. *Incipit*: "Dya-
logus doctoris venerabilis magistri Guillermi Okam tres tractatus continet." *Explicit*: "Abbreviatio dyalogi Okam quam fecit magister Petrus de Alliaco,
episcopus Cameracensis et postea cardinalis." Salembier, *Cardinal*, p. 369, dates it
between 1372 and 1395.

word for word; [18] and this is no accident for this particular section of Ockham's work has been described as the section most influential for later Conciliar thinking.[19] In his last major work, however—the *Tractatus de ecclesiastica potestate* which he read to the Council of Constance in October 1416—d'Ailly draws upon the third part of the *Dialogus,* and it is here that he is most unambiguously dependent upon Ockham. Almost the whole of his extensive discussion concerning papal election is taken from the *Dialogus,* without acknowledgment, but in many passages verbatim.[20] Nor is this the sum of his borrowings from Ockham in this tract; in another place he goes on to repeat Ockham's arguments concerning the disposition of the right to elect the Pope in the event of the normal electors having failed to fulfill their duty.[21]

In his theology d'Ailly was indebted to Ockham more than to any other single thinker, and, if we take it as a whole, we may say the same of his legal and political thinking. Certainly the names of the two men were linked together by later writers; the French nominalist and Conciliarist, Jacques Almain,[22] for ex-

18. Thus, compare *Utrum Petri ecclesia lege reguletur,* Dupin, *1,* 666–67, with *Dialogus,* I, V, caps. 12–13, and 25–31; Goldast, 2, 481–83 and 494–503; also Dupin, *1,* 668–69, with *Dial.* I, V, cap. 21; Goldast, 2, 488–89; also Dupin, *1,* 669–71, with *Dial.* I, V, caps. 24–25; Goldast 2, 492–95; also *Utrum Petri ecclesia rege gubernetur,* Dupin, *1,* 689, with *Dial.* I, V, cap. 25; Goldast, 2, 494.

19. Brian Tierney, "Ockham, the Conciliar Theory, and the Canonists," *Journal of the History of Ideas, 15* (1954), 66.

20. Some of these strikingly similar texts are printed in parallel by Roberts, "Pierre d'Ailly," pp. 140–42. The relevant section of d'Ailly's, *Abbreviatio,* is printed below, Appendix II, p. 243. Roberts (p. 136) states that "the argument had been noted at some length and largely in Ockham's own words in d'Ailly's *Abbreviatio . . . .* Thence, apparently, he transferred it, practically untouched, to his tract *De potestate ecclesiastica.*" Comparison of the texts reveals, however, that this is not the case, for d'Ailly took more (verbatim) from the *Dialogus* than he had included in his *Abbreviatio.* If he used the *Abbreviatio,* he used it only as a guide to the original from which he drew his material directly. The same also seems to hold true of his borrowings from *Dial.* I, V; see above, n. 18.

21. Dupin, 2, 932; *Dial.* III, II, III, caps. 11 ff.; Goldast, 2, 941 ff.; cf. *Abbreviatio,* f. 101v.

22. Almain (d. 1515) has attracted less attention than he deserves and his name is well-nigh forgotten today. For a brief biographical sketch, see *Dict. de théol. catholique,* s.v. "Almain, Jacques."

ample, repeatedly cited d'Ailly's works, along with those of Gerson and John of Paris, in his commentary on Ockham.[23] While d'Ailly's dependence on Ockham is admitted and overt, and was already recognized in his own day, it is to Almain that the credit must go for indicating his borrowings from John of Paris, whose name, to my knowledge, d'Ailly never even mentions.[24] The influence of John's teaching on the kingship of Christ is evident in one of d'Ailly's early disputations,[25] but it was only when he came to write his *Tractatus de ecclesiastica potestate*—the most complete statement of his Conciliar views—that this influence became preponderant. In that work, four long passages are dependent both in thought and language upon John's earlier tract. We have already had occasion to examine three of these passages: that which concerns the relation of the ecclesiastical authority to temporal power and temporal possessions,[26] that which defines the authority of the Pope over the goods of clerics and laymen,[27] and that which concerns the form of government appropriate to the Church.[28] This last one constitutes a good warning against taking medieval citations at their face value, for d'Ailly is ostensibly arguing at firsthand on the basis of Aristotle's classification of policies, whereas in fact he is to a considerable extent merely repeating the words of John of Paris, who in turn (though he too does not acknowledge the fact) was drawing much of his material from Aquinas. Almain indicates a fourth dependent passage when he tells us, quite correctly, that the classification of ecclesiastical powers which constitutes

23. *Expositio circa decisiones magistri Guillielmi Occam,* Dupin, 2, 1015, 1047, and esp. 1078–79, where, linking d'Ailly's views with those of Ockham, he cites them at length against Fitzralph's doctrine of dominium. See also his *Tractatus de authoritate Ecclesiae et Conciliorum generalium,* Dupin, 2, 980 and 1011.

24. See Almain, *Tract. de auth. eccl.,* Dupin, 2, 980: "De aliis autem Potestatibus Ecclesiasticis a coërcitiva, quas optime declarat Joannes de Parisiis, et consequenter Petrus de Alliaco, in hoc Tractatu nihil dicere intendo"; cf. Dupin, 2, 1047.

25. *Utrum Petri ecclesia rege gubernetur,* Dupin, 1, 677–78; cf. John, *Tract. de pot.,* cap. 8–9; Leclercq, pp. 190–94.

26. Above, pp. 49 ff.; below, pp. 241–42, where the texts are printed in parallel.

27. Above, p. 50.

28. Above, pp. 117–18.

the opening section of d'Ailly's tract was inspired by John's work.[29]

This work, then, should be added to Ockham's *Dialogus* as a primary source of d'Ailly's ecclesiastico-political views. On d'Ailly's specifically Conciliar teaching, John of Paris undoubtedly exercised an influence greater even than that of Ockham, for whereas Ockham had drawn back on the brink of an assertion of Conciliar supremacy and reiterated the more conservative views of the thirteenth-century canonist Huguccio,[30] John had not, and d'Ailly, repeating his words, forsook the Ockhamist position and went on to assert in unambiguous terms the superiority of the Council to the Pope.[31]

But what then of the *Defensor pacis* of Marsilius of Padua, which must surely loom large in any discussion of late medieval political thought and especially of Conciliar theory? It is true that d'Ailly never mentions Marsilius, but neither does he mention John of Paris, and that is by no means enough, therefore, to eliminate the possibility of Marsilian influence. So far as the evidence goes, Marsilius cannot wholly be eliminated from the list of possible sources, but he is an unlikely choice, and for several reasons. In the first place, just as there are in d'Ailly's writings no citations of the *Defensor pacis,* neither are there, to my knowledge, any unidentified borrowings from it. There is,

29. *Expositio,* Dupin, 2, 1015: "De Alliaco, post Joannem de Parisiis, assignat sex species Potestatis Ecclesiasticae immediate a Christo traditas." Compare d'Ailly's *Tract. de eccl. pot.* (Dupin, 2, 927–32) with John's *Tract. de pot.,* cap. 13; Leclercq, pp. 211–16.

30. Tierney, "Ockham, the Conciliar Theory and the Canonists," pp. 60–62; cf. Georges de Lagarde, "L'Idée de représentation dans les oeuvres de Guillaume d'Ockham," *Bulletin of the International Committee of the Historical Sciences, 9* (1937), 446–48, and also "Ockham et le Concile général," *Album Helen Maud Cam,* Studies Presented to the International Commission for the History of Representative and Parliamentary Institutions, *23* (1960), 83–94, where he notes some of Ockham's qualifications concerning the authority possessed by a General Council.

31. Thus John's tract "provides by far the most consistent and complete formulation of conciliar doctrine before the outbreak of the Great Schism" (Tierney, *Foundations,* p. 177). For d'Ailly's arguments see above, pp. 000 ff. Roberts, "Pierre d'Ailly," p. 137, somewhat oversimplifies, then, when she asserts that d'Ailly borrowed from Ockham "the framework of his ecclesiastical constitution."

furthermore, an element of truth in the rather sweeping assertion that "the work of extreme secularists like Marsiglio of Padua was of little use to the churchmen," [32] and it is possible, as Martin claims, that d'Ailly regarded some of Marsilius's ideas as positively dangerous,[33] since it was his concern to reform the Papacy and neither to destroy it nor to deny its divinely appointed character. Finally, although it is true that d'Ailly in common with Marsilius stressed, for instance, the idea that the ultimate authority in any polity must, in some sense, remain with the whole community, so, too, did Ockham and John of Paris, and they went on to deduce from it various conclusions which were less radical and (in John's case at least) more immediately applicable to the problems that d'Ailly faced.

It would seem therefore that if we are to indicate the chief sources of d'Ailly's political ideas, we are justified in pointing not to Marsilius, but rather to John of Paris and principally to William of Ockham, the master who had already provided him with the main outlines of his general theology. To abandon the question at this point, however, would be to plead guilty to E. F. Jacob's accusation that "in Conciliar studies . . . we are frequently told that this or that view 'is to be found in Ockham,'

32. Roberts, "Pierre d'Ailly," p. 124. It has long been known that the *De modis uniendi et reformandi ecclesiam in concilio universali* (1410), now firmly attributed to the radical reformer Dietrich of Niem (d. 1418), contains material drawn from the *Defensor Pacis,* and it has recently been asserted that there are similar borrowings in the *De concordantia catholica* of Nicholas of Cusa—see Paul E. Sigmund, Jr., "The Influence of Marsilius of Padua on XVth-Century Conciliarism," *Journal of the History of Ideas, 23* (1962), 392–402. For Dietrich's borrowings, see also Haller, *Papsttum,* p. 508; Martin, "Comment c'est formée la doctrine de la supériorité du concile," pp. 273–74, n. 3; E. F. Jacob, *Essays in the Conciliar Epoch* (2nd ed., Manchester, 1953), pp. 41–42. Martin stresses, however, the antipathy to Marsilian ideas of leading Gallican theologians like Gerson and d'Ailly; cf. his *Origines du Gallicanisme, 2,* 132 and 134–62, and Haller, *Papsttum,* p. 342.

33. *Origines du Gallicanisme, 2,* 132; also the article cited above, pp. 273–74, n. 3. But I know of no evidence for Martin's accompanying claim that it was "in great part to combat Marsilian ideas that d'Ailly wrote his *Tractatus de ecclesiastica potestate.*" The remarks which d'Ailly makes in the text to which Martin refers (Dupin, *2,* 926) do not support such a contention; indeed, they could hardly do so, for most of them are pre-Marsilian, being taken verbatim from John of Paris; see below, pp. 241–42.

and there the matter is unsatisfactorily left," [34] a crime the more heinous in that it is no longer completely excusable on the grounds of lack of knowledge of Ockham's sources, or indeed of the sources of John of Paris. Hamman's perception of the close parallel between some of Ockham's ideas and those of John of Paris is not particularly helpful [35] (Almain had noticed it already at the start of the sixteenth century),[36] but his observation that the greater part of Ockham's patristic quotations was taken from Gratian's *Decretum* and the subsequent collections of decretals is more promising,[37] the more so in that more recent scholars have fruitfully exploited this approach. It has been remarked that "in the manipulation of the texts and concepts that were the *loci communes* of canon and Roman law . . . Ockham displays an almost terrifying efficiency," [38] and Tierney, in two illuminating articles,[39] has marshalled a persuasive array of facts in favor of his argument that in his methods of manipulating and interpreting canonistic texts nothing sharply distinguished Ockham's technique from that of the great canonists themselves, and that in several of those doctrines central to his view of ecclesiastical authority, Ockham and John of Paris too were repeating arguments which had already been elaborated by the thirteenth-century canonists, in particular by Huguccio of Pisa and Hostiensis.[40]

This argument, moreover, forms part of Tierney's general thesis that the foundation of Conciliarist theories is to be sought, not in the reactions of Conciliarists to the problems confronting them, nor in the theories devised in earlier times of crisis by

34. *Essays in the Conciliar Epoch*, p. 85.

35. P. A. Hamman, *La doctrine de l'église et de l'état chez Ockham* (Paris, 1942), p. 186.

36. See *Expositio circa decisiones . . . Occam,* Dupin, 2, 1047.

37. Hamman, p. 29.

38. C. C. Bayley, "Pivotal Concepts in the Political Philosophy of William of Ockham," *Journal of the History of Ideas, 10* (1949), 199.

39. Brian Tierney, "A Conciliar Theory of the Thirteenth Century," *Catholic Historical Review, 36* (1951), 415–40, and "Ockham, the Conciliar Theory and the Canonists," *Journal of the History of Ideas, 15* (1954), 40–70.

40. For a more complete discussion of the work of John of Paris and his dependence on canonistic sources, see Tierney, *Foundations,* pp. 157–78.

John of Paris or William of Ockham, but rather in the slowly developing legal tradition which was the outcome of the attempts of generations of canonists to rationalize the structure both of the individual churches and of the Universal Church.[41] Extensively employing Decretist and Decretalist literature, Tierney has argued that two separate doctrines of Church unity are to be found in the canonist glosses of the centuries preceding the Great Schism:

> The more conspicuous one, which has usually been regarded as the canonistic principle *par excellence,* insisted that the unity of the whole Church could be secured only by a rigorous subordination of all the members to a single head, and to make that subordination effective, it developed the familiar theory of papal sovereignty. But side by side with this there existed another theory, applied at first to single churches and then, at the beginning of the fourteenth century, to the Roman Church and the Church as a whole, a theory which stressed the corporate association of the members of a church as the true principle of ecclesiastical unity, and which envisaged an exercise of corporate authority by the members of a church even in the absence of an effective head.[42]

41. Tierney expounds his thesis in *Foundations,* in which, taking as his point of departure the fragmentary suggestions made over the years by Gierke, Arquillière, Martin, and Ullman, he sets out to prove that Conciliar theories, far from being a reaction against canonist views, were the logical culmination of certain strands of canonist thought itself. He does, in fact, succeed in tracing the principal Conciliar ideas back beyond publicists like John of Paris and Ockham to their source in the writings of the Decretists and Decretalists, in particular of Huguccio and Hostiensis. See above, Ch. 4 and 5; Gierke-Maitland, p. 50; Arquillière, "L'Appel au concile sous Philippe le Bel," pp. 51–55; Martin, "Comment c'est formée la doctrine de la supériorité du concile," pp. 121–43; Ullmann, *Origins,* pp. 184–85, and *The Growth of Papal Government in the Middle Ages* (London, 1955), pp. 452–53. Thus, for example, Tierney, *Foundations,* p. 45, traces back to Huguccio the fundamental distinction, which appears in the works of most of the major Conciliarists, "between the local *Romana Ecclesia* and the Roman Church understood as the whole *universitas fidelium*—often regarded as a contribution of Ockham to Conciliar thought." For further evidence of Decretist attitudes, see Tierney, "Pope and Council: Some New Decretist Texts," *Mediaeval Studies, 19* (1957), 197–218.

42. Tierney, *Foundations,* p. 240.

It is not, therefore, to the Imperial or French publicist literature of the early fourteenth century—literature in which the
works of Ockham and John of Paris bulk large—that we should
look for the ultimate sources of Conciliar theory, nor even, as
Figgis suggested, to the constitutional example of secular states,[43]
but to the canon law and the complex commentaries of the canonists. These were responsive both to the exacting requirements
of the ancient doctrines of the Church and to the practical
exigencies of day-to-day ecclesiastical life. No "practicable system of Church government," whether Conciliar or not, could
ignore them; "the Conciliar theory . . . sprang from the im-
pregnation of Decretist ecclesiology by Decretalist corporation
concepts." [44]

The dependence of d'Ailly's political thought upon the views
of Ockham and John of Paris is also then—at least in part—a
secondhand dependence upon the theories of the canonist glossators. This revelation gains added significance in the light of
d'Ailly's own extensive canonistic citations; despite his repeated
attacks on the jurists,[45] in his later tracts he cites more frequently
than any other sources Gratian's *Decretum*, the official collections of papal decretals, and the works of the famous glossators.
The *Tractatus de materia* alone affords an impressive demon-
stration of his familiarity with the works of many of the glossators as well as with the texts of the *Decretum* and of the Decretals
of Gregory IX.[46] In it d'Ailly quotes the glosses of the Decretists
Huguccio (d. 1210), Johannes Faventinus (d. ca. 1220), Laurentius Hispanus (d. 1258), and Bartholomaeus Brixiensis (d. 1258),
as well as of the Decretalists Goffredus Tranensis (d. 1245),
Henricus Boik (d. ca. 1250), Innocent IV (d. 1254), Hostiensis
(d. 1271), Guido de Baysio (d. 1313), and Joannes Andreae (d.

43. Figgis, *Studies*, pp. 35–36.
44. Tierney, *Foundations*, p. 245.
45. See above, pp. 163–64.
46. The *glossa ordinaria* to the *Decretum* was the work of Joannes Teutonicus
(d. 1246), and that to the *Decretals* of Gregory IX was the work of Bernardus
Parmensis (d. 1266). D'Ailly also quotes, though less frequently, the *Liber Sextus*,
the *Clementinae*, and the *Extravagantes Joannis XXII*. At times his own text
reads like a work of canonistic scholarship; cf. his *Tract. de eccl. pot.*, Dupin, 2,
956–57, which is a tissue of material from the glosses.

1348)—an extensive and formidable list. Two of his early non-Conciliarist works reveal that he had long been familiar with some, at least, of these glosses,[47] and in his *Tractatus de ecclesiastica potestate,* many of these glossators are again referred to, and along with them the Decretalists Joannes Monachus (d. 1313) and Petrus Bertrandi (d. 1349).[48]

D'Ailly's dependence on the canonistic literature is indisputable and it is something more than the fruit of a secondhand acquaintance with the ideas of the glossators. His canonistic erudition certainly seems to have exceeded that of John of Paris who influenced his Conciliar thinking so profoundly. Indeed, on the crucial issue of the rôle of the cardinals in the Church, it enabled him to go beyond John's position, and citing Hostiensis, Guido of Baysio, and Joannes Monachus, to indicate his adherence at least to some of the oligarchic views expressed by those canonists.[49]

In this direct as well as indirect dependence upon the theories of the canonist glossators, d'Ailly again betrays something which we have already, in the context of specific problems, had more than one occasion to note—his ultimate but fundamental indebtedness to Romano-canonical corporation theory, the fruitful elaboration of which had kept pace with the vast extension both

47. Thus, in his *Utrum indoctus in jure divino,* Dupin, *1,* 654–56, he takes sharp issue with the exalted position ascribed to the study of canon law by Hostiensis, and (p. 661), cites the commentary of Petrus Bertrandi on the Clementines. Similarly, in his *Tractatus II adversus Cancellarium Parisiensem,* Dupin, *1,* 745–78, he relies very heavily on the authority of Hostiensis, and also cites, among others, Bartholomaeus Brixiensis, Henricus Boik, and Joannes Monachus.

48. Dupin, *2,* 925–60. In addition to the two mentioned, he quotes Huguccio, Bartholomaeus Brixiensis, Joannes Andreae, Innocent IV, Hostiensis, and Guido de Baysio. The last name deserves particular attention because d'Ailly refers here (col. 935), as well as in the *Tract. de mat.* (below, App. III, 290 n. 8 and 320 n. 6) to Guido's *Rosarium,* a massive and influential gloss on the *Decretum* through which many early and forgotten Decretist opinions, some of them semi-Conciliarist, "acquired a new currency in the fourteenth century" (Tierney, "Ockham, the Conciliar Theory, and the Canonists," p. 43).

49. *Tract. de eccl. pot.,* Dupin, *2,* 933. D'Ailly was not, however, as precise in these matters as was Zabarella. For the views of Hostiensis, Guido de Baysio, Joannes Monachus, and Zabarella, see Ullmann, *Origins,* pp. 203–210; Tierney, *Foundations,* 151–53, 179–90, 220–37.

of secular and ecclesiastical corporate associations.[50] Figgis could stress the *damnosa hereditas* of the Roman law,[51] but as d'Entrèves pointed out, its influence was by no means totally on the side of the ruler, and the scholarship of recent years has increasingly stressed how much the development of medieval constitutionalism—and in particular the growth of representative assemblies—owed to the contributions of the Roman and of canon law.[52] The question of the subsequent influence of d'Ailly's political views will therefore have an added interest in that it will also serve to elucidate the enduring impact of this contribution.

II

About a century after his death, d'Ailly's views on dominium were cited by Almain, though along with the whole doctrine of dominium as contingent on grace they were soon to be forgotten.[1] More than a century and a half later, a revealing remark made by the learned Cambridge Platonist Ralph Cudworth indicated that d'Ailly's natural law theory had played at least a discernible part in the establishment of that voluntaristic tradition of natural law thinking which historians have usually ignored, but which was to exercise a profound influence over the

50. This helps to explain why, despite the similarity of some of their ideas, there is no adequate ground for assuming any necessary link between the thought of d'Ailly and that of Marsilius of Padua. It has long been assumed, at least by some of his historians, that Marsilius's work reflected the political experience of the corporately organized Italian communes (see above, Ch. 4, n. 4, p. 115), and it has recently been observed that very close parallels exist between some of his key ideas and the corporate concepts applied to the Church by Hostiensis (Tierney, "A Conciliar Theory of the Thirteenth Century," pp. 415–26).

51. J. N. Figgis, *Churches in the Modern State* (London, 1913), p. 226.

52. A. P. d'Entrèves, *The Medieval Contribution to Political Thought* (Oxford, 1939), pp. 17–18. See C. H. McIlwain, *Constitutionalism Ancient and Modern* (Ithaca, N.Y., 1958), pp. 41–60, and the articles of Gaines Post cited above, pp. 135 ff. The general case for the relevance of canonistic studies to the history of medieval political theory and medieval constitutionalism is well stated by Brian Tierney, "The Canonists and the Medieval State," *Review of Politics, 15* (1953), 378–88.

1. *Expositio*, Dupin, 2, 1078–79.

ethical, legal, and scientific thinking of the sixteenth and seventeenth centuries.[2] The heart of d'Ailly's political theory, however, lies in his Conciliar thinking; the particular question of the influence of his political ideas is, of course, inextricably bound up with the broader issue of the subsequent history of the Conciliar movement and of Conciliar theory. The triumph of the Papacy over the Council of Basel marked the defeat of Conciliarism, but Jedin has clearly shown that despite the subsequent widespread tendency "to revert to the monarchical conception of the Church's constitution" and its powerful justification by Torquemada, the "idea of the Council" was not completely abandoned, and survived into the "era of the papal restoration."[3] The strength of the idea, he admits, lay less in its connection with the strict Conciliar theory than "in the combination of the demand for a Council with the actual need of reform," the great concern being "not so much the question of the supremacy of the Council as the holding of a Council there and then."[4] But the Conciliar theory itself was by no means dead. It found in Spain, it is true, a hostile environment, but in Italy it retained support among the canonists and jurists, if not among the theologians. Similarly, it was favored until the failure of Basel by the Continental universities north of the Alps, with the sole exception of Heidelberg. It lost ground during the years that followed, but it did so slowly.[5] Even in England, where no

2. Cudworth (d. 1658) was an indefatigable opponent of the voluntaristic ethic and he tells us that "though the ancient Fathers of the Christian Church were very abhorrent from this doctrine . . . yet it crept up afterwards in the scholastic age, Ockham being among the first that maintained . . . 'That there is no act evil but as it was prohibited by God, and which cannot be made good if it be commanded by God.' . . . Herein Petrus Alliaco and Andreas de Novo Castro, with others quickly followed him." *Treatise concerning immutable morality*, Bk. I, Ch. 1, § 5; (New York, 1838), p. 11. For some comments on the importance of the voluntarist tradition in political and scientific thinking, see my articles "Medieval Theories of Natural Law: William of Ockham and the Significance of the Voluntarist Tradition," *Natural Law Forum*, 6 (1961), 65–83, and "Laws of Nature," 433–57.

3. Hubert Jedin, *A History of the Council of Trent*, trans. Ernest Graf (St. Louis, 1947), *1*, 27–61.

4. Jedin, p. 61.

5. Jedin, pp. 34–42.

strong Conciliar tradition had grown up at the universities, it seems to have enjoyed something of a vogue in the early Reformation era, at least among the Henrician pamphleteers, some of whom categorically affirmed the superiority in spiritual matters of a General Council both to the Pope and to the king, and appealed not only to the example of the early ecumenical councils and of those of Constance and Basel but also to the writings of such Conciliarists as Gerson and d'Ailly.[6]

Nevertheless, it is true to say both of the fifteenth and sixteenth centuries that "Gallican France was the real stronghold of the strict Conciliar theory, and the University of Paris its citadel."[7] Even after the failure of Basel, Paris continued to throw its weight behind the theory, publicly defending the more disputable decrees of Constance and Basel, and compelling would-be opponents—such as the Dominican, John Munerii, in 1470—to recant their views. It was in accordance with this position that it sent representatives to the antipapal *conciliabulum* of Pisa in 1511, and in March 1518 reacted against the concordat which the French king had concluded in 1516 with the Pope by appealing to a General Council.[8] These events were the occasion for forceful and influential reiterations of Conciliar principles by the Parisian theologians John Major and Jacques Almain, the former in his *Disputatio de authoritate concilii supra pontificem maximum*,[9] and the latter in his *Tractatus de authoritate*

---

6. F. Le van Baumer, *The Early Tudor Theory of Kingship* (New Haven, 1940), pp. 50–53; W. Gordon Zeefeld, *Foundations of Tudor Policy* (Cambridge, Mass., 1948), pp. 133–35; P. A. Sawada, "Two Anonymous Tudor Treatises on the General Council," *The Journal of Ecclesiastical History, 12* (1961), 197–214.

7. Jedin, pp. 32–34. Jedin does not, however, take note of the parallel strength of Conciliar ideas in Scotland throughout the fifteenth century. See J. H. Burns, *Scottish Churchmen and the Council of Basle* (Glasgow, 1962), and his "The Conciliarist Tradition in Scotland," *Scottish Historical Review, 42* (1963), 89–104.

8. The text of the appeal is printed in J. Thomas, *Le Concordat de 1516* (Paris, 1910), *3*, 429–37. The legal sections of Luther's appeal to a council (November, 1518) are dependent, even in expression, upon this earlier appeal. For a comparison, see Thomas, *3*, 72–74.

9. Dupin, 2, 1131–45. John Major (1469–1550), the last famous British scholastic, taught at Glasgow, Paris, and St. Andrews, and numbered among his pupils the Scottish reformers John Knox and George Buchanan. The best biographical sketch of Major is that by Aeneas J. G. Mackay in the introduction to *John Major's His-*

ecclesiae et conciliorum generalium, written in 1512 in reply
to Cajetan's attack upon the Council of Pisa.[10] Both of these
men claimed that they were merely giving expression to a tradition of the University of Paris dating back to the time of the
Council of Constance,[11] and the claim is clearly a justifiable one.
It was in this tradition that doctrinal support was found for the
"liberties" from papal control demanded by the Gallican
Church; later Gallican writers, according to Martin, merely
echoed the ideas of d'Ailly and Gerson.[12]

In the cases of Major and Almain this is certainly true, and
it is underlined by their frequent citations of d'Ailly and Gerson.[13] It is only a little less true of the theological Gallicans of

---

tory of Greater Britain, trans. A. Constable (Edinburgh, 1892), pp. xxix ff. But it
should now be read in conjunction with J. Durkan, "John Major: After 400
Years," *Innes Review, 1* (1950), 131–39, and J. H. Burns, "New Light on John
Major," ibid., 5 (1954), 83–100. My article "From Constance to 1688: The Political
Thought of John Major and George Buchanan," *The Journal of British Studies, 2*
(1962), 1–31, ventures (pp. 12–19) upon a preliminary analysis of Major's political
thought. Dr. Burns is engaged upon a detailed study.

10. Dupin, 2, 976–1012. In an attempt to defend the Pope, Cajetan had written
his *Auctoritas papae et concilii sive ecclesiae comparata,* and Louis XII had called
upon the Faculty of Theology at the University of Paris for a refutation. Almain's
tract is a direct outcome of that appeal and Major's work was closely connected
with it; see Aimé-Georges Martimort, *Le Gallicanisme de Bossuet* (Paris, 1953),
pp. 100–01. D'Ailly's name figures prominently in the controversial literature
evoked by the Council; see the survey by Josef Klotzner in his *Kardinal Domini-
kus Jacobazzi und sein Konzilswerk* (Romae, 1948), pp. 209 ff.

11. Major, Dupin, 2, 1132: "Super praefata quaestione sunt modi dicendi oppo-
siti, quorum unus tenet Papa esse supra Concilium Universale: hunc . . . tenent
communiter Thomistae . . . . Alium modum semper nostra Universitas Parisiana,
a diebus Concilii Constantiensis imitata est; sic quod in ea, qui praedictam viam
tenuerit, in campo cogitur eam revocare"; cf. also col. 1144. Almain, Dupin, 2,
1070: "est conclusio quam tenent omnes Doctores Parisienses et Galli, quod Potestas Papae est subjecta Potestati Concilii . . . . Dicunt communiter omnes Doctores Parisienses, quod Potestas Papae, est sub Potestate Concilii, quantum ad
hoc quod Concilium potest certis Legibus Papam arctare, ita quod teneatur
Papa judicare secundum Leges, et Constitutiones a Concilio latas: et quantum
ad hoc, est expressa determinatio Concilii Constantiensis et Basiliensis."

12. Martin, *Origines du Gallicanisme, 2,* 125 and 148.

13. See, e.g., Dupin, 2, 980, 1011, 1015, 1062, 1078, 1136, 1144, 1150. D'Ailly and
Gerson were the predecessors of Major and Almain not only at the University
of Paris but also at the College of Navarre; see Jean Launoy, *Academia Parisiensis Illustrata* (Paris, 1682), *1,* 93, 97, 208, 400–01. For a different link between

the seventeenth and early eighteenth centuries.[14] Three examples must, however, suffice to illustrate this latter contention
—for the seventeenth century, Edmond Richer and Bishop
Bossuet, and for the eighteenth, Louis Ellies du Pin. In the case
of Richer,[15] who was Syndic of the Sorbonne and a staunch
defender of the Gallican liberties and the strict Conciliar theory,
this dependence is obvious. His famous and controversial *Libellus de ecclesiastica et politica potestate,* published in 1611, embodies extensive citations and quotations from the works of
those who might be said to belong to the "Navarre school"—
d'Ailly, Gerson (whom he refers to as "the disciple of Cardinal
Alliacenus"),[16] Major, and Almain—and incorporates several
passages from d'Ailly's *Tractatus de ecclesiastica potestate.*[17]
The same is true of his posthumously published *Apologia pro
Joanne Gersonio,*[18] and in yet another work he published d'Ailly's *De ecclesiastica potestate* along with works of Gerson,

---

d'Ailly and Major, see J. H. Baxter, "Four 'New' Medieval Scottish Authors,"
Scottish Historical Review, 25 (1928), 90–97. Baxter draws attention to the Scottish Conciliarist, Thomas Livingstone—who was active at the Council of Basel
and who later became an associate of Nicholas of Cusa—and claims him as "a
direct and essential link in the chain which connects Buchanan and Major back
to d'Ailly and Gerson." But Livingstone was by no means the only Scottish Conciliarist before Major; see the works cited above, n. 7, and also J. H. Burns,
"John Ireland and 'The Meroure of Wyssdome,' " *Innes Review,* 6 (1955), 77–98.

14. Viscount St. Cyres, "The Gallican Church," *C Mod H* (New York, 1908), 5,
75, contrasts theological Gallicanism with political Gallicanism as follows: "Theological Gallicanism maintained that the supreme infallible authority of the
Church was committed to Pope and Bishops jointly. Political Gallicanism declared that no amount of misconduct, or neglect of Catholic interests, justified the
Pope in interfering with a temporal sovereign."

15. Edmund Richer (d. 1631), philosopher, theologian, and sometime partisan
of the Catholic *Ligue.* For a biographical sketch, see *Dict. de Théol. Cath.,* s.v.
"Richer." See also Aimé-Georges Martimort, *Le Gallicanisme de Bossuet* (Paris,
1953), esp. pp. 48–56.

16. I.e., d'Ailly, *Libellus de eccl. et pol. pot.* (Paris, 1660), p. 60.

17. *Libellus,* pp. 58 ff., 184 ff., 100, 102, 104, 124, 181, and 246.

18. *Apologia pro Joanne Gersonio . . . adversus Scholae Parisiensis, et ejusdem
Doctoris Christianissimi obtrectatores* (Lyons, 1676); see e.g. pp. 71, 120, 154, 8,
and 32. This work is of added interest because it clearly reveals a voluntarist conception of the natural law similar to that held by Gerson as well as d'Ailly (see
esp. pp. 5–7). For Gerson's view of law see L. Vereecke, "Droit et morale chez Jean
Gerson," *Rev. hist. de droit français et étranger, 32* (1954), 413–27.

Almain, Major, and significantly, John of Paris.[19] Later on in the century, Bossuet, Bishop of Meaux and adviser to Louis XIV, proclaimed his adherence to the strict Conciliar position, supporting his stand by citing the views of d'Ailly and Gerson, and indicating that Almain and Major had adhered to these same views.[20] At the start of the next century, which was to witness the decline of clerical Gallicanism,[21] the example of Richer and Bossuet was followed by Louis Ellies du Pin, who not only included—in his 1706 edition of Gerson's complete works—numerous tracts of d'Ailly, Major, Almain, and other Conciliarists, but also in 1707 claimed that the University of Paris had always held, "as a fundamental point of its ecclesiastical discipline," that the Council is above the Pope,[22] and supported his argument with frequent references to the works of d'Ailly and Gerson.[23]

D'Ailly may, then, be regarded as one of the founders of a long-enduring tradition in the Faculty of Theology at the University of Paris, and his Conciliar ideas, and the works in which he expressed them, were by no means forgotten in the centuries following his death. It would be surprising if this had not been the case, for many of his other works continued to be read—at least into the fifteenth and sixteenth centuries—and at times when some of them, at least, can have been of no polemical value.[24] Nor does it seem that the appeal of his greatest Conciliar

19. *Vindiciae Doctrinum Majorum scholae Parisiensis . . . contra defensores Monarchiae universalis et absolutae Curiae Romanae* (Cologne, 1683). He also included works of these men in his influential edition of the works of Gerson: *Joannis Gersonii . . . Opera, 1* (Paris, 1606), 675–934.

20. See e.g.: *Appendix ad defensionem declarationis Cleri Gallicani* (1682), Lib. I, caps. 5, 6, 7 and 8; in *Oeuvres complètes de Bossuet, 9* (Paris, 1836), 528–34. Cf. Martimort, *Le Gallicanisme de Bossuet*, pp. 361 ff.

21. V. Martin, *Le Gallicanisme et la Réforme Catholique* (Paris, 1919), p. 403.

22. *Traité de la puissance ecclésiastique et temporelle* (n.p., 1707), pp. 475–76. Dupin (d. 1719), who taught at the Sorbonne, was primarily an ecclesiastical historian; see *Dict. de théol. cath.*, s.v. "Dupin."

23. *Traité de la puissance*, pp. 372–542, and esp. 441, 443, 450, 476, 487, and 537.

24. Among other of his works, d'Ailly's *Imago mundi, Conceptus et insolubilia, Sententiae, Tractatus et sermones*, and *Tractatus de anima* were printed in the late fifteenth and early sixteenth centuries (several of them more than once). There was clearly a survival of interest in his geographical, logical, theological,

work, the *Tractatus de ecclesiastica potestate,* was limited to those with Conciliar sympathies, for the arguments therein contained—in favor of an aristocratic ecclesiastical constitution in which the cardinals would possess the right to a share in the government of the Church—helped to stimulate, Jedin tells us, "a literary movement" in favor of the idea.[25] This movement survived the failure of Basel, and among the people subsequently influenced by d'Ailly's oligarchic views was the papalist Torquemada himself.[26]

There can be little doubt, therefore, about the real influence of d'Ailly's political ideas upon later theories concerning the nature of the ecclesiastical polity. We are now faced with those more difficult questions that concern the alleged influence of

---

and philosophical views; both his *Sententiae* and *Tractatus de anima* went through multiple editions in the years between 1478 and 1505. Of all his works, however, the *Tractatus de reformatione* (his redaction of the third part of the *De materia*) seems to have been the most popular in the two centuries after his death. It was published separately in 1510, 1525, 1551, 1600 (this last in a German translation), and in 1671, as well as being reprinted in the collections of Hardt, Dupin, and others. See Salembier, *Alliaco,* pp. XXI–XXVI. Salembier does not list the 1510 edition nor does he mention that the work is printed, along with excerpts from Marsilius of Padua, Gerson, Dietrich of Niem, and others in *Speculum Ecclesiae Pontificiae Nicolaus Clemangis Archidiaconus Baiocensis . . . de corrupto Ecclesiae statu* (London, 1606).

25. Jedin, *History, 1,* 79–84; see above, p. 128.

26. Torquemada never mentions d'Ailly's name but the views on the papal plenitudo potestatis, which he attributes to "a certain number of the masters" at Constance and then attacks are in fact drawn verbatim from d'Ailly. See Juan de Torquemada, *Summa de ecclesia* (Rome, 1489), Lib. II, cap. 70 (no foliation); cf. d'Ailly, *Tract. de eccl. pot.,* Dupin, 2, 951. Earlier on in his work, however, Torquemada had reproduced without acknowledgment a good deal of d'Ailly's arguments concerning the rôle of the cardinals in the government of the Church. Compare Torquemada, *Summa,* Lib. I, caps. 80–81, with d'Ailly, *Tract. de eccl. pot.,* Dupin, 2, 929 ff. Jedin, *History, 1,* 83 n. 1, notes, too, that Domenichi, the papalist Bishop of Vercelli, though uninfluenced by d'Ailly's views on this matter, later noted his agreement with these views on the manuscript of his *Tractatus de cardinalium creatione.* Denis the Carthusian (d. 1471) also had drawn heavily on d'Ailly's oligarchic arguments (sometimes verbatim) in his *De auctoritate summi pontificis et generalis Concilii,* in *Opera omnia, 36* (Tornaci, 1908), 613–27 (esp. 615 and 624–25). Nicholas of Cusa was familiar with these arguments. He owned a copy of the *Tractatus de ecclesiastica potestate* and was influenced by it on more than one matter. See P. Sigmund, *Nicholas of Cusa and Medieval Political Thought* (Cambridge, Mass., 1963), pp. 103–07, 170.

Conciliar thought upon later secular political theorizing. Is "the road from Constance to 1688" a direct one? [27] Is there any evidence to support Sabine's assertion that "from the Conciliar theory of the 15th century there is a directly developing line of thought to the liberal and constitutional movements of the 17th and 18th centuries"? [28] And in particular can d'Ailly's political thought be assigned any individual part in this development?

It might well be expected a priori that a good case could be made for the existence of this type of influence. After all, the "constitutional" movement in the Church merely paralleled analogous secular movements and differed from them only, perhaps, in the abstract and universal quality of its theoretical expression.[29] D'Ailly regarded his basic political concepts as true not merely of the ecclesiastical but of any "rightly ordained polity," and indeed justified their application to the Church on this very ground. Nor had the predecessors of the Conciliarists, the Decretists and Decretalists to whom they owed so much, regarded the "juristic principles of ecclesiastical polity" as inapplicable to matters of secular government; Huguccio, for example, in an attempt to prove that the barons of a tyrannical king might, under certain circumstances, depose him, had made use of the canonist doctrine that an heretical pope was liable to deposition.[30] Moreover, as Jedin points out, "it is a common-

27. See above, p. 5, n. 8.

28. George H. Sabine, *A History of Political Theory* (2nd ed., New York, 1950), pp. 326–27.

29. Figgis, *Studies,* p. 36, says of the Conciliarists that "they raised the constitutionalism of the past three centuries to a higher power, expressed it in a more universal form and justified it on grounds of reason, policy and Scriptures."

30. Brian Tierney, "The Canonists and the Medieval State," *Review of Politics, 15* (1953), 381. The relevant text in Huguccio is quoted in S. Mochi Onory, *Fonti Canonistiche dell'idea moderna dello stato* (Milan, 1934), p. 156. Professor Tierney has kindly drawn to my attention two parallel texts. The first is that of the English canonist Alanus in the Apparatus *Jus naturale* on the *Decretum:* gloss ad C. 15, q. 6, c. 3: "sicut nec populus romanus ex quo semel contulit omne jus suum in imperatorem eum possit deponere, nec concilium nisi de heresi papam judicare, ar. supra di. xvii Hinc etiam, di. xl Si papa" (Paris, Bibl. Nat. *Ms.* 3909). Again, in the *Summa duacensis,* a work of the early thirteenth century and probably French, gloss ad C. 15, q. 6, c. 3: "Set et quod nec concilium potest papam deponere ut ix q. 111 Nemo, xxi Nunc autem. Idem etiam de omni rege qui jurisdictionem non habet ab alio" (*Ms.* Douai 649, f. 123rb).

place with the writers of the period of restoration that the democratic ideas of the epoch of the Councils were a danger for the monarchy as an institution." [31] Considerations such as these, together with the obvious similarities between the Conciliar views of the nature of political association and the ideas of seventeenth-century constitutional thinkers, naturally predispose one to accept without question the generalizations of Figgis, Laski, and Sabine.

With the exception, however, of the rather general statements of Figgis, little historical evidence has been adduced in support of these generalizations, and as a result not all historians have been willing to recognize their validity.[32] The Protestant Reformation still dominates the historical landscape of the period, and blocks out more distant prospects. Yet this was not so for many of those who lived closer to the event. In their works we may catch precious glimpses of the continuing influence of Conciliar ideas in general, and sometimes even of d'Ailly's ideas in particular. Sir Robert Filmer complained in a famous passage that the idea of government as based upon the consent of the people dates back to the "time that school divinity began to flourish," [33] and David Owen, writing in 1610, argued more precisely that the "leud learning" that invested "the people and nobles with the power over kings to dispose of their kingdoms" went back over "220 years in the Christian world: The first Authors of it being Johannes de Parisiis, Jacobus Almain and Marsilius Patavinus." "From these," he said, "the Puritans have learned their error of the power of Statesmen over Kings." [34]

31. *History, 1*, 137 n. 1.

32. Figgis, *Studies*, pp. 31 ff. The dominant attitude among historians and even historians of political thought has been one of indifference to the whole issue. Thus Janet and Carlyle seem to have regarded Conciliar thinking as irrelevant, strictly speaking, to the history of political theory; P. Janet, *Histoire de la science politique*, (3rd ed. Paris, 1887), *1*, 471 n. 1; Carlyle, *History*, 6, 163–67, and esp. 247, where he contrasts "ecclesiastical questions of the relation between the Pope and the General Council" with "political principles."

33. *Patriarcha*, I; ed. Peter Laslett, *Patriarcha and Other Political Works of Sir Robert Filmer* (Oxford, 1949), p. 53.

34. D. Owen, *Herod and Pilate Reconciled* (London, 1663), Ch. 8, p. 39. This was the third edition of the work. It had previously appeared under the same title in 1610, and in 1643 under the significant title *Puritano—Jesuitismus.*

The works of these men, along with those of Ockham, d'Ailly, Gerson, Zabarella, and Major were repeatedly cited during the course of the seventeenth century as having championed the right of the people to resist tyranny.[35] In this respect John Maxwell (1590?–1647) is not uncharacteristic, for in 1644 he claimed that the sectaries had learned such doctrines not from "the sound Protestants of the Reformed Churches" but from Papists such as Boucher and Rossaeus; these, he conjectured, had borrowed them in turn from

> the Sorbonists, and others of that kinde; who to oppose the Pope his infallibilitie in judgement, his unlimited power, and to subject him to a Councell, did dispute themselves almost out of breath, to prove that *potestas spiritualis summa* was by Christ first and immediately given *unitati*, or *communitatis fidelium* . . . that howsoever for the time it was virtually in the Pope, yet he had it onely from the communitie of the faithfull *communicatively*, and in the case of defailance, in them it was suppletive; and in the case that the power of the Church was abused to heresie or tyrannie, the Pope was deposable (not onely censurable) by a Councell.[36]

One might object that both Owen and Maxwell, as opponents of such resistance theories, had much to gain by smearing them with the taint of Popery. After all, Maxwell's own insistence on the matter sprang, as he himself admitted, from the desire to show that "these tenets came not into the world with Luther and Calvin, but were long before there was any word of a Reformer." Ockham, John of Paris, Gerson, and Almain all lived

35. In addition to Owen and such French writers as Cardinal Perron, see William Barclay, *De regno et regali potestate* (Paris, 1600), Bk. VI, cap. 24, p. 512; Robert Burhill, *De potestate regia et ursurpatione papali* (Oxford, 1613), pp. 193–215; Hugo Grotius, *De jure belli et pacis,* ed. William Whewell (Cambridge, 1853), Bk. I, ch. 4 § 11, pp. 190–91; William Prynne, *The Soveraigne Power of Parliaments and Kingdoms* (London, 1643), Pt. 3, pp. 136 and 144, and App., p. 161; Samuel Rutherford, *Lex Rex: The Law and the Prince* (London, 1644), pp. 50, 418, 449.

36. *Sacro-sancta Regum Majestas* (Oxford, 1644), pp. 14–16.

prior to the Reformation, and "Our Rabbies . . . have drawn these doctrines out of their polluted cisterns." [37] But this can hardly be said either of William Bridge (1600?–1670) or of his more famous contemporary William Prynne, for both of them, as Parliamentarians, were anxious to vindicate such doctrines of resistance. Yet Bridge, intent upon showing that these doctrines were "no new upstart opinion," did not hesitate to appeal to "the judgment of the Divines in the Council of Basel" and to the analogy they had drawn between the subordination of the Pope to the authority of the whole Church and that of the King to his kingdom.[38] Similarly Prynne, who in the course of defending the maxim *rex singulis major, universis minor,* which had been a cliché of sixteenth-century resistance theories, could argue that "the Papists were the first broachers of it long agoe." It is true that he was far from viewing the maxim as the invention of the Conciliarists but he did argue that it "was so authentike in those dayes, and after times, that the great Councell of Basel Anno 1431 when this mighty question was debated; whether a Pope were above a generall Councell or a Councell above him? such a Councell was at last resolved to be above the Pope." And he went on to cite Conciliar theory and practice at some length.[39]

The authors cited above are nearly all English, but their familiarity with Conciliar theory will not surprise us unless we are prone to regard English constitutional history as something wholly insulated from changes in the political temperature and pressure of the rest of Europe. It will be remembered that the Conciliar theory enjoyed something of a vogue in England during the reign of Henry VIII, and though the duration of this vogue was short and its scope limited, the memory of the Conciliar movement persisted into the seventeenth century, refreshed by the publication of works such as John White's *The Way to the True Church.* This book cited not only the events

37. Ibid., p. 16.

38. William Bridge, *The Wounded Conscience Cured, the Weak One Strengthened and the Doubting Satisfied* (London, 1642), pp. 7–8.

39. William Prynne, *The Soveraigne Power,* Pt. I, pp. 5–7, 31, 68, and 73.

at Constance and Basel but also the Conciliar views of Ockham, d'Ailly, Gerson, Nicholas of Cusa, Major, and Almain,[40] and from it Prynne himself was to derive much of his knowledge of Conciliar history. It appeared at the height of the controversy occasioned by the imposition of the Oath of Allegiance on English Roman Catholics in the wake of the Gunpowder Plot, a controversy kept alive by the attempt of the Estates-General in 1614–15 to require a similar oath in France. This coincidence was not without its significance, for the dispute not only served, as Salmon has argued, to direct the attention of a number of Englishmen to the political attitudes characteristic of the Gallican Church, to the history and thought of the French Religious Wars, and to the writings of the medieval thinkers from whom Jesuit and Calvinist resistance theories had been drawn, but also, and more precisely, it served to underline the relevance to secular politics of the theories of the Conciliar thinkers.[41]

Aenius Sylvius Piccolomini tells us that at the beginning of the Council of Basel one of the Spanish bishops had argued that

> The Pope is in the Church as a King is in his kingdome, and for a King to be of more authority than his kingdome, it were too absurd; Ergo, Neither ought the Pope to be above the Church. . . . Verily, as reason doth perswade, even so doth the use thereof also teach us: It seemeth also agreeable unto reason that the same should be done in the Church, that is, in the Councel, which is done in any kingdome. And so is this sufficiently apparent, that the Pope is subject unto the Councell.[42]

The lesson was by no means lost upon English political thinkers of the seventeenth century. The English version cited above is

40. J. White, *The Way to the True Church* (London, 1608). See esp. sec. 36, pp. 161–209.

41. J. H. M. Salmon, *The French Religious Wars in English Political Thought* (Oxford, 1959), pp. 69–79; cf. Charles H. McIlwain, *The Political Works of James I* (Cambridge, Mass., 1918), pp. lix–lxxix.

42. *De gestibus Basiliensis Concilii,* Bk. I, in Pius II, *Opera quae extant omnia* (Basel, 1571), p. 8.

taken from Prynne's *Soveraigne Power of Parliaments and King-doms* and Prynne was not alone in appreciating the analogy between the civil and ecclesiastical polities.[43] Over a century earlier Jacques Almain and John Major following d'Ailly and Gerson had made it quite explicit that they regarded their po-litical principles as equally applicable to both types of polity,[44] and at the beginning of the seventeenth century the Oath of Allegiance controversy had focused attention once again upon their writings.[45] One should not be misled by the fact that advo-cates of the Oath cited these writings, along with those of John of Paris, Ockham, d'Ailly, and Gerson, in support of their own contentions. These advocates—men such as Robert Burhill or James I himself—were anxious to prove that even Roman Cath-olic theologians had denied the Pope any temporal authority over kings or any right to depose kings. But what they over-

43. Pt. I, p. 6. The passage was also cited by William Bridge, *The Wounded Conscience Cured*, p. 8.

44. See, e.g., Almain, *Quaestio resumptiva . . . de dominio naturali, civili et ecclesiastica*, Dupin, 2, 964; Major, Dupin, 2, 1135.

45. As also on the works of John of Paris, Ockham, d'Ailly, Gerson, Zabarella, and Nicholas of Cusa. Much of the polemical literature relating to the controversy is not readily accessible, but in the following works, which I have been able to consult, numerous references will be found to the views of all of these men: William Barclay, *An et quatenus in Reges et Principes seculares jus et imperium habeat* (London, 1609), pp. 2, 134, 182, 219, and 328; John Barclay, *Pietas sive publicae pro regibus et principibus et privatae pro Guil. Barclaio parente vindi-ciae adversus Bellarmino* (1611), in Goldast, *3*, 1104 and 1131; Roger Widdring-ton, *Apologia Cardinalis Bellarmini pro jure principum* (1611), Goldast, *3*, 690–91, 695, 707–12, 717, 722, 752, 754, and 758; also his *A Cleare, Sincere and Modest Confutation of . . . Fitzherbert* (n.p., 1616), pp. 34, 39, 42, 75–76, 87–97, 111, 117, 124–25, 129, and 188; William Warmington, *A Moderate Defence of the Oath of Allegiance* (n.p., 1612), pp. 38–39, 59, 88, and 98; Robert Burhill, *De potestate regia et usurpatione papali*, pp. 193–215; Jacques Davy, Cardinal du Perron, *An Oration made on the Part of the Lordes Spirituall in the Chamber of the Third Estate*, delivered in 1614, translated into English (St. Omer, 1616), pp. 44, 46–50, 63, 121–22; James I, *A Premonition to all most mightie monarches*, and *A Re-monstrance for the Right of Kings and the Independence of their crownes*, both in McIlwain, *Political Works*, pp. 119–20, 202–06, and 208–09 (where he cites D. 40, c. 6); Archbishop Bancroft's summary of the statements of the Archpriest Blackwell before the High Commission, *Quaestio bipartita in Georgium Blackuel-lum Angliae Archipresbyterum*, Goldast, *3*, 591, 598, and 602–05; cf. McIlwain, *Political Works*, p. lix, n. 3.

looked, and what opponents such as Cardinal Perron were quick to make clear, was that the very theologians whom they were citing still believed the Pope to retain the right to *condemn* kings who were guilty of heresy, and denied him the right of *deposition* simply because this right belonged to "the whole body of the Realme." [46] James could bluster that Perron had misrepresented the views of these men, but one of his own quotations from the works of Major inadvertently revealed that Major himself was far from denying the right of a people to depose their king.[47] This point was surely not missed by Prynne who, defending the right of subjects to resist tyranny, not only cited Major but also commented that "lest any should think that none but Puritanes maintained this opinion K. James himself in his Answer to Cardinal Perron justifieth the French Protestants taking up Defensive Arms in France." [48]

Enough has been said to illustrate the continuing influence of Conciliar ideas in the seventeenth century. At the start of the century, the works of some of the famous Conciliarists—including d'Ailly's *Tractatus de ecclesiastica potestate* and *Tractatus de reformatione ecclesiae*—were made available to the public in new editions.[49] These works were read and cited not only by Gallican opponents of papal pretensions or by their Anglican counterparts but also by some of the English advocates of constitutional doctrines, men who had perceived that Conciliar principles were applicable to the political order of the secular world as well as to the ecclesiastical polity.[50] Paradoxically, the

46. Perron, *Oration*, pp. 47–49, 59 and 63.

47. *A Remonstrance*, McIlwain, *Political Works*, p. 202. Here James, denying that Childeric was deposed by Pope Zacharias, adds: " 'The word, Hee deposed,' saith Major, 'is not to bee understood as it is taken at the first blush or sight; but hee deposed is thus expounded in the glosse, Hee gave his consent unto those by whom he was deposed.' " For Major's own words see his *Disputatio de statu et potestate Ecclesiae*, Dupin, 2, 1128–29.

48. Prynne, *The Soveraigne Power*, Pt. III, pp. 144–45.

49. See above, notes 19 and 24, p. 216. Supply would seem to indicate demand and Perron, *Oration*, pp. 49 and 121–122, attests to the rôle played by Richer's 1606 edition of the works of Gerson. This edition also seems to have been the source of Warmington's knowledge of Almain; see *A Moderate Defence*, pp. 88 and 38–39.

50. See above, n. 45, p. 223. In addition to the numerous references to the

most striking evidence of the influence of Conciliar ideas on the political thinking of the seventeenth century is to be found in the political literature of the previous century. For if *some* of the seventeenth-century constitutionalists drew directly upon the ideas of the leading Conciliarists, nearly all of them drew heavily upon the theories formulated by their more immediate predecessors, the Catholic and Protestant monarchomachs of the sixteenth century.[51] Had these more proximate and more influential predecessors shown themselves to have been unaware of— or even uninfluenced by—the Conciliar precedent, then Figgis, Laski, and those historians who agreed with them would surely have exaggerated.

This, however, was not the case. It is true that the Catholic monarchomachs are not at all helpful on this issue. Many of the positions adopted by the writers of the Catholic *Ligue* parallel Conciliar ideas, and in the case of some of the views expressed by Rossaeus, the parallel has been said to be a close one.[52] But if a preliminary examination of his lengthy and little-read tract, the *De justa reipublicae Christianae authoritate,* and of Boucher's *De justa abdicatione Henrici Tertii,* can be regarded as an adequate sampling of the views of those associated with the *Ligue,* we are left without much unambiguous evidence of the influence of Conciliar ideas.[53] Similarly, in the writings of the Jesuit monarchomachs, their conscious Ultramontanism

----

works of Almain and Major (themselves indebted to d'Ailly), the latter is himself quoted or referred to in White, *The Way to the True Church,* pp. 159, 181, 192, 199–200, and 269; Widdrington, *Apologia,* in Goldast, *3,* 708, and *A Cleare, Sincere and Modest Confutation,* p. 34; Warmington, *A Moderate Defence,* pp. 38–39; Blackwell, in *Quaestio bipartita,* Goldast, *3,* 598. The works cited are his *Recommendatio Sacrae Scripturae, Utrum Petri ecclesia lege reguletur, Utrum Petri ecclesia rege gubernetur, Tract. de eccl. pot.,* and *Tract. super ref. ecclesiae.*

51. Salmon, *French Religious Wars,* indicates very clearly and documents very fully the extent of this indebtedness.

52. Figgis, *Studies,* p. 140; Rossaeus (William Rainolds?), *De justa reipublicae Christianae in reges impios et haereticos authoritate* (Paris, 1590).

53. Jean Boucher, *De justa Henrici Tertii abdicatione e Francorum Regno* (Lyons, 1591). J. W. Allen, *A History of Political Thought in the Sixteenth Century* (New York, 1960), p. 345, cites a *Ligue* pamphlet of 1589 which argued that "the King . . . must obey the Estates just as a Pope must obey a General Council."

served to eliminate any overt indication of indebtedness to Conciliar thinking, for it was their desire, as Figgis pointed out, "to emphasize the difference between ecclesiastical jurisdiction, which comes from above, and civil, which springs from below." [54]

No such problems plagued the Protestant advocates of resistance theories, yet if we begin with the works of John Knox, or of Christopher Goodman, the Marian exile, we are again faced with disappointment. The interests of both of these men were only incidentally political, and their theories of resistance were formulated ad hoc and upon an almost exclusively religious basis. The political ideal of Knox seems really to have been the theocracy advocated and partly established in Scotland by his successor, Andrew Melville,[55] and Goodman's book [56] has well been described as "a long and tedious sermon on the text: 'We must obey God rather than man.' " [57]

In four important works, however, at least three of which exercised an immense influence upon the political thinking of seventeenth-century England, there is clear evidence of depend-

---

54. Figgis, *Studies*, p. 156. The same is true of the famous work of Reginald, Cardinal Pole, written before the defeat of Conciliarism at Trent. In it, while we find many "constitutional" ideas which would have been congenial to the Conciliarists, we also find that Pole was anxious to desecularize the notion of the *corpus mysticum*, and to stress the differences rather than the similarities between the Church and the secular state. This was understandable in a man who was writing with the express purpose of defending against Henry VIII an ecclesiastical unity which, in his opinion, depended on the preservation of the papal primacy. See his *Ad Henricum Octavum Britanniae Regem pro ecclesiastica unitatis defensione* (Rome, 1536), ff. 16r, 41r–42r, and 101r; cf. the comment of Kantorowicz, *King's Two Bodies*, pp. 229–30. The reverse was true of many of the later French writers who, because of the association of theological Gallicanism with the cause of the French monarchy, restricted the application of its Conciliar constitutionalism to the Church alone.

55. See Knox's *First Blast of the Trumpet Against the Monstrous Regiment of Women* (1557) and his *Appellation* (1558); David Laing, *The Works of John Knox* (Edinburgh, 1855), *4*, 349–422, 461–520. For the life of Andrew Melville see *Dict. Nat. Biogr.*, s.v. "Melville, Andrew."

56. Christopher Goodman, *How Superior Powers Oght to be Obeyd* (Geneva, 1558); reprinted in facsimile (New York, 1932).

57. Christopher Morris, *Political Thought in England from Tyndale to Hooker* (Oxford, 1953), p. 152.

ence upon Conciliar political ideas. The first of these is the *Shorte Treatise* written in 1556 by John Ponet, exiled Bishop of Winchester, which has the distinction of containing the first complete doctrine of resistance formulated by a Protestant thinker on other than purely religious grounds.[58] The second is the *De jure regni apud Scotos*, written about 1567 by the Scottish humanist, George Buchanan (who was to be tutor to the future James I), but published only in 1579.[59] The third is the *Du droit des magistrats* usually attributed to Theodore Beza, Calvin's successor at Geneva.[60] The fourth is the *Vindiciae contra tyrannos*, which appeared in 1579 and was destined to become the most famous of all the Huguenot tracts.[61]

Ponet seems to have been familiar with some at least of the works of John Major,[62] and it is in his very able *Shorte Treatise*[63] that the most extensive of all these appeals to Conciliar theory and practice is to be found. There the analogy between the respective positions of Pope and king is drawn in two passages;[64] in the second of these Ponet reveals a clear grasp of the history of the fifteenth-century Councils and of the principles of Conciliar theory, which interestingly enough he ascribes to

58. *A Shorte Treatise of Politicke Power* (Strassburg, 1556); a facsimile edition is printed in Winthrop S. Hudson, *John Ponet (1516–1556): Advocate of Limited Monarchy* (Chicago, 1942). The Lutheran *Bekenntnis* of Magdeburg (1550) was, of course, the first formal declaration by an "orthodox" Protestant group of a right of active resistance to tyranny.

59. In G. Buchanan, *Opera Omnia* (Edinburgh, 1715), *1*, § 8.

60. In *Mémoires de l'Estat sous Charles IX*, ed. Simon Goulart (Paris, 1577), *2*, 753–90. For a discussion of Beza's views, see Pierre Mesnard, *L'Essor de la philosophie politique au XVIe siècle* (Paris, 1936), pp. 309–26.

61. *Vindiciae contra tyrannos . . . Being a Treatise Written in Latin and French by Junius Brutus, and Translated Out of Both into English* (London, 1689), p. 142. This work was attributed to Hubert Languet and more recently, at least in part to du Plessis Mornay. See Raoul Patry, *Philippe du Plessis Mornay, un huguenot homme d'état* (Paris, 1933), pp. 275–82; cf. Allen, *History of Political Thought*, p. 313.

62. Ponet cites few authorities, but Hudson, *John Ponet*, p. 172, claims that there is material drawn from Major's *History of Greater Britain* in the *Shorte Treatise*.

63. Morris, *Political Thought in England*, p. 146, regards Ponet as "the acutest of English political thinkers between Tyndale and Hooker."

64. *A Shorte Treatise*, ed. Hudson, pp. [60], and [102]–[106].

the canonists. "For," he says, "the canonistes (the pope's own championes), grounding themselves upon this lawe of nature, saye that popes . . . maie be depryved by the body of the churche. And so at one clappe, in the counseil holden at Constaunce . . . were three popes popped out of their places." [65] After considerable elaboration, he draws the familiar conclusion that "if it be lawfull for the body of the churche to depose and punishe a Pope . . . how muche the more by the like argumentes, reasones, and authoritie, maie Emperours, kings, princes and other governours, abusing their office, be deposed and removed out of their places and offices, bi the body or state of the Realme or commonwealthe." [66]

Buchanan was a pupil of John Major, and his influential work, which surely in part reflects the teaching of his master,[67] contains a similar passage, in which he appeals to the practice of Constance and Basel and concludes that he is unable to understand how kings "can think that it takes anything away from their dignity to be held responsible before the law" while "the Roman Pontiffs who graciously permitted kings to kiss their feet . . . these same Pontiffs, when they were summoned to appear for trial, obeyed; and, upon the orders of their judges, have abdicated their offices." [68] Again, the *Du droit des magistrats* is explicit enough on this particular point to make it possible for Owen to describe the work as one "wherein it is said that the people have the same right to depose kings that are tyrants

65. Hudson, p. [103].

66. Hudson, pp. [104]–[105].

67. Buchanan studied briefly under Major at the University of St. Andrews, and seems to have followed his teacher to Paris in 1525; see P. Hume Brown, *George Buchanan; Humanist and Reformer* (Edinburgh, 1890), p. 47. Buchanan never cites Major in the *De jure regni* but there is a striking similarity between some of his arguments and those of his master, in minor as well as major positions. See my article "From Constance to 1688," where I analyze and compare the political theories of the two men, and present a case for Buchanan's partial dependence on Major. See also Burns, "The Conciliarist Tradition in Scotland," pp. 102–03, where he points out the similarities and dissimilarities in the political thinking of the two men, and notes that Buchanan held "at one stage in his career conciliarist ideas partly derived no doubt from Major."

68. *Opera Omnia, 1,* 36; cf. p. 30, translated by Charles F. Arrowood, *The Powers of the Crown in Scotland* (Austin, Texas, 1949), pp. 136–37; cf. 118–19.

228

which a general counsell hath to displace a Pope that is a Heretique." [69] Finally, in the *Vindiciae contra tyrannos,* which has been described as "the most important book on the subject previous to Locke's work," [70] there is yet another lengthy appeal to Conciliar theory and practice, concluding that if the Council can depose the Pope, who regards himself "as much in dignity above the Emperor, as the Sun is above the Moon," then

> who will make any doubt or question, that the general Assembly of the Estates of any Kingdom, who are the representative body thereof, may not only degrade and disthronize a Tyrant, but also disthronize and depose a King, whose weakness and folly is hurtful or pernicious to the State. [71]

A conclusion by now familiar to us and one which cannot have been uncommon at the time.

Summing up this discussion, then, it may be concluded that d'Ailly's political ideas, enshrined in the enduring Conciliar tradition which he had done so much to establish at the University of Paris, exercised, broadly speaking, a twofold influence. In the first place, that full formulation of his thought about the government of the ecclesiastical polity which is to be found in his *Tractatus de ecclesiastica potestate* remained, along with the teaching of his pupil Gerson and of their disciples, Major and Almain, the abiding inspiration of theological Gallicans such as Richer, who himself continued to espouse the strict Conciliar theory, and also to a certain extent d'Ailly's aristocratic constitutional ideal. [72] In the second place, this Conciliar tradition was a living tradition in the sixteenth and seventeenth centuries, and as such it helped to mould secular as well as ecclesiastical political thinking. The works of the leading Conciliarists were consulted and quoted by many, including

69. *Mémoires de l'Estat,* 2, 777; Owen, *Herod and Pilate Reconciled,* p. 43.

70. Figgis, *Studies,* p. 134.

71. *Vindiciae,* p. 142.

72. *Apologia pro Joanne Gersonio,* pp. 41 and 44–48.

some of the English advocates of constitutional doctrines in the early seventeenth century. They must also be numbered among the direct sources of the political views at least of Beza, Ponet, Buchanan, and the author of the *Vindiciae*—views which, precisely because they were grounded upon political principles of more universal validity and appeal than those drawn more exclusively from scriptural precedents [73] or national constitutional practice,[74] were of immense value in more than one country, and not least in England, where constitutionalism triumphed.[75] Two of these works—the *Vindiciae* and Buchanan's dialogue—were probably the most important of all the political works opposing absolute monarchy written in the two centuries before the appearance of Locke's *Second Treatise*. Both were certainly well known in England. An edition of the *Vindiciae* was published there as early as 1579, and three English editions appeared in the seventeenth century, two during the Civil War period and another in 1689.[76] Similarly, some indication of Buchanan's enduring notoriety is given by the governmental condemnations of his work in 1584, 1660, 1664, and 1688, and by the public censure of his works pronounced by the University of Oxford in 1683.[77]

If these facts are kept in mind, it may not seem unreasonable to suggest that the history of early modern political theory should be viewed a little less in terms of the upheaval occasioned by the Protestant Reformation and a little more in terms of late medieval antecedents. This is in no way to question the

73. As, e.g., Goodman's *How Superior Powers Oght to be Obeyd*.

74. As, e.g., François Hotman's *Franco-Gallia* (1573); cf. Mesnard, pp. 327–36.

75. Even Ponet's work, perhaps the least well-known of them all, was reprinted twice on the eve of the Civil War. See Hudson, pp. 210–11.

76. See Salmon, *The French Religious Wars*, p. 173; R. H. Murray, *The Political Consequences of the Reformation* (Boston, 1926), p. 209.

77. For a full discussion of the immediate popularity of the work and of its later influence see W. S. McKechnie, "De Jure Regni Apud Scotos," in *George Buchanan: Glasgow Quatercentenary Studies* (Glasgow, 1907), pp. 211–24, 276–96. Of the Oxford condemnations Salmon remarks (p. 145) that "it was an indication of the persistent influence of monarchomach theory that the *Vindiciae contra tyrannos* and the *De jure regni apud Scotos* should be listed beside the many English and Scottish works which in the preceding forty years had reproduced French doctrines of resistance."

immense importance of the political consequences of the Reformation, but it is to suggest that these consequences were practical rather than theoretical in character. For it was "reluctantly and in spite of themselves" that "religious societies were led by practical necessities to employ upon their own behalf doctrines which are now the common heritage of the Western World"; [78] and, it should be added, it was the failure of all the religious groups (both old and new) to command a universal allegiance rather than any necessary theoretical deductions from their doctrinal premises that contributed to the revival or, more properly, ensured the survival of constitutional ideas.

From 1450 onwards, Figgis argued, it seemed to most practical statesmen and to all monarchs that absolute monarchy was the most civilized form of government. Constitutional movements in every country were regarded by men like Strafford and Richelieu, or sovereigns like Elizabeth I and Charles I, as "inefficient clogs upon the wheels of government," and as "not merely wrong but stupid." [79] The fact that constitutional limitations on the monarchy survived in England is to be attributed not to their unique quality—for they were common to the greater part of medieval Europe—but rather to what McIlwain called "the unexampled toughness of the ancient English common law," [80] to the alienation from the Crown of so many of the property-owning gentry, and most of all to the existence of a strong religious minority which belligerently refused to conform to the beliefs of the established Church. It is true that perhaps the strongest section of this religious minority tended, in rejecting the doctrine of the divine right of kings, to do so in terms of an opposing divine right inherent in the spiritual kingdom of the faithful, and the contest was therefore one between two forms of divine right, the monarchical and the ecclesiastical. But it may be doubted whether the quasitheocratic principles of those Puritans were as important a factor in providing an

78. Figgis, *Studies*, p. 5.
79. Ibid., p. 60.
80. C. H. McIlwain, *Constitutionalism Ancient and Modern* (Ithaca, N.Y., 1958), p. 95.

initial theoretical and unifying justification for the opposition
to monarchical absolutism as that "Whig" tradition of thought
which was so well expressed in the *Vindiciae* and in the works
of Ponet and Buchanan. This tradition was not the offspring
of the Reformation but rather the legacy of the Middle Ages,
and it had received its clearest and most universal theoretical
formulation in the thought of the fourteenth- and fifteenth-
century Conciliarists, not least in that of Pierre d'Ailly. It is
because of this that Laski was correct in asserting that the road
from Constance to 1688 was a direct one and again that the
Council of Constance was "the real watershed between medieval
and modern politics." [81] For as Ponet himself said, "by this lawe
and argumentes of the canonists and example of deprivacion
of a Pope, are all clokes (wherewith Popes, bishoppes, priestes,
kaisers and kinges use to defende their iniquitie) utterly taken
away." [82]

81. *C Med H, 8,* 636.
82. Hudson, p. [105].

Conclusion

Despite the complexity of d'Ailly's political thinking his guiding principles are fundamentally quite simple. His position is
predicated on the belief that under the present divine dispensation, the will of God, expressed in the form of the immutable
dictates of the natural law, is accessible to the right reason of
all men. In accordance with these rationally accessible norms,
and interpreted in terms of them, the common good or common
interest is declared to be the end for which political authority
is instituted. "Mixed monarchy"—which embraces oligarchic
and democratic elements as well as monarchical—is the form
of government least likely to defect from this end. If, however,
a political authority fails to fulfill the functions for which it is
instituted, although measures such as tyrannicide and popular
revolt are forbidden, the natural law dictates that the community must nevertheless possess the authority to rectify the situation. Although political authority depends ultimately upon
God, it is at least mediately derived from the community, which
retains therefore the authority to prevent its own ruin. It can
exercise this authority either directly or through its representatives to the extent of judging, correcting, and even deposing
its ruler.

Most of these principles are not unfamiliar. The assertion of the popular origin of political authority and the belief that the common interest is the criterion of the legitimacy of governmental acts would serve by themselves to locate d'Ailly's political thinking within the long and hallowed tradition of European constitutionalism. This tradition came fully of age only under the maturing and transforming conditions of seventeenth-century political life, but its origins have to be sought in the day-to-day practices of medieval political life, both civil and ecclesiastical. For it was neither in the constitutional conflicts of seventeenth-century England, nor in the French religious wars of the previous century, but in the influential theories hammered out earlier on during the Conciliar era, that this constitutional tradition, freed at last from the particularizing elements of national and regional custom, received its first universal theoretical formulation.

The belief in the value of mixed monarchy is almost as familiar as the constitutionalist tradition but it is by no means coterminous with it. Historians have often read the idea of mixed monarchy into the distinctions of Sir John Fortescue, but McIlwain has insisted that the idea was fundamentally alien to the medieval brand of constitutionalism, which, he says, received its classic expression in the work of Bracton.[1] Legal limitations on the exercise of royal authority—these the medieval constitutionalists knew; but it was only in the seventeenth century that an element of political control was added to them, and then only in England, and after a revolutionary struggle. This is not to say that the classical idea of mixed monarchy was unknown during the Middle Ages, but rather that it represented little more than "a literary tradition" until it came into its own in England during the Civil War period. Previous to this it "touched the political life of the time" only on infrequent occasions. The Conciliar period, however, was definitely one of those occasions. It witnessed one of the few medieval attempts to transcend the fundamental weakness of medieval constitutionalism by buttressing the customary theoretical limitations on

1. McIlwain, *Constitutionalism*, pp. 67–122; cf. Francis D. Wormuth, *The Origins of Modern Constitutionalism* (New York, 1949), pp. 30–31, 50–58.

234

absolutism with some viable structure of administrative control. The importance of the political thinking of d'Ailly and Zabarella derives in no little part from the fact that, more explicitly than any of the other leading Conciliar thinkers, and long before constitutionalists in the national monarchies, they saw in the old idea of mixed monarchy the possibility of securing "a sanction short of force" for legal limitations on papal absolutism, and sought to naturalize this sanction by rooting it in the ancient oligarchic traditions of the Roman curia. The experiment failed, but it did so only after repeated and protracted attempts to make it work.[2]

One principle remains for comment, and it is a less familiar one. Few, if any, historians of political thought would deny that the belief in the existence of an immutable natural law accessible to the right reason of all men was well-nigh universal during the Middle Ages. But some might well be disposed to question whether medieval disagreements about the *nature* of natural law fall within their legitimate province as historians of *political* thought. Some have identified the natural-law tradition with the tradition of metaphysical "realism" or "essentialism," and have been prone therefore to assume that the nominalism of Ockham and his followers eliminated the very possibility of their having possessed any meaningful concept of natural law.[3] Others, accepting this diagnosis but acquainted also with the fact that the Ockhamists continued obstinately to appeal to the standards of the natural law, have concluded that their legal thinking must have enjoyed some sort of illogical immunity from the corrosive effects of their more radical philosophical assumptions.[4] Others still, conceding that this was not the case, and realizing that the realist–nominalist split had as its counterpart a rationalist–voluntarist divide in natural-law

2. See Hubert Jedin, *A History of the Council of Trent,* trans. Ernest Graf (St. Louis, 1957), *1,* 76–100.

3. Thus H. A. Rommen, *The Natural Law: A Study in Legal and Social History and Philosophy,* trans. Thomas R. Hanley (St. Louis, 1959), pp. 58–60.

4. Thus Max A. Shephard, "William of Ockham and the Higher Law," *The American Political Science Review,* 26 (1932), 1009; cf. George H. Sabine, *A History of Political Theory* (2nd ed. New York, 1959), p. 306.

thinking, have been inclined, nevertheless, to dismiss the difference as "unreal and trivial," perhaps even as characteristically scholastic.[5]

Such arguments are far from convincing. We ourselves have seen that the nominalism of the Ockhamists was the outcome of a fundamental voluntarism and that their legal thinking was not immune to the impact of this voluntarism. We have seen, too, that this lack of immunity by no means entailed the denial of a meaningful concept of natural law. What it did entail was a radical reinterpretation of the nature of natural law; this reinterpretation, far from being a mere scholastic quibble, marked a shift in political thinking, a shift significant both because of its causes and because of its consequences.

Political theorizing can take place on a variety of levels. Its inspiration may as easily be practical in nature as disinterestedly philosophical, and the approach to political questions of the adherents of the constitutional tradition was not usually a philosophical one. But d'Ailly was a theologian and philosopher, and as such he was unable, in articulating the structure of his political theory, to allow himself the gratuitous support of a host of assumptions which are no less philosophical in nature for being unconsciously or uncritically held. He was forced, instead, to attempt the prior task of consciously postulating a view of the world. This is in no way to suggest that we should expect his political theory to be deducible from his fundamental philosophical and theological premises, for that would be to misconceive the nature of a philosophical system,[6] but rather that we should expect to see in it the clear impress of his individual view of the world. While his political thought has been found to possess an independent coherence and importance of its own, its significance can hardly be fully assessed unless it is seen in the context of his broader theological and philosophical predilections.

5. Thus J. W. Gough, *John Locke's Political Philosophy* (Oxford, 1956), p. 4.

6. As has been said in relation to a greater (and more systematic) thinker, the system of a philosopher lies "not in an architectonic structure" but in the "thought which pervades its parts"; see Michael Oakeshott, ed., *The Leviathan of Thomas Hobbes* (Oxford, 1946), p. xix.

Not every historian of philosophy or of political theory is inclined to view with sympathy such a suggestion. Deriding as "an adventure" attempts to derive Ockham's political ideas from "his so-called Metaphysics," Philotheus Boehner claimed, a few years ago, that these ideas "in their great outlines could have been developed . . . from any of the classical metaphysics of the 13th century." [7] May not the same be true of d'Ailly's political ideas? The bulk, after all, of his political tracts were written later in his life than were his principal philosophical and theological works, and under very different circumstances. Moreover, the central arguments which they put forward can hardly be regarded as simply derived from his philosophico-theological principles since, as we have seen, they are rooted in the Conciliar theories elaborated by his canonist and publicist predecessors.

Nevertheless, Boehner himself was willing to admit that there were "inner connections" between Ockham's metaphysics and his political ideas, and Baudry and de Lagarde alike have been insistent about the importance of these continuities.[8] Nor are such continuities lacking in the case of d'Ailly. The basic tenet of his thought is the unity, freedom, and omnipotence of God. From this follows his conception of the universe as one in which an utterly free God boldly confronts a fragmented world of "absolutes," of isolated singular entities radically contingent upon Him. More than once we have had occasion to insist that this conception does not entail a denial of the existence of any moral or natural order in the universe. D'Ailly circumvents this, as did Ockham before him, by distinguishing between the absolute and ordained powers of God. What the conception does

---

7. "Ockham's Political Ideas," *The Review of Politics,* 5 (1943), 465–66.

8. L. Baudry, "La philosophie et la politique dans Guillaume d'Ockham," *Archives d'hist. doct. et litt. du M.A., 14* (1939), 209–30; Lagarde, *Naissance, 5* and *6,* esp. *5,* Ch. 1. Note that Lagarde (5, 27) is careful to stress that there can be no *deduction* of Ockham's political ideas from his general philosophical principles, but this has not saved him from criticism by J. B. Morrall, who has insisted on "the discontinuity between Ockham's philosophical and political thinking" in "Some Notes on a Recent Interpretation of William of Ockham's Political Philosophy," *Franciscan Studies, 9* (1949), 335–69.

involve is an unambiguous assertion of the fundamental relativity of that moral and natural order, and along with it a limitation of the segment of knowledge to which absolute validity can be ascribed. Just as the natural order which we perceive in the world is not proof against an incursion of the absolute power of God, neither is the natural moral law to which right reason is (though only in the present economy) our infallible guide. The banishing of the greater part of knowledge to the limbo reserved for the probable, or at best for the conditionally evident, is but one of the more immediate corollaries.

Such drastic changes can hardly leave the world of political ideas untouched. Even the most fundamental of these ideas can lay no claim to absolute evidence, and the bulk of them move in the shadowed world of the merely probable. The basic assumption underlying d'Ailly's Conciliar arguments is the belief that the community is the ultimate human source of political authority. It is because of this that it possesses the right to elect its ruler, either directly or indirectly via its representatives. D'Ailly grounds this right in the immutable mandates of the natural law. Yet even so fundamental a right as this is but a relative one, since the dictates of the natural law are immutable only in the presently ordained divine economy, and of His absolute power God could substitute for them other, perhaps even diametrically opposed provisions. Election, it is true, is one of the "created circumstances" or "titles" which God associates in the disposition of political authority with His approving will. But He does so only de facto or by His ordained power, and if He chooses to endow such titles with the concurrence of His approving will He does so freely. Of His absolute power He could equally well refrain from doing so, or could even bestow such political authority directly, in spite of, or without the coincidence of, such human titles, just as, for that matter, He could obligate us directly without the medium of any created law, either natural or human, or again, in the world of nature, directly effect whatever He normally effects indirectly by means of secondary causes.

It is d'Ailly himself who draws these important analogies between the workings of obligating law, the bestowal of political authority, and the operation of natural causality, and his ideas about all three are clearly responsive to the exigencies of his natural theology. This is apparent even if we confine our reading to the works in which he discusses the disposition of political authority, for subtle harmonics of his fundamental philosophico-theological positions can be detected both in his refusal to consider a political community as anything other than the aggregate of its members,[9] and in his specification of the command of a law-making authority as the constitutive element of human law. If in these works we hear little of the *potentia dei absoluta,* d'Ailly himself occasionally reminds us that he has not forgotten the qualifications that it imposed on his arguments. Thus he warns us that we cannot know in any evident way, but only with a degree of probability, whether or not a particular prelate or prince has a just title to his authority. Or again, he insists that God could create a pope even in opposition to the provisions of canon law, and given the confusion and protracted scandal of the Schism, he clearly thinks that such a miraculous interposition in the affairs of the Church is not altogether unlikely.[10]

Considerations such as these might well serve as the starting point for less restrained speculations,[11] but in the present context they will have proved their value if they serve to underline the one fact that it would be easy especially for historians of Conciliar thought to overlook, namely that d'Ailly's political ideas are the outcome of the encounter with political realities

9. This is clearly reflected in his definition of the Church: "Ecclesia militans proprie sumpta pro ecclesia universali potest isto modo describi: ecclesia est omnis homo fidelis, vel omnes homines fideles, in mortali corpore naturaliter viventes" (*Utrum Petri ecclesia lege reguletur,* Dupin, *1,* 666).

10. See above, Ch. 3, n. 45, p. 91.

11. One might, for example, be tempted to see in the striking parallels between his conception of political society and his "idea of nature" a tentative anticipation of that interpenetration of natural philosophy and political theory which became so prominent in the thinking of the eighteenth-century *philosophes.* But for a few preliminary remarks on this subject, see my article "Medieval Theories of Natural Law: William of Ockham and the Significance of the Voluntarist Tradition," *Natural Law Forum, 6* (1961), 78–83.

of d'Ailly the philosopher as well as d'Ailly the churchman, and bear the impress not only of the legal and political context in which he lived and thought, or of the ecclesiastical exigencies with which he grappled, but also of his fundamental philosophico-theological view of the world.

APPENDIX I[1]
D'Ailly and John of Paris

D'Ailly, *Tractatus de ecclesiastica potestate;* Dupin, 2, col. 926.

"circa ecclesiasticam potestatem, medium docet veritas catholica, inter duos errores: nam error Waldensium fuit, quod successores Apostolorum, scilicet Papa et praelatis ecclesiasticis repugnat dominium in temporalibus nec eis licet habere divitias temporales. Unde Ecclesiam Dei, et successores Apostolorum, et veros praelatos Ecclesiae, durasse dicunt tantum usque ad Silvestrum, a quo (donatione facta Ecclesiae per Constantinum Imperatorem) dicunt incepisse Romanam Ecclesiam, quae modo est, quae secundum ipsos non est Dei Ecclesia; sed Dei Ecclesiam jam defuisse dicunt, nisi in quantum in ipsis est continuata per ipsos vel reparata, ad quod inducunt auctoritates Evangelii, quae suadent consilium Evangelicae paupertatis. Ex quibus, quasi de consilio volentes facere praeceptum, dicunt Ecclesiae praelatos, Apostolorum successores non debere in temporalibus divitiis habere dominium. . . . Alius vero error fuit Herodianorum: Herodes enim audiens Christum Regem natum, credidit ipsum esse re-

John of Paris, *Tractatus de potestate regia et papali;* Leclercq, pp. 173–75.

"circa potestatem ecclesiasticorum pontificum veritas medium ponit inter duos errores. Nam error Valdensium fuit successoribus Apostolorum scilicet Pape et prelatis ecclesiasticis repugnare dominium in temporalibus nec eis licere habere divitias temporales. Unde Ecclesiam Dei et successores Apostolorum et veros prelatos Ecclesie Dei durasse dicunt tantum usque ad Silvestrum a quo donatione facta Ecclesie per Constantinum Imperatorem dicunt incepisse Romanam Ecclesiam que modo secundum ipsos non est Dei Ecclesia. Sed Dei Ecclesiam jam defecisse dicunt, nisi in quantum in ipsis est continuata vel per ipsos reparata. Ad quod inducunt inter cetera illud Matthei VI: Nolite thesaurizare vobis thesauros in terra" . . . etc . . . "Ex quibus dicunt prelatos Dei Ecclesie, successores Apostolorum, no debere habere dominium in temporalibus divitiis. Alius vero error fuit Herodis qui audiens Christum regem natum credidit ipsum regem esse terrenum. Ex quo derivari videtur opinio quorumdam modernorum qui

1. For a discussion of these texts see above, pp. 49–50.

gem terrenum. Ex quo derivari videtur error quorundam, qui in tantum ad oppositum praedicti errores Waldensium declinant, ut asserere praesumant, Papam, inquantum est loco Christi in terris ab ipso immediate habere primariam auctoritatem, dominium, et jurisdictionem in temporalibus bonis, non solum Ecclesiae donatis, seu alias juste acquisitis, sed etiam principibus secularibus subjectis, licet dicant quod Papa in his non habet executionem immediatam, nisi in quibusdam casibus notatis in *Extravagante, qui filii sunt legitimi. Per venerabilem.*

Inter hos autem duos errores contrarios. Catholica medium tenet Ecclesia; videlicet quod Papae et praelatis Ecclesiae, non repugnat habere dominium in temporalibus, et jurisdictionem, contra primum errorem: nec tamen eis debetur per se, ratione status sui, inquantum sunt Vicarii Christi et Apostolorum successores, contra secundum errorem. Sed eis convenire potest habere talia, si eis ex devotione collata fuerint vel aliunde, justo titulo acquisierint."

in tantum supradictum errorem declinant ad oppositum totaliter deflexi ut asserant dominium Papam in quantum est loco Christi in terris habere dominium in temporalibus bonis principum et baronum et cognitionem et jurisdistionem. Dicunt etiam quod hanc potestatem in temporalibus habet Papa excellentius quam princeps quia Papa habet eam . . . a Deo immediate, princeps autem habet eam a Deo mediante Papa. Et iterum quod Papa non habet executionem immediatam nisi in quibusdam casibus notatis *Extra. Qui filii sunt legitimi, Per venerabilem.* . . . Inter has ergo opiniones tam contrarias, quarum primam erroneam omnes putant, puto quod veritas medium ponit, quod scilicet prelatis Ecclesie non repugnat habere dominium in temporalibus et jurisdictionem, contra primam opinionem erroneam. Nec tamen eis debetur per se ratione status sui et ratione qua sunt Vicarii Christi et Apostolorum successores. Sed eis convenire potest habere talia ex concessione vel permissione principum si ab eis ex devotione aliquid hujusmodi collatum fuerit vel si habuerint aliunde."

APPENDIX II[1]
Abbreviatio dialogi Okam

Abbreviatio dialogi Okam, Paris, Bibliothèque Nationale, *Ms. Lat.* 14,579, fol. 101r.

Sextum capitulum ostendit quod extendendo jus divinum ad omne jus naturale, Romani ex jure divino habent jus eligendi summum pontificem, *et ibi nota distinctionem de jure naturali valde bonam.*

Item qualiter omne jus naturale potest vocari jus divinum, quia est a Deo qui est conditor naturae et quia aliquo modo explicite vel implicite continetur in jure divino et in divinis scripturis.

Item quod Romani de jure naturali tertio modo dicto habent jus eligendi summum pontificem, quia supposito quod aliquis sit aliquibus praeficiendus, praelatus, princeps, vel rector, evidenti ratione colligitur quod, nisi per illum vel illos quorum interest ordinetur contrarium, illi quibus praeficiendus habent jus ipsum ordinarie eligendi. Unde nullus debet dari ipsis invitis et hoc probat. *Et ibi nota quod Christus et non papa potuit privare Romanos jure eligendi summum pontificem. Hoc tamen Christus non fecit* sed magis oppositum docuit.

Item nota quare magis dicitur quod Romani habent praedictam potestatem jure divino vel naturali quam jure gentium. Enim quia ad gentium jus non spectat habere episcopum catholicum etc. (Italics mine.)

1. For a discussion of this text see above, pp. 141, 177–79.

Tractatus de materia

Tractatis de materia concilii generalis:
Introduction

1. *The Manuscripts* [1]

A: Paris, Bibliothèque Nationale, *Ms. Lat.* 1571. Paper, 17th century, 1 fol. and 98 pp., 240 mm x 185 mm, written in one column, averaging 29 lines to the column. It is written in a clear post-humanist hand. Fol. 1 is taken up by notes made by Baluzius; page 1 bears the superscription *Petri de Alliaco Episcopi Cameracensis Tractatus de Materia Concilii Generalis,* and page 98, the following note: *Descripsi ex veteri codici ms. anno MDCXCVII, mense aprili. Stephanus Baluzius.*

Consult *Bibliothèque Nationale, Catalogue Général des Mss. Lat.,* 2 (Paris, 1940), 72–73.

B: Paris, Bibliothèque Nationale, *Ms. Lat.* 1480, fols. 84r–120r. Parchment and paper, 15th century, 295 mm x 225 mm, written in one column, averaging 34 lines to the column. It is copied in a Gothic script, showing cursive influence, but usually clear. Fol. 83r bears the title *De Materia Concilii Generalis,* and fol. 84r the superscript *Episcopi Cameracensis.*

Consult *Bibliothèque Nationale, Catalogue Général des Mss. Lat.,* 2, 30.

---

1. I have been able to see these four manuscripts only in microfilm, and, in the cases of *Mss. C* and *V,* my description depends to a large extent upon my own examination of the microfilms. For the information, however, that *Ms. V* is copied on parchment I am indebted to Meller, *Studien,* p. 289.

C: Paris, Bibliothèque Nationale, *Ms. Lat.* 3124, fols. 27r–55v. Paper, 15th century, approximately 290 mm x 210 mm, written in one column, averaging 35 lines to the column. It is copied in a Gothic script that shows quite considerable cursive influence. It bears no title.

Consult *Bibliothèque Nationale, Catalogue Général des Mss. Lat., 4* (Paris, 1958), 175–76.

V: Vatican, *Ms. Vat. Ottob., lat.* 3074, fols. 1r–43r. Parchment, 15th century, written in one column averaging 34 lines to the column. It is copied in a somewhat difficult Gothic script that shows cursive influences. It bears no title, and has been described in no catalogue. Many of the folios seem to be stained, perhaps by dampness.

The classification of these manuscripts by the "genealogical" or "common faults" system indicates the existence of two manuscript traditions. *Mss. A* and *B* are very closely related to one another—in faults, omissions, variants, and word order.[2] Similarly, word order, common omissions, and variants suggest a close relationship between *C* and *V* too, but some variants and omissions common to *V* and *B*, but not to *C* and *V*, suggest that *V* may be a *conflated* manuscript.

Such a classification clearly gives no one manuscript any priority over the others. The text presented here is that of *Ms. V;* the variant readings of the other manuscripts are located in the footnotes. Two main considerations indicated this choice: the first, that *Ms. V* needs less correction than any of the others; the second, that its readings agree in the vast majority of cases with those contained in the fragments of the treatise which d'Ailly included in other of his works.

2. *The Edition*

The *Tractatus de materia concilii generalis* has never hitherto been edited in full.[3] Until recently, only three fragments of the treatise

2. The large number of omissions and variants unique to *A*, and the existence of a few readings common to *A* and *C*, or *A* and *V*, but not to *A* and *B*, necessitate the rejection of the obvious hypothesis that *A*, dating to 1697, is a copy of *B*.

3. In 1954, Meller edited the first two parts of the treatise (*Studien*, pp. 290–336). This edition came to my attention in 1955 when my own was nearing completion, and I saw fit to continue my work because Dr. Meller has not edited the full treatise, and because his version of the first two parts contains a surprising number of errors. These are too numerous to indicate in footnotes to the following text, but for a discussion of them, and for illustrations of their main types, see below, Appendix IV.

had been printed, none of these in its original form, and one of them incorrectly attributed.

The first fragment, which contains in abbreviated form the first seven *considerationes* of the *Prima Pars* along with additional material foreign to the *De Materia*, is to be found among the works of Gerson under the title *De concilio generalis unius obedientiae*.[4] This work was attributed in toto to Gerson,[5] and marginal annotations in *Mss. C* and *V* indicate that scholars or scribes became aware of the fact that part of the matter included in the *De materia* was to be found in the *De concilio*.[6] Salembier, however, seems to reject the attribution to Gerson of any part of the latter treatise,[7] and one can sympathize with his view. While it is extremely unlikely that any man would borrow undocumented arguments if he had to go to the trouble of finding the references from which those arguments drew their force, the reverse process of abbreviation is not at all uncommon, and the first part of the *De concilio* undoubtedly reads like a synopsis of d'Ailly's treatise.[8] But such an argument, plausible though it may be, is mistaken, for this problem of attribution can be settled in a definitive way simply by reference to a brief remark of d'Ailly's which seems, unfortunately, to have gone unnoticed. This remark occurs in his *Apologia concilii Pisani*, where, speaking of the *De materia*, he bluntly asserts that he took the first seven considerations of the *Prima Pars* from the writings of Gerson, adding to them other useful material.[9] Salembier was mistaken, therefore, in ascribing the *De concilio* to d'Ailly, and we are left with only two authentic printed fragments.

The first of these is to be found at the end of d'Ailly's later work, the *Tractatus de potestate ecclesiastica*, where he actually refers back

4. Dupin, 2, 24–32.

5. E.g., by Dupin and Valois. The latter, indeed, was unaware of any correspondence between parts of the *De concilio* and of the *De materia*, though he dates the two works similarly and upon the same grounds; see Valois, *France, 3,* 249, n. 3, and 270, n. 2.

6. See below, p. 253, n. 8.

7. Salembier, *Schisme,* p. 198, n. 1.

8. Dupin, 2, 24–29.

9. Printed in Tschackert, *Ailli,* Appendix XII, pp. [31]–[41]; see p. [41]: "mitto vobis tractatum, de quo supra tetigi, quem super materia generalis concilii dudum composui. In cujus prima parte septem considerationes satis utiles ex scriptis praememorati Johannis cancellarius Parisiensis recepi, aliqua iis non inutiliter superaddens."

to the *De materia* as the source of his concluding arguments.[10] The second, which is d'Ailly's redaction under the title *Tractatus de reformatione ecclesiae* of the third part of the treatise, was published many times during the fifteenth and sixteenth centuries,[11] but as we shall see later on, it differs from the original in more than one respect. The passages alien to the original treatise but included in this last fragment have been given, for easy reference, in appendices at the end of the edition.

In the course of preparing the edition several problems arose toward which definite policies had to be adopted. These were:

(1) *Ms. C* contains many marginal annotations (rarely fully legible on the microfilm) which together form an index to the treatise. It has been my policy to ignore these in the footnotes, but to include any annotation that seems to constitute a genuine gloss on the text. The same policy has been adopted towards the other manuscripts, although *Mss. A* and *B* contain few such notes.

(2) Concealed lacunae in d'Ailly's quotations from other authors are by no means infrequent, and where I have thought it desirable, lacunae have been indicated thus: ⟨. . .⟩

(3) The word order often differs in the several manuscripts but it has not been deemed necessary to indicate such differences in the *apparatus criticus*. The same policy has been adopted towards differences and peculiarities in spelling, for it is doubtful whether a treatise of this type would provide any reliable arguments for those interested in philology. A system of spelling therefore has been adopted which, I trust, is sufficiently uniform to ensure a readable text. With the exception of these differences in word order and spelling, all variants in the four manuscripts have been indicated, even in cases when they seemed to be trivial. Similarly, the pagination or foliation of all the manuscripts has been indicated in the text, and all quotations have been italicized.

(4) Where d'Ailly has quoted another author and the text of *Ms. V* has conflicted with that of the standard edition of the author quoted, I have adopted the reading given in that edition, though only if it is also contained in one or more of *Mss. A, B,* and *C.* It

10. Dupin, 2, 956 D–960 C.

11. Also known under the titles *De Emendatione Ecclesiae, De squaloribus Ecclesiae Romanae, Canones super reformatione Ecclesiae, De reformatione Ecclesiae.* The editions most readily available are those in Dupin, 2, 903–16, and Hardt, 1, 407 ff. Cf. Salembier, *Alliaco,* p. XXXII.

247

should be noted that this has concerned only individual word variants, and also that it accounts for most of the cases in which the readings of *Mss. A, B,* or *C* have been preferred to those of *V*.

3. *The Treatise*

There is a certain confusion over the date of the composition of this work. Salembier correctly dismissed the assumption of Louis Ellies Dupin and others that it was written in 1416, and concluded that 1403, *vel circiter,* was the correct date.[12] More precisely, he maintained that it was not written before May 1403, adducing as evidence the reference to the instructions of the delegation sent by the Sacred College to the French king,[13] for he said this delegation, consisting of the Cardinals de Saluces and de Malesset, did not see the King before May 1403.[14] Valois, on the other hand, ascribes the composition to the latter months of 1402 or the beginning of 1403,[15] quoting as proof two passages, the first of which indicates that Benedict was still imprisoned in the besieged palace at Avignon at the date of composition [16]—which would mean that d'Ailly must have been writing before March 11, 1403, the date of Benedict's escape [17]—and the second of which indicates that some of the countries recognizing the Avignonese succession and possibly all (other than France) had restored obedience to Benedict.[18] Now Provence had restored obedience around May 1401, Louis II of Anjou did so in August 1402, and Henry III of Castile in February 1403.[19] It follows, therefore, that the treatise was probably written between August 1402 and March 1403.

We are presented, then, with two possible conclusions: either that

12. Salembier, *Alliaco,* p. 266, n. 1.
13. "Inde concludere est tractatum Alliaceni non ante mensem maii 1403 fuisse lucubratum" (ibid., p. 268, n. 2).
14. Salembier, *Schisme,* p. 197.
15. Valois, *France, 3,* 249, n. 3.
16. "Immo videntur magis posse argui de saevo et crudeli odio illi qui eum in domo sua propria hostiliter invaserunt et adhuc incarceratum detinent" (below, p. 299).
17. Valois, *France, 3,* 325.
18. "Facilius ista restitutio et reductio tractari poterit in solo regno Franciae, si verum sit quod omnes alii jam restituerunt obedientiam, aut in ea permanserunt" (below, p. 257).
19. Valois, *France, 3,* 238–39, 273–75, 281–82.

the *De materia concilii generalis* consists of a group of fragments composed at different times and put together by d'Ailly later on, or that either Salembier or Valois was mistaken in his dating. The latter solution is the correct one. Salembier's argument depends upon his confusion of two distinct delegations sent by the Sacred College to the French king, on different business and at different dates. The text indicates quite clearly that d'Ailly is referring to the delegation which spoke out *against* Benedict and not on his behalf (after all, the *Secunda Opinio* holds *indistincte* that a restitution of obedience is not to be made).[20] The delegation in question was not therefore that of May 1403, but that consisting of the Cardinals de Malesset, de Thury, and de Saluce which the Sacred College sent to Paris in 1398, and which in January 1399 accused Benedict, in the presence of the King, of heresy, perjury, and other crimes.[21]

The way is clear, then, for an acceptance of the dating suggested by Valois, which is supported by another passage to which neither Valois nor Salembier referred,[22] and from which it is to be deduced that the treatise was written before the Eastern Emperor embarked for Constantinople at Venice in April 1403.[23] The conclusion follows that the *De materia concilii generalis* was written in the months between August 1402 and March 1403.

The unrest caused throughout Europe by the seemingly endless prolongation of the Great Schism provides the setting for the treatise, as, more particularly, does the strengthening of ecclesiastical disunity not only by the Schism itself, but also by the most important, though abortive, attempt to bring it to an end—the withdrawal of obedience from Benedict XIII, sponsored by France and adopted by other countries of the Avignonese obedience.

Such is the context in which we must view the treatise if we are

20. "Secunda opinio praedictae contraria indistincte tenet quod hujusmodi restitutio obedientiae in casu praesenti non est facienda. Et fundatur in quibusdam oppositionibus quae fiunt contra Dominum Benedictum, sicut patet in instructionibus Dominorum Cardinalium missorum ad Regem Franciae ex parte Sacri Collegii" (below, p. 288).

21. Valois, *France, 3,* 209–10.

22. "Quod nunc maxime opportune fieri posse videtur, dum eorum Imperator inter Latinos degens a Romana Ecclesia et Dominis temporalibus, praecipue a Francorum Rege, contra infideles cogitur auxilium et subsidium postulare" (below, p. 321).

23. See, L. Bréhier, *Le monde Byzantin: vie et mort de Byzance* (Paris, 1947), pp. 471–72.

to perceive its historical significance. It presents us, in the first place, with an analysis of ways and means to terminate the Schism made by a man who was both a prominent ecclesiastic and a distinguished academician (and one who, though a proponent of the Conciliar movement, was no extremist). It states, in the second place, the same man's program for reforming the Church "in head and members."

The *Pars Prima* treats of the matter and form, not of a General Council, but of the Council of the Avignonese *obedience* which was to discuss the matter of the Schism, maintaining among other things that such a council should refrain from hearing accusations of heresy and perjury brought against Benedict, and stating that innovations were to be avoided because they might lead to disaster and because the three well-publicized ways for ending the Schism—cession, compromise, and a general council—were adequate.

In the *Pars Secunda* d'Ailly sets forth the three current opinions upon the much discussed question of whether obedience was to be restored to Benedict before the convocation of such a council; the third opinion, and the one to which he himself probably subscribed,[24] was that only those prerogatives which were due by divine right to the Pope as head of the Church should be restored, while those which were accidental to the Papal office (such as reservations for ecclesiastical benefices) should not.

Finally, the *Tertia Pars*. It consists of d'Ailly's program for the reformation of the Church at every level of its hierarchy, from the Pope down to the laity, a program which, as the footnotes indicate, anticipated to a considerable extent the reforming decrees of the Council of Trent. This latter fact should not be overstressed, for it is less indicative of d'Ailly's prescience than of the persistent nature of the problems which plagued the late medieval—or rather the pre-Tridentine—Church.

This program of reform, d'Ailly, as we have seen, revised and presented at the Council of Constance on November 1, 1416, under the title of *Tractatus super reformatione ecclesiae*.[25] It should be noted that this latter work is not, as both Tschackert and McGowan seem to believe, a redaction of the *Tractatus agendorum in concilio generali de ecclesiae reformatione*, since that work was written as

24. Salembier, *Schisme*, p. 200, comments: "la connaissance que nous avons du caractère et des autres oeuvres de d'Ailly nous permet de croire que ce tiers parti est bien celui auquel appartenait l'auteur."

25. Cf. above, n. 11.

late as 1409.[26] Nor is it the same text as the third part of the *De materia,* for besides abbreviating in order to eliminate anchronisms and superfluous matter, d'Ailly also omitted one passage and interpolated two new ones. These changes deserve mention because they reflect certain developments in his position.

When he wrote the *De materia,* d'Ailly was still a mere bishop, and in two distinct passages [27] he did not hesitate to attack the cardinals. Granted that in the second passage he adds that he himself does not approve of the opinion there expounded that the cardinalate should be abolished; [28] nevertheless, when he came, as a cardinal, to write the *Tractatus super reformatione,* he omitted the first of the passages in question, and substituted for the second a condemnation of the opinion that the cardinalate should be suppressed, stating that such an opinion is erroneous.[29] These changes, however, are probably less indicative of his own self-interest than of the strengthening of the conservative and moderate elements of his character, for it is clear from the original text that he was never an extremist.

Perhaps more significant is a further passage which he interpolated towards the end of the work,[30] at the point at which he is discussing the duty of princes to encourage reform. In this passage he criticizes

26. See Salembier, *Alliaco,* p. XXXI; cf. Tschackert, *Ailli,* pp. 259–60; J. P. McGowan, *Pierre d'Ailly and the Council of Constance* (Washington, 1936), p. 70. Tschackert may be excused for his mistake because the manuscripts, and therefore the contents of the *De materia,* were unknown to him, though he did know that d'Ailly had written some tract of this nature (see p. [38], n. 3). This fact is relevant also to the old dispute about the authorship of the *Tractatus* or *Capita agendorum,* for Tschackert's arguments in favor of attributing this work to d'Ailly and not to Zabarella depend upon his misinterpretation of certain references made by d'Ailly to the *De materia.* Unaware of the existence of the *De materia,* Tschackert asserted that these references were to the *Capita agendorum* and concluded that this latter work must, therefore, have been written by d'Ailly (see p. 166, n. 1). Strangely enough most subsequent writers on d'Ailly, though they have been aware of the existence of the *De materia,* have accepted without question Tschackert's attribution to him of the *Capita agendorum* (see, e.g., Meller, *Studien,* p. 7, n. 50).

At a later date I hope to examine this particular problem of attribution. I am inclined to think that the *Capita agendorum* was not, in fact, written by d'Ailly.

27. See below, pp. 322 ff., 328 ff.

28. "Ideo fuit quorundam opinio, quam tamen non approbo . . . quod ille Cardinalium status tanquam male stabilis, caderet, sicut olim status Chorepiscoporum" (below, p. 328).

29. See Appendix V.

30. See Appendix VI.

the system of voting by "nations," declaring it to be a civil rather than an ecclesiastical procedure, and suggesting voting by ecclesiastical provinces as an alternative.[31] He had had nothing to say when the original resolution had been adopted,[32] but it may be assumed that the proceedings of the Council had speedily made it clear to him that voting by nations served only to foster division by exacerbating political jealousies and international rivalries.

An introduction of this kind is not the place in which to attempt a precise assessment of the influence which the *De materia concilii generalis* may have exercised upon the course of historical events. But three considerations which have emerged from our discussion, and which are relevant to such an assessment, should be indicated. In the first place, the policy proposed in the third opinion of the *Prima Pars* (i.e. that obedience should be restored to Benedict, but only in part), was the policy that was finally adopted by France in 1406. Secondly, the *Tertia Pars* anticipated many of the reforming decrees of the Council of Trent. And thirdly, the same *Tertia Pars*, in its revised form, was repeatedly published in several countries, being translated into German as late as 1600.[33]

4. *Text*

TRACTATUS DE MATERIA CONCILII GENERALIS PETRI DE ALLIACO EPISCOPI CAMERACENSIS [1]

Ad honorem Sanctae Trinitatis tractatus iste tres partes continebit. Prima erit de quibusdam generalibus considerationibus tam circa materiam quam circa formam Concilii occasione praesentis schismatis celebrandi. Secunda erit de diversis et adversis opinionibus circa illam quaestionem: utrum ante hujusmodi Concilium subtracta Papae oboedientia eidem debeat restitui? Tertia erit de quibusdam

---

31. D'Ailly was obviously exercised by the fear that the *episcopelli* of the multitudinous Italian dioceses would have too much power, for he wrote in certain safeguards to make the ecclesiastical provinces more evenly balanced. See Appendix VI.

32. Cf. J. P. McGowan, *Pierre d'Ailly and the Council of Constance*, p. 48.

33. Repeated publication implies demand, and the *Tractatus super Reformatione Ecclesiae* seems to have been used by the Reformers as anti-Romanist propaganda, being published at Basel in 1551 under the significant title *De squaloribus Ecclesiae Romanae* (see Salembier, *Alliaco*, p. XXXII).

1. This is the title to be found in *Ms. A;* cf. above, p. 244.

specialibus considerationibus circa necessariam reformationem universalis Ecclesiae Christi.

In quibus omnibus lectorem praemonitum esse volo et in singulis pro generali protestatione praesuppositum esse cupio, nihil assertive aut determinative, sed solum recitative et disputative, per me fore dicendum; his tantummodo [2] exceptis, quae sanctae [3] Ecclesiae approbat [4] auctoritas.

SEQUITUR PRIMA PARS HUJUS TRACTATUS

Quia scriptum est: *Audiens sapiens sapientior erit,*[5] ideo daturus occasionem sapientibus ut sapientiores fiant, propono eorum examinationi octo considerationes, quae sequuntur, super materia et forma communis Concilii hujus oboedientiae; ex quibus patebit citius, si sit expediens Concilium hujusmodi celebrari, et si [6] sic, quae cautela debeat observari.

Prima,[7] non videtur expedire fieri hujusmodi Concilium ad tractandum determinative materias fidei.[8] Ratio ad hoc, quia esset dare occasionem scandali et periculi (2) magni in fide nostra, si aliquid determinaret ista pars sive altera in materia quae omnes tangit, et quae ab omnibus debet approbari,[9] quemadmodum patuit de Latinis et Graecis.[1] Facile enim esset et verisimile, quod determinationem in hac parte factam non approbaret altera pars; praesertim si in aliquo tangi videretur status eorum in materia hac schismatis, sicut [2]

2. Omnimodo *AB.*

3. *Add.* matris *AB.*

4. *Add.* aut approbabit *AB.*

5. Prov. 1:5.

6. *Om. A.*

7. *Om. AB.*

8. Ea quae sequuntur, sunt de dictis domini Joannes de Gersonno, Cancellarii Parisiensis, *in marg. C;* cf. above, p. 246, and below, n. 3, p. 266.

9. Cf. the maxim of Justinian: "quod omnes similiter tangit, ab omnibus comprobetur" (C. 5, 59, 5, § 2), the emphasis being on the summoning of all parties interested because of their rights. For a discussion of this and related texts see above, p. 112, note 27, and p. 145.

1. The case, for instance, of the breach between the Greek and Latin Churches associated with the name of Michael Cerularius: cf. Mansi, *19,* 811 ff.; J.-P. Migne, *Patrologiae Cursus Completus . . . series Graeca* (Paris, 1880), *120,* 735–48; L. Bréhier, *Le Schisme Oriental du XIe siècle* (Paris, 1899), pp. 123 ff.

2. Sic *C.*

tamen tangeretur, et jam apud istam par-(1v)-tem et forte apud aliam dicuntur multae assertiones de fide, in quibus est adversissima sententia inter diversas oboedientias, immo et inter multos ejusdem oboedientiae; ut super materia appellationis a Papa, et super eo, quod renuens cedere aut cessionem offerre est schismaticus, et quod non adhaerens subtractioni est suspectus de schismate vel Ecclesia adversus, vel in latitudine schismatis. Et ita de similibus multis.

Constat quod (84v) de prima istarum propositionum est controversia in regno Franciae apud theologos et decretistas et inter multos de consilio et de parlamento Regis et alios de Universitate et inter se mutuo.[3] De aliis duabus assertionibus similiter et amplius, quoniam altera oboedientia nunquam tales concederet, immo reputaret erroneas. Propterea perspicuum est non esse tutum talia determinare per modum auctoritatis Concilii generalis. Sed nec deberent tales assertiones leviter a particularibus etiam poni, quia (27v) deputatur hoc ab aliis in injuriam suam: ut dicere, quod error sit in fide, si asseratur, quod stante dubio probabili de papatu apud duos contendentes alteri (3) sit adhaerendum, quia non videtur esse possibile majus dubium probabile quam sit in casu praesentis schismatis. Et tamen utraque oboedientia dicit [4] esse oboediendum suo. Et ita de similibus: ut quod non sit alia via humanitus [5] invenibilis ad sedandum schisma quam via cessionis, cum tamen videatur jam reddita per se inefficax, nisi concurrat saltem Concilium generale, quod excludere non bene saperet, et quia certe circunstantiis negotiorum variatis possunt viae et remedia ad unitatem habendam vario modo reperiri, sicut et necessarium esse experientia praesens notum facit.

Unde qui sine auctoritate scripturae, Ecclesiae, vel Concilii, tales assertiones dogmatizat, videtur temerarius judicandus juxta doctrinam Hostiensis in prologo Summa suae,[6] quia scilicet: *prudentiae*

3. For a discussion of the withdrawal of obedience of 1398 and of the problems which it raised, consult Valois, *France, 3,* Ch. 2 and 3; also Salembier, *Schisme,* pp. 162 ff., and G. Barraclough, "Un Document inédit sur la soustraction d'obédience de 1398," *Rev. d'hist. ecclésiastique, 30* (1934), 101–15. The text of the withdrawal is to be found in Mansi, *26,* col. 841.

4. dixit *AB.*

5. humanitas *A.*

6. Henry of Segusia, Cardinal-Bishop of Ostia, d. 1271; *Summa Hostiensis super titulis decretalium, cum summariis et adnotationibus N. Superantii,* Proemium, § Septimo (Lyons, 1542), f. 2r.

suae innititur; et capitaneam sententiam veritati praeponit: 37 dist.
"Relatum," [7] *De constitutione cap. 1* [8] *et cap. "Ne innitaris,"* [9,1] ubi
allegatur auctoritas (2r) Salomonis: *Ne innitaris prudentiae tuae*
⟨. . .⟩ *ne sis sapiens apud temetipsum.*[2]

Non videtur expedire fieri concilium hujusmodi ad tractandum
reformationem Ecclesiae in moribus per modum determinationis.
Ratio ad hoc est quoad multa eadem sicut ad praecedentem propositionem; addito quod reformatio Ecclesiae universalis fieri non
potest in moribus sine abolitione multorum statutorum super excommunicationibus et ceteris traditionibus nimis multiplicatis,
quia [3] nec observantur nec observari possunt rationabiliter ubique
propter varietatem morum et temporum.

Circa quod advertendum est, (4) quod—sicut recitat Cantor
Parisiensis in Verbo Abbreviato cap. LXXII [4]—*in Lateranensi Con-*
cilio, sedentibus patribus ad condendum nova decreta, ait Johannes
Carnotensis: [5] *"Absit,"* inquit *"nova (85r) condi, vel plurima ve-*
terum reintingi vel renovari. Multitudine enim inventorum prae-
gravamur, cum dicat auctoritas,[6] *quia etiam de utilibus aliqua post-*
ponenda sunt, ne multitudine utilium gravemur." Potius elabo-
randum esset *"ut evangelium observaretur, cui nunc pauci oboediunt.*
Timeamus, ne dicat nobis Dominus: [7] *Irritum facitis praeceptum Dei*
propter traditiones vestras." [8] Haec ille. Ex quibus patet, quod
multiplicatio humanorum constitutionum restringenda esset potius
quam amplianda. Et tamen tales remotiones [9] statutorum et canonum
antiquorum aut additiones novorum fieri nequeunt rationabiliter

7. D. 37, c. 14.
8. X, 1, 2. c. 1.
9. initatis *B*.
1. X, 1, 2, c. 5.
2. Prov. 3: 5–7.
3. quae *AB*.
4. Peter Cantor, master of theology at Notre Dame in Paris, d. 1197. Cf. P.
Feret, *La Faculté de Théologie de Paris, 1* (Paris, 1894), 58–67. The reference is
to *Verbum abbreviatum*, cap. 79, § 206; PL *205*, 235.
5. The third Lateran Council, convoked by Pope Alexander III in 1179. The
debates at this Council are not extant, but John, Bishop of Chartres, is listed
among the dignitaries present, in Mansi, *22*, 239. Cf. Hefele-Leclercq, *5*, 1087.
6. Cf. PL, *205*, 474, § 483, note: "auctoritas intelligitur ut supra indeterminate
pro veteribus auctoribus."
7. deus *C*.
8. Matt. 15:6.
9. renovationes *C*.

pro tota Ecclesia sine consensu communi.[1] Alias posset esse [2] diversitas nimia in moribus et judiciis quoad ea quae Papae et Concilia statuerunt. Si vero diceretur, quod multa ibi bona possent advisari et discuti, sed non determinari, pauca esset ista utilitas quoad hoc in comparatione tanti facti. Nam pauci viri litterati et probi faciliter, et forte congruentius, ista consiliarent, extraherent, et ordinarent. Nolo tamen dicere, quin in multis particularibus [3] posset Ecclesia per suas partes reformari, prout [4] hoc necesse esset. Sed ad hoc agendum sufficerent Concilia provincialia, et ad quaedam satis essent Concilia dioecesana et (28r) synodalia; (2v) prout super hac re jam aliqua scripta sunt et avisata, si quis vellet ad opus manum mittere et ad fortia. Sed heu *desolatione desolata est omnis terra, quia nemo (5) est qui recogitet* [5] *corde,*[6] et *quaerunt omnes, quae sua sunt.*[7]

Non videtur expedire fieri Concilium generale hujus oboedientiae ad tractandum et sententiandum de criminibus Domini Benedicti sibi per quosdam impositis, ut puta de perjurio et schismate et haeresi, aut de suspicione vehementi super istis.[8] Ratio: [9] primo, quia oboedientia ista in se et partibus suis divisa est circa judicium de actis per Papam,[1] aliis dicentibus quia bonus est et sufficienter obtulit, praesertim novissime; aliis contrarium asserentibus. Tractare igitur talia coram multitudine tam multipliciter divisa esset potius induratio et nova multiplicatio divisionum quam illarum sedatio, attento quod ita requireret Dominus Benedictus fieri discussionem super dictis haereticis et actis per Cardinales et eorum moribus, super gestis etiam aliorum qui sibi subtraxerunt. Et sic ista tractare non esset, nisi detrahere et discordiam parare. Quod prohibetur 46 dist. § 1 [2] et cap.[3] *Clericus invidens.*[4]

1. Cf. above, n. 9, p. 253.
2. *Add.* statim *AB.*
3. partibus *AB.*
4. immo *AB.*
5. recogitat *AB.*
6. Jerem. 12:11.
7. Philipp. 2:21.
8. Benedict's chief accusers at the Council of 1398 were Simon de Cramaud, Pierre le Roy, and Pierre Plaoul; cf. Valois, *France, 3,* 148 ff.; Salembier, *Schisme,* p. 168; Mansi, *26,* 841.
9. *Om.* ratio *AB.*
1. Cf. above, n. 3, p. 254.
2. *Pars I Gratiani?*
3. Perhaps this originally read: 46 dist § 1 et *specialiter* cap. etc.
4. D. 46, c. 7.

Secundo, quia Concilium hujusmodi ad hunc finem aut fieret secundum (85v) formam scriptam [5] a jure, aut nova adinventione. Si primo [6] modo,[7] constat quod Benedictus deberet praeesse, etiam sine nova summissione. Et tamen, rebus stantibus ut stant, non videtur quis locus esset aptus sibi [8] ad securitatem, cum detineatur inclusus. Nec videtur quod permanentes in subtractione suae vocationi [9] oboedirent. Et ita nihil ageretur. Si autem fieret Concilium per novos modos praeter formam juris, non videtur modus verisimilis ante celebrationem Concilii quomodo [1] praelati et principes in unum concordarent, uno volente unum modum, altero alium. Et esset tractus in tractando hoc dispendiosissimus et sumptuo—(6)—sissimus sine fructu magno.

Tertio, quia [2] in determinatione hujus materiae necesse esset multa concurrere (3r) et allegare tangentia fidem et mores. Sed tales materias non expedit in hoc Concilio ventilare ad determinandum hic, prout dictum est in prima consideratione.

Quarto, quia nunc omnia possunt fieri ad unitatem universalem Ecclesiae erga alios procurandam, quemadmodum, si tota haec materia esset in concilio isto terminata, sive Papa remaneret, sive non, attento quod offert omnia quae noviter electus quicunque posset offerre. Immo apud talem aut pro tali noviter electo fieri possent novae colligationes et confirmationes pejores prioribus, et fieret verisimiliter nova divisio, aut jam facta continueretur in hac oboedientia.

Non videtur expedire pro restituendo obedientiam Papae in spiritualibus fieri Concilium generale.

Primo, quia videtur implicatio, sicut tactum est, quod maneat subtractio (28v) hujusmodi a Papa, et quod fiat concilium.

Secundo, quia facilius ista restitutio et reductio tractari poterit in solo regno Franciae, si verum sit quod omnes alii jam restituerunt oboedientiam, aut in ea permanserunt, si verum sit etiam quod subtractio non est facta a Papa etiam in [3] regno, nisi sub conditione

---

5. praescriptam *AB*.
6. prima *C*.
7. *Om.* modo *C*.
8. *Om.* sibi *A*.
9. *Om.* suae vocationi *AB*.
1. quoquo modo *A*.
2. *Om. C.*
3. sub *AB*.

explicita, ut quidam dicunt, aut saltem implicita, et quae de jure et aequitate debet intelligi. Haec conditio est: quousque Papa fecerit debitum suum et concesserit illa quae sibi petebantur,[4] et propter quorum negationem fiebat subtractio: Nam cessante causa, cessare debet effectus.[5] Addito hoc, quod subtractio nullo modo fieri potuit juste, nisi ad finem unionis tanquam (7) medium ad hoc necessarium. Alioquin tantum malum et tam insolitum (86r) inoboedientiae nullo modo posset a culpa defendi. Si ergo nunc videatur quod subtractio non prodest ad unionem, vel non est necessaria propter condescensionem Papae ad illa quae petebantur, cessare ipsa debet: quia, si rebus stantibus ut stant erga Papae promptitudinem de cedendo, non posset de novo fieri subtractio, sicut concedere habent adversarii, ut videtur, non potest aut debet (3v) eisdem rebus stantibus eadem subtractio continuari.

Tertio,[6] quia restitutio hujusmodi oboedientiae quoad spiritualia fieri commodius et brevius potest per assensum Cardinalium et reconciliationem mutuam indulgendo praeterita, et ratificando quae ratificanda essent ad cautelam futurorum, et emendationem securiorem praeteritorum et conscientiarum serenationem et ad abolendam omnem infamiae aut rebellionis notam, et quatenus in viam pacis communi animo et eodem pede procederet haec oboedientia concordius; quoniam faciendo restitutionem debitis modis, nec subtrahentes nec ille a quo est facta subtractio remanerent notati de talibus; quod [7] difficilius esset evadere, si per concilium aliquod fieret determinativa decisio. Et ad talem reconciliationem Papae et Cardinalium et pacificationem animorum, injuriarum quoque omnium oblivionem, pro concordi modo procedendi in hac materia facilius obtinendo deberent laborare omnes [8] principes catholici, exemplo Imperatoris qui in Concilio Nicaeno jurgia episcoporum sedavit, ut *his omissis, illa quae ad fidem Dei pertinent absque ulla*

---

4. patebantur *C.*

5. St. Thomas Aquinas, *ST* 1, qu. 96, art. 3, objection 3; also in the form: "remota causa, removetur effectus," *ST* 1a 2ae, qu. 85, art. 5 and elsewhere. The principle is also employed in the canon law: "quod ergo necessitas pro remedio reperit, cessante utique necessitate debet cessare pariter quod urgebat" (C. 1, q. 7, c. 7).

6. taceo *A.*

7. quos *A.*

8. *Om.* omnes *ABC.*

animorum contentione, disceptarent, sicut legitur in Historia Ecclesiastica lib. 10, cap. 2,[9] et saepe (8) recitatur in canone.[1]

Non videtur expedire concilium tale celebrari pro restituendo
oboedientiam Papae in administrationibus beneficiorum et aliorum
hujusmodi: quae licet annexa sint spiritualibus, tamen possunt temporalia nominari.[2]

Primo, quia rationes aliquae priores de non expediendo reformationem Ecclesiae universalem in moribus tractare faciunt pro hac
parte. Et pro ista [3] materia animadvertendum est, quod secundum
multorum opinionem, et si concederetur Papam habere de jure
divino dominium universale respectu omnium, tamen constat quod,
pro diversitate (29r) temporum et locorum et statuum, nec Papa
nec Ecclesia habuerunt aut habere debent in talibus dispensatio-
nibus et administrationibus beneficiorum et temporalium jurisdic-
tionum universaliter exercitium aut executionem aut usum. Itaque
notum est (4r) quod Ecclesia tempore Christi et Apostolorum nullum habuit exercitium aut executionem juridicam et (86v) civilem
circa hujusmodi temporalia. Immo Christus plus videtur facto et
verbo tale exercitium jurisdictionis civilis prohibuisse quam per-
misisse, licet non dicam quod prohibuerit aut oppositum consuluerit
nisi pro loco et tempore. Quia enim Ecclesia tunc multiplicanda
erat per discursum Apostolorum et fidelium, ideo talis jurisdictio
temporalis et possessiones fuissent eis ad impedimentum; et tales
sunt ad hoc congruentiae multae. Sed pro tempore Silvestri et Constantini magni placuit Domino ad dilatationem Ecclesiae suae
inspirare tum Constantino quod tales possessiones daret, tum
Ecclesiae quod reciperet.[4] Et duravit hujusmodi dotatio Ecclesiae
usque ad tempora nostra (9) per successiones sanctissimorum
patrum Gregorii et Ambrosii et aliorum, quos non est credibile in
retentione talium errasse contra Christi jussionem. Sed longe aliter

9. The reference is to the Latin paraphrase by Rufinus Aquileiensis of the
Ecclesiastical History of Eusebius, Book I, c. 1; PL *21*, 468–69.

1. Cf. D. 15, c. 1 and 3; D. 16, c. 9.

2. The passage which follows is discussed above, p. 44.

3. illa *C.*

4. That the *Donatio Constantini* was a forgery was demonstrated shortly after
this treatise was written, by Nicholas of Cusa, Lorenzo Valla, and Reginald Pe-
cocke, Bishop of Chichester. For the text of the *Donatio* consult Mansi, 2, 603 ff.
For a bibliography of secondary authorities, cf. *Lex. für theol. u. Kirche, 6* (1934),
167–68.

in primitiva dotatione distribuebantur bona talia quam postmodum tempore praelatorum, qui coeperunt paulatim refrigescere a sanctitate priorum. Tandem abusi sunt taliter collationibus beneficiorum et hujusmodi administratione, quod Papae paulatim et successive ad se multa revocaverunt, usque adeo quod finaliter, datis occasionibus et acceptis, quas non est hic opus recitare, quasi tota collatio et jurisdictio talis penes Papam et ejus curiam remanebat, ita ut vix esset praelatus qui posset minimum beneficium conferre. Concurrebant ad hoc [5] exactiones multiplices pro statu Papae et cardinalium. Et si fraudes et abusus et simoniae committerentur, relinquo judicandum expertis.

Contra [6] hanc usurpationem Romanae Curiae advertendum est, quod scribit Cantor Parisiensis in Verbo Abbreviato, cap. 37,[7] ubi specialiter reprobat exemptiones, et eas facientes et procurantes multis auctoritatibus et exemplis concludit [8] esse schismaticos. Et in fine capituli contra se obiciens ait: *Sed* [9] *dicitur mihi: "Os tuum ponis in caelum."* [1] *Respondeo quod non. Haec enim non asserendo, sed opponendo induco.* Et quasi ironice loquens subdit: *Non enim licet mihi dicere Domino Papae: "Cur ita facis?"* (4v) *Sacrilegium enim est opera ejus redarguere et vituperare. Veruntamen horum solutionem, vel qua ratione his obvietur, non video. Scio enim* [2] *quia auctoritate veteris* [3] *ac novi canonis non fiunt haec in Ecclesia, sed speciali auctoritate sedis apostolicae, quam non patitur Dominus errare. Forte* (10) *enim instinctu et familiari consilio Spiritus Sancti legeque privata hoc* [4] *agit, sicut Samson se cum hostibus occidit.*[5] (87r) Ex qua similitudine patet, quod haec locutio ironica est. Unde finaliter concludit applicando verbum poetae de Caesare, et inferioribus potestatibus saecularibus ad Papam et inferiores Praelatos. *Sic, inquit, sublati sunt Consules et Proconsules de medio, ut vel pauca vel nulla imperent, et omnia sit* (29v) *Caesar qui omnia*

---

5. haec *AB*.

6. circa *AB*.

7. Peter Cantor, *Verbum abbreviatum,* cap. *44,* § 114; PL *205,* 139–40; cf. above, n. 4, p. 255.

8. probat *A*.

9. *Om. A*.

1. Ps. 72:9.

2. *Om. CV*.

3. *Om. AB; Add.* doctorum *AB*.

4. haec *AB*.

5. Cf. Judges 16:30.

sicut omnibus imperet, juxta illud Lucani: *Omnia Caesar erat,*[6] vel illud: Omnia Caesar avet, id est, avide cupit. Haec idcirco dixi, quoniam forte aliquibus videretur, quod sit expediens Ecclesiae universali redire omnia ad pristinum statum Ecclesiae tempore Silvestri et Gregorii, quando quilibet praelatus dimittebatur in sua jurisdictione et sollicitudinis parte, et Papa tenebat quae sua erant absque tot reservationibus et continuis magnisque exactionibus pro sustinendo statum Curiae et capitis nimis forte crescentem super caeteros membrorum status; vel saltem in his esset modificatio et moderatio inferioribus ecclesiis et praelatis tolerabilis [7] adhibenda. Ad sciendum igitur istud cum multis appendenciis de provisione clericorum sufficientium etc, et ad providendum expediens est fieri determinationem et reformationem universalem Ecclesiae. Nam universalem statum tangit. Sed dictum est prius, quod reformatio talis fieri non debet in concilio solius oboedientiae istius, saltem determinative. Non dico tamen, quin ibi possent multa utilia tam in fide quam in moribus et reformationibus statuum praeadvisari,[8] postea in generali omnium fidelium concilio conclusive terminanda.[9]

Si vero quis obiciat, quod istud sic stare non potest cum (11) eis quae (5r) dicta sunt de restitutione oboedientiae quoad spiritualia, quin esset ita bene periculum inoboedientiae culpabilis in uno sicut in alio, respondetur, quod latissima est differentia in spiritualibus et temporalibus quoad hoc. Et utinam bene fuisset semper intellecta a prioribus et modernis. Forte quod adhuc starent Graeci cum Latinis. Patet enim ex priori deductione, quod Papa potest manere [1] Papa universalis in perfectione magna, immo majori quam erat Silvester, et tamen nullum habebit exercitium actuale circa temporalia Ecclesiae universalis per dioeceses, quantumcunque habeat dominium vel plenitudinem potestatis in habitu. Quae potestas ex causis certis potest cohiberi et artari,[2] immo debet, ne exeat in actum, sed dimittat singula singulis ministrare, sicut caput in humano corpore dimittit (87v) singula membra singulis officiis inservire, juxta similitudinem quam applicat Apostolus ad corpus Ecclesiae in prima

6. M. Annaeus Lucanus, *De bello civili,* III, line 108. Cited Cantor, *Verbum abbreviatum,* cap. 32; PL 205, 117.

7. tolerabiliter *ABC.*

8. praevisari *AB.*

9. For a discussion of the parallel passages and of the idea of *status ecclesiae* see above, pp. 110–12; cf. p. 145.

1. moenere *A.*

2. arceri *AB.*

epistola ad Corinthios [3] et in aliis multis locis. Nonne Christus fuit Ecclesiae caput principale et Papa perfectissimus? Nonne similiter post eum Petrus? Ipsi tamen omne exercitium abdicaverunt a se in talibus, quamquam Christus cum summa facilitate illud obtinere potuisset. Nihil ergo de perfectione status Summi Pontificis diminuitur, si pro causa rationabili removetur ad tempus aut suspenditur sibi tam anxia sollicitudo tot curarum immortalium et periculosissimarum in anima et corpore pro hujusmodi exercitio circa temporalia distribuenda atque conferenda. Augetur potius sua perfectio, et gratulari profecto deberet in Domino.

Videtur ulterius per [4] hoc multis quod non expedit unum solum caput praeesse in tali (30r) exercitio administrationis temporalium, sicut expedit, immo sicut necesse est unum solum praeesse in [5] spiritualibus respectu omnium. Cujus ratio est, quia ea quae fidei sunt debent eadem [6] esse (12) apud omnes. Et haec identitas et unitas vix aut nunquam perpetuari posset, nisi recursus esset finalis ad unum caput. Sed de traditionibus (5v) humanis pro regimine temporalium Ecclesiae totaliter oppositum invenitur, quoniam secundum varietatem temporum, locorum, et gentium, et rituum, variandae sunt decretales et ordinationes super collationibus et regimine talium temporalium. Et ideo exercitium et adminstratio talium non videtur ad unum solum pertinere, sed ad multos. Et ad hoc faciunt auctoritates Apostoli quas in dicto capitulo Cantor allegat: [7] *Omnis,* inquit, *anima potestatibus sublimioribus subdita sit.*[8] (Non ait *potestati,* sed potestatibus ordinatis a Deo in Ecclesia.) Quibus *qui resisti,* sicut ait idem Apostolus, *ordinationi Dei resistit.*[9] Item: *Oboedite praepositis* [1] *vestris.*[2] Glossa *majoribus et minoribus.*[3,4]

3. I Cor. 12:12–28.

4. pro *AB.*

5. *Om.* tali exercitio . . . unum solum praeesse in *AB.*

6. *Om. C.*

7. *Verbum abbreviatum,* cap. 44; PL 205, 137; cf. above, n. 4, p. 255, and n. 7, p. 260.

8. Rom. 13:1.

9. Rom. 13:2.

1. principibus *AB.*

2. Heb. 13:17.

3. Cf. *Liber vite* . . . *Biblia cum glossis ordinariis* (Venice, 1495), f. 1312r. For a discussion of the problem of the medieval Biblical gloss, consult B. Smalley, *The Study of the Bible in the Middle Ages* (Oxford, 1952), pp. 46 ff.

4. *Om.* et minoribus *AB.*

Ex his omnibus, quae latius multo possent deduci, probabiliter vellet aliquis dicere: non esse expediens fieri concilium decisivum super restitutione universali temporalis administrationis Papae, sed super hoc concilium debet universale celebrari. Nec oportet illos esse vel dici schismaticos, qui occasione data et accedente [5] talem in temporalibus fecerunt aut continuabunt subtractionem: quia etiam [6] stante unitate Ecclesiae talis subtractio vel in toto vel in parte fieri fortassis debuisset, et hoc si absque graviori scissura in spiritualibus hoc potuisset contingere. Et ita sapientissima lucet in hac parte Dei providentia, quae ex malo schismatis alia bona sciet elicere. Et si petatur de quo (88r) viverent [7] interim Papa et cardinales, respondetur, quod si faciant debitum suum laborando et diligenter inquirendo finem schismatis praesumendum est quod cito invenient. Et tunc providebit (13) eis concilium generale qualiter erit expediens et honestum pro statu tantorum dominorum. Similiter de modo provisionis sufficientium clericorum tunc tractandum esset pro futuro.

Item, ex praemissis posset elici talis ratio, quia si in hujusmodi concilio tractaretur et determinaretur de restitutione hujusmodi temporalium, vel per talem determinationem concluderetur talia esse Papae restituenda, vel non. Si dicatur primum, hoc esset ligare perpetuo Ecclesiam Gallicanam, (6r) et alios [8] qui subtraxerunt, ad talia onera importabilia, subeunda, quia Papa et Romana Curia semper dicerent se illa auctoritate concilii habere, quae ut supra tactum est, ab aliquibus dicuntur eos hactenus in aliorum praelatorum et ecclesiarum praejudicium usurpasse.[9] Et sic postea non posset circa haec [1] rationabilis moderatio faciliter adhiberi. Si [2] dicatur secundum, scilicet quod talia per concilium non concluderentur restitui, sed in toto vel in parte subtrahi, tunc illi qui subtraxerunt, tum ex possessione jam habita, tum ex auctoritate concilii superveniente, semper starent in tali subtractione, nec forte possent postea etiam per generale concilium reduci. Et sic esset divisio schismatica forte perpetua quantum ad hoc. Quod quantum sit periculum

---

5. *Om.* et accedente *A.*
6. etiamsi *A.*
7. viveret *AB.*
8. alias *V.*
9. Cf. above, n. 7, p. 260.
1. hoc *AB.*
2. *Add.* vero *C.*

advertant illi qui haec agitant. Immo (30v) generaliter considerent: quicquid per hanc oboedientiam determinabitur, alii non reputabunt alicujus momenti, nec ad talem determinationem se teneri. Immo reputabunt se contemptos, et propterea (14) fortasse provocabuntur[3] ad oppositum determinandum; sicut exemplum habemus de cessione et subtractione quas sine eis fecimus, quia omnia acta nostra calumniari student et pro posse irritari. Et ideo determinatio alicujus oboedientiae sine alia ad aliquem certum actum[4] vel procedendi modum est nimis periculosa et perpetui schismatis dispositiva, sicut de Graecis et Latinis videmus per hujusmodi determinationes contigisse.[5] Quare videtur honestius et omnino securius ante omne concilium talem oboedientiam in temporalibus sicut prius restitui, illo saltem titulo, quia etiam praedo restituendus est. Vel de consensu Papae et collegii posset quoad hoc aliqua moderatio adhiberi, postea in generali concilio confirmanda vel corrigenda. (88v) Ad hoc autem propositum de hujusmodi restituenda oboedientia nihil hic allego, quia circa hoc plura inferius dicenda sunt.

Non videtur expedire concilium praefatum fieri tanquam viarum unionis tantummodo repertivum. Ratio est, quoniam materia hujusmodi jam totaliter aperta est et discussa quoad possibilitatem viarum et rationabilitatem vel irrationabilitatem (6v) earum; et non restat nisi convenire istam oboedientiam cum altera in aliquam[6] viarum. Hoc autem fieri potest, si unquam debeat fieri, absque tali concilio hujus oboedientiae; quoniam non videtur quod alia conclusio ibidem concluderetur, quam quod summarentur adversarii de aliqua via assumenda. Si enim una particularis via limitaretur, incideremus in inconveniens quale patimur.

Ex his omnibus non determinative aut assertive positis, (15) sed tantummodo examinative, videtur sequi septima consideratio, quod nullo modo expedit nunc concilium[7] istius oboedientiae fieri ad aliquid determinative concludendum vel definiendum, nisi forte solum ad habendum liberam in consulendo deliberationem et plenam concordiam capitis et membrorum ad invicem super modo et forma uniendi hanc oboedientiam secum et cum alia, et hanc unionem concorditer prosequendi. Ad quod amplius declarandum possent adduci, particulares circumstantiae super diversis affectioni-

---

3. vocabunt *AB*.
4. *Om. AB.*
5. Cf. above, n. 1, p. 253.
6. aliqua *CV*.
7. *Add.* congregare *C.*

bus et intentionibus diversorum, et super periculo maximo novarum dissensionum suboriendarum et vix unquam sopiendarum in spiritualibus et temporalibus, nisi prius ante omnia limitarentur ea [8] quae tractanda essent in concilio et super quibus fieret, nisi praeterea fieret talis provisio super praemissis non determinandis, quae tangunt fidem et universalem Ecclesiam, quod convocato concilio nulli super ipsis disceptare aut saltem determinare praesumerent. Denique constat aliquos affectare totalem penitus destitutionem Benedicti, et alii nequaquam hoc volunt, sed totis viribus obniterentur; nec est ratio patens ad sui restitutionem [9] statim sic invenienda ut dicunt.[1] (31r)

Restat igitur communi et concordi concilio [2] vel deliberatione tantummodo quaerere cum aliis viam aliquam, in qua nobiscum conveniant pro uniendo Ecclesiam: sive illa via sit conventio, sive compromissio (89r) habens vim concilii generalis in modificatione sua, sive concilium generale formaliter, sive cessio, sive omnes viae in unum, si debeat perfectus haberi finis, (16) prout multi doctores opinantur.[3] Nam et cessio, ut dicunt (7r) fieri nequit quae unionem det veram in Ecclesia sine [4] concilio generali, et per consequens neque absque conventione et praesertim renuente cedere altero contendentium; quoniam per concilium taliter artabitur quilibet vel [5] artari poterit, quod non requiretur eorum consensus. Nam si dissenserint [6] oboedire concilio, erunt palam schismatici; et si schismatici, erunt deponendi. Quibus depositis, procedendum erit ad novam electionem libere fiendam sicut eis a vita separatis aut libere cedentibus. An vero ista sola causa ultimo [7] tacta [8] sit sufficiens causa ad hoc quod pro expedientiori aut de necessitate celebrandum sit hujusmodi [9] concilium commune hujus [1] oboedientiae, attenta difficultate in convocando, et expensis et periculis in continuando, judicent illi ad quos spectat, et inconvenientibus majoribus prudenter occurrant.

8. omnia C.

9. destitutionem V.

1. Concerning the problem of the restitution of Benedict, cf. above, n. 3, p. 254, and n. 8, p. 256.

2. consilio A.

3. For the three ways, consult Denifle, 2, 611–15; Salembier, *Schisme,* pp. 131 ff.

4. sive BC.

5. aut ABC.

6. desierint C.

7. ultima C.

8. *Om. C.*

9. *Om.* hujusmodi ABC.

1. istius ABC.

Advertendum est etiam, quod si fiat concilium hujus oboedientiae ad finem praedictum, erit expediens [2] non determinative sed consultive aliqua deliberare pro universali reformatione Ecclesiae; quia talia possent ibidem tractari ad hanc reformationem utilia, quae possent aliam oboedientiam inducere et attrahere ad breviorem et faciliorem totius Ecclesia unionem, sicut inferius apparebit.[3, 4]

Praemissis his considerationibus, quae videntur tangere materiam tractandorum in hoc concilio, tangendum est de modo ipsius et forma; de quo sit haec octava consideratio.[5]

Non videtur expedire hujusmodi concilium fieri in forma seu per [6] novas adinventiones fabricata, sed (17) solum in forma juris communis a sanctis patribus in sacris canonibus instituta.[7] Ratio ad hoc. Primo,[8] quia praesumptuosum videretur in materia tam ardua uti novis adinventionibus, spretis vel obmissis canonicis institutionibus sanctorum patrum in jure et historiis ecclesiasticis satis expressis. Facit ad hoc, et pro rationibus sequentibus, decretum Alexandri Papae [9] dicentis: *quid enim aliud est reicere mandatum* (89v) *Dei quam privato consilio, aut humano judicio novis rebus constituendis liberius delectari? Unde et scriptum est: "Ne transgrediaris terminos antiquos,* (7v) *quos posuerunt patres tui."* [1] *Terminos indubitanter transgreditur, qui statuta patrum postponit atque confundit.* Haec ibi, et habentur in sexto titulo Libri Conciliorum,[2] ubi multa notanda (31v) leguntur.

2. *Om. C.*

3. *Add.* Praedictam pro majori parte posuit Jo. Cancellarius Parisiensis, alia quae sequuntur P. Episcopus Cameracensis *C;* cf. above, n. 8, p. 253. After Jo. Cancellarius, de Gerson *in marg. C;* after P. Episcopus Cameracensis, de Alliaco *in marg. C.*

4. Praemissis considerationes pro majori parte posuit Jo. Cancellarius Ecclesiae Parisiensis; alias quae sequuntur P. Episcopus Cameracensis, *in marg. V.*

5. Ea quae sequuntur sunt de dictis Petri de Alliaco, Episcopi Cameracensis, postmodum Cardinalis, *in marg. C.*

6. super *C.*

7. For the meaning that d'Ailly attached to the expression "common law" see above, pp. 173–74.

8. *Om. C.*

9. Alexander I, 109–119; Hinschius, p. 95, cap. 1.

1. Prov. 22:28.

2. The reference is to the Pseudo-Isidorian Decretals; Hinschius, p. 95. The *Breviarum canonum apostolorum* (Hinschius, p. 25) gives an approximate indication of the old divisions of the collection, to which d'Ailly refers throughout the treatise under the name of *Liber conciliorum.*

Item ex novis adinventionibus praeter vel [3] contra jus commune jam in hac materia videmus inconvenientia processisse; et ita ex praeteritis conjecturando futura timendum est verisimiliter in proposito simile.

Item valde periculosum esset novam formam adinvenire, quia Papa et sui adhaerentes vellent unam, et alii aliam. Et sic esset nova divisio periculosior prima. Quia si nunc fieret concilium, et propter discordiam talium modorum diversorum recederemus sine concordi unitate, esset periculum perpetui schismatis, sicut fuit inter Latinos et Graecos,[4] nec esset spes ulterius postea congregandi inter nos, et multo magis inter alios contrariae oboedientiae. Item, cum forma sit de essentia rei, si non servaretur forma juris canonici, jam non esset concilium, sed conciliabulum seu conventiculum suspectum. Et sic [5] omnia ibi facta carerent auctoritate et (18) roboris firmitate, et eadem facilitate respuerentur sicut reciperentur.

Item, si nunc liceret in hoc concilio a forma juris deviare, eadem ratione et in aliis conciliis in posterum fiendis. Et sic [6] si in futurum insurgeret aliqua haeresis in concilio tractanda, si essent multi et potentes talis haeresis defensores, dicerent: "Non placet nobis forma juris communis, sed volumus talem formam rationabilem observari." Et allegarent quod sicut alias fuisset forma juris immutata ita [7] et tunc posset. Et per consequens non possent per concilium generale convinci. Et istud inconveniens videtur mirabiliter ponderandum: quia sic velle immutare formam conciliorum, esset [8] asperire viam ad haereses et errores varios in futurum.

Item, velle novam formam concilio imponere est aequivalenter concilium impedire: quia Papa et sui adhaerentes non possunt cogi concilium (8r) acceptare nisi in forma juris, nec est verisimile eos in ipsum aliter consentire et novis adinventionibus adversariorum condescendere. Quare forma canonica est (9or) sequenda et ex decretis ac [9, 1] decretalibus [2] ac historiis ecclesiasticis fideliter extra-

3. et *AB*.
4. Cf. above, n. 1, p. 253.
5. *Om. C.*
6. *Om.* sic *ABC*.
7. *Om. A.*
8. esse *B*.
9. aut *C*.
1. et *AB*.
2. Cf. D. 15, 16, 17, 18, etc.; and the *Ordo de celebrando concilio,* in Hinschius, pp. 22 ff.

henda,[3] et principibus et praelatis sine contentione proponenda.

Quae autem sit haec forma? Videtur sub brevitate eam posse ad tres conditiones reduci. Prima est, quod fiat de consensu et auctoritate Papae. Secunda, quod omnes episcopi convocentur. Tertia, quod auctoritas statuendi et definiendi pertineat ad episcopos. Et hoc patet [4] ex definitione concilii universalis, per quam differt a conciliis particularibus sive provincialibus, (19) quam ponit Huguccio, et post eum Bartholomaeus Brixiensis 17 dist., cap. 1: [5] *Universale,* inquit, *est quod a Papa vel ejus legato cum omnibus episcopis statuitur.* Et postea dixit [6] quod *universale concilium non debet fieri sine auctoritate Papae, sicut nec particulare sine auctoritate Metropolitani vel Primatis, nec episcopale sine auctoritate episcopi.* Ex quibus clare patet prima conditio, (32r) quam tamen intelligo regulariter. Potest enim in duplici casu, ut videtur, concilium fieri sine Papae auctoritate. Primus, sede vacante, si occurreret urgens necessitas vel evidens utilitas. Secundus, si vivente Papa, ipse recusaret [7] concilium facere, rationabiliter requisitus, sicut hoc infra jure divino probabitur.

Secunda conditio, quod omnes episcopi convocentur,[8] patet ex illo verbo posito in definitione concilii, *cum omnibus episcopis.*[9] Si enim, spretis aliquibus, alii vocarentur, inde mala et periculosa suspicio oriretur, et evacuaretur auctoritas concilii.

Tertia conditio, quod ad episcopos pertineat statuendi, id est, definiendi, auctoritas, patet ex [1] verbo *statuitur.*[2,3] Nam licet alii possint et debeant in concilio interesse, sive ad concilium [4] discussionis, sive ad testimonium veritatis, sive ad auxilium executionis,

---

3. Cf. Eusebius-Rufinus, *Historia ecclesiastica,* I, caps. 2, 20, etc., in PL *21,* 467 ff. And M. Aurelius Cassiodorus, *Historia tripartita,* II, caps. 1 ff., in PL *69,* 919 ff.

4. haec patent *ABC.*

5. Huguccio, Bishop of Ferrara, glossator of the *Decretum,* Professor at Bologna, d. 1210. Bartholomew of Brescia, glossator of the *Decretum,* d. 1250 or 1258. D. 17, pars Ia Gratiani *in v.* Generalia quoque concilia.

6. dicit *AB.*

7. refutaret *AB.*

8. Non qui sunt (?) vocandi ad concilium generali, *in marg. V.*

9. Cf. above, n. 5.

1. *Add.* illo *C.*

2. Cf. above, n. 5.

3. D'Ailly later modified this position. For a discussion of this and of related texts see above, pp. 152 ff.

4. Concilium *ABC; corr. in marg.* consilium *A.*

sicut patet in decretis [5] et historiis ecclesiasticis,[6] tamen soli episcopi principaliter sunt ibi ad judicium definitionis. Ideo in quatuor conciliis principalibus soli numerantur episcopi ad ostendendum quod in eis consistit [7] auctoritas concilii, ut patet (8v) per Isidorum 7. Etymologiarum, cap. 18 [8] et habetur 15 dist. cap. 1.[9] Et idem de omnibus conciliis approbatis, ut 16 dist.[1] quasi per totum. Insignum hujus etiam in definitionibus (20) conciliorum primi subscribuntur [2] episcopi, ut patet in Libro Conciliorum [3] et in multis locis Decreti, et specialiter 17 dist. in fine.[4] Unde etiam in Chalcedonensi Concilio reprehenditur Dioscorus Alexandrinorum Episcopus, quia in synodali (9ov) definitione clericos fecerat subscribere primos, quia, sicut ibi dicitur: *Synodus est episcoporum,* et [5] non clericorum.[6]

Ad majorem certitudinem praemissorum videtur expediens inducere aliquos auctoritates sacrorum canonum.

Et primo Isidorus in prologo Libri Conciliorum [7] ex multis decretorum sententiis hanc quasi principium juris praemittit dicens: *Synodorum vero congregandarum auctoritas apostolicae sedi privata commissa est potestate, nec ullam synodum ratam esse legimus quae ejus non fuerit auctoritate congregata vel fulta. Haec canonica testatur auctoritas, haec historia ecclesiastica roborat, haec sancti patres confirmant.*

Item in Chalcedonensi Concilio Dioscorus Alexandrinorum [8] Archiepiscopus inter alia condemnatur quia *synodum ausus est facere sine auctoritate* [9] *sedis* apostolicae.[1] Nam, sicut ibidem, dicitur, hoc

5. Cf. D. 15.

6. Cf. Cassiodorus, *Historia tripartita,* II, cap. 1; PL *69,* 921–22: in praesenti siquidem choro multitudo erat episcoporum, numerum trecentorum excedens, sequentibus eos presbyteris, ac diaconibus, et acolythis, quorum numerus non poterat comprehendi.

7. constitit *V.*

8. Isidore of Seville, *Etymologies,* VI, cap. 16; PL *82,* 243–45, § 2 *ad finem.*

9. D. 15, c. 1.

1. Cf. D. 16, c. 7, 9 and 12.

2. subscribunt *AB.*

3. In the *Ordo de celebrando concilio;* Hinschius, pp. 23–24.

4. D. 17, c. 6.

5. *Om. AB.*

6. In Mansi, *6,* 607.

7. *Praefatio,* cap. 8; Hinschius, p. 19.

8. *Om. A.*

9. auctoritatem *A.*

1. The fourth ecumenical Council at Chalcedon, 451. For the incident consult Mansi, *6,* 582; Hefele-Leclercq, 2, 670; cf. above, n. 6.

nunquam rite factum est nec fieri licuit. Item, idem ostendit Gratianus per totam dist. 17, et specialiter auctoritate Pelagii scribentis ad episcopos *qui convenerant ad illicitam vocationem Johannis Constantinopolitani,* in cap. *Multis denuo* [2] *apostolicis et canonicis atque ecclesiasticis historiis* [3] *instruimur regulis: non debere absque sententia,* id est licentia, *Romani Pontificis Concilia,* scilicet generalia, *celebrari. Quapropter recte* [4] *non concilium sed vestrum conventiculum vel conciliabulum cassatur, et quicquid in eo actum est, irritum habeatur* [5] *(21) et vacuum. Vos quoque deinceps videte, ut nullius hortatu talia praesumatis, si apostolicae sedis communione carere non vultis.* Item eadem dist. cap. *Concilia* in § *Hinc etiam* [6] manifeste patet quod licet (32v) concilium tempore Theodorici Regis in urbe Roma convenisset ut *judicaret de his quae Papae Symmacho ab adversariis ejus dicebantur impingi,* (9r) quamvis, ut ibi dicit glossa,[7] etiam accusatus fuerit de haeresi, tamen ab episcopis dictum est: ipsum debere synodum convocare.[8] Episcopi vero auctoritate ejusdem Symmachi dixerunt: [9] *Symmachus Papa, sedis apostolicae praesul, ab hujusmodi oppositionibus impetitus quantum ad homines respicit, sit immunis et liber, cujus causam totam Dei judicio reservamus. De clericis vero memorati Papae qui ab episcopo suo ante tempus,* id est, ante definitionem concilii, *contra regulas discesserunt, et schisma fecerunt, hoc fieri decrevimus, ut satisfacientes episcopo suo misericordiam consequantur,*[1] *et officiis ecclesiasticis set gau-(9ir)-deant restitui.*

Ex quibus patent tria documenta.

Primum, quod Papa, etiam de haeresi suspectus vel accusatus, potest concilium convocare et ibidem interesse.

Secundum, quod episcopi in tali casu possunt etiam auctoritate Papae decernere et definire, et quod haec auctoritas debet ad solos principaliter episcopos pertinere.

2. D. 17, c. 5.
3. *Om. AB.*
4. *Om. C.*
5. habeant *B.*
6. D. 17, c. 6, § Hinc etiam.
7. D. 17, c. 6, § Hinc etiam *in v.* Praecepisset: "Isti episcopi venerunt ad citationem Regis: non quod venire tenerentur, sed ut revocarent eum ab errore suo etc."
8. D. 17, c. 6, § Hinc etiam.
9. D. 17, c. 6, § Hinc etiam.
1. *Om. C.*

Tertium, quod clerici non debent a Papa etiam suspecto de
haeresi ante definitionem concilii discedere et quod [2] hoc est
schisma facere, et quod hoc facientes, si misericordiam consequi debeant, satisfacere (22) tenentur. Alioquin officiis ecclesiasticis privantur, ut 8 q. 4, cap. *Nonne*.[3] Et haec plenius patent in Libro
Conciliorum [4] in illis sex conciliis sub Symmacho celebratis, specialiter in quarto, ubi Gratianus ista recepit,[5] et in quinto, ubi
quartum concilium confirmatur, et approbatur Liber Ennodii
Diaconi,[6] qui contra clerum Romanum acriter invehit. Et patet ibi,
quod isti clerici Romani erant cardinales. Ideo etiam in definitionibus conciliorum istorum, ubi contra eos fertur sententia, non subscribunt, sicut in aliis faciunt. Unde pro casu praesenti et ejus de-
pendenciis valde expedit videre Librum Conciliorum,[7] ubi ad
plenum legitur quod a Gratiano truncate diversis in locis recitatur.[8]
Ideo Johannes Faventinus,[9] Laurentius,[1] et Archidiaconus [2] in hac
materia ad Librum Conciliorum remittunt.[3]

Si autem contra dictum cap. *Nonne* [4] et illud quo hic dictum est
de clericis qui *ante tempus sententiae ad episcopo* discedunt, obiciatur cap. *Anastasius* 19 dist.[5] Respondet ibi glossa quod hic clerici
*non recesserunt a Papa ante sententiam, quia inciderat in haeresim
jam damnatam, ut 24, q. 1, c. 1,*[6, 7] ubi in fine dicitur: *Quicunque
enim in haeresim semel damnatam labitur, ejus damnatione se ipsum
involvit.* (9v)

2. ac per *C.*
3. C. 8, q. 4, c. 1.
4. Hinschius, pp. 662 ff.
5. This chapter, however, is taken from the *Libellus Ennodii,* which was approved at the fifth synod; Hinschius, p. 669.
6. *Libellus Ennodii;* Hinschius, pp. 664 ff.
7. Cf. Hinschius, pp. 664 ff.
8. Cf. C. 8, q. 4, c. 1; C. 9, q. 3, c. 14.
9. Johannes Faventinus (John of Faenza) d. 1190. Glossator of the *Decretum.*
1. Laurentius Hispanus, Archdeacon of Bologna, who taught in that city in the
13th century. Glossator of the *Decretum.*
2. Guido de Baysio, Archdeacon of Bologna, d. 1313. Glossator of the *Decretum.*
3. remittant *A.*
4. C. 8, q. 4, c. 1.
5. D. 19, c. 9, *in v.* Abegerunt: "Sed contra 8 q. 4 nonne, ubi dicitur quod ante
tempus sententiae non possunt clerici recedere ab episcopo. Sed hic non recesserunt ante sententiam: quia inciderant in haeresim jam damnatum" etc.
6. *Om.* c. 1 *A.*
7. C. 24, q. 1, c. 1.

Item in § praedicto [8] *Hinc etiam,*[9] valde notandum est quod licet ibi dicatur: cum auctoritas Theodorici Regis ad urbem Romam sacerdotes, id est, episcopos *convenire praecepisset,* tamen ibi dicit glossa [1] quod isti episcopi venerunt ad citationem Regis, non quia *venire tenerentur, sed ut eum ab errore suo revocarent. Sed* (33r) glossa non declarat a quo errore. Et licet Vincentius, in (23) Speculo Historiali, 22 libro,[2] dicat quod iste Rex fuit Arianus, quod etiam testatur Johannes Papa in epistola ad Episcopos Italiae,[3] tamen de hujusmodi errore Arianorum nihil tractatur in consiliis sub Symmacho celebratis.[4] Quare credendum est dictos episcopos venisse ad praeceptum dicti Regis ut eum revocarent ab errore, quo sinistre informatus (91v) a clericis Romanis male de dicto Symmacho sentiebat. Et nihilominus iste rex noluit in praedicto concilio praesidere aut definire, sed, sicut ibidem subditur,[5] episcopis *Deo inspirante respondit: "synodalis esse arbitrii in tanto negotio sequenda praescribere, nec aliquid ad se praeter reverentiam de ecclesiasticis negotiis pertinere, committens etiam,"* id est, remittens, *"potestati Pontificum, ut quod* [6] *magis putarent utile deliberarent."*

Ex quibus patet iterum quod supra dictum est,[7] scilicet ad solos episcopos, et non ad principes seu quoslibet alios, auctoritatem definitivam concilii principaliter pertinere, nec eos in concilio debere interesse causa praesidendi aut definiendi seu auctoritative determinandi, sed bene causa se informandi et veritatem confirmandi et per executionem potentiae roborandi, ut probatur ex his, quae leguntur 96 dist. quasi per totum, et specialiter in capitulo *Nos ad fidem* [8] *confirmandum, non ad potentiam,* scilicet definitivam et

8. in dicto § *AB.*

9. D. 17, c. 6, § Hinc etiam.

1. D. 17, c. 6, § Hinc etiam, *in v.* Praecepisset; cf. above, n. 7, p. 270.

2. Vincent of Beauvais (d. 1294), *Speculum historiale,* Lib. 21, cap. 1 (Venice, 1494), f. 262. Theodoric is not said in this chapter to be an Arian, but in one of the versions of the *Liber Pontificalis*—from which the greater part of the chapter is taken—he is called "the heretic"; cf. L. R. Loomis, *The Book of the Popes* (New York, 1916), p. 117. For a bibliography on Vincent, consult F. Ueberweg and B. Geyer, *Grundriss der Geschichte der Philosophie* (Berlin, 1928), 2, 733.

3. John I (523–526); Hinschius, pp. 695 ff.

4. *Om. AB.*

5. D. 17, c. 6, § Hinc etiam; cf. above, n. 6 ff., p. 270.

6. quid *V.*

7. See above, p. 268, and n. 3.

8. D. 96, c. 2.

auctoritativam, *ostendendam exemplo religiosissimi Principis Constantini synodo interesse volumus.* Et in capitulo *Ubi,*[9] dicit Nicolaus Papa: *Ubinam legistis Imperatores, antecessores vestros, synodalibus conventibus interfuisse, nisi forsan* [1] *in quibus de fide tractatum* [2] *est?* etc., ubi (24) super verbo *interfuisse* [3] dicit glossa non eos in aliis conciliis interfuisse *nisi rogatos, ut 63 dist. "Adrianus."* [4] De exemplo vero religiosi (10r) Constantini, de quo in dicto capitulo *Nos* [5] fit mentio, habetur infra eadem dist. cap. *In scripturis narratur.*[6] Et plenius de hoc legitur in Ecclesiastica Historia Lib 10,[7] cap. 2,[8] et in Tripartita, Lib. 2, cap. 5,[9] ubi haec notanda verbo ponuntur: *Convenientibus igitur universis, maximam domum in regalibus praeparavit Imperator, sedes* [1] *et subsellia* [2] *in ea poni praecipiens, quae sufficerent ordini sacerdotum. Ita decentem praeparans eis honorem, invitavit ingredi, et de praesentibus habere consilium. Intravit* [3] *autem et ipse princeps ultimus cum paucis laude dignam sui magnitudinem habens, et mirabilem speciem mirabilioremque gerens dignitatem pudoris in fronte. Minori vero sede quam aliis posita in medio eorum sedit, primo tamen petens hoc sibi episcoporum jussione concedi. Tunc cum eo residit sacratissimus ille chorus.* Haec ibi. De hujus quoque Imperatoris religiositate plenius habetur in Libro Conciliorum in 34 rubrica,[4] ubi agitur de Concilio Nicaeno, in (92r) praefationibus dicti concilii,[5] et in edictis ejusdem Constantini.[6]

Item notandum est quod in dicto § *Hinc etiam* [7] ex illo verbo,

9. D. 96, c. 4.
1. forsam *CV.*
2. tractandum *CV.*
3. D. 96, c. 4, *in v.* Interfuisse.
4. D. 63, c. 2.
5. Cf. above, n. 8, p. 272.
6. D. 96, c. 8.
7. 2° *C.*
8. Eusebius-Rufinus, *Historia Ecclesiastica,* I, cap. 2; PL *21,* 468–69.
9. M. Aurelius Cassiodorus, *Historia tripartita,* II, cap. 5; PL *69,* 924 D.
1. sedens *AB.*
2. substellia *C.*
3. introivit *ABV.*
4. Hinschius, pp. 247 ff.
5. Hinschius, pp. 254 ff.
6. Cf. Hinschius, pp. 249–54.
7. D. 17, c. 6, § Hinc etiam; cf. above, n. 6 ff., p. 270.

cujus causam totam Dei judicio reservamus, posset aliquibus [8] videri, quod Papa non posset a concilio judicari, quia etiam 10, q. 3, cap. *Nemo* [9] dicitur quod licet Papa a nemine potest (33v) judicari. Sed sciendum est quod licet Papa nullius personae singularis possit subire judicium, nisi forte spontanee illi se subiciat, ut 2, q. 7, *Nos*,[1] tamen judicio concilii generalis subjectus est in certis casibus et [2] pro certis criminibus, maxime in [3] tangentibus fidem, ut 40 (25) dist., *Si Papa*, cum his quae notantur in glossa.[4, 5] Unde etiam dicit Gratianus 2, q. 7, cap. ⟨Item⟩ *Cum Balaam*,[6] in fine, quod *Symmachus Papa in Romana Synodo dignitate sua exspoliatus, prius statui* [7] *pristino reddi decernitur, ut tunc veniret ad causam, et si ita recte videretur, accusantium propositionibus responderet, digna res visa est maximo numero sacerdotum,* id est episcoporum, *atque meretur effectum, et cum postmodum ordinaretur quomodo esset accusandus praefatus* [8] *Papa, ut causam diceret, occurrebat;* (10v) *sed ab aemulis est impeditus.* Et ista plenius habentur in quarto concilio supra allegato,[9] ubi etiam praemittitur, quod hujusmodi concilium voluntate dicti Symmachi a dicto Rege Theodorico congregatum est. Et super hoc litterae ipsius Papae postulatae [1] sunt, quas ab eo directas constabat, quas Rex dari sacerdotibus sine tarditate constituit. Et sic Papa Symmachus basilicam, ubi erat congregatio, ingressus Regi [2] gratias tulit, et rem desiderii sui evenisse testatus est. Unde ibi concluditur: *Causa ergo de sacerdotum animis, quae de concilio nondum firmato tristitiam ministrabat, abscissa est.* Ex quo patet quod hujusmodi concilium non fuisset solide firmatum, nec efficax ad judicandum in hac causa, nisi fuisset de consensu dicti Papae congregatum.[3] Sed ipso sic firmato, ut superius

---

8. alicui *C*.

9. C. 9, q. 3, c. 13: "Prima sedes nullius judicio subjacet."

1. C. 2, q. 7, c. 41.

2. *Om. AB*.

3. *Om. AB*.

4. D. 40, c. 6, and gloss *in v.* a fide devius.

5. For parallel passages see below, pp. 300 ff.; the texts are discussed above, pp. 112, 148 ff.

6. C. 2, q. 7, c. 41, § Item cum Balaam.

7. *Add.* suo *V*.

8. *Om. AC*.

9. Cf. Hinschius, pp. 662 ff.; Hefele-Leclercq, 2, 964 ff.; cf. above, n. 5, p. 271.

1. congregatae *AB*.

2. rege *B;* regis *V*.

3. Cf. D. 17, c. 6, § Hinc etiam.

dictum est, concilium judicavit, et in causa tangente Papam et Ecclesiam Romanam sententiam tulit. Non ergo ibi dictum est *causam Dei judicio reservari*,[4] quia per concilium non potest Papa judicari, maxime super crimine haeresis; sed quia aemuli sui per invidiam eum accusaverant, et crimen probare non poterant, ut supra tactum est. Ideo tanquam occultum debebat divino judicio (26) (92v) reservari, cum apud homines idem sit judicium de his quae non sunt et quae non apparent, ut De consecratione, dist. 1, cap. *Solemnitates*[5] [1] et 32 dist. *Erubescant*.[6] Quod autem legitur in cap. *Nunc autem*, 21 dist.,[7] de Marcellino et de[8] Sixto Romanis Pontificibus, quod Papa a suis inferioribus non judicatur, et quod ipsi suo dimissi sunt judicio. Dicendum est[9] quantum ad Marcellinum, quod crimen idolatriae suae erat notorium, de quo ipsemet publice confessus et poenitens, contra se ipsum dictavit sententiam. Ideo dicit ibi Hugutio[1] quod non fuit condemnandus, quia non fuit pertinax. Unde aliter fuisset per concilium judicandus. Quantum autem ad Sixtum, dicendum quod accusabatur de moribus mali rumoris, non de fide aut pertinentibus ad fidem. Ideo non fuit judicandus a subditis, (34r) ut probatur 2, q. 7, multis auctoritatibus canonum et sanctorum; et specialiter in[2] capitulo Oves[3] hoc confirmatur, et habetur in principio quintae synodi sub Symmacho, ubi dicitur: (11r) *Oves quae pastori suo commissae fuerunt eum nec reprehendere, nisi a recta fide exorbitaverit, praesumant, nec ullatenus* pro quacunque re alia accusare audeant.

Sed numquid in casu praesentis schismatis deberet concilium de his duobus contendentibus et de facto electionis cardinalium judicare. Visum est quibusdam[4] quod sic per cap. *Si duo*, 79 dist., ubi dicit glossa: concilium debere vocari quando est contentio se duobus electis.[5] Alii dicunt[6] quod illud capitulum non habet hic locum,

4. Cf. D. 17, c. 6, § Hinc etiam; Hinschius, pp. 662 ff.
5. D. 1, c. 16, *de cons.;* cf. *esp.* D. 1, c. 16, *in v.* Iteratum.
6. D. 32, c. 11.
7. D. 21, c. 7.
8. *Om. C.*
9. *Om. AB.*
1. D. 21, c. 7, *in v.* Marcellinus.
2. ibi *AB.*
3. C. 2, q. 7, c. 13.
4. D'Ailly himself, presumably, was one of these.
5. D. 79, c. 8, *in v.* Contra fas.
6. Baldus de Ubaldis, the civilian and canonist (d. 1400), was probably one of those to whom d'Ailly refers here; cf. *Allegationes Baldi pro Urbano VI:* "in casu

quia dicit textus: *si duo contra fas temeritate concertantium fuerint ordinati, nullum ex eis futurum sacerdotem permittimus.* In quo casu dicit glossa: Cardinales non debere esse (27) judices, quia *essent judices in proprio facto,* ex eo scilicet quod [7] una pars ipsorum cardinalium certat contra aliam pro duobus electis. Sic autem non est in propisito, quia in electione cujuslibet electi ipsi cardinales dicuntur fuisse concordes. Sed prima facie videretur quod licet isti casus non sint similes, tamen simili aut majori ratione videretur habere locum opinio glossae [8] de concilio congregando propter concertationem duarum partium Christianitatis super electionibus et assertionibus cardinalium variis multipliciter dubitantium et suo electo diu irrevocabiliter adhaerentium, quia major est (93r) et majori remedio indigere videtur talis dubitatio duarum partium Christianitatis sic periculose concertantium,[9] quam dubitatio procedens [1] ex temeritate concertationis duarum partium Cardinalium contra se invicem divisorum. Ubi autem majus periculum, ibi cautius et cum majoris auctoritatis discretione providendum, ut in cap. *Ubi ⟨periculum⟩ majus,* De electione, Lib. Sexto.[2] Facit autem plurimum ad propositum praesentis schismatis et terminationis ejusdem illud [3] quod legitur in Concilio Chalcedonensi, Actione *XI,*[4] de duobus contendentibus in sede Ephesina, scilicet Bassiano et Stephano; quorum uterque per decretum concilii rejectus est, et judicatum est tertium eligendum.

Ultimo juxta verbum *Digna res visa est maximo numero sacerdotum, atque meretur effectum,* supra allegatum in cap. ⟨*Item cum*⟩ *Balaam,*[5] (11v) notandum est quod licet de jure illud quod in concilio a majori numero episcoporum definitum est, sit inviolabiliter observandum; tamen (28) in hoc concilio super hoc esset summopere providendum: quia, si [6] secus fieret, esset error pejor priore,

---

dubii ipsi tenetur habere electum pro papa, ut expresse legitur et notatur 79 d. cap *si duo forte* . . . unde non habemus legem neque instrumentum legis in hoc casu"; in Caesar Baronius, *Annales Ecclesiastici, 26* (Angers, 1872), 588; cf. also Ullmann, *Origins,* Ch. 8.

7. quia *ABC.*
8. glosso *C.*
9. concertantis *AB.*
1. praecedens *ABC.*
2. VI⁰, 1, 6, c. 3.
3. *Om. C.*
4. Cf. Mansi, 7, 271–94; Hefele-Leclercq, 2, 755 ff.
5. C. 2, q. 7, c. 41, § Item cum Balaam; cf. above, n. 6, p. 274.
6. *Om. B.*

et sequerentur inremediabilia pericula; sicut contigit etiam in schismate contra dictum Symmachum per Laurentium excitato,[7] qui eo vivente per contentionem ordinatus est, et postea ejectus, et damnatus per concilium, et sui adhaerentes sicut narrat Vincentius lib. 22 [8] allegans [9] multa ex Libro Pontificali.[1] Unde ibidem sic habetur: Symmachus Romanae Ecclesiae XLIX-us praesidet, ordinato contra eum per contentionem Laurentio. Quae res [2] discidium Ecclesiae grave diu et usque ad ipsa protraxit homicidia, donec tandem hanc altercationem compressit Theodorici Regis Ostrogothorum (34v) regnantis in Italia, quamvis Ariani, potentia, hoc aequitatis judicio obtinente ut Symmachus Papa esset quia prior ordinatus fuerat, eique pars maxima faveret. Et post aliqua alia sequitur: *Aliqui Romanorum ex clero et senatu, maxime Festus et Probinus interminaverunt [3] Symmachum Papam, et subornaverunt testes falsos, quos miserunt Ravennam ad Regem Ostrogothorum Theodoricum, accusantes Beatum Symmachum, et occulte revocaverunt Laurentium,* quem ipse Papa Symmachus in Nucerinam [4] civitatem intuitu misericordiae ordinaverat episcopum, *Post libello Romae facto fecerunt schisma. Et* (93v) *divisus est iterum clerus, alii adhaerentes Symmacho alii Laurentio. Tunc Festus et Probinus Senatores miserunt Regi Theodorico relationem, et coeperunt agere ut visitatorem, id est [5] vicarium, daret Rex sedi apostolicae. Tunc Rex dedit Petrum Altimae [6] civitatis Episco-*(29)*-pum, quod canones fieri prohibebant.* Item ibidem subjungitur: *Eodem tempore, Beatus Symmachus Papa centum quindecim episcopos congregavit, et facta synodo purgavit se a crimine objecto. Damnatusque est Petrus Altimae [7] civitatis Episcopus, et Laurentius Nucerinae [8] Episcopus,*

---

7. excitatum *BCV*.

8. Vincent of Beauvais, *Speculum Historiale, 21*, cap. 1 (Venice, 1494), f. 262; cf. above, n. 2, p. 272; Hefele-Leclercq, 2, 957 ff.

9. alligans *ABC*.

1. Cf. *Le Liber Pontificalis*, ed. L. Duchesne (Paris, 1886), *1*, 260–61; cf. above, n. 2, p. 272. It should be indicated that the words which follow (up to *aliqui Romanorum*), constitute a paraphrase, not a quotation, of Vincentius and of the *Liber Pontificalis*.

2. questes *B*.

3. interminaverant *C*.

4. Micerinam *BC*.

5. idque *B;* atque *A*.

6. Altinae *A*.

7. Altinae *A*.

8. Nucerinus *A;* Micerinae *C*.

qui vivo Papa Symmacho pervaserant [9] (12r) *sedem ejus. Tunc ab omnibus ⟨episcopis⟩, presbyteris et diaconis, et omni clero et plebe, Beatus Symmachus apud Sanctum Petrum in sede sua restituitur. Sed exinde Festus et Probinus invidia ducti caedes et homicidia in clero et populo catholico* [1] *intra Ecclesiam et extra, solummodo contra eos se opponente Fausto Senatore, exercuerunt.* Haec ibi. Ad terrorem autem illorum, qui sic praesumerent sedem apostolicam turbare, vel definitioni concilii [2] contraire allegandae sunt poenae juris, quae leguntur in Libro Conciliorum,[3] et objurgationes quas contra tales facit Ennodius in Libro suo per concilium approbato,[4] ubi inter alia dicit verbum notabile: *Pingues,* inquit, *hostias litat diabolo, qui contristat Ecclesiam.* Similiter inducendum exemplum, quod tangit Vicentius, ubi supra,[5] et narrat Gregorius in quarto Dialogorum, de Pascasio, sedis apostolicae Diacono: [6] qui licet *mirae sanctitatis vir fuerit,* ita ut miraculum ibidem fecisse legatur, quia tamen *in contentione quae inter Symmachum et Laurentium facta est Laurentium elegit et in sua sententia usque ad diem mortis perstitit, illum praeferendo, quem episcoporum judicio praeesse sibi Ecclesia refutavit,* ideo Germanus Episcopus eum postea mortuum in poenis vidit, cui dixit: *Pro nulla alia causa in hoc poenali loco deputatus sum,* (30) *nisi quia in parte Laurentii contra Symmachum sensi ⟨. . .⟩ Quia tamen non malitia, sed ignorantiae errore peccaverat, purgari post mortem potuit a peccato.* Caveant ergo qui ex certa malitia tale schisma fieri procurarent.

Admonendi itaque sunt principes, ut definitiones conciliorum reverenter suscipiant, et executioni mandari faciant exemplo Constantini in Concilio (94r) Nicaeno et Marciani in Concilio Chalcedonensi, de quibus supra tactum est,[7] et in Libro Conciliorum [8] poterit plenius apparere. Admonendi sunt etiam (35r) ut episcopis ad synodum convenientibus libertatem consulendi ac definiendi

---

9. persuaserant *B.*

1. catholicae *AB.*

2. *Add.* vel majoris partis *ABC.*

3. Cf. Hinschius, p. 704.

4. *Libellus Ennodii;* Hinschius, p. 673.

5. Vincent of Beauvais, *Speculum historiale,* 22, cap. 93, (Venice, 1494), f. 286 v; cf. above, n. 8, p. 277. This section of the *Speculum historiale* is extracted from the writings of Pope Gregory I, 492–96.

6. Gregory I, *Dialogi,* IV, cap. 40; PL 77, 397.

7. Cf. above, n. 1, p. 269.

8. Hinschius, pp. 247 ff., 288 ff.

habere permittant atque procurent, attendentes quod ea quae in concilio libere definiuntur, velut Spiritu Sancto (12v) praesente atque dictante instituta censentur: quia, sicut in Concilio Chalcedonensi dicitur, *si Dominus simul [9] duobus episcopis [1] in nomine suo congregatis se interesse promisit, quanto magis pluribus [2]* etc. Ideo in conciliis Spiritus Sancti praesentia orationibus humiliter imploranda est, sicuit docet Isidorus in primo capitulo Libri Conciliorum,[3] ubi tractat de religiosa et devota forma in eis congregandis observanda. Admonendi sunt propterea principes ut omnem illicitam violentiam, tanquam Spiritui Sancto contrariam, arceant. Nam, sicut legitur in epistola Damasi Papae [4] quam rescripsit [5] Aurelio Carthaginensi Episcopo, et quam praemisit idem Isidorus in principio Libri Conciliorum,[6] *violatores voluntarie [7] canonum graviter a Sanctis Patribus judicantur, et a Spiritu Sancto (cujus instinctu ac dono ditati sunt), damnantur quoniam blasphemare Spiritum Sanctum non incongrue videntur qui [8] contra eosdem sanctos canones ⟨. . .⟩ proterve agunt,[9] aut (31) loqui praesumunt, aut facere volentibus sponte consentiunt.* Ideo in Concilio Chalcedonensi [1] etiam damnatus est Dioscorus [2] quia in congregatione synodali vi militari usus est. Unde ibidem dicitur: *Ubi gladii et fustes sunt, qualis sy-*

9. *Om. C.*

1. *Om.* episcopis *C; Add.* sic discipulis *C.*

2. Cf. Matt. 18:20; cf. PL *54*, 951 B, 959 C.

3. *Ordo de celebrando Concilio;* Hinschius, pp. 22–24.

4. Cf. C. 25, q. 1, c. 5.

5. scripsit *AB.*

6. Hinschius, p. 21.

7. voluntarii *AC.*

8. quoniam *V.*

9. *Om.* damnantur quoniam . . . canones proterve agunt *A.*

1. This was the complaint of the *Orientals:* "Minabatur nobis damnatio, minae exilii, tendebantur, milites cum fustibus et gladiis instabant: timebamus et fustes et gladios. Ubi gladii et fustes, qualis synodus est?" Mansi, *6*, 602; cf. Hefele-Leclercq, *2*, 669–85.

2. Licet magis credendum sit ea quae hic dicuntur esse accipienda ante depositionem Petri de Luna supradicti in Concilio Pisano factam circa annos [sic] Domini 1407, pro subtractionem factam eidem per Ecclesiam Gallicanam, ex voluntate et ordinate Regis Francorum congregato. Qui post depositionem factam in illo Pisano Concilio, quod fuit universale et in quo cardinales et praelati duarum oboedientiarum conveneruntur, non videtur dubium si bene damnatus et depositus fuit, licet ipse et pauci qui cum eo erant et qui illi universali concilio non oboediverunt, hoc procurarent . . . (?) . . . restitui ad oboedientiam rem, *in marg. C.*

nodus est? [3] *Quod autem a libertate conciliorum violentia excluditur,* non solum de reali, sed etiam de verbali, intelligendum est; de qua quidam ait:

> *Est orare ducum species violenta jubendi,*
> *Et quasi nudato supplicat* [4] *ense potens* (13r).

EXPLICIT PRIMA PARS.[5]

SEQUITUR SECUNDA ⟨PARS⟩.[6]

Post tractatum de considerationibus habendis circa generalem convocationem seu commune concilium hujus oboedientiae, conveniens videtur aliquid tractare de illa perplexa quaestione quae nunc inter multos communiter agitatur, videlicet: utrum (94v) ante hujusmodi concilium subtracta Papae oboedientia eidem restitui debeat? [7] Et quia circa hoc diversae et adversae inveniuntur sententiae, nihil determinative, sed solum disputative propono dicere, sed varias opiniones cum aliquibus earum motivis ad majorem declarationem materiae recitare, ut quid melius eligendum sit doctiores instruant.

Prima ergo opinio [8] est quae indistincte ponit hujusmodi oboedientiam debere [9] restitui.[1] Et pro hac esse videntur plures aucto-

3. Non contra Pisana synogoga, *in marg. B.*

4. supplecat *A.*

5. *Om.* explicit prima pars *AB.*

6. *Om.* sequitur secunda *AB.*

7. By the time that this treatise was written, dissatisfaction about the withdrawal of obedience was rampant in France, the University of Toulouse being particularly outspoken in its demands for a restitution of obedience to Benedict XIII; cf. Valois, *France, 3,* 255–79.

8. Forte huic primae opinioni posset servire quidam tractatus, in fine hujus libri positus inter praemissimum (?) Dominum Sigismundum (tunc Regem Romanorum et postmodum Imperator), super augusta ac numera sacri generalis Concilii Constanciensis, ex una, et Petrum de Luna, olim Benedictum XIII vocatum, ex altera, licet fuerit inutilis finaliter, *in marg. C.*

9. *Om. A.*

1. Among the supporters of this opinion were Pierre Ravat, Nicholas of Clamanges, Jean Fiot, and the Duke of Orléans; cf. Valois, *France, 3,* 259–71. Salembier, *Schisme,* p. 199, claims that Jean Gerson too was a supporter of the opinion, but it is clear that the latter was not without his reservations on the subject of a full restitution of obedience, and sought a suitable via media. In an opuscule written at this time Gerson specifically says "quod oboedientia nec simpliciter neganda est, nec ex toto restituenda; sed modificationes quaedam sunt apponendae" etc. (Dupin, *2,* 34).

ritates sanctorum canonum.[2] Unde in prologo Libri Conciliorum, Isidorus hanc sententiam velut regulam seu (35v) principium juris praemisit: [3] *Nullus,* inquit, *qui (32) suis est rebus spoliatus, aut a sede propria vi* [4] *aut terrore pulsus, antequam omnia sibi ablata ei legibus restituantur, et ipse pacifice diu suis fruatur honoribus, sedique propriae regulariter restitutus, ejus multo tempore libere potiatur honore, juxta canonicam accusari, vocari, judicari aut damnari institutionem* [non] [5] *potest. Unde et Ecclesiastica Historia ab Eusebio Caesariensi Episcopo* [6] *confecta de muliere quadam, quae pro castitate a marito accusabatur, ait: "Praeceptum vel indictum est ab Imperatore lege lata, ut primo permitteretur ei rem familiarem libere diutius ordinare, tum deinde responderet objectis." Haec omnes leges tam ecclesiasticae quam ut* [7] *vulgares publicaeque praecipiunt.*[8] *Horum vero concinnantia,* id est, concordantia, *si omnia ponerentur, ante deficeret dies, quam horum similia, et nimis prolixa fieret epistola. Ex pluribus tamen aliqua hic ad provocationem aliorum inserere judicavimus. Ait namque Sanctus Leo Romanae Ecclesiae antistes, in epistola Chalcedonensi Concilio missa,*[9] *cujus initium est: "Leo Episcopus Synodo Chalcedonensi. Optaveram quidem, dilectissimi," et reliqua. In qua inter cetera sic testatur dicens:* (13v) *"Quia vero non ignoramus per pravas aemulationes multarum ecclesiarum statum fuisse turbatum, plurimosque fratres injuste sedibus suis pulsos et in exilia deportatos, atque in locum superstitum alios substitutos; his primitus vulneribus adhibeatur medecina justitiae. Nec quisquam ita careat propriis, ut alter (33) utatur alienis. Quem ita errorem omnes relinquant, ut nemini quidem perire honor debeat, sed prioribus episcopis cum omni privilegio suo jus proprium reformetur." Eadem et antiqui Apostoli qui fuerunt ante Synodum Nicaenam sanxerunt.* (95r) *Eadem synodus quae habita est in Larissa sub Valeriano loquitur. Eadem plurimae Romanae synodi testantur. Eadem Papa Symmachus et ceteri sancti patres sanxerunt. Quorum instituta prolixitatem vitantes hic inserere distulimus. Si quis autem haec plenius scire et legere voluerit, suis in auctoribus*

---

2. E.g. C. 3, q. 2, c. 8; C. 5, q. 2, c. 4.
3. *Praefatio,* cap. 6; Hinschius, pp. 18–19.
4. *Om. A.*
5. Hinschius, p. 18, omits *non.*
6. Eusebius, *Historia ecclesiastica,* IV, 17.
7. quamve *A; Om.* ut *C.*
8. recipiunt *C.*
9. Leo I, *Ep.* 93; PL *54,* 935–40.

*invenire et legere pleniter poterit. Nobis vero haec in praefatiuncula
ista sufficiant. Et sicut militi ex multis armis illa sufficiunt quae ferre
congruenter super se poterit, sic nobis de multis sententiis una vel
duae vel quantum tunc temporis necesse fuerit, sufficiunt, quoniam
sicut cum uno telo aut duobus inimicum vincimus, sic cum una aut
duabus sententiis auctoritate plenis aemulum superamus. Si de
mulieribus et saecularibus hominibus haec constituta sunt, multo
magis ecclesiasticis viris et sacerdotibus sunt concessa. Haec eadem
vero et ecclesiastica jura jubent et saeculi leges praecipiunt.* Haec ibi.

Item in Libro Conciliorum XV° titulo, in (36r) decretali epistola
Zepherini Papae [1] ita scribitur: *Patriarchae vero vel primates [2] accu-
satum discutientes episcopum, non ante sententiam proferant finiti-
vam, quam apostolica fulti auctoritate, aut reum se ipse confiteatur,
aut per innocentes et regulariter examinatos convincatur testes. Qui
minori non sint (34) numero quam illi discipuli fuerunt, quos
Dominus ad adjumentum Apostolorum eligere praecepit, id est, septuaginta duo. Detractores quoque,[3] (14r) qui divina auctoritate
eradicandi sunt, et auctores inimicorum ab episcopali submovemus [4]
accusatione vel testimonio, nec summorum quispiam minorum [5]
accusationibus impetatur aut desperet, neque in re dubia certa
judicetur sententia, nec ullum judicium, nisi ordinaliter habitum
teneatur. Absens vero nemo judicetur, quia et divinae et humanae
hoc prohibent leges. Accusatores autem eorum omni careant suspicione, quia columnas suas Dominus firmiter [6] stare voluit,[7] non a
quibuslibet agitari. Nullum namque eorum sententia a non suo
judice dicta constringat, quia et leges saeculi id ipsum fieri praecipiunt. Duodecim enim judices quilibet episcopus accusatus, si
necesse fuerit, eligat, a quibus ejus causa juste judicetur, nec prius
audiatur aut excommunicetur vel judicetur, quam ipsi ⟨per se⟩ eligantur et regulariter vocatus ad suorum primo conventum episcoporum per eos causa juste audiatur et rationabiliter discernatur.
(95r) Finis vero ejus causae ad Sedem Apostolicam deferatur, ut
ibidem terminetur [8] nec ante finiatur, sicut ab Apostolis vel suc-*

1. Hinschius, pp. 131–32, caps. 2–6.
2. *Om.* vel primates *AB.*
3. vero *C.*
4. submonemus *BC.*
5. modorum *C.*
6. *Om. CV.*
7. noluit *B.*
8. determinetur *ABC.*

cessoribus eorum olim statutum est, quam ejus auctoritate fulciatur. Haec ibi, et plura alia ex quibus patet quanta solemnitas in condemnatione [9] episcoporum et multo magis Summi Pontificis debeat adhiberi.

Postea vero in epistola ejusdem sequenti ad episcopos Aegypti [1] magis ad propositum sic habetur: *Praeceptum est ergo antiquis statutis, episcopos (35) ejectos atque suis rebus exspoliatos in ecclesiis propriis recepi, et primo omnia sua sibi reddi, et demum si quis eos juste accusare voluerit aequo periculo facere. Judices esse decernentes, episcopos recta [2] sapientes et in Ecclesia convenientes, ubi testes essent singulorum qui oppressi videbantur.*

Item simile legitur [3] eodem libro, titulo 23,[4] ubi Stephanus Papa de accusatoribus episcoporum ita scribit: *Audivimus enim vos a quibusdam accusari non tam pro vestra culpa, quam pro eorum libitu; ut vestra rapere possint, et ideo vos nimis affligi et concuti (14v) in tantum, ut etiam a propriis sedibus pellamini, et tali occasione Ecclesiae facultates vestraeque vastentur ac depraedentur. Ista, carissimi, non oportet fieri, nec denuo replicari. Tamen necesse est quae totiens usurpantur, saepius replicentur et prohibeantur. Nam quicquid in sacratis Deo rebus et episcopis injuste agitur pro sacrilegio reputabitur, quia sacra (36v) sunt, et violari a quoquam non debent. Nullus enim episcoporum, dum suis fuerit rebus exspoliatus, aut a sede propria [5] qualibet occasione pulsus, debet accusari, aut a quoquam ei potest crimen obici, priusquam integerrime restauretur, et omnia quae sibi ablata quocunque ingenio fuerant, legibus reintegrentur, et ipse propriae sedi et pristino statui regulariter reddatur, ita ut omnes possessiones et cuncta sibi injuste ablata atque fructus omnes ante coeptam accusationem, primates et synodus episcopo [6] de quo agitur funditus (36) restituant, quia hoc non solum ecclesiasticae, sed etiam saeculi leges fieri prohibent.*

Item, simile habetur expressius eodem libro, titulo 26, in epistola Felicis Papae ad episcopos Galliarum,[7] ubi [8] auctoritate sanctae

9. condemnationibus *A.*
1. Hinschius, p. 133, cap. 12.
2. erecta *ABC.*
3. loquitur *A.*
4. Hinschius, p. 184, caps. 4–6.
5. *Add.* pro *A.*
6. *Om. C.*
7. Hinschius, p. 201, cap. 10; cf. C. 3, q. 2, c. 8.
8. *Om. AB.*

synodi ita dicit: *Nam si quis suis rebus fuerit aut Ecclesiae sibi commissae exspoliatus, aut, quod absit, quod alienum (96r) ab omnibus esse debet fidelibus a sede propria ejectus, aut in detentione aliqua a suis ovibus fuerit sequestratus, tunc canonice, antequam in pristino restituatur cum omni privilegio suo honore, et sua omnia quae insidiis inimicorum suorum ei ablata fuerunt legibus reintegrentur, nec vocari judicari poterit, nisi ipse pro sua necessitate, minime tamen judicandus, advenire sponte elegerit. Nullatenus ergo a quoquam respondere rogetur antequam integerrime omnia quae per suggestiones inimicorum suorum amiserat potestati ejus ab honorabili concilio legali ordine reintegretur; praesul vero cum omni honore statui pristino reddatur, et ipse dispositis ordinatisque libere ac secure diu suis tunc regulariter infra quatuor vel quinque aut septem menses, (15r) juxta quod possibilitas ei fuerit, et non ante convocatus ad tempus concilio in [9] legitimo et canonico [1] veniat ad causam, et si ita juste videtur, accusantium propositionibus respondeat.*

Item eodem libro valde multa similia leguntur in decretis Summorum Pontificum et definitionibus conciliorum, ut titulo 28, in decretis Gaii Papae,[2] et titulo 30, in decretis Marcelli,[3] et titulo 31, in decretis Eusebii Papae et specialiter in epistola ad Aegyptios,[4] et titulo 106, in decretis Symmachi Papae,[5] de quo (37) supra meminit Isidorus,[6] et maxime ac expressissime in quinta synodo sub eo celebrata.[7] Quae omnia hic recitare longum esset, sed ad originale habeatur recursus.

Haec [8] autem hic inducere dignum duxi, quia si hoc in minoribus episcopis servandum est, multo magis in Summo Pontifice, sicut etiam de supradicto Symmacho Papa servatum esse legimus: ut patet ex [9] quarta synodo sub eo celebrata,[1] et habetur 17 dist., cap. *Consilia*, in § *Hinc etiam*, ubi dicit glossa quod accusatus fuerat de

---

9. *Om. V.*

1. legitime et canonice *V.*

2. Hinschius, pp. 214–15, caps. 3–4; cf. C. 3, q. 1, c. 1.

3. Hinschius, p. 227, cap. 8.

4. Hinschius, p. 237, cap. 12; cf. C. 3, q. 1, c. 4.

5. Hinschius, pp. 664 ff.

6. Cf. above, n. 3, p. 281.

7. Hinschius, p. 676.

8. hoc *C.*

9. in *AB.*

1. Hinschius, pp. 662–64.

haeresi.[2] Et tamen 2, q. 7, cap. ⟨*Item*⟩ *cum Balaam* [3] in fine dicitur quod *Symmachus Papa, in Romana Synodo dignitate sua exspoliatus, prius statui pristino reddi decernitur etc.*

Item ad propositum scribit Gratianus 3, q. 1 et q. 2 [4] quasi per totum, ubi probat multis juribus et aliquibus decretis supra allegatis quod exspoliatis vel ejectis episcopis restitutio danda est, antequam ullum crimen eis obici possit, quodque induciae post restitutionem praestandae sunt (37r) antequam ad synodum convocentur. Unde in principio hujus Causae dicit glossa: [5] *Est* (96v) *autem regulare quod spoliatus ab alio quam a judice, vel etiam si a judice est spoliatus sine ordine juris, semper statim* [6] *est restituendus, non obstante exceptione alicujus criminis vel non canonicae institutionis, ut patet Extra., De restitutione spoliatorum, cap. "In litteris,"* cum suis concordanciis.[7] Quae jura ad majorem claritatem praemissorum expedit inducere. Dicitur ergo in cap. *In Litteris,* et est responsio Alexandri tertii Episcopo Briciensi, *super quaestione illa,* (15v) *videlicet, cum quis dicit se de possessione violenter ejectum,*[8] *et adversarius dicit eum non* (38) *fuisse canonice institutum; respondemus, prius de violenter ejectione quam de* [9] *canonica institutione agi* [1] *debere, quia praedo, secundum rigorem juris est restituendus.* Ubi dicit Innocentius: [2] *Hoc verum est, quando non confitetur se praedonem, vel quando non constat proprietatem ad alium spectare secundum quosdam.* Facit ad hoc cap. *Item,* eodem titulo,[3] ubi idem Alexander scribit Exoniensi [4] Episcopo: *Cum quis dicit se de possessione violenter ejectum vel adversarium clam possessionem intrasse, et adversarius ejus crimen obicit, ut eum a sua intentione ratione criminis repellat, non occurrit,* id est, non videtur *nobis, quod illius objectio admitti debeat vel principalis causae*

---

2. D. 17, c. 6, § Hinc etiam, *in v.* praecepisset; cf. above, n. 4, p. 275.
3. C. 2, q. 7, c. 41, § Item cum Balaam, § 10; cf. above, n. 5, p. 276.
4. C. 3, q. 1 and 2, passim.
5. C. 3, q. 1, *in v.* quod restitutio.
6. statui *ABC.*
7. X, 2, 13, c. 5; and X, 2, 13, c. 6 and 7.
8. ejectus *B.*
9. *Om. AB.*
1. agere *A.*
2. X, 2, 13, c. 5; Innocent IV, 1243–54—the actual words cited here are not his; cf. Innocentius, *In quinque libros Decretalium* (Venice, 1578), f. 95r, § 14.
3. X, 2, 13, c. 6.
4. Oxoniensi *V.*

*propter hoc executio retardari, quoniam criminaliter adversus eum
ante restitutionem agere non potest, cum praesumatur ejus existere
inimicus.*

Ex praemissis, aliis quoque juribus pluribus satis patet praedicta
regula, quod spoliatus a non judice vel sine juris ordine restituendus
est., etc. Tamen, sicut ibi notat glossa,[5] hoc fallit in certis casibus.

Primus [6] casus est intrusio, ut ead. 3, q. 1, § finali: *Patet ergo.*[7] Ubi
obicit Gratianus quod *ubi non fuit legitima institutio, ibi nec potest
esse restitutio. Non enim probatur destitutus qui prius non fuit
institutus, ac per hoc nec restaurationem postulare potest. Illi ergo,
quorum electio vitiosa est, vel qui a clero non sunt electi, vel a
populo expetiti, vel qui [8] per simoniam irrepserunt, non sunt habendi
inter episcopos. Et ideo, si a sedibus, quas tenere videbantur, expulsi
fuerint, non possunt restitutionem petere, antequam vo-*(97r)-*centur
ad causam.* Et allegat ad hoc Gra-(39)-tianus, cap. *Si quis pecunia,*
supra in Tractatu Ordinandorum, 79 dist.,[9] ubi dicitur quod si quis
populari aut militari tumultu sine canonica electione Apostolicae
sedi fuerit inthronizatus, liceat cardinalibus talem *invasorem ana-
thematizare et humano auxilio ab Apostolica sede pellere,* et quem
dignum judicaverint (16r) praeponere etc. Sed istud contrarium
solvit Gratianus dicens quod hoc in *eo casu tantum intelligitur quo
Apostolica sedes per violentiam occupatur. Quo casu judex non
invenitur, cujus officio ille apostaticus possit excludi.* Et ideo ex hoc [1]
§ bene concludit ibi glossa, quod hoc est speciale in Papa. Ex quo
patet quod illi minus juridice loquuntur, qui dicunt Bartholo-
maeum aut ejus successorem [2] debere restitui, antequam nobiscum [3]
ad generale [4] concilium conveniat, cum ejus intrusio in Papatum
(37v) per tumultum populi facta fuerit notoria.

In aliis autem casibus praeterquam in intrusione Papatus objectio supradicta, sicut dicit Gratianus,[5] *locum non habet, cum*

---

5. X, 2, 13, c. 6, *in v.* Clam possessione intrasse.

6. post *A; corr. in marg.* primus *A.*

7. C. 3, q. 1, c. 6, § *Patet ergo.*

8. quia *AB.*

9. D. 79, c. 9.

1. in illo *C.*

2. Bartholomew Prignano, later Pope Urban VI, 1378–89; his successor was
Peter Thomacelli, Boniface IX, 1389–1404.

3. *Om. C; Add.* vel istud *C.*

4. *Om. AB.*

5. C. 3, q. 1, c. 6, § *Patet ergo;* cf. above, n. 7.

violenta possessio, nisi per judicis sententiam, violento detentori detrahi non possit. Ideo finaliter concludit: *Si ergo episcopi a sedibus, quas quoquomodo tenere videbantur, non per judicem, sed violenter ejecti fuerint, post ejectionem restituendi sunt ante regularem ad synodum vocationem.* Si autem hoc verum est de minoribus episcopis, quanto magis de Summo Pontifice, qui superiorem non habet, ut 9, p. 3, *Aliorum.*[6] Licet autem praeallegata glossa [7] plures alios casus enumeret, in quibus fallit praedicta regula de restitutione spoliati, illos tamen hic non prosequor, quia secundum hanc primam opinionem, quam (40) nunc tracto, non habent locum in Papa quominus oboedientia sit ei restituenda, cum de ejus causa non liceat subditos definire vel ejus facta judicare, ut 9, q. 3, cap. *Nemo,* et capitulis sequentibus.[8] Unde ibi dicit Innocentius Papa: [9] *Nemo judicabit primam sedem justitiam temperare desiderans. Neque enim ab Augusto,* id est, Imperatore, *neque ab omni clero, neque a regibus, neque a populo judex judicabitur.* Et in cap. *Aliorum* supra allegato.[1] dicit textus: *Aliorum hominum causas Deus voluit per homines terminari, sed sedis istius praesulem suo sine quaestione reservavit arbi-*(97v)*-trio. Voluit Beati Petri Apostoli successores caelo tantum debere innocentiam.* etc. Et licet hoc allegat Gratianus a Symmacho Papa, tamen est dictum Ennodii Diaconi; sed quia ejus liber approbatus fuit in quinta synodo (16v) sub Symmacho celebrata, ideo inter ejus decreta connumeratur. Ad idem facit capitulum *Facta,* eadem quaestione,[2] ubi dicit Anterus Papa: *Facta subditorum judicantur a nobis, nostra vero a Domino judicantur.* etc. Et cap. *Isti sunt,*[3] ubi dicit Gelasius Papa: Sedem Apostolicam *ad nullius commeare judicium, nec de ejus unquam judicio judicari,* sed ipsius *potius sequenda decreta.* Simile in sequenti capitulo, *Cuncta per mundum,*[4] ubi dicitur: *Sacrosancta Romana Ecclesia fas de omnibus habet judicandi, neque cuiquam de ejus liceat judicare judicio.* etc. Et infra sequitur: *Sed nec illa praeterimus, quod Apostolica Sedes sine ulla synodo praecedenti et solvendi quos iniqua* [5]

6. C. 9, q. 3, c. 14.
7. X, 2, 13, c. 6, *in v.* Clam possessione intrasse; cf. above, n. 5, p. 286.
8. C. 9, q. 3, c. 13, *et seq.*
9. C. 9, q. 3, c. 13.
1. C. 9, q. 3, c. 14.
2. C. 9, q. 3, c. 15.
3. C. 9, q. 3, c. 16 (*Ipsi* sunt).
4. C. 9, q. 3, c. 17.
5. jamque *AB.*

synodus damnaverit, et damnandi, nulla existente synodo, quos oportet habuit facultatem. Et hoc nimirum pro suo principatu, quem Beatus Petrus Apostolus Domini voce tenuit et semper tenebit. Et hoc quod (41) hic de synodo dicitur, non de universali rite celebrata intelligendum est quia ejus sententiae nunquam a Sede Apostolica damnatae leguntur, sed de particulari synodo intelligi potest,[6] vel de universali non canonice celebrata, sed sine Apostolica auctoritate vocata, quia quae in talibus synodis acta sunt, regulariter revocata sunt: ut patet in fine Libri Conciliorum Isidori, in altercatione Liberii Papae et Constantini Imperatoris,[7] ubi synodalis sententia contra Athanasium lata per dictum Liberium reprobatur; ubi inter cetera, cum eidem [8] diceret Imperator: *Plurimorum namque episcoporum debet valere sententia; tu solus es, qui amicitias illius scelerati (38r) defendis. Liberius respondit: Imperator, nunquam audivimus absente accusatore [9] judicem ejus scelera proferentem, nisi quia propria videntur haec odia.*

Ex praemissis omnibus tenentes hanc opinionem concludunt [1] per plurium episcoporum aut aliorum particulariter congregatorum et auctoritate saecularis principis vocatorum sententiam contra Papam absentem non potuisse ca-(98r)-nonice subtractionem oboedientiae eidem fuisse factam, ac ideo sibi a [2] dicta oboedientia spoliato eam debere restitui, antequam de ejus causa aut factis ipsius [3] possit (17r) per concilium generale tractari. Et haec de prima opinione sufficiant.

Secunda opinio praedictae contraria indistincte tenet quod hujusmodi restitutio oboedientiae in casu praesenti non est facienda. Et fundatur in quibusdam oppositionibus quae fiunt contra Dominum Benedictum, sicut patet in instructionibus Dominorum [4] Cardinalium missorum ad Regem Franciae ex parte Sacri Collegii.[5] Et possunt hujusmodi oppositiones reduci ad aliquos de illis casibus

6. *Om.* quia ejus . . . synodo intelligi potest *A.*

7. *Dialogus Liberii Episcopi Romani et Constantii Imperatoris;* PL *8,* 1364. D'Ailly is paraphrasing rather than quoting.

8. ei *A.*

9. accusatorem *C.*

1. Cf. above, n. 1, p. 280.

2. *Om. C.*

3. ejus *C.*

4. duorum *V.*

5. These were the three cardinals, de Malesset, de Thury and de Saluces, whom the Sacred College sent to Paris in 1399. They accused Benedict of heresy, perjury, dissoluteness, and injustice; cf. Valois, *France, 3,* 209–11.

quos tangit glossa 3, q. 1, in principio Causae.[6] In quibus casibus fallit regula de restitutione spoliati secundum glossam ibidem, (42) quam sequuntur multi doctores. Et de multis ibidem tactis solum octo casus hic tangam, quia alii non possunt ad propositum convenienter aptari.

Primus casus est dilapidatio, cap. *Quia ea,* 3, q. 2,[7] ubi auctoritate Pelagii Papae dicitur quod ab administratione submoveatur qui res Ecclesiae male ministrat, donec de causa cognoscatur. Et licet dicat glossa [8] praedicta quod hoc hodie non tenet, quia non est spoliandus quis nisi probata suspicione; ut Extra, De simonia, *Licet,*[9] ubi Abbas a monachis delatus de simonia, perjurio, dilapidatione ac insufficientia, tamen propter hoc [1] non prius mandatur ab administratione spoliari, antequam facta fuerit inquisitio de praemissis et legitima probatio. Sed hoc non obstante, ubi dilapidatio esset notoria, non videretur esse opus probatione. Quod notatur eod. cap. *Licet,* ex illo verbo, *ut de notoriis excessibus taceatur,* ubi super verbo *taceatur* dicit Johannes Andreae [2] quod tacendo exprimit. Ex hoc opponitur contra Dominum Benedictum quod notorium est ipsum esse insufficientem et inutilem ad regimen Papatus ac dilapidatorem et dissipatorem Ecclesiae, et maxime in eo quod negligens erat circa sedationem schismatis, et cardinalibus ac aliis circa hoc laborantibus et ipsum ad hoc excitantibus obtemperare nolebat aut negligebat, et multa hujusmodi contra ejus [3] mores dicta et scripta sunt. Quare (17v) concludit haec opinio subtractionem administrationis eidem merito factam esse et restitu-(98v)-tionem sibi fieri non debere.

Secundus casus criminis enormitas, 2, q. 5,[4] *Super causa;* (38v) ubi Gillandus Presbyter de morte episcopi sui infamatus, honore suo spoliatus fuerat. Et tamen Alexander Papa mandat prius ipsum episcopo suo judicialiter praesentari et accusatores exami-(43)-nari, antequam restituatur. Et ibi dicit glossa [5] quod *iste officio et beneficio*

6. C. 3, q. 1, *in v.* quod restitutio; cf. above, n. 5, p. 285.

7. C. 3, q. 2, c. 9.

8. C. 3, q. 2, c. 9, *in v.* Donec causa.

9. X, 5, 3, c. 31.

1. haec *ABC.*

2. *Joannis Andreae . . . In Quintum Decrelatium Librum Novella commentaria* (Venice, 1581), ad X, 5, 3, c. 31, f. 29v. Joannes Andreae, d. 1348, was a Professor at Bologna and glossator of the *Liber sextus, the Clementines,* and the *Decretals.*

3. hujusmodi *AB.*

4. C. 2, q. 5, c. 11.

5. C. 2, q. 5, c. 11, *in v.* Beneficia.

privatus fuerat, quia graviter erat [6] infamatus. Et maxime hoc locum habet ubi est exceptio haeresis, ut notavit [7] glossa in cap. *Quo jure,* 8 dist.,[8] ubi addit Archidiaconus quod dicit Innocentius in cap. *Inter dilectos, De excessibus praelatorum:* [9] *Si quis agit de* [1] *possessorio ad repetendum beneficium, vel dignitatem amissam,*[2] *tunc distingue: quia si obicitur crimen vel aliquid aliud, quod ipso* [3] *jure inducit* [4] *privationem,*[5] *utpote quod sit haereticus vel sententialiter de crimine condemnatus, admittenda est hujusmodi exceptio, argumento capituli "Quo jure,"* [6] *et 23, q. 7,*[7] *cap. 1 et 2.*[8] Sed si aliud *crimen sibi obiciatur, ut quod sit adulter, perjurus, vel simoniacus, quia per hujusmodi crimina non amittit jus suum, non credit hujusmodi exceptiones admittendas.* Idem notat [1] Bernardus Compostellanus cap. *Quod sic, De elect.,*[2] et Henricus in cap. *Inter dilectos* praeallegato.[3] Et corcordat Hostiensis in Summa, Rubrica De restitutione spoliatorum,[4, 5] ubi inter casus in quibus restitutio denegatur, ponit decimo septimo, quod *haereticus non potest petere restitutionem rei ecclesiasticae* quia nec potest possidere, ut 23, q. 7, cap. 1 et 2.[6]

6. fuerat *AB.*

7. notabat *AB.*

8. D. 8, c. 1; Guido de Baysio (Archidiaconus, cf. above, n. 2, p. 271), *Lectura . . . super Decreto; quam ipse Rosarium appellavit* (Lyons, 1516), f. 8r, § 15.

9. X, 5, 31, c. 11; Innocent IV, in *Quinque Libros Decretalium* (Venice, 1578), f. 216v, § 1.

1. *Om. AB.*

2. admissam *V.*

3. non *AB.*

4. induxit *C.*

5. probationem *A.*

6. D. 8, c. 1.

7. 8 *AB.*

8. C. 23, q. 7, c. 1 and 2.

1. notant *ABC.*

2. Bernard, Archdeacon of Compostella, a 13th century canonist, often referred to as *Antiquus.* See Bernardus Compostellanus, *Lectura aurea super Primo Libro Decretalium* (Venice, 1588), ad X, 1, 6, c. 28 f. 192v, §§ 24–25. The words are practically the same as those of Innocent: cf. above, n. 9.

3. X, 5, 31, c. 11; Henricus Boik, 1310–ca. 1350?

4. spoliati *CV.*

5. Henry of Segusia, *Summa Hostiensis super titulis Decretalium,* Rubrica: De restitutione spoliatorum, § 4 (Lyons, 1542), fol. 89r; cf. above, n. 6, p. 254.

6. C. 23, q. 7, c. 1 and 2.

Tertius casus in quo, secundum praeallegatam glossam,[7] fallit regula de restitutione spoliati etc., *est infamia et criminis evidentia, ut 2, q. 5, Presbyter,*[8] *et q. 1, Scelus,*[9] *et cap. Manifesta.*[1] Unde in dicto capitulo Presbyter, auctoritate Concilii Ilerdensis, sic dicitur: *Presbyter si a plebe sibi commissa mala opinione infamatus fuerit, et episcopus si*[2] *legitimis testibus approbare non potuerit, suspendatur usque ad dignam satisfactionem, ne populus fidelium in eo scandalum patiatur.* Ubi super verbo suspendatur dicit glossa.[3] *Hoc verum est secundum distinctionem, si fuerit* (18r) *notorium vel* (44) *manifestum vel famosum, ut Extra, De cohabitatione clericorum et mulierum, cap. "Vestra,"*[4] *et cap. ultimo.*[5] *Et*[6] *etiam refert, si fuerit famosum, sine scandalo vel cum scandalo, ut ibidem cap. "Tua."*[7] In praeallegato autem cap. *Manifesta,*[8] et cap. *Scelus*[9] probatur quod sine accusatione manifesta crimina judicantur et puniuntur. Et ibi notat glossa[1] quod *aliud est fama, aliud manifestum, aliud notorium, et quod notorium triplex est, scilicet no-*(99r)*-torium facti, notorium juris, et notorium praesumptionis.* De quibus ibi et in Doctoribus plenius videndum est. Ex praedictis haec opinio contra Dominum Benedictum opponit et concludit ut supra,[2] quia asserit eum commisisse enorme crimen, scilicet fautoriam schismatis, et incurrisse etiam suspicionem haeresis multa dicendo[3] et faciendo contra proprium juramentum circa materiam pacis et unionis universalis Ecclesiae, et de hoc laborare contra eum infamiam et criminis evidentiam, etiam cum scandalo notorio tam apud suos cardinales quam plures saeculares[4] principes et alios suae oboedientiae. Quare, etc.

Quartus casus in quo non fit restitutio spoliati, secundum glossam

7. C. 3, q. 1, *in v.* quod restitutio; cf. above, n. 6, p. 289.
8. C. 2, q. 5, c. 13.
9. C. 2, q. 1, c. 21.
1. C. 2, q. 1, c. 15.
2. *Om. C.*
3. C. 2, q. 5, c. 13, *in v.* suspendatur.
4. X, 3, 2, c. 7.
5. X, 3, 2, c. 10.
6. *Om. C.*
7. X, 3, 2, c. 8.
8. C. 2, q. 1, c. 15.
9. C. 2, q. 1, c. 21.
1. C. 2, q. 1, c. 15, *in v.* manifesta.
2. Cf. above, n. 5, p. 288.
3. docendo *A.*
4. *Om.* quam plures saeculares *C.*

(39r) praedictam,[5] est contumacia: ut 3, q. 9, decrivimus,[6,7] ubi auctoritate Bonifacii probat Gratianus quod sententia feriendus est, qui causae suae negligit adesse. Et licet istud capitulum de directo non faciat ad propositum, quia loquitur de eo qui evocatur est ad judicium, et ideo praesumitur confiteri crimen, quia, sicut ibidem dicitur: *purgandi se occasione non utitur,* tamen hoc potest induci contra Dominum Benedictum per argumentum a simili, quia scilicet neglexit adesse causae suae in prosecutione unionis Ecclesiae et contumaciter, ut videtur, contempsit credere consilio cardinalium suorum et principium notabilium, qui causam (45) dictae unionis prosequi per viam convenientiorem, scilicet per viam cessionis, instantissime suadebant et humiliter requirebant. Quare dicta opinio eum ex his conclusit contumacem ac ideo ab administratione suspendendum nec esse restituendum. (18v)

Quintus casus faciens ad propositum quem tangit dicta glossa est scandalum: ut [8] probatur 3, q. 6, *Haec* [9] *quippe,*[1] ubi, auctoritate Nicolai Papae, ostendit Gratianus quod *quorundam depositionem* [2] episcoporum, contra vel praeter *conscientiam Romani Pontificis factam* tolerat Ecclesia pro pace servanda inter quosdam reges et ecclesiarum scandalo evitando.[3] Unde in fine capituli concluditur: *Non enim ecclesias Domini per discordias regum divisionis aliqua pati damna necesse est, cum (quantum ex se est) pacem, quam praedicant, servare studeant invicem et in omnes.* Sic similiter in proposito dicit ista opinio, quod subtractio contra Dominum Benedictum facta pro tollendo scandalum schismatis et (99v) restauranda pace universalis Ecclesiae toleranda et continuanda est usquequo unitas habeatur. Posset etiam ista objectio vel exceptio de scandalo convenientius applicari ad casum supra tactum et [4] cap. *Presbyter,* 2, q. 5,[5] quia dicit ista opinio quod populus fidelium sub Domino Benedicto et ejus facto scandalum patitur, in hoc scilicet quod viam cessionis contumaciter refutando et, ut dicunt aliqui,

---

5. C. 3, q. 1, *in v.* quod restitutio; cf. above, n. 7, p. 291.
6. decernimus *AC.*
7. C. 3, q. 9, c. 10.
8. *Add.* probat dicta glossa, ut *AB.*
9. hoc *C.*
1. C. 3, q. 6, c. 10.
2. dispositionem *V.*
3. vitando *C.*
4. ex *ABC.*
5. C. 2, q. 5, c. 13; cf. above, n. 8, p. 291.

impugnando crimen schismatis et vehementem suspicionem haeresis incurrisse famatur. Ideo juxta dictum capítulum [6] *usque ad dignam* [7] *satisfactionem* merito suspenditur.[8]

Sextus casus applicabilis ad propositum, in quo secundum praedictam glossom non fit restitutio spoliatorum,[9] est cum a muliere obicitur saevitia viri, ut Extra, De restitutione spoliatorum, *Ex transmissa,*[1] ubi dicitur: (46) *Si autem capitali odio ita vir mulierem persequeretur,*[2] *quod merito de ipso diffidat, alicui probae et honestae mulieri, usque ad causae decisionem custodienda studiosius committatur in loco, ubi vir vel parentes ejus mulieri nullam possint violentiam inferre.* Sic in proposito, per argumentum a simili, concludit ista opinio quod si fieret Domino Benedicto oboedientiae restitutio, quia, ut asseritur, valde (39v) crudelis et vindicativus est, timenda esset (19r) ejus saevitia et capitale odium in eos, qui bona intentione subtractionem fecerunt ad finem unionis Ecclesiae. Quare usque ad causae decisionem, id est, schismatis terminationem, hujusmodi restitutio reservanda est.

Septimus causus notatus in glossa praedicta,[3] ubi spoliatus non restituitur, est exceptio jurisjurandi vel pacti secundum quosdam: ut Extra, De restitutione spoliatorum, *Accepta.*[4] Sic similiter in proposito videretur quod contra Dominum Benedictum opponi potest exceptio de jurejurando seu de juramento facto ante et post electionem suam in Papatum, quo obligabatur laborare ad unionem Ecclesiae omnibus viis et modis rationabilibus, etiam usque ad viam cessionis, etc. Et quia hoc non fecit, ad subtractionem oboedientiae processum est, a qua non est discedendum, saltem usquequo efficaciter impleverit juramentum.

Octavus et ultimus casus in dicta glossa tactus, et magis ad propositum faciens, est quod non restituitur a possessione sua spoliatus quando sub conditione possidet, ut Extra, De restitutione spoliatorum, *Olim.*[5] Nunc autem ista opinio asserit quod Dominus Benedictus recepit et possedet Papatum sub conditione expressa in

6. C. 2, q. 5, c. 13.
7. condignam *AB.*
8. suspendetur *A.*
9. spoliati *A.*
1. X, 2, 13, c. 8.
2. prosequeretur *ABC.*
3. C. 3, q. 1, *in v.* quod restitutio; cf. above, n. 5, p. 292.
4. X, 2, 13, c. 3.
5. X, 2, 13, c. 16.

ju-(100r)-ramento praedicto. Et ideo, quia conditionem non implevit, fuit merito a possesione spoliatus, nec ad eam (47) restituendus est.

Ex praemissis igitur et aliis multis similibus, quae tamen ad octo supradictas objectiones videntur posse reduci, fundatur opinio supradicta.

Tertia opinio media est inter duas extremas et contrarias opiniones praedictas,[6] asserens quod in casu praesenti restitutio oboedientiae in aliquibus facienda est et in aliquibus non; quia distinguit quod ea, in quibus ante subtractionem dabatur oboedientia, erant in duplici differentia. Nam quaedam erant essentialia et necessario annexa dignitati Papatus, scilicet illa jura, illae praeeminentiae et illi honores, qui tam ratione ordinis (19v) quam ratione jurisdictionis de jure divino debentur Papae tanquam supremo capiti universalis Ecclesiae. Alia erant accidentalia et adventitia et, ut quibusdam videtur, usurpata in praejudicium praelatorum et ecclesiarum inferiorum, sicut dispositiones et collationes episcopatuum in praejudicium electionum, reservationes beneficiorum ecclesiasticorum in praejudicium collationum ordinariorum, receptiones vacantium in praejudicium et saepe in maximam destructionem ecclesiarum, retentiones et reservationes procurationum in praejudicium visitationum et correctionum ac reformationum status ecclesiastici et in grave scandalum et periculum animarum, ac etiam multa (40r) alia hujusmodi, quae vocabantur jura Camerae Apostolicae. Et haec omnia antiquitus non erant annexa Papatui, nec Petrus nec plures ejus sanctissimi successores Papae perfectissimi talibus utebantur; sed ab aliquibus temporibus introducta sunt, magis de facto quam de jure, cum ista contra jus commune immo etiam contra jus divinum esse videantur. Juxta hanc distinctionem respondet haec opinio ponendo duas conclusiones.

Prima est, quod quantum ad illa quae in primo (48) membro distinctionis comprehenduntur, restitutio oboedientiae est Papae facienda. Et in hoc concordat cum prima opinione, et fundatur in auctoritatibus pro ea superius introductis, junctis cum eisdem rationibus prius tactis in quarta consideratione primae partis hujus tractatus.

Secunda conclusio (100v) est, quod quantum ad illa quae in secundo membro praedictae distinctionis exprimuntur, non est Papae danda oboedientia.[7, 8] Et in hoc concordat cum secunda opinione,

6. This is the opinion which triumphed at the Council of 1406—cf. Valois, *France, 3,* 455 ff.; see above, n. 24, p. 250.

sed non fundatur in allegationibus pro eo factis, sed magis in rationibus prius tactis in quinta consideratione primae partis hujus tractatus. Et possent ad hoc induci plures probationes tam de jure
divino quam humano.

Sed contra hanc secundam conclusionem obicit prima opinio per
illa quae superius pro ea et pro prima conclusione producta sunt:
quia ex quo Dominus Benedictus et sui praedecessores fuerunt in
possessione et usu praemissorum, et ipse per subtractionem fuerit[9]
spoliatus, videtur quod ante omnia restituendus sit (20r) juxta
superius allegata et ea quae leguntur 2, q. 2, per totum,[1] ubi probatur multis auctoritatibus, quod ante litem contestatam[2] possessori
omnes possessiones restituendae sunt, et quod nullus episcopus debet
accusari dum suis rebus fuerit spoliatus, nec vocari ad synodum, nec
in aliquo judicari. Et si haec in minoribus episcopis, tanto magis in
Summo Pontifice servanda sunt.

Ad hanc objectionem secundum hanc tertiam opinionem videtur
posse dupliciter responderi. Primo, quod quantum ad ea quae contra
episcopos et ecclesias inferiores fuerunt a Romana Curia usurpata,
Dominus Benedictus non fuit per subtractionem proprie loquendo
spoliatus, quia secundum Gofredum, in Summa, Rubrica, De restitutione spoliatorum,[3] definitur spoliatio, quid *est a possessione rei
immobilis violenta et injuriosa ejectio* (49) *vel mobilis rei ablatio.*
Et sicut ipse ibidem subdit, *injuriosa* propter hoc adicitur *quia non
quotienscunque quis de possessione violenter eicitur, injuriose*[4] *eici
intelligendus est, ut cum quis alium eiciens incontinenti et quasi
bello continuato reicitur. Nam etsi per violentiam excludatur, non
tamen restituitur, ut infra eod. tit. Olim,*[5] *3, q. 1, § Patet.*[6] *Cod. Unde
vi*[7] *l.1.*[8]

7. *Add.* Usquequo per generale concilium aliter fuerit ordinatum. *C.*

8. Usquequo per generale concilium aliter fuerit ordinatum, *in marg. V.*

9. fuit *C.*

1. C. 2, q. 2, c. 1, 2, 3, and 4.

2. litis contestationem *C.*

3. Geoffrey de Trani, Cardinal, glossator of the Decretals, d. 1245. For a bibliography consult *Lex. für Theol. u. Kirche* (1932), *4*, 564. The reference here is to
his *Summa . . . in Titulis Decretalium omnibus utilis et necessaria,* Rubrica: De
restitutione spoliatorum, § 1 (Venice, 1564), p. 189.

4. injuriosa *V.*

5. X, 2, 13, c. 16.

6. C. 3, q. 1, c. 6, § Patet ergo; cf. above, n. 7, p. 286.

7. *Om.* unde vi *C; Add.* vᵃ 3 *C.*

8. Cf. the law of Justinian: C., 8, 4, 4.

Ex quibus nunc arguere possunt episcopi et ecclesiae inferiores quod Papa et praedecessores sui contra eorum jura, ipsis quantum potuerunt renitentibus, vel (40v) saltem invitis et renitere non audentibus, usurpaverunt, et nunc per subtractionem, quasi bello (101r) continuato, hujusmodi usurpationem rejecerunt, et ad antiquam jurium suorum possessionem redierunt, nec in hoc Papae injuriam inferunt. Quare nec ipsum spoliant, quia, sicut dici solet: *qui jure suo utitur, nemini facit injuriam*. Immo quod episcopi ab hac possessione, in qua nunc sunt, et in qua alias antiquitus fuerunt, non sint vel fuerint nunc vel alias spoliandi, videntur probare jura contra hanc secundam conclusionem et pro prima opinione superius allegata.

Secundo, potest responderi ad praedictam objectionem quod supposito quod concederetur improprie [9] loquendo, quod Papa a praedicta possessione fuerit spoliatus, tamen non oportet concedere quod in hoc sit (20v) restituendus; quia (ut supra allegatum est ex glossa 3, q. 1) [1] multi sunt casus in quibus fallit regula de restitutione spoliati, quorum aliqui videntur ad propositum pertinere.

Unus est, cum incontinenti spoliator vult probare exceptionem: ut Extra, De restitutione spoliatorum, cap. *Per* [2] *litteras*,[3] ubi patet quod *si contra petentem* (50) *restitutionem conjugis opponatur consanguinitas* [4] *in gradu prohibito, et offerantur probationes paratae* ⟨. . .⟩ *negabitur restitutio quoad thorum,* quae tamen plenaria fieret, si probationes promptae non essent. Modo in casu praesenti praelati incontinenti et prompte possunt probare exceptionem docendo de jure proprietatis, quia omnia jura communia sunt pro eis, et maxime jura antiqua a sanctis patribus instituta. Et si aliquae novae decretales epistolae seu papales constitutiones in favorem dictae possessionis emerserint, illae per generale concilium retractandae et corrigendae sunt vel saltem moderandae juxta ea quae dicta sunt in quinta consideratione primae partis hujus tractatus.

Secundus casus ad propositum faciens, in quo [5] juxta praeallegatam glossam, non fit restitutio spoliato, est, si ex gratia vel precario possedit, ut Extra, De excessibus praelatorum, cap. *Cum ad quo-*

---

9. proprie *AB*.
1. C. 3, q. 1, *in v.* quod restitutio; cf. above, n. 3, p. 293.
2. *Om. BV.*
3. X, 2, 13, c. 13.
4. consanguineitas *BCV*.
5. qua *B*.

rumdam,[6] et 10, q. 3. *Quia cognovimus.*[7] In quo capitulo auctoritate Concilii Toletani statuitur, ut *ultra morem antiquum,* a subditis nihil exigatur, et ut alia episcopis quae nunc usque *praesumpta sunt denegentur.* Et causa ibi subditur, *ne videamur in Ecclesia Dei, exactores potius quam Dei Pontifices nominari.* Et ibidem super verbo *praesumpta sunt* notat (101v) glossa [8] quod longinqua possessio non facit jus, ut 93, dist., *Illud,*[9] et 24, q. 1, *Schisma,* cum aliis concordanciis ibidem allegatis.[1] Notat etiam, quod sua auctoritate quis potest detinere quod de jure non praestitit, licet illud diu solverit, quia tempus non inducit obligationem, ut Extra., De censibus, *Pervenit.*[2] Et facit ad confirmationem praemissorum, quod [3] Hostiensis in (41r) Summa,[4] Rubrica De restitutione spoliatorum, inter XXIV casus, in quibus restitutio denegatur ponit tres: *Si petenti resti-*(51)*-tutionem obiciatur spoliatio.*[5] Et de hoc vide ibi: [6] Modo in proposito dicunt et obiciunt episcopi, quod fuerunt suis juribus spoliati. Ex quibus concluditur ut supra, et respondetur (21r) ad objectionem praedictam, confirmando praemissam conclusionem secundam.[7]

Sed contra conclusionem primam sunt omnia illa quae praedicta sunt pro secunda opinione, in qua octo objectiones inductae sunt contra Dominum Benedictum, ad probandum quod ei non debeat fieri aliqua restitutio oboedientiae. Ad quas omnes objectiones respondet ista opinio.

Primo, quod Dominus Benedictus et illi qui ei non subtraxerunt, aut qui oboedientiam reddiderunt, negant omnia illa crimina quae sibi in dictis objectionibus opponuntur, et per consequens negant illa esse notoria seu evidentia. Et super his offert idem Dominus Benedictus de se [8] omni poscenti reddere rationem, ut patet in litteris ejus

---

6. X, 5, 31, c. 7.

7. C. 10, q. 3, c. 6.

8. C. 10, q. 3, c. 6, *in v.* praesumpta.

9. D. 93, c. 22.

1. C. 24, q. 1, c. 34; cf. also, X, 5, 3, c. 9; X, 5, 3, c. 8; C. 1, q. 1, c. 100.

2. X, 3, 39, c. 5. The reference is rather to the gloss *in v.* Census ignorantiae, than to the text.

3. *Add.* notat *AB.*

4. sola *CV.*

5. Henry of Segusia, *Summa Hostiensis super titulis Decretalium* (Lyons, 1542), f. 89r, § 3. Cf. above, n. 6, p. 254.

6. *Om. C; Add.* id est 6 *C.*

7. praedictam *AB.*

8. *Om.* de se *AB.*

scriptis archiepiscopis et episcopis Regni Franciae. Quare super his non est sibi deneganda audientia.[9] Immo injustissimum videtur ipsum non auditum puniri et a non judice suo spoliari.

Secundo dicit ista opinio quod, supposito quod Dominus Benedictus in materia ista aliquo modo peccasset vel errasset, tamen in errore non perseveravit, sed quicquid in materia Ecclesiae ab eo petitum est ad instantiam Regis Franciae concessit, sicut patet ex publicis instrumentis super hoc factis et manu sua propria subscriptis; nec fuit obstinatus aut pertinax, ut patet ex protestationibus per eum saepe factis, quibus se et fidem suam ac omnia dicta et facta in materia unionis, submisit correctioni ac determinationi Ecclesiae. Quare non potest dici schismaticus aut haereticus (52) juxta [1] dictum commune Augustini: *Errare potero,* (102r) *sed haereticus non ero.*[2, 3] Et hinc patet, quod hic non habet locum exceptio haeresis, de qua 8, dist., cap. *Quo jure.*[4] Dicit glossa [5] hic: *quod petenti restitutionem obstat exceptio haeresis. Haeretico enim nihil est licitum possidere, ut 23, q. 5, Si vos,*[6] *et q. 7, cap. 1 et 3.*[7] Haec namque locum habent in eo qui pertinaciter est haereticus, vel qui tenet obstinate haeresim manifestam et alias damnatam, ut in cap. *Anastasius,* 19 dist.,[8] ubi legitur quod ab eo se subtraxerunt clerici. Sed dicit ibi glossa [9] quod hoc ideo fecerunt, quia incidebat [1] in haeresim jam damnatam, et patet in textu quod etiam communicabat notorie cum manifesto haeretico,[2] (21v) ejus [3] errorem fovendo, et in eo contumaciter perseverando. Ideo etiam ibi dicitur quod *nutu divino percussus est.*

Tertio ex hoc concludit ista opinio quod cum notorium sit subtractionem non fuisse conclusam in Regno Franciae—nisi sub conditione, scilicet quousque Dominus Benedictus concordaret viam

---

9. oboedientia *AB*.

1. *Add.* illud *AB*.

2. The idea is St. Augustine's, cf. *De Trinitate*, I, c. 3; PL *42*, 822–23; also *De Haeresibus* in the Preface; PL *42*, 20 ff. The actual words, however, are St. Bonaventure's, *Sent., 4*, dist. 13, dub. 4.

3. *Add.* etc. *AB*.

4. D. 8, c. 1, *in v.* Nam jure divino.

5. *Add.* habes *CV*.

6. C. 23, q. 5, c. 35.

7. C. 23, q. 5, c. 1 and 3.

8. D. 19, c. 9.

9. D. 19, c. 9, *in v.* Abegerunt.

1. inciderat *BC*.

2. haeretice *A*.

3. Cujus *ABC*.

cessionis, etc.—consequens est, ex quo paratus est conditionem (41v) adimplere, ut dictum est, quod ei debeat oboedientia restitui, saltem quoad illa quae in prima conclusione dicta sunt, quia cessante causa subtractionis, cessare debet subtractio juxta dictum philosophi: *Cessante causa cessat effectus.*[4]

Quarto dicit opinio praedicta quod per hujusmodi subtractionem non est sedatum scandalum schismatis, immo magis prima [5] schisma firmatum, et in hac oboedientia aliud schisma subortum. Quare supposito quod ab aliquibus facta fuerit bono zelo, scilicet intentione sedandi schismatis [6] tamen cum experientia nunc doceat subtractionem ad hoc non proficere, sed obesse, et majus (53) scandalum generare a subtractione cessandum est. Alioquin deinceps dabitur occasio scandalis contra doctrinam Evangelii: *Vae ⟨homini⟩ illi per quem scandalum venit.*[7, 8]

Quinto dicit ista opinio quod minus juste arguitur Dominus Benedictus de saevitia aut odio capitali in eos qui subtractionem facerunt, cum ad debitam indulgentiam se paratum esse spoponderit, nec propter suspicionem de contrario videtur in carcere detinendus, quia aliter, et multo justius et honestius posset super hoc provideri. Immo videntur magis posse argui de saevo et crudeli odio illi, qui eum in (102v) domo sua propria hostiliter invaserunt et adhuc incarceratum detinent, cum tamen hoc in deliberatione subtractionis minime conclusum fuerit. Immo per Regem Franciae, ut ex ejus litteris patet,[9] tales violentiae nec ratificatae fuerunt nec approbatae, sed potius contra eas Dominus Benedictus in salva gardia Regis receptus est. Et ideo qui in eum talem violentiam continuant, evidenter se esse ejus hostes manifestant. Quare contra eum convenienter [1] esse non possunt testes aut judices, prout omnia jura clamant.

Sexto,[2] quantum ad materiam septimae et octavae oppositionis, respondet haec opinio quod (22r) ex juramento Domini Benedicti

---

4. The principle does not seem to be Aristotelian; cf. above, n. 5, p. 258.

5. primum *ABC*.

6. schisma *AB*.

7. Matt. 18:7.

8. *Add.* etc. *ABC*.

9. The reference is to the letter of safeguard delivered to Benedict XIII on April 10, 1399, by the ambassador of Charles VI, and to the letter of August 1, 1401, disavowing the war and violence organized by the Sacred College. Cf. Valois, *France, 3*, 216 ff. and 325, n. 3.

1. *Om.* se esse ejus . . . eum convenienter *AB*.

2. *Om. AB*.

facto ante vel post ejus electionem, non concluditur quod ejus electio
vel receptio in Papatum fuerit conditionalis vel sub conditione
facta, quia Papae electio conditionalis esse non potest. Et nihilominus ad purificandum et implendum conditionem in dicto juramento expressam Dominus Benedictus, ut supra dictum est se paratum exhibet. Et sic quantum in se est juramentum adimplet. Quare
ad administrationem Papatus restituendus est, cum etiam (54) subtrahentes ipsum habere jus in Papatu negare non possint, quia
ipsum Dominum Benedictum nominant (quod non est nomen personae, sed officii et dignitatis papalis) [3] et etiam quia post subtractionem petierunt ab eo viam cessionis, etc. Et tamen, si ipse Papa
non esset, Papatui cedere non posset; sicut ad haec et omnia praemissa possent jura plurima induci. Sed transeo causa brevitatis.

Septimo, pro generali responsione ad omnes hujusmodi objectiones dicit haec opinio quod jura allegata in illis octo (42r) casibus
supra tactis, in quibus non fit restitutio spoliato, non loquuntur de
episcopis, sed solum de inferioribus personis, sicut inductive patet
in omnibus capitulis ibidem allegatis, excepto capitulo *Haec* [4] *quippe,*
3, q. 6.[5] Et tamen ibi non loquitur secundum juris dispositionem,
sed per tolerantiam seu permissionem. Modo sic est secundum jura et
auctoritates pro prima opinione inductas et quae faciunt ad probationem primae conclusionis hujus opinionis tertiae, quod regulare
et speciale est in episcopis a suis sedibus vel honoribus spoliatis, eos,
priusquam ad synodum valeant evocari, debere restitui. Quae regula
in proposito maxime observanda videtur; quia Papa non minus, sed
magis privilegiatus est (103r) aliis inferioribus episcopis, sicut clamant jura tam divina quam humana. Et sic patet conclusio prima.

Sed adhuc ad confirmationem hujus conclusionis faciunt aliqua
jura allegata in fine opinionis primae: quae non solum videntur
probare quod Papae debeat fieri hujusmodi restitutio, sed etiam
quod nec fieri potuit debite subtractio, quantum ad ea quae necessario sunt annexa Papatui, ex (55) eo scilicet quia secundum illa
jura Papa non potest nec debet a suis subditis (22v) judicari. Et
hoc regulariter concedit ista opinio.

Sed occasione capituli *Nemo* [6] ibidem allegati, ubi de Papa dicitur,
Neque ab omni clero judex judicabitur, oritur hic specialis diffi-

3. *Om. AB.*
4. hoc *A.*
5. C. 3, q. 6, c. 10.
6. C. 9, q. 3, c. 13; cf. above, n. 8, p. 287.

cultas, quia ex illo verbo, *neque ab omni clero,* et aliis capitulis et concordanciis inductis 9, q. 3, tam in textu quam in glossa videtur aliquibus quod Papa non possit etiam per generale concilium judicari.[7] Unde ibi dicit glossa super verbo *ab omni clero,* quod hic est argumentum, quod *concilium non potest Papam judicare, ut Extra, De electione, "Significasti."* [8] *Unde si totus mundus sententiaret in aliquo negotio contra Papam,*[9] *videtur quod sententiae Papae standum esset, ut 24, q. 1, "Haec est fides".*[1, 2] *Sed est argumentum contra, quia orbis est major urbe, ut 93,*[3] *dist. "Legimus".*[4] Licet autem glossa non solvat nec concordet hic ista contraria, tamen in eodem capitulo [5] remittit ad capitulum *Si Papa,* 40 dist.,[6] ubi de hoc determinavit. Ibi autem dicit textus: *Si Papa suae et fraternae salutis negligens deprehenditur inutilis et remissus in operibus suis.* etc. Et sequitur: *tamen hujusmodi culpas redarguere praesumit hic nullus* [7] *mortalium, quia cunctos ipse judicaturus a nemine est judicandus, nisi deprehendatur a fide devius.* etc. Et ibi super verbo *a fide devius,* dicit glossa [8] *quod hoc intelligit Huguccio, cum Papa non vult corrigi. Si enim paratus esset corrigi, non posset accusari, ut 24, q. 1, "aperte",* cum suis similibus.[9] Et concordat cum eo quod supra dictum est in octava consideratione primae partis hujus tractatus de Marcellino Papa in cap. *Nunc autem,* 21 dist.[1, 2]

Sed quaerit glossa praedicta: *quare* (56) Papa [3] *non potest accusari de alio crimine* quam de haeresi? *Ponamus enim quod notorium sit crimen ejus, vel per confessionem vel facti evidentiam. Quare non accusatur vel de crimine simoniae* (103v) *vel adulterii, et cum admonetur, incorrigibilis est,* (42v) *et scandalizatur Ecclesia per causam*

7. C. 9, q. 3, c. 14 and 15; cf. above, n. 1, p. 287. Cf. also X, 1, 6, c. 4; C. 24, q. 1, c. 14.
8. X, 1, 6, c. 4.
9. *Om.* contra Papam *AB.*
1. Hoc non probat c. 1 *Haec est fides* si bene consideretur *in marg. B.*
2. C. 24, q. 1, c. 14.
3. 23 *ABC.*
4. D. 93, c. 24.
5. C. 9, q. 3, c. 13; cf. above, n. 7.
6. D. 40, c. 6.
7. *Om. AB.*
8. D. 40, c. 6, *in v.* a fide devius.
9. C. 24, q. 1, c. 36; cf. also C. 24, q. 1, c. 14 and 35.
1. D. 21, c. 7.
2. For the parallel text referred to see above, p. 275.
3. *Om. C.*

ejus seu per[4] *crimen?* Et ad hoc respondendo dicit glossa: *Certo credo quod si notorium est crimen ejus quodcunque, et inde scandalizetur Ecclesia, et incorrigilis sit, quod inde possit accusari. Nam contumacia dicitur haeresis, ut 81 dist., "Si qui Presbyteri",*[5] *et contumax dicitur (23r) infidelis: ut 27 dist., "Nullus".*[6] *Hic tamen fit mentio specialiter de haeresi, ideo quia et si occulta esset haeresis, de illa*[7] *posset accusari,*[8] *sed de alio occulto crimine non posset.*

Et postea quaerit eadem glossa: *Nunquid Papa posset statuere, quod non posset de haeresi accusari? Respondet quod non, quia ex hoc periclitaretur tota Ecclesia, quod non licet, ut 25, q. 1, "Sunt quidam",*[9] *ubi dicit textus: Si enim quod docuerunt Apostoli et Prophetae destruere, quod absit, niteretur non sententiam dare, sed magis errare convinceretur.* Et sicut dicit ibi glossa praedicta, *in eo casu Papa desineret esse caput Ecclesiae, et ita non teneret ejus constitutio.*

Et hanc glossam tenet et approbat tertia opinio supradicta,[1] et secundum hoc intelligit cap. *Mandastis,* 2, q. 4,[2] ubi scribit Sixtus Papa omnibus episcopis: *Mandastis, ut scriberem vobis qualiter instans*[3] *jurgium contra me suscitatum sit, vel a quo, ut vestro adminiculo pelleretur, et causa mea firmaretur. Scitote me criminari a quodam Basso et injuste (57) persequi. Quod audiens Valentinianus Augustus nostra auctoritate Synodum jussit congregari; et facto concilio, cum*[4] *magna examinatione satisfaciens omnibus, licet evadere aliter satis potuissem suspicionem tamen fugiens, coram omnibus me purgavi, me scilicet a suspicione et aemulatione liberans; sed non aliis qui noluerint aut sponte hoc non elegerint, faciendi formam dans.*[5] Ubi dicit glossa[6] super verbo *licet aliter evadere satis potuissem,* quod hoc ibi dicitur *quia Papa a nullo potest judicari nec etiam ab universali concilio, ut 17 dist., § "Hinc etiam".*[7]

4. *Add.* per *ABC.*
5. C. 1, q. 7, c. 1.
6. D. *38,* c. 16.
7. *Om.* de illa *C.*
8. *Add.* de illa *C.*
9. C. 25, q. 1, c. 6.
1. Vera doctrina catholica, *in marg. V.*
2. C. 2, q. 5, c. 10.
3. *Om. A.*
4. *Om. AB.*
5. formans *AB; Om.* dans *AB.*
6. C. 2, q. 5, c. 10, *in v.* potuissem.
7. D. 17, c. 6, § Hinc etiam; cf. above, n. 3, p. 274.

Et hoc intelligendum est secundum priorem glossam quantum ad crimina occulta,[8] ut superius dixi de Symmacho Papa in dicto §, super verbo *cujus causam Dei judicio reservamus*.[9] Et intelligo hic crimina occulta, id est, quae non sic sunt (104r) scandalosa ut ex eis tota turbetur Ecclesia juxta modum loquendi glossae praedictae. Et consimiliter intelligendum est cap. *Nemo*, cum suis similibus.[1]

Vel potest dici quod ibi [2] illud verbum, nec *ab omni clero judex judicabitur*,[3] non capitur collective pro toto clero universali (23v) seu concilio generali, sed capitur distributive, ut sit sensus quod a nullo clero, id est,[4] nulla parte seu a nullo collegio cleri particulari Papa judicandus est. Vel capitur ibi omnis clerus pro Collegio Cardinalium seu toto clero Romano vel Romanae dioecesis, sicut etiam supra sumitur in § *Hinc etiam*,[5] sicut dictum est in octava consideratione primae partis. Ex quibus omnibus concludit opinio supradicta quod Papa potest in certis casibus per generale concilium judicari, sicut in praedicta consideratione praetactum est.

Sed contra hoc obiciunt aliqui [6] quia major non judicatur (43r) a minori nec superior ab inferiori, ut 22 dist., *Quia ergo*.[7] Sed Papa est major et superior (58) concilio. Ergo non judicatur ab eo. Immo ultra dicunt quod in concilio generali Papa dumtaxat judicat et definit, et si eo praesente ibi [8] aliqua statuantur, concilium nihil statuit sed suadet et consulit, ut De bap., cap. finali,[9] ubi dicit Papa *sacro concilio suadente districte praecipimus* et in cap. *Ad apostolicae*, De re. jud., lib. 6,[1] dicitur,[2] *de consilio concilii*, et circa finem: *Nos itaque ⟨. . .⟩ cum fratribus nostris et sancto concilio nostro deliberatione praehabita*, etc. Et aliqua similia habentur in jure. Ex quibus notant aliqui doctores canonistae quod Papa non habet necesse sequi deliberationem vel suasionem concilii. Quare

8. D. 40, c. 6, *in v.* a fide devius; cf. above, n. 8, p. 301.
9. D. 17, c. 6, § Hinc etiam.
1. C. 9, q. 3, c. 13, 14 and 15; cf. above, n. 5, p. 301.
2. *Om. AB.*
3. C. 9, q. 3, c. 13.
4. *Add.* a *ABC.*
5. D. 17, c. 6, § Hinc etiam.
6. Cf. the speech of William Philastre (then Dean of Rheims) at the Council of Paris in 1406—Chastenet, pp. 125 ff.
7. D. 22, *Prima pars Gratiani.*
8. *Om. C.*
9. X, 3, 42, c. 6.
1. VI°, 2, 14, c. 2.
2. dicit *ABC.*

multo minus potest ab eo judicari. Unde Joannes Andreae, in Novella cap. *Significasti,* De elect.,[3] dicit super verbo *robur: Ergo videtur standum sententiae Papae, si contradicat Ecclesia vel concilio.
De hoc 4 dist., cap. "In istis",*[4] et 15 dist., "Sicut", in fine,[5] et 19
dist., cap. paenultimo,[6] 9,[7] q. 1, "Nemo",[8] 24, q. 1, "Quodcunque"* [9]
Johannes Andreae.

Ad hanc autem [1] rationem respondetur primo quod major rationis,
licet regulariter sit vera, tamen quandoque fallit. Nam Rex Franciae,
qui est major et superior in toto regno, saepe in aliquibus casibus
judicatur et contra eum fertur sententia in suo parlamento.[2] Similiter Papa in foro conscientiae (104v) a simplici sacerdote judicatur.
Etiam in foro exteriori potest judicari ab inferiori suo, si se ei
sponte subiciat, ut 2, q. 7: [3] *Nos, si incompetenter aliquid egimus*
etc., ubi Leo (24r) Papa loquens Imperatori dicit: *vestro ⟨. . .⟩
cuncta volumus emendare judicio,* etc.

Secunda ad praedictam objectionem dicitur quod minor rationis
non est vera, scilicet quod Papa est major et (59) superior concilio,
licet sit major et superior in concilio [4] cum sit caput omnium
membrorum. Et ad hoc probandum videtur esse ratio evidens, quia
omne totum sua parte majus est.[5] Sed Papa est pars concilii, sicut
caput pars corporis. Ergo totum concilium majus est Papa, et per
consequens auctoritas totius concilii major auctoritate Papae. Unde
dicit Hieronymus: [6] *Si auctoritas quaeritur, orbis major est urbe.*
Ubi dicit glossa in cap. *Legimus* [7] supra allegato, quod hic sumitur
argumentum *quod statutum concilii praejudicat statuto Papae.* Et

3. *Joannis Andreae . . . In Primum Decretalium librum Novella Commentaria*
(Venice, 1581), ad X, 1, 6, c, 4 f., 74r; cf. above, n. 2, p. 289.
    4. D. 4, c. 3.
    5. D. 15, c. 2.
    6. D. 19, c. 9.
    7. 60 *AB.*
    8. C. 9, q. 3, c. 13.
    9. C. 24, q. 1, c. 6.
    1. ergo *C.*
    2. D'Ailly is referring, presumably, to the frequent condemnation by the *Parle-
ment* of royal officers, or to the clashes with the King over alienations of the royal
domain; see above, pp. 53 and 123.
    3. C. 2, q. 7, c. 41.
    4. *Om.* licet . . . in concilio *AB.*
    5. loquendo de toto respectu suarum partium integralium, *in marg. V.*
    6. St. Jerome, *Ep.* 146; PL 22, 1194; cf. D. 93, c. 24.
    7. D. 93, c. 24, *in v.* major est.

19 dist., cap. Anastasius,[8] dicitur quod *multi clerici se a communione ipsius abegerunt, eo quod sine concilio episcoporum* communicasset cum Photino haeretico. Ubi dicit glossa: [9] *quod Papa tenetur requirere concilium episcoporum, ubi de fide agitur, et tunc synodus major est Papa, ut 15 dist., sicut"*.[1] Et 24, q. 1, cap. 1, *Achatius,* super verbo *quicunque in haeresim semel damnatum labitur* dicit glossa: [2] *Hic est casus ⟨. . .⟩ in quo Papa in canonem latae sententiae incidit. Nec obviat regula illa, quia par parem solvere aut* (43v) *ligare non potest: quia si Papa haereticus est, in hoc minor est quolibet catholico, 12, q. 1, "Scimus"* [3] multo magis ergo minor [4] et inferior generali concilio.[5]

Tertio ex his sequitur quod illud falsum est, quod ultimo in illa [6] ratione assumitur, scilicet quod in concilio generali solus Papa judicat et definit: quia licet in conciliis generalibus communiter proferat sententiam, tamen auctoritative et consensu concilii. Nec bene concludunt illi doctores qui [7] arguunt: *Concilium consulit et deliberat, ergo non definit vel judicat.* Nam contrarium expresse legitur in multis locis Libri Conciliorum et etiam Decreti et Decretalium,[8] ubi sic [9] dicitur: [1] *Placuit sancto concilio,* vel *Concilium definit,* vel *statuit sanctum concilium.* Papa etiam quandoque dicit: *sacri auctoritate concilii et* (60) *consensu atque reliquorum fidelium et cunctorum* [2] *consiliariorum nostrorum consultu definitum est.* De auctoritate quoque (105r) conciliorum 15 dist., cap. *Sicut* [3] (24v) dicit Beatus Gregorius: *Sicut Sancti Evangelii quatuor libros, sic quatuor concilia suscipere et venerari me fateor.* Et in fine capituli causam subdit: *quia universali consensu constituta sunt.* Non dicit:

8. D. 19, c. 9.
9. D. 19, c. 9, *in v.* Consilio.
1. D. 15, c. 2.
2. C. 24, q. 1, c. 1, *in v.* haeresim.
3. C. 12, q. 1, c. 9.
4. *Add.* est *C.*
5. *Om.* multo magis . . . generali concilio *AB.*
6. ultima *C.*
7. Cf. above, n. 6, p. 303.
8. Cf. Hinschius, pp. 354–62; D. 16, c. 7, § 1.
9. saepe *ABC.*
1. ut supra allegatum est capitula secunda tertiae partis *in marg. V.* The reference is not to the *De materia* but to the *De ecclesiastica potestate,* Part III, Ch. 2; Dupin, 2, 951–53.
2. *Om.* et cunctorum *AB.*
3. D. 15, c. 2; cf. above, n. 1.

quia papali [4] sed *quia universali consensu.* Similiter in conciliis Symmachi [5] dicunt episcopi: *decernimus, et synodali auctoritate roboramus,* et *synodalis ordinatio vigeat.* Et in subscriptionibus episcoporum dicitur: [6] *"his constitutis synodalibus a nobis probatis atque firmatis."* Et multa alia hujusmodi. Quae verba magis sunt notanda et sequenda quam cujuscunque novelli [7] doctoris opinio contrarium asserentis.

Quarto, dicitur ad confirmationem praedictae solutionis quod illi qui, ut praemissum est, sic deprimunt auctoritatem definitivam conciliorum exaltando et magnificando auctoritatem Summorum Pontificum, non solum docent contra jura humana praeallegata, sed etiam contra jus divinum. Nam in primo concilio celebrato Hierosolymis (de quo habetur Actuum 15) Jacobus, qui erat Episcopus Hierosolymitanus, etiam praesente Petro protulit sententiam. Unde ibi dicit: *Propter quod ego judico non inquietari eos,*[8] etc. Et ibidem scripta est epistola cujus initium est: *Apostoli et seniores fratres his qui sunt Antiochae,* etc.[9] Sequitur: *Placuit nobis collectis in unum eligere viros,* etc.[1] Sequitur: *Visum est Spiritui Sancto et nobis nihil ultra imponere,* etc.[2] Ex quibus omnibus patet quod auctoritas definiendi seu determinandi in concilio non ibi [3] attribuitur Petro, quamvis esset caput Ecclesiae, sed toti concilio Apostolorum (61) et seniorum, quorum consensu lata est et publicata sententia.

Quinto ex his concludit praedicta opinio quod auctoritas et determinatio concilii attribuenda est determinationi Spiritus Sancti; quia ibi dicitur: *Visum est Spiritui Sancto et nobis,* etc. Cui concordat quod dicitur 25, q. 2, cap. Igitur,[4] ubi dicit Leo Papa: *sanctorum patrum canones, spiritu Dei conditos et totius mundi* (44r) *reverentia consecratos.* Et hinc trahitur secundum aliquos [5] quod concilium generale non potest errare in his quae sunt fidei. Quod etiam probatur ex illo verbo Christi: *Petre, rogavi pro te ut non*

---

4. papa *C.*
5. Hinschius, pp. 658, 677, 684.
6. *Add.* et *ABC.*
7. *Om.* novelli *ABC.*
8. Acts 15:19.
9. Acts 15:23.
1. Acts 15:25.
2. Acts 15:28.
3. *Om. C.*
4. C. 25, q. 2, c. 5.
5. *Om.* secundum aliquos *ABC.*

deficiat fides tua,[6] (25r) quia hoc non est dictum de fide personali Petri, cum ipse erraverit, sed de fide universalis (105v) Ecclesiae, quae repraesentatur in concilio generali, de qua etiam ibidem dictum est: *et portae inferi non praevalebunt adversus eam,*[7] scilicet Ecclesiam. Non enim dictum est *adversus te,* scilicet Petrum. Ex quibus patet, quod judicium concilii praeferendum est judicio Papae, cum ipse in his quae fidei sunt possit errare; sicut et Petrus, de quo dicit Paulus ad Galatas, 2 cap., quod ei *restitit in faciem, quia repraehensibilis erat,* non recte ambulans ad veritatem evangelii, etc.[8, 9]

Ex his sexto infertur quod quamvis Papa concedatur esse caput Ecclesiae, tamen hoc est sub principali et essentiali capite Christo. Et ideo subordinatio corporis Ecclesiae ad Papam est solum accidentalis; sed[1] essentialis ad Christum, a quo immediate habet auctoritatem et illud privilegium quod non potest errare in fide. Quod privilegium non habet a[2] Papa. Et ideo licet auctoritas Papae in illis[3] quibus non errat, sit a jure divino[4] immediate juxta verbum Christi: *Et ego dico tibi quia tu es Petrus et super hanc petram aedificabo Ecclesiam meam,* etc:[5] tamen (62) ex hoc non sequitur, sicut aliqui volunt concludere, quod reliqua auctoritas et tota potestas Ecclesiae sit a Papa immediate. Nam hoc potest multiplicam pati calumniam.

Primo, quia auctoritas sacerdotalis, quae[6] major est in Ecclesia, non semper immediate derivatur a Papa, cum stet aliquem esse Papam et non sacerdotem, et per consequens tunc posse proprie conferre ordinem sacerdotalem.

Secundo, et magis ad propositum, quia nullo etiam existente Papa, habet Ecclesia multiplicem potestatem tam ordinis quam jurisdictionis, quae tunc non derivatur nec dependet a Papa.

6. Luke 22:32.
7. Matt. 16:18.
8. Gal. 2:11–14.
9. Tamen secundum aliquos, hoc est speciale privilegium Universalis Ecclesiae quod non potest errare in fide, licet hoc idem pie credatur de concilio generali, videlicet quando innititur divinae scripturae, vel auctoritati, quae a Spiritu Sancto inspirata est. Alias saepe errasse legitur, *in marg. V.*
1. *Add.* est *ABC.*
2. *Om. AB.*
3. *Add.* in *AC.*
4. *Om. C; Add.* a Christo *C.*
5. Matt. 16:18.
6. quod quantum ad potestatem ordinis sacramentalis, *in marg. V.*

Tertio, hanc auctoritatem habet Ecclesia universalis, ut dictum est, quod in fide errare non potest; et haec nec mediate nec immediate a Papa dependet, quia illam non habet.

Ex quibus omnibus sequitur quod potestas seu auctoritas Ecclesiae immediate [7] est a Christo, et non a Petro. Et hoc notatur (25v) in verbo Christi, quia non dicit: *Tu es Petrus et super hanc petram aedificabis,* sed *aedificabo;* nec dicit *tuam,* sed *Ecclesiam meam.*[8] Item ad hoc facit quod ait Augustinus (106r) Libro De Agone Christiano, cap. 22,[9] ubi dicit quod *Ecclesiae claves regni caelorum datae sunt, cum Petro datae sunt;* et quod *ei dicitur, ad omnes dicitur.*[1] Et super Johannem,[2] sermone 116,[3] dicit quod non est dictum Petro, *Tibi dabo claves regni caelorum,* quia solus ligandi et solvendi acceperat potestatem, sed *ideo unus pro omnibus, quia unitas est in omnibus.* Et ibidem, sermone 122,[4] dicit quoniam nec solus Petrus, sed universa Ecclesia ligat et solvit peccata.

Septimo, ex hoc verbo (44v) et aliis praecedentibus, infertur quod Ecclesia debet oboedire Petro et ejus vicario tanquam capiti suo in his quae pertinent ad Ecclesiae aedificationem, et non ad ipsius destructionem. Quod (63) etiam expresse probat Apostolus 2, Ad Corinthios, 10 cap.,[5] ubi ait: *Nam, etsi [6] amplius ⟨aliquid⟩ gloriatus fuero de potestate nostra, quam nobis dedit Dominus in aedificationem, et non in destructionem.* Et ibidem cap. ultimo: [7] *Ut non praesens durius agam secundum potestatem, quam Dominus dedit mihi in aedificationem et non in destructionem.* Et ideo ubi Papa utitur potestate sua in aedificationem Ecclesiae, multa specialia privilegia habet, quae sibi soli competunt, quae in cap. *Cum ex generali privilegio,* De translat. episc., notat glossa [8] his versibus:

7. *Om. C.*

8. Mt. 16:18; cf. d'Ailly's earlier work, *Recommendatio sacrae scripturae,* Dupin, *1,* 604.

9. St. Augustine, *Liber de agone Christiano,* cap. *30;* PL *40,* 308.

1. *Om. AB.*

2. domini *AB.*

3. St. Augustine, *In Joannis Evangelium tractatus CXXIV,* Tractatus 118, § 4; PL *35,* 1949.

4. St. Augustine, *In Joannis Evangelium tractatus CXXIV,* Tractatus *124,* § 5; PL *35,* 1973.

5. 2 Cor. 10:8.

6. si *CV.*

7. 2 Cor. 13:10.

8. X, 1, 7, c. 1, *in v.* Pertinet.

Restituit Papa solus, deponit et ipse,
Dividit, ac unit; eximit, atque probat:
Articulos solvit, synodumque facit generalem,
Transfert et mutat: appellat nullus ab ipso.

Et de his remittit pro concordanciis ad cap. *Sicut unire,* De excess, praelat. § 1,[9] et De off. leg., *Quod per translationem,* in glossa.[1] Et Goffredus dicit [2] quod haec singula per jura probantur, 2, q. 6, *Ideo,*[3] 3, q. 6, *Quamvis,*[4] *et Dudum,*[5] 16, q. 1, *Praecipimus,*[6] 2, q. 1, *Et*[7] *temporis,*[8] 16, q. 1, *Frater noster,*[9] 17 dist., *Regula,*[1] 24, q. 1, *Quotiens,*[2] 17 dist., cap. 1, 2, 3,[3] et 7, q. 1, *Temporis qualitas,*[4] 7, q. 1, *Mutationes,*[5] (26r) 9, q. 3, *Cuncta.*[6] Sed haec privilegia non habet Papa in destructionem Ecclesiae, ut 25, q. 2, cap. *Si ea destruerem.*[7]

Octavo,[8] ex omnibus praemissis concludit ista opinio quod tam de jure humano quam divino concedendum est Papam posse ab universali Ecclesia vel a generali concilio eam repraesentante in multis casibus judicari et condemnari, et ab eo ad concilium in multis casibus posse appellari, videlicet in casibus Ecclesiae destructionem tangentibus. Et hoc ultra praemissa probatur ratione, quia aliter (64) (106v) sequeretur ipsum Christum verum et supremum caput

9. X, 5, 31, c. 8, *in v.* Pertinere.

1. X, 1, 30, c. 4, *in v.* Reservata.

2. *Summa D. Goffredi Tranensis . . . in Titulis Decretalium omnibus utilis et necessaria,* Rubrica: De Officio legati, § 3 (Venice, 1564), p. 205. Cf. above, n. 3, p. 295.

3. C. 2, q. 6, c. 17.

4. C. 3, q. 6, c. 7.

5. C. 3, q. 6, c. 9.

6. C. 16, q. 1, c. 53.

7. *Om. C.*

8. C. *16,* q. 1, c. 48.

9. C. 16, q. 1, c. 52.

1. D. 17, c. 2.

2. C. 24, q. 1, c. 12.

3. D. 17, c. 1, 2 and 3.

4. C. 7, q. 1, c. 44.

5. C. 7, q. 1, c. 34.

6. C. 9, q. 3, c. 17 and 18.

7. C. 25, q. 2, c. 4.

8. The passages which follow (pp. 309–14) are cited along with parallel texts from other of d'Ailly's works above, pp. 112, 148 ff.

Ecclesiae et institutorem [9] ejus sapientissimum eam non perfecte et sufficienter ordinasse. Quod est haereticum et contra illud Deuteronomii 32: *Dei perfecta sunt opera.*[1] Et tamen patet consequentia, quoniam illa communitas non est sufficienter ordinata quae perditioni suae et demolitioni publicae non potest occurrere. Sic esset de ecclesiastica politia in casu quo papa per haeresim manifestam, aut tyrannidem apertam aut aliud notorium crimen conaretur eam subvertere et nemo ei dicere posset: *Cur ita facis?* silicet per viam juris eidem resistendo, id est, ab eo appellando, eum accusando, et per concilium judicando. Hoc enim esset Papae concedere potestatem, non in aedificationem, sed in destructionem (45v). Quod est contra praemissam sententiam Apostoli,[2] quam non solo[3] verbo docuit, sed exemplo firmavit, quando scilicet Petro restitit in facie, ut dictum est. Ubi considerandum est quod licet Petrus a Paulo fuerit[4] reprehensus et rationabiliter reprehensus,[5] quia scilicet non recte ambulabat ad veritatem Evangelii, tamen nec ex textu vel[6] glossa[7] apparet quod Petrus fuerit haereticus, nec erraverit errore haeresis. Quare similiter Papa in aliquibus casibus, ubi non est haeresis, potest reprehendi et corrigi. Nec oppositum sufficienter probant aliqui ex illis capitulis supra allegatis, scilicet ex cap. *Oves,*[8] et ex cap. *Si Papa.*[9] Immo magis sequitur propositum (26v) ex illis verbis: *nisi a recta fide exorbitaverit,* et *nisi deprehendatur a fide devius,* quia tunc semper[1] Papa a recta fide exorbitat et deviat quandocunque non recte ambulet ad veritatem Evangelii, cum veritas Evangelii (65) sit recta fides. Sed hoc potest contingere in multis casibus aliis quam in casu haeresis, sicut in illis in quibus scandalose turbaret et manifeste destrueret[2] Ecclesiam, et per consequens in illis posset corrigi, accusari et judicari.

Et si quaeratur: Si Papa in his casibus recuset convocare con-

9. instructorem *ABC.*
1. Deut. 32:4.
2. Gal. 2:11–14; cf. above, n. 8, p. 307.
3. Solum *C.*
4. fuisset C.
5. reprehensibilis *V* and *corr. in marg. A.*
6. nec *A; Add.* ex *A.*
7. Cf. PL *114,* 573–74.
8. C. 2, q. 7, c. 13.
9. D. 40, c. 6; cf. above, n. 8, p. 303.
1. *Om. AB.*
2. *Om.* et manifeste destrueret *A.*

cilium, quid fiet? Respondet ista opinio quod in hoc [3] casu [4] si hoc recuset sufficientur requisitus, faciendum esset sicut si sede vacante similis occurreret necessitas. Nam in his duobus casibus, sicut supra [5] octava consideratione tactum est, poterit concilium sine Papa vel sine ejus auctoritate celebrari, scilicet (107r) auctoritate Christi et universalis Ecclesiae, et convocabitur per majores praelatos, vel in juris subsidium ad eorum instantiam per principes saeculares, sicut saepius legitur esse factum. Et ad hoc est evidens ratio: quia nisi, sede vacante, vel etiam Papa renuente concilium celebrare, posset per Ecclesiam modo praedicto remedium adhiberi, sequeretur quod Ecclesia non haberet sufficientem fecunditatem et fecundam virtutem ad se conservandum et continuandum. Et sic posset penitus deficere Politia Christiana, quod est contra [6] dictum Christi: *Ego vobiscum sum ⟨omnibus diebus⟩ usque ad consummationem saeculi.*[7] Et tamen patet consequentia. Quia si nullo existente Papa, cardinales obstinati essent non velle eligere, vel in Ecclesia seditionem facere vellent et eam hostiliter perturbare, vel etiam si a nova electione essent a principibus tyrannice impediti aut carceraliter detenti, vel omnes mortui, aut si Papa et ipsi fierent haeretici manifesti, constat quod si in talibus vel similibus casibus residuum Christianitatis, quod tunc esset Ecclesia, non posset concilium facere et novum Papam per alium clerum eligere et (66) contra casus praedictos aut [8] similes salubriter providere, necesse esset perire et deficere Ecclesiasticam Politiam. Quapropter consequens est ut ad obviandum tanto discrimini concedatur universalem Ecclesiam (27r) posse auctoritate Christi generale concilium in praedictis (45v) casibus congregare. Cui condorat illud dictum Christi: *Ubi duo vel tres congregati fuerint in nomine meo, in medio illorum sum.*[9] In qua auctoritate considerandum est et super omnem [1] auctoritatem juris humani ponderandum, quod ait Christus, *in nomine meo.* Non ait *in nomine Petri,* vel *nomine seu auctoritate Papae,*[2] sed *in nomine meo,* quod est nomen Jesu, id est salvatoris et salutis, juxta aliud

3. *Om. C.*
4. *Add.* isto *C.*
5. *Om. C.*
6. *Add.* illud *ABC.*
7. Matt. 28:20.
8. et *AB.*
9. Mt. 18:20.
1. *Om. AB.*
2. *Add.* vel cardinalium *ABC.*

311

ejus simile dictum: *Quodcunque petieritis patrem in nomine meo,*[3] id est, quicquid petieritis pertinens ad salutem. Ex quo datur intelligi ad salutem Ecclesiae posse congregationem fidelium fieri, si illi, ad quos regulariter pertinet, non possint aut velint hoc exsequi.[4]

Et si dicatur auctoritatem intelligi communiter de congregatione fidelium ad orandum, respondetur, quod eadem ratione (107v) debet intelligi de congregatione fidelium ad salutarem cujuscunque dubii decisionem pro salute Ecclesiae deposcendam juxta verbum *Quicquid petieritis.*[5]

Et ad hoc facit auctoritas Synodi Chalcedonensis, quae illud applicat ad congregationem concilii generalis, prout superius tactum est.[6] Et si obiciatur contra hoc de his quae supra dicta sunt in octava consideratione primae partis, et de ca. *Confidimus,* 25, q. 1,[7] ubi dicitur quod prima sedes, id est, Romana Ecclesia, *unamquemque* (67) *synodum sua auctoritate confirmavit,* et de cap. *Significasti,* Ext., De elect.,[8] ubi dicitur quod *omnia concilia per Ecclesiae Romanae auctoritatem et facta sint et robur acceperint.* Ad hoc[9] respondet ista opinio quod si hic capiatur sedes seu Ecclesia Romana pro Ecclesia universali, sicut saepe in sacris canonibus intelligere necesse est, tunc ista non probant oppositum, sed propositum. Si autem Romana Ecclesia caperetur pro Collegio Cardinalium vel clero Romanae dioecesis, talis Ecclesia Romana nullam super (27v) generali concilio conceditur auctoritatem habere. Immo tale particulare Collegium, quantum ad electionem Papae vel alia ejus privilegia, a generalibus conciliis auctoritatem accepit, et forte contra ea plurima usurpavit. Si autem in illis capitulis et aliis similibus capiatur sedes aut Ecclesia Romana pro Papa, sicut saepe sumitur in jure, sic conceditur quod ab eo concilia regulariter confirmata et facta sunt, et robur acceperunt, scilicet quia ejus auctoritate congregata sunt,[1] sicut probant jura in octava consideratione superius allegata, et quod ejus auctoritate debeant congregari. Hoc rationabiliter statuit Ecclesia, et ex justis causis suam in hoc auctoritatem

3. John 14:13, 16:23.

4. For citation and discussion of this and the following passage and of parallel texts from other of d'Ailly's works see above, pp. 54, 122–24, 147.

5. *Add.* etc. *ABC.*

6. Cf. above, n. 1, p. 269.

7. C. 25, q. 1, c. 1.

8. X, 1, 6, c. 4.

9. haec *ABC.*

1. *Om.* et robur . . . congregata sunt *A.*

restrinxit, quae tempore Apostolorum nondum sic erat limitata, sicut patuit in illo Concilio Hierosolymitano de quo supra allegatum est Actuum 15.[2] Ideo cum omnibus juribus humanis postea conditis stat quod jure divino et a Christo immediate Ecclesia sua habuit et semper habebit [3] specialem potesta-(68)-tem et auctoritatem concilium (46r) congregandi et ibi definiendi et determinandi, maxime in casibus supradictis.

Sed quod in dicto cap. *Significasti* [4] dicitur quod Ecclesiae Romanae nulla concilia legem praefixerunt, et quod (108r) in eis *et eorum statutis Romani Pontificis patenter* [5] *excipitur auctoritas.* Respondet haec opinio quod hoc [6] regulariter et [7] in pluribus verum est, sed tamen in aliquibus fallit, quae particulariter declarare non est praesentis [8] operis. In casibus autem praemissis manifesta est instantia, sicut ratione et divina auctoritate probatum est.

Generaliter tamen in dicto cap. *Confidimus* [9] dicit Gelasius Papa: *Uniuscujusque synodi constitutum, quod universalis Ecclesiae probavit assensus, nullam magis exsequi sedem prae ceteris oportere, quam primam,* scilicet Romanam Ecclesiam. Ubi super verbo *oportere* dicit glossa [1] quod *hoc verbum "oportet" est hic verbum honestatis* et non necessitatis. Et hoc ideo dicit (28r) *quia princeps legibus solutus est,* ut in dicto cap. *Significasti.*[2] *Tamen honestum est ut secundum legem vivat,* ut testatur Imperator. Sed quod dicit hic glossa, quod princeps est solutus legibus, intelligit haec opinio de legibus humanis ab ipso editis. De legibus autem divinis aut divina auctoritate ab universali Ecclesia institutis generaliter et in omnibus verum esse non concedit, et maxime in his quae totum corpus et universalis Ecclesiae statum tangunt.[3] De particularibus [4] autem personis et in certis potest Romana Ecclesia circa statuta conciliorum et

2. Acts 15:4–30.
3. habet *A.*
4. X, 1, 6, c. 4.
5. *Om. CV.*
6. cum suis similibus, *in marg. V.*
7. *Add.* ut *AB.*
8. hujus *ABC.*
9. C. 25, q. 1, c. 1.
1. C. 25, q. 1, c. 1, *in v.* Oportet.
2. X, 1, 6, c. 4.
3. See above, p. 145, where this text is cited and discussed; cf. also, pp. 53 and 111–12.
4. peculiaribus *A.*

leges suas, quae mores humanos respiciunt, sua auctoritate ordinare et dispensare, (69) et pietatis vel necessitas intuitu [5] rationis aequitate considerata, semel a se concessa valet vel in totum vel in partem commutare: ut ostendit Gratianus 25, q. 2 § *His ita respondetur*.[6] Et quantum ad ista intelligendum est quod notavit Joannes Andreae in Novella, cap. *Significasti*, super verbo *robur*,[7] ubi dicit quod per hoc videtur quod solus Papa sine concilio vel ejus parte possit interpretari statuta concilii. Ad idem 17 dist., *Nec licuit*,[8] ubi de hoc. Et hoc verum est, ut infra cap. *Statutum*, et cap. *Constitutio*,[9] De sent. excom., *Constitutionem*,[1, 2] et cap. *Statutum*,[3] Libro Sexto, et in Clementinis,[4] *Ne Romani*, § *Sane*,[5] et cap. *Constitutionem*.[6] Nec mirum, cum illa etiam immutet et corrigat, eod. Libro, De rescriptis, *statutum*, Jo. Andreae.[7] Et haec de tertia opinione sufficiant.

In hac ergo (108v) opinionum diversitate et adversitate det nobis Dominus Jesus Christus [8] id eligere, quod scit utilius esse et convenientius ad honorem sui nominis et salutem Ecclesiae suae sanctae. Amen.

EXPLICIT SECUNDA PARS [9]
SEQUITUR TERTIA [1] ⟨PARS⟩

(29r) Restat aliqua considerare circa reformationem Ecclesiae Christianae: quae quam necessaria jamdudum fuerit, et amplius modo sit, evidenter (46v) ostendunt lamentabilia verba Beati Ber-

---

5. *Om. C.*

6. C. 25, q. 2, c. 21, § His ita.

7. Cf. above, n. 3, p. 304.

8. D. 17, c. 4.

9. These two chapters are identical with those referred to immediately below, n. 1 and 3.

1. VI°, 5, 11, c. 9.

2. *Add.* etc. *V.*

3. VI°, 5, 11, c. 13.

4. Clementina *A*.

5. *Clem.* 1, 3, c. 2, § Sane.

6. *Clem.* 1, 3, c. 4.

7. VI°, 1, 3, c. 11; the reference to Joannes Andreae is a general one to the *Glossa ordinaria* of the Liber Sextus; cf. above, n. 2, p. 289.

8. *Om. AB.*

9. *Om.* Explicit secunda pars. *AB.*

1. *Om.* Sequitur tertia *ABV.*

3¹4

nardi, sermone 33, super Cantica,[2, 3] ubi sic ait: [4] *Serpit hodie putrida tabes per omne corpus Ecclesiae, et quo latius, eo desperatius; eoque periculosius, quo interius. Namsi insurgeret apertus haereticus, mitteretur foras, et aresceret; si violentus inimicus, absconderet se forsitan ab eo. Nunc vero quem ejiciet,[5] aut a quo abscondet se? Omnes amici, et omnes inimici; omnes necessarii, et omnes [6] adversarii; omnes (70) domestici, et nulli pacifici; omnes proximi, et omnes quae sua [7] sunt quaerunt. Ministri Christi sunt, et serviunt Antichristo. Honorati incedunt de bonis Domini, qui Domino honorem non deferunt.* Et enumeratis quibusdam excessivis abusibus ecclesiasticorum subdit. *Olim praedictum est, et nunc tempus impletionis advenit: "Ecce in pace amaritudo mea amarissima".[8] Amara prius in nece martyrum, amarior post in conflictu haereticorum, amarissima nunc in moribus domesticorum. Non fugare,[9] non fugere eos potest. Ita invaluerunt et multiplicati sunt super numerum. Intestina et insanabilis est plaga Ecclesiae. Et ideo in pace amaritudo ejus amarissima. Sed in qua pace? Et pax est, et non est pax. Pax a paganis, pax ab haereticis. Sed non est profecto a filiis. Vox plangentis in tempore isto: "Filios enutrivi et exaltavi,[1] ipsi autem spreverunt me".[2] Spreverunt et maculaverunt me a turpi vita, a turpi quaestu, a turpi commercio a negotio denique perambulante in tenebris.* Si haec a Beato Bernardo dicta sunt, nunc multo magis dici possunt; quia ex tunc Ecclesia de malis ad pejora processit: et in omni tam spirituali quam saeculari statu, abjecto decore virtutum, (29v) in variam cecidit turpitudinem vitiorum.

Propterea ex tunc quidam spirituales mala haec subtilioris intelligentiae oculo [3] praevidentes, praesentem Ecclesiae persecutionem et hujus schismatis (109r) horrendam monstruosamque divisionem, subtractionem quoque oboedientiae ab Ecclesia Romana, et alia plura scandalosa inde secutura praedixerunt, sicut patet in libris

---

2. canonica *C*.
3. St. Bernard of Clairvaux, *Sermo* XXXIII; PL *183*, 959.
4. Vide Fasciculum rer. expetendar., fol. 203 verso, *in marg. A.*
5. ejicit *AB*.
6. *Om. AB*.
7. *Om. V.*
8. Is. 38:17.
9. fugere *A*.
1. exaltvi *AB*.
2. Is. 1:2.
3. titulo *AB*.

Abbatis Joachim [4] et Hildegardis,[5] quos non esse contemnendos quorundam magnorum doctorum probat auctoritas.[6]

Haec (71) autem Deus misericordissimus, qui solus ex malis bona novit elicere, ideo permittere credendus est ut eorum occasione Ecclesia sua in melius reformetur. Quod nisi celeriter fiat, audeo dicere quod licet magna sint quae videmus, tamen in brevi incomparabiliter majora videbimus, et post ista tonitrua tam horrenda, alia horribiliora in (47r) proximo audiemus. Eapropter summopere vigilandum est circa reformationem Ecclesiae, de qua in concilio generali hujus oboedientiae aliqua poterunt utiliter pertractari, non quidem definitive,[7] sed solum dispositive, ut postea in generali utriusque oboedientiae concilio definiantur et concorditer confirmentur. Quae etiam tam justa, tam rationabilia, et toti Christianitati tam utilia esse poterunt quod ambas oboedientias schismatice divisas ad unionem et concordiam disponere, inducere, et attrahere verisimiliter praevalebunt. Ideoque circa hoc aliquas considerationes particulares scribere et prudentum examinationi proponere dignum duxi, nec omnes quidem, quia ad hoc et majori libro et majori

4. Joachim of Flora, ca. 1132–ca. 1202, abbot of the Cistercian monastery of Corrazzo, later head of an independent house near Flora. Cf. H. Bett, *Joachim of Flora* (London, 1931). In d'Ailly's own lifetime there had been a revival of interest in the prophecies of Joachim, because of the activities of a certain Telesphorus of Cosenza. He claimed to find the Great Schism and all the troubles of the Church predicted in the prophecies of Joachim, and wrote a book entitled *Liber de magnis tribulationibus* with the purpose of applying those prophecies to his own age; cf. Bett, pp. 173–75. It is probably to this book (no longer extant) that d'Ailly is referring. See also his "Sermo secundus de adventu Domini," in *Sermones*, f. s6v ff., and his "Sermo tertius de adventu Domini," ibid., f. t6r. Telesphorus clearly favored the cause of Clement, and his prophecies were taken seriously enough for Henry of Langenstein to have refuted them in 1392; cf. Valois, *France*, *1*, 373.

5. St. Hildegarde, ca. 1100–ca. 1179, abbess of Disenberg and later of Rupertsberg. For a modern study of the abbess, consult F. M. Steele, *The Life and Visions of St. Hildegarde* (London, 1914). The reference is probably to the *Liber divinorum operum*, PL *197*, 1017. D'Ailly refers to this work again in his sermon "De Sancto Francisco," *Sermones*, f. C7v.

6. William of Auvergne eulogized Joachim thus: "Istud donum scilicet donum intellectus, tantae claritatis est et acuminis in quibusdam, ut valde assimiletur spiritui prophetiae; qualem crediderunt nonnulli fuisse in abbate Joachim et ipsemet de seipso dixisse dicitur, quia non erat ei datus spiritus prophetiae, sed spiritus intelligentiae. Si quis autem Apocalypsim et super Concordiam duorum Testamentorum, mirabitur donum intellectus in eo." *De virtutibus;* in *Opera Omnia*, *1* (Paris, 1674), 152. St. Bernard, too, had commended St. Hildegarde; cf. E. Vacandard, *Vie de Saint Bernard*, 2 (Paris, 1927), 313–27.

7. *Add.* ut supra parte prima dictum est *AB;* and *in marg. v.*

ingenio opus esset, sed utiliores et meo judicio magis necessarias, et per quas ad omnes alias via proterit facilius aperiri. Prima autem consideratio erit de reformandis circa corpus Ecclesiae. Secunda, de reformandis circa ejus caput, scilicet circa statum Papae et Romanae Curiae. Tertia, de reformatione principalium Ecclesiae partium, scilicet praelatorum. Quarta, de reformandis circa religiones et religiosos. Quinta, de (30r) reformandis circa ceteros ecclesiasticos. Sexta, de reformatione laicorum Christianorum, et maxime principum. (72)

Prima ergo consideratio est de his quae viderentur reformanda circa totum corpus universalis Ecclesiae. Ubi primo occurrit esse expediens et necessarium quod saepius quam hactenus factum sit generalia (109v) concilia celebrentur, scilicet de trigesimo in trigesimum, vel ad tardius de quinquagesimo in [8] quinquagesimum annum. Et propter plures congruentias videretur conveniens quod celebraretur in anno Jubileo, et quod sine nova vocatione seu alio speciali mandato Apostolico in Roma vel alio convenienti loco ubi Romana Curia resideret omnes episcopi vel eorum procuratores relaturi quae in suis provinciis et dioecesibus viderentur reformanda comparerent.[9] Et si aliqui alii devoti principes aut viri ecclesiastici et religiosi scientifici ibidem adesse vellent, per hoc acquirerent indulgentias Romanas perinde ac si loca sanctorum Romae corporaliter visitarent. Item videtur [1] expediens quod etiam saepius celebrarentur concilia provincilia: quia, ut patet 18 dist. Decreti,[2] sancti patres propter Ecclesiae utilitatem primo statuerunt ea bis in anno celebrari. Postea vero propter fatigationes, et ut opportune haberentur, hi qui congregandi sunt statuto synodali definierunt omni excusatione remota modis omnibus semel in anna fieri et depravata [3] corrigi.

Unde et episcopi qui ad synodum venire contempnunt, et principes qui hoc prohibent vel impediunt, vel metropolitani qui absque rationabili causa hoc agere negligunt, canonicis poenis subjacent, ut haec (47v) probantur in dicta distinctione [4] quasi per totum et multis

---

8. ad *C*.

9. For this and d'Ailly's related views on the constitution of the Church see above, p. 123.

1. videretur *V*.

2. D. 18, c. 1 and 2.

3. damnata *AB*.

4. D. 18.

canonibus conciliorum, ut in secundo capitulo Carthaginensis Concilii tertii,[5] et in septimo capitulo Toletani (73) Concilii sexti,[6] et in tertio capitulo quarti Concilii Toletani,[7] ubi sic legitur: *Nulla paene res disciplinae mores ab Ecclesia Christi magis expellit quam negligentia sacerdotum,* (30v) *qui contemptis canonibus ad corrigendos ecclesiasticos mores synodum facere negligunt,* etc.[8] Et certe hodie docet experientia quot et quanta mala ex hujusmodi negligentia proveniunt. Et ideo necesse est providere ut hujusmodi concilia saepius fiant, et si non semel in anno juxta rigorem canonum, saltem de triennio in triennium ad evitandum vexationes itinerum, laborum, et expensarum, et quia omne rarum pretiosum. Et si di- (110r)-catur quod hodie non est opus generalia aut provincialia concilia congregare,[9] sicut fuit in primitiva Ecclesia,[1] et quod ad tollendum vexationes praelatorum in hujusmodi conciliis Romana Ecclesia seu Papalis Curia potest sufficienter casibus emergentibus providere, respondetur quod hoc non est utique verum; tum primo quia experientia docet quod propter defectum conciliorum, et maxime generalium totius Ecclesiae, quae sola potest audacter et intrepide omnes corrigere, ea mala quae universalem tangunt Ecclesiam diu remanserunt impunita, incorrecta, et adeo creverunt et inveterata sunt quod tandem multa injusta et iniqua sub praetextu fictae et corruptae consuetudinis licita reputantur. Item, multi suspicantur quod haec dissimilaverit Romana Curia et super his concilia fieri neglexerit ut posset ad suae voluntatis libitum plenius dominari et jura aliarum ecclesiarum liberius usurpare. Quod non assero esse verum. Sed quia contra eam hujusmodi laborat infamia, deberet ad eam purgandam super (74) congregatione conciliorum generalium et provincialium providere. Alioquin, juxta dictum Augustini,[2] si [3] *famam suam neglegit, crudelis est.*

Item illa sanctissima Romana Curia, scilicet Petri et Apostolorum, licet potuisset sine congregatione [4] concilii per epistolas vel aliter causas et negotia Ecclesiae faciliter terminare, tamen legitur quatuor

5. Hinschius, p. 297.
6. Hinschius, p. 378.
7. Hinschius, p. 364.
8. *Om. C.*
9. congregari *A.*
1. *Add.* seu papalis curia potest sufficienter casibus emergentibus *C.*
2. St. Augustine. *Sermo* 355, cap. 1; PL *39,* 1569.
3. qui *C.*
4. convocatione *ABC.*

concilia celebrasse, sicut patet Actuum primo, 6, 15 et 21 capitulis.[5] Unde per hoc exemplum instructionis [6] de saepe congregandis conciliis suis posteris (31r) relinquerunt.[7] Nam sicut Christi, sic et Apostolorum suorum actio nostra est instructio, juxta illud Apostoli: *Imitatores mei estote,* sicut et ego Christi.[8] Item 14 dist., cap. *Canones,*[9] dicit Isidorus quod quia ante tempora Constantini *non erat episcopis licentia conveniendi in unum,* scilicet publice per modum concilii generalis, ideo Christianitas in diversas haereses scissa est. Et ita dicere possumus modo, quod propter defectum celebrationis conciliorum Ecclesia in diversa Schismata et alia innumerabilia mala forte etiam ad haereses disponentia, proh dolor! lapsa est, sicut experientia (48r) docet. Item, si concilia saepius celebrata fuissent, verisimile est quod hoc nephandum schisma non tamdiu perdurasset, nec forte schisma Graecorum.[1] Unde hujusmodi schismatibus (110v) debuisset cito per concilium generale provideri; ut in primitiva Ecclesia docuerunt Apostoli, prout legitur Actuum sexto,[2] quod quia ortum *est murmur Graecorum adversus Hebraeos,* etc., statim duodecim Apostoli ipsum convocata multitudine sedaverunt. Similiter Actuum 15 [3] orta discessione propter observantiam legalium, statum Paulus et Barnabas [4] ascenderunt ad Apostolos in Hierusalem.

Unde patet quod damnabiliter peccaverunt illi seu principes seu praelati qui pro sedatione hujusmodi schismatum convocationem concilii neglexerunt aut impediverunt.

Item aliqui sunt casus ardui necessario reformandi, in quibus non potest commodius quam per generale concilium provideri; sicut patet primo de (75) reformatione Romanae Curiae quae, ut infra dicetur,[5] necessaria est, et tamen non nisi per generale concilium fieri potest: quia secundum aliquos illius judicio subest, sicut superius in secunda parte diffuse tactum est. Cui etiam concordare videtur Augustinus in epistola ad Donatistas,[6] ubi, loquens de Col-

---

5. Acts 1, 6, 15, and 21.
6. instructiones *C.*
7. relinquerunt *BC.*
8. Philipp. 3:17.
9. D. 15, c. 1.
1. Cf. above, n. 1, p. 253.
2. Acts 6:1.
3. Acts 15, the question of circumcision and the Council of Jerusalem.
4. Bernardus *AB;* Barnabas *corr. in marg. A.*
5. Cf. below, p. 322, *Secunda consideratio.*
6. St. Augustine, *Epistola* 43, cap. 7; PL *33,* 169.

legio Papae et Cardinalium, dicit: *Quasi vero adhuc dici possit et injustissime: Ecce putas illos episcopos qui Romae judicaverunt, non bonos judices fuisse. Restabat adhuc plenarium Ecclesiae universale concilium, ubi etiam cum ipsis judicibus causa posset agitari,* (31v) *ut si male judicasse convicti essent, eorum sententiae resolverentur.*[7] Unde quod in arduis et magnis dubiis et per consequens in tangentibus reformationem et dispositionem Romanae Ecclesiae, finaliter ad concilium generale pervenire oporteat ostendit. Idem Augustinus in principio libri De gratia et libero arbitrio:[8] *Contra,* inquit, *haeresim,* scilicet Pelagianam, *cum fuisset diutius disputatum etiam ad concilia episcopalia novissima necessitate est perventum.* Et ideo non debet Romana Curia indignari seu respuere a generali[9] concilio reformari, sicut nec contempsit a generali concilio plures sui principatus honores recipere: quia licet principaliter Romana Ecclesia principatum habuerit a Domino, tamen secundario a concilio, ut dicit glossa, 17 dist., super capitulo *Concilia.*[1]

Item (111r) reformatio totius corporis Ecclesiae et particularis Ecclesiae Romanae est de arduis pertinentibus ad fidem. Nam ejus generalis deformatio non mediocriter fidem tangit, et per consequens.[2] Ideo in hoc non debet Papa aut ejus curia deliberationem generalis conciliis respuere; quia: (sicut dicit glossa, 19 dist., super capitulo *Anastasius*)[3] *Papa tenetur requirere concilium*[4] *episcoporum ubi agitur de fide.* Quod non solum intelligo de articulis fidei, sed de arduis tangentibus[5] universalem statum fidelis Ecclesiae. Quod notavit Archidiaconus, 15 dist., in capitulo *Sicut,*[6] ubi dictam glossam approbans addit quod nimis periculosum esset fidem nostram committere arbitrio unius hominis, et idcirco Papa in casibus novis et arduis ad deliberationem concilii recurrere (76) consuevit.[7]

Item,[8] (48v) duo sunt arduissimi casus fidem et fideles omnes

---

7. *Add.* et *C.*
8. St. Augustine, *De gratia et libero arbitrio,* cap. 4; PL *44,* 886.
9. *Add.* episcoporum *ABC.*
1. D. 17, c. 6, *in v.* Jussione Domini.
2. *Add.* ejus reformatio *C;* ejus reformatio *in marg. V.*
3. D. 19, c. 9, *in v.* Consilio.
4. consilium *A.*
5. *Add.* fidem et *C.*
6. D. 15, c. 2; Guido de Baysio (Archidiaconus, cf. above, n. 8, p. 290), *Lectura . . . super Decreto: quam ipse Rosarium appellavit* (Lyons, 1516), f. 15r, § 1.
7. For a discussion of parallel texts see above, pp. 112–13 and 145.
8. Ideo *C.*

mirabiliter et miserabiliter concernentes, quibus esset per generale concilium necessarium providendum. Unus est de modo providendi contra Sarracenos et alios infideles fidem et Christianitatem impugnantes et nunc multo periculosius quam a multis retroactis temporibus fecerint contra Ecclesiam Catholicam insurgentes: quibus si non celeriter obvietur, timendum est ne Constantinopolitanum imperium jam ab eis multipliciter laceratum et vexatum (32r) penitus destruant,[9] ac deinde Romanum imperium jam divisum et paene ad ruinam praeparatum invadant, et sic Ecclesiam destruant jam schismatice laceratam, ut sic via praeparetur adventui Antichristi, de quo praedicit[1] Apostolus: *nisi venerit discessio primum,* etc.[2] Quod exponit glossa[3] de duplici discessione seu divisione, una ab imperio, alia ab Ecclesia Romana, quae praevenire debet Antichristum; et utramque jam praesentialiter videre multi devoti fideles non immerito pertimescunt. Alius casus est de modo providendi circa Graecos, ut ad unitatem Romanae Ecclesiae reducantur. Quod nunc maxime opportune fieri posse videtur, dum eorum Imperator inter Latinos degens a Romana (111v) Ecclesia[4] et dominis temporalibus, praecipue a Francorum Rege, contra infideles cogitur auxilium et subsidium postulare.[5, 6]

De viis autem et modis circa dictos casus reservandis scripserunt plures fidei zelatores, et specialiter Frater Humbertus de Romanis, quondam Magister quintus Ordinis Praedicatorum, tractatum utilem composuit ut super his provideretur in Concilio Generali Lugdunensi, sub Gregorio Papa X celebrando;[7] ad quem pro futuro concilio recurrendum esse arbitror.

---

9. After the defeat of the Christian armies by the Sultan Bayazet at Nicopolis in 1396, the position of the Eastern Empire was indeed perilous; cf. L. Bréhier, *L'Église et l'orient au moyen âge* (Paris, 1907), pp. 314 ff.

1. dixit *C.*

2. 2 Thess. 2:3.

3. *Liber vite. Biblia cum glossis ordinariis* (Venice, 1495), f. 1276r.

4. curia *C.*

5. On the advice of the French soldier Baucicant, the Emperor Manuel visited the West in person in order to plead for help, leaving Constantinople in December 1399 and arriving back in June 1403; cf. L. Bréhier, *Le monde Byzantin, vie et mort de Byzance* (Paris, 1947), *1,* 471–72.

6. At this point in *Ms. V.* there is a marginal annotation which is illegible on the microfilm.

7. Humbert of Rome, ca. 1194–ca. 1277, Dominican Master-General; cf. Mortier, *Histoire des Maîtres-Généraux de l'Ordre des Frères-Prêcheurs* (Paris, 1903), *1,* 415–664. The reference is to his *Liber de tractandis in Concilio Lugdunensi;*

Secunda consideratio est de his quae reformanda videntur circa caput corporis Ecclesiae, id est, circa statum Papae et suae Romanae Curiae. Et primo tollendus esset ille detestabilis abusus a quo praesens schisma originem traxit; scilicet quod una natio sive regnum, aliquando ultra, aliquando citra montes, in scandalum residui Christianitatis ita diu Papatum tenuit ut (77) posset dicere: *Hereditate possideamus sanctuarium Dei.*[8] Quod quam detestabile sit, praecipue in Papatu, ostendit ille qui ait: *In veritate comperi quod non sit personarum acceptor Deus,* etc.[9] Et ideo ad providendum circa hoc esset inviolabiliter observandum quod nunquam de eodem regno vel provincia bina vice successive eligeretur Papa, sed alternatis vicibus, nunc de una, nunc de alia (32v) natione, omni carnali favore et affectione cessantibus, ut collegio eligentium successorem Petri posset dici illud quod a Christo Petro dictum est: *Caro et sanguis non revelavit tibi.*[1]

Item propter idem[2] esset statuendum quod nunquam bina vice successive eligeretur Papa de Collegio Cardinalium, quia non est praesumendum quod extra Collegium non possit reperiri sufficiens; nec apud (49r) multos caret mala suspicione vel carnalis affectionis vel simoniacae pravitatis vel alterius secretae et illicitae conspirationis quod Cardinales ut[3] communiter unum eligunt ex se ipsis, et vix reperitur instantia, ut jam proverbialiter dicitur, nisi Spiritu Sancto inter eos discordiam operante. Et in hoc et aliis pluribus sua potestate eligendi taliter sunt abusi quod nunc, proh dolor! multorum est opinio[4] quod hujusmodi potestate seu privilegio eligen-(112r)-di essent merito privandi juxta capitulum *Privilegium,* 11, q. 3, cum suis concordanciis,[5] et de aliis electoribus ac aliis, electionis modis esset per generale concilium providendum, cum hujusmodi potestatem non habeant immediate a Christo, sed a concilio; quia per multa tempora, ut patet in ecclesiasticis historiis,[6] non fiebat

---

Mansi, *24,* 109–32. This work was written on the demand of Gregory X for the fourteenth Ecumenical Council, held at Lyons in 1274. Cf. Hefele-Leclercq, *6,* 167.

8. Ps. 82:13 (Vulgate) or 83:12.

9. Acts 10:34.

1. Matt. 16:17.

2. ut quibusdam videtur, *in marg. V.*

3. *Om. C.*

4. quod non approbo quia nimis est rigorosa, *in marg. V.*

5. C. 11, q. 3, c. 63.

6. E.g. Cassiodorus, with whose *History* d'Ailly was familiar, makes no mention of the rôle of the cardinals; cf. *Historia tripartita,* X, cap. 29; PL *69,* 1184.

electio Papae per Cardinales, sed postea potestas electiva ipsius devoluta fuit ad eos in quadam Romana synodo, 113 episcoporum praesidente Nicolas Papa celebrata,[7] de qua idem ait: *Primo namque, inspectore Deo, est statutum ut electio Romani Pontificis in potestate cardinalium episcoporum sit,* etc. Sed absit ut ad rigorem dictae opinionis oporteat procedere et propter abusionem privilegii Cardinales dictam potestatem perdere et in alios transferri,[8] dum tamen eorum consensu abusus praeteriti (78) corrigantur, et pro futuris temporibus et praemissis et aliis convenientibus remediis provideamur.[9]

Item pro dicta provisione esset statuendum quod de cetero major pars cardinalium non posset assumi de uno regno sive de una natione, (33r) sicut quandoque hactenus factum est in magnum scandalum plurimorum, sed quod de diversis regnis et provinciis indistincte juxta personarum merita assumantur: quia sicut apud Deum, ita apud Dei ministros non debet esse acceptio personarum.

Et videretur sufficere quod de una provincia solum esset unus cardinalis, ut sic in eorum promotione et multiplicatione tolleretur vel saltem restringeretur et artaretur carnalis affectio promoventis, et ut per assumptos de diversis provinciis diversitas morum et statuum [1] eorundem [2] Romanae Ecclesiae innotesceret ad utilitatem et salutarem provisionem incolarum. Item quia una causa praesentis schismatis fuit quod cardinales nimis tardaverunt declarare et fideles sufficienter informare quod primam electionem fecissent vi aut metu,[3] ideo ad tollendum quod alias similis scandali non detur occasio, expediens videretur artare aliquod tempus infra quod talis exceptio metus deberet allegari, et ultra quod, nec illa, nec alia exceptio contra Papae electionem posset per cardinales opponi; et esset etiam per concilium (112v) declarandum quis de hujusmodi causa metus haberet cognoscere; quia Johannes Andreae [4] super

7. Nicholas II, 1058–1061, at the Council of Rome in 1059; Mansi, *19*, 897. For a study of the edict itself, and of the problems related to it, consult Hefele-Leclercq, *4*, 1139 ff.

8. transferre *AB*.

9. See above, pp. 148–49, where this passage is cited and discussed.

1. statutum *C*.

2. ejusdem *AB*.

3. Cf. Ullmann, *Origins*, esp. pp. 69 ff., Valois, *France, 1*, Ch. 1. Other causes were, according to d'Ailly in a letter to John XXIII: "Romani populi seditio, seu tumultus" and "ambitio Papatus, quia videlicet una Orbis Natio diu Papatum tenuerat" (Dupin, *2*, 882).

4. *Om. C.*

Clementina [5] De electione quaerit: [6] quis de hujusmodi causa metus cognoscere haberet, si allegaretur circa electionem Papae? et respondens dicit quod *ista nondum decisa nec provisa egebunt provisione.*

Item, necessaria erit reformatio et provisio circa gravamina quae Romana Ecclesia [7] infert aliis inferioribus ecclesiis et praelatis, et maxime in tribus, de quibus conqueritur praeallegatus Frater Humbertus in dicto tractatu suo parte secunda, cap. 11,[8] ubi dicit quod causa dispositiva schismatis Graecorum inter (79) (49v) alias una fuit propter *gravamina Romanae Ecclesiae in exactionibus, excommunicationibus,*[9] *et statutis.* De primo gravamine dictum fuit in tertia opinione secundae partis hujus tractatus, et in quinta consideratione primae partis. Et contra (33v) hanc multitudinem et magnitudinem exactionum providendum esset tripliciter. Primo, per diminutionem pomposorum [1] statuum et excessivarum expensarum, ut sic Romana Ecclesia minus esset onerosa subjectis, et ut etiam eis esset exemplum humilitatis et forma virtutis instar Christi, cujus ipsa vicariatum,[2] et a quo primatus honorem tenet, qui ait: *Discite a me quia mitis sum et humilis corde.*[3] Secundo, per diminutionem et artationem hujusmodi exactionum, sic scilicet quod certa summa rationabilis determinaretur et limitaretur pro moderato statu [4] Papae et cardinalium subjectis ecclesiis imponenda et per dioeceses proportionaliter distribuenda et a dioecesanis recolligenda et in certis terminis solvenda Romanae Curiae; ultra quam summam nova exactio non posset imponi sine auctoritate et consensu generalis concilii. Tertio per diminutionem numeri cardinalium, ita quod non esset tantus nec tam onerosus numerus ipsorum sicut hactenus fuit, ne Romanae Curiae dici possit: *Multiplicasti gentem, et non magnificasti laetitiam.*[5] Item, circa statum cardinalium et

5. *Read* Clementinis (?).

6. *Clem.* 1, 3, c. 2, *in v.* Compellant. Johannes Andreae was the author of the *Glossa ordinaria;* cf. above, n. 2, p. 289.

7. *Om.* quae Romana Ecclesia *B.*

8. Humbert of Rome, *Liber de tractandis in Concilio Lugdunensi,* II, cap. 11; Mansi, *24,* 125–26; cf. above, n. 7, p. 321.

9. *Om. AB.*

1. *Om. C.*

2. *Add.* tenet *AB.*

3. Matt. 11:29.

4. *Om. C.*

5. Is. 9:3.

aliorum ecclesiasticorum [6] providendum esset quod deinceps non tenerent illam monstruosam et multipliciter scandalosam beneficiorum multitudinem,[7] cujus occasione plurimae ecclesiae depauperantur et destruuntur (113r) ac dignis rectoribus et scientificis viris privantur, divinus in eis cultus diminuitur mala fidelibus exempla praebentur, et aliis ecclesiasticis et saepe indignissimis audacia datur ambiendi pluralitatem beneficiorum et eam damnabiliter occupandi. De quo abusu antiqui sapientes conquesti sunt, sicut Guilelmus,[8] Episcopus Parisiensis in speciali tractatu [9] quem de hoc composuit, et Cantor Parisiensis in Verbo (80) Abbreviato, capitulo ⟨33?⟩,[1] et auctor, De virtutibus et vitiis, capitulo de signis avaritiae ecclesiasticorum.[2] (34r) Quorum rationes expediret diligenter examinare et pro sedatione conscientiarum, quid super hoc re tenendum sit declarare.

De secundo gravamine supra tacto, scilicet de multiplicitate excommunicationum, et ex consequenti irregularitatem, quas Romana Ecclesia in suis constitutionibus poenalibus et maxime in quibusdam novis decretalibus imposuit,[3] et saepe per suos collectores in multorum scandalum fulminavit, et ad cujus exemplum alii praelati leviter et pro levibus causis, ut pro debitis, vel [4] hujusmodi, pauperes excommunicatione crudeliter feriunt, necesse est providere,[5] cum hoc sit contra jura, ut 11, q. 3, cap. *Nullus*, cum suis concor-

---

6. *Om.* et aliorum ecclesiasticorum *ABC*.

7. Cf. *Conc. Trid.*, Sess. 24, De Reform; c. 17, pp. 271–72.

8. Guilermus *A*.

9. William of Auvergne, Professor of Theology at the University of Paris, and Bishop of Paris, d. 1249; for a brief review and bibliography consult E. Gilson, *History of Christian Philosophy in the Middle Ages*, Part 6, Ch. 3 (New York, 1955), pp. 250–58, 658–60. William wrote the tract referred to here—"Tractatus de collatione et singularitate beneficiorum," *Opera*, 2 (Paris, 1674), 248–60—before 1228, and in that year he conducted a campaign against the plurality of benefices, inducing the doctors of the University solemnly to declare that they could not in conscience possess two benefices when a single one would suffice to support them; cf. P. Ferét, *La Faculté de Théologie de Paris et ses docteurs les plus célèbres, 1* (Paris, 1894), 211–12.

1. Peter Cantor, *Verbum abbreviatum*, cap. 33, § 93; PL *205*, 118–19; cf. above, n. 4, p. 255.

2. For information on this work, cited also by Gerson, see M. Lieberman, "Chronologie Gersonienne," *Romania, 81* (1960), 89–90.

3. Cf. *Extr. Joan. XXII,* 13, c. 1.

4. et *AB*.

5. Cf. *Conc. Trid.*, Sess. 25, De Reform., C. 3, pp. 301–02.

danciis.[6] Nam gladius Ecclesiae scilicet excommunicatio, qui in primitiva Ecclesia veneranda raritate formidabilis erat, jam propter abusem [7] contrarium [8] contemptibilis effectus est, sicut ostendit (50r) Doctor subtilis Johannes Scoti, super quarto Sententiarum, dist. 18.[9] Qui tamen contemptus valde periculosus est; quia excommunicatio major, quae anathema dicitur, aeternae est mortis damnatio, et non nisi pro mortali debet imponi crimine, et illis qui aliter non potuerint corrigi, ut habetur 11, q. 3, cap. *Nemo*.[1] Cui concordat glossa, Ext., De verbor. signif., *Ex parte*.[2] Quod autem excommunicatio dicatur *perpetua damnatio* intelligendum est secundum glossam in dicto cap. *Nemo*,[3] cum ipsa contempnitur, alias non, ut 24, q. 3, *Notandum*,[4] et 2, q. 1, *Multi*.[5] Et ideo vae illis qui eam per irrationabilem ipsius multiplicationem contemptibilem efficiunt: quia excommunicatione nulla est major poena in Ecclesia, ut 24, q. 3, *Corripiantur*.[6] Et ideo, sicut dicit ibi glossa,[7] non est infligenda pro levibus criminibus, sed solum pro contumacia, ut 11, q. 3, *Absit*.[8] (113v)

De tertio gravamine Romanae Ecclesiae scilicet quod imponit aliis in onerosa multitudine statutorum, (81) canonum et decretalium, et maxime illorum (34v) quae viderentur ad graves poenas et praecipue ad mortales culpas obligare, et eadem ratione de similibus statutis aut constitutionibus synodalibus praelatorum, providendum erit de rationabili, alleviatione hujusmodi onerum, ne de praelatis Ecclesiae verificetur quod de Pharisaeis et sacerdotibus synagogae a Christo improperando dictum est: [9] *Imponunt onera gravia et importabilia in umeris hominum; digito autem nolunt ea movere*. Et de hac re scripsit Cantor Parisiensis, sicut supra alle-

---

6. C. 11, q. 3, c. 42.
7. *Om. AB.*
8. *Om. C.*
9. John Duns Scot, *In IV Sent.*, dist. 19, qu. 1; *Opera Omnia, 18* (Paris, 1894), 642–43, § 17.
1. C. 11, q. 3, c. 41.
2. X, 5, 40, c. 23, *in v.* Pro contumacia.
3. C. 11, q. 3, c. 41, *in v.* Mortis.
4. C. 24, q. 3, c. 37.
5. C. 2, q. 1, c. 18.
6. C. 24, q. 3, c. 17.
7. C. 24, q. 3, c. 17, *in v.* Major.
8. C. 11, q. 3, c. 14.
9. Matt. 23:4.

gatum est [1] in consideratione secunda primae partis.[2] Super qua materia matura deliberatione opus esset.

Item super quibusdam aliis gravaminibus per Romanam Ecclesiam aliis praelatis et ecclesiis superinductis adhibenda erit provisio, scilicet super collationibus beneficiorum et electionibus dignitatum, de quibus supra in prima et secunda parte tactum est. Etsi in his utile visum fuerit observare antiqua jura communia, providendum erit contra abusum praelatorum in collationibus beneficiorum et capitulorum ac conventuum in electionibus praelatorum, ut beneficiis et utilitatibus ecclesiarum magis quam personis aut eorum [3] privatae commoditati succurratur. Similiter super concessionibus exemptionum quas Romana Ecclesia pluribus religionibus [4] abbatibus et conventibus ac capitulis in praejudicium praelatorum concessit, de quibus jam olim plures devoti ecclesiae zelatores conquesti sunt, sicut Beatus Bernardus [5, 6] et Cantor Parisiensis, ubi supra allegatum est quinta consideratione primae partis.[7] Similiter de pluribus aliis honoribus, reverentiis et praeeminentiis quos cardinales et quidam alii officiarii Romanae Curiae super alios praelatos usurpaverunt, et multis eorum particularibus (50v) excessibus, de quibus longum esset per singula discutere, perutilis et necessaria erit provisio.[8] Et ut de aliis (82) silvam, hunc abusum monstruosam indignantissime (35r) ferunt plurimi, quod [9] non solum cardinales episcopi aut presbyteri, sed etiam diaconi, contra decretum Hieronymi, 93. dist., cap. *Legimus,* cum multis similibus,[1] immo (114r) etiam quandoque simplices clerici protonotarii, et quidam alii officiarii Romanae Curiae singulis praelatis, non solum episcopis, sed archiepiscopis, primatibus, et patriarchis praeferuntur, et quod intolerabilius est,

---

1. *Add.* et *C.*

2. Peter Cantor, *Verbum abbreviatum,* cap. 79, § 206; PL *205,* 235.

3. earum *B.*

4. *Om.* religionibus *AB.*

5. in libro De Consideratione ad Eugenium Papam et alii, *in marg. V.*

6. St. Bernard of Clairvaux, *De consideratione libri quinque ad Eugenium Tertium,* Lib. II, cap. 4; PL *182,* 766–69.

7. Peter Cantor, *Verbum abbreviatum,* cap. 44, § 114; PL *205,* 139–40.

8. See Appendix V.

9. Vide P. de Alliaco to I Gerson, pag. 904, *in marg. A.* This reference is to d'Ailly's *Tract. de eccl. pot.,* cap. 2, in Edmond Richer, ed., *Joannis Gersonii. Opera, 1* (Paris, 1606), 904; cf. Dupin, 2, 933.

1. D. 93, c. 24.

cardinales non solum supra ceteros [2] praelatos, sed etiam aliquo modo se contra suum caput, scilicet Summum Pontificem, erexerunt, aliorum praelatorum statum deponendo, quia [3] et jamdudum quidam ipsorum praesumpserunt assumere hanc audaciam, ut dicerent Papam non posse cardinalem deponere. Unde Hostiensis et post eum quidam canonistae tenuerunt [4] quod in casu quo depositio cardinalis immineret facienda, generale concilium foret congregandum.[5]

Haec autem omnia, ut quidam dicunt, non tam in divina auctoritate quam in [6] humana adulatione fundatur, cum cardinalitus non sit ordo nec gradus ecclesiasticae hierarchiae a Christo institutus, nec ordini aut gradui Apostolorum aut discipulorum succedens, sicut episcopatus et sacerdotium. Quare nec introductus divinitus, sed humanitus adinventus. Propter quod non videtur gradui episcopali a Christo instituto praeferendus juxta cap. *Dominus noster,* § *Meminisse,* 92 dist.[7, 8] Ideo fuit quorundam opinio, quam tamen non approbo, quod expediret Ecclesiae Papam habere loco cardinalium aliquos praelatos de diversis regnis et provinciis eidem pro consilio assistentes, et quod ille cardinalium status, tanquam male stabilis, caderet, sicut olim status chorepiscoporum,[9] qui olim propter insolentiam suam, qua [1] episcoporum officia usurpabant, ab Ecclesia (83) in generali concilio sub Leone Papa prohibiti sunt, ut legitur 68 dist., *Chorepiscopi,*[2] ubi dicitur: *Chorepiscopi tam ab*

2. ceteres *B.*

3. *Om.* aliorum praelatorum statum deponendo quia *ABC; Add.* sicut jam docet experientia *ABC.*

4. Henry of Segusia, cf. above, n. 6, p. 254. He does not seem to have expressed this precise doctrine either in his *Summa* or his *Commentary on the Decretals.* He does, however, exalt the position of the cardinals and states that they can be judged only by the Pope and the Sacred College: "Cardinales non possunt judicari nisi a Papa, et collegiis suis"—*In Quinque Decretalium libros commentaria doctissimorum virorum quam pluribus adnotationibus illustrata* (Venice, 1581), 2, f. 17v, § 5. Cf. above, pp. 127–28.

5. cur non ita de aliis praelatis, *in marg. V.*

6. *Om. C.*

7. D. 93, c. 25, § Meminisse.

8. At this point there are two marginal annotations in *Ms. V.,* the first of of which is illegible and the second: Utinam ista opinio in hoc concilio repellatur.

9. The *chorepiscopi* were rural bishops who exercised their office in distant or rural localities as delegates of the bishop of the city, and who did not possess the right of exercising the most important powers of a bishop; cf. Th. Gottlab, *Der abendliche Chorepiskopat* (Bonn, 1928).

1. quia *A.*

2. D. 68, c. 5.

hac sacra sede quam ab episcopis totius orbis prohibiti sunt. Nimis enim [3] *eorum institutio improba est et prava.* Quod si *de summo sacerdotis ministerio,* id est, episcopali, *aliquid praesumant, omnino auctoritate carent. Nam non amplius, quam duo ordines inter discipulos Domini esse* [4] *cognovimus, id est, duodecim Apostolorum* (35v) *et LXXXII discipulorum. Unde iste tertius processerit, ignoramus. Et quod ratione caret extirpandum est.* Et super verbo *unde* [5] *processerit* dicit glossa: [6] *id est, ex qua causa* processerit *quoad talem praesumptionem* ignoramus. Sed nonne per totum orbem fuerunt Chorepiscopi. Ergo praesumendum est quod fuerunt ab Apostolis vel a conciliis (114v) instituti, ut 12 dist., *Illa.*[7] (51r) Sed hic non negat eos ab Apostolis institutos, sed causam institutionis ignorari dicit. Et hic est argumentum quod a quocunque auctore aliquid sit institutum, et quantumcunque diu obtentum,[8] si non subest causa, vel si onerosum est, extirpandum est, ut 12 dist., *Omnia,*[9] De consecratione, dist., 1, *Placuit,*[1] 10, q. 1, *Hanc,*[2] 63,[3] dist., § *Verum,*[4] Ext., De censi., *Pervenit.*[5] Ex hac glossa [6] a fortiori arguit dicta opinio quod cum iste status cardinalium non fuerit vel a Christo, vel ab Apostolis institutus, nec causa institutionis necessaria appareat, et sit valde onerosus, ut dictum est, quod magis quam status chorepiscoporum prohibendus est et ab Ecclesia extirpandus. Sed avertat Deus ut ad hujus rigoris executionem procedere oporteat; sed provideat ejus clementia ut Romana Ecclesia hunc statum (84) et alios sic ratione temperare studeat quod ei rationabiliter obtemperare et suo regimini subesse Christi fideles non taedeat, juxta verbum Senecae: *Multos reges, si ratio te rexerit.*[7]

Tertia consideratio erit de reformatione Ecclesiae circa partes ejus

3. *Om. C.*
4. causae *ABV.*
5. *Om. C.*
6. D. 68, c. 5, *in v.* Unde et processerit.
7. D. 12, c. 11; the reference is rather to the gloss on the word *intelligi* than to the text itself.
8. *Om. AB.*
9. D. 12, c. 12.
1. D. 1, c. 26. *de cons.*
2. C. 10, q. 1, c. 15.
3. *Om. C.*
4. D. 63, c. 28, § *Verum.*
5. X, 3, 39, c. 5.
6. D. 12, c. 11, *in v.* intelligi; cf. above, n. 7.
7. Seneca. *Ep. Mor.* XXXVII, 4.

principales, scilicet majores praelatos. Unde providendum erit quod tales eligantur [8] qui non sint juvenes indiscreti [9] aut immoriginati aut carnales spiritualium ignari sed graves aetate et moribus eminentes spirituali scientia et doctrina, qui in suis non sint rebus strenui et in ecclesiasticis (36r) remissi, nec propria magis quam communia jura procurent, qui angarias vel impositiones vel hujusmodi gravamina subjectis non imponant, qui per singulos annos parrochias suas cum fructuoso effectu visitent, qui potentes et tyrannos populi oppressores arguant et corripiant, qui divinis scripturis studeant, et non scientiis practicis et litigiosis totaliter inhaereant,[1] qui verbis aut ludis joculatorum et mimorum aut publicis spectaculis vel superfluis conviviis non delectentur, sed moderato habitu et temperato victu contenti [2] etiam in mensa lectioni divinarum scripturarum intendant, et ut breviter dicam, in omnibus tales sint ut ceteris sint fidelibus in exemplum, sicut et esse [3] tenentur, cum illis in officio succedant quibus a Christo dictum est: *Vos estis lux mundi,*[4] et *vos estis sal terrae* etc.,[5] et multa similia.[6]

Item ut tales ad praelaturas assumerentur, et non indigni (115r) et insufficientes, providendum esset quod electiones praelatorum non faciliter aut leviter, sed cum diligenti et gravi (85) examinatione confirmarentur, etiamsi nullus se opponeret: quia non sufficit bono patrifamilias constituenti custodem thesauri sui quod nihil mali sibi de illo opponatur, nisi etiam ipse, aliis tacentibus, de ejus idoneitate diligenter inquirat.

Item quia stultum esset patremfamilias thesaurarium facere sine thesauro, sic similiter facere episcopum sine subjecto populo, sicut saepe fecit [7] Romana abusio in contemptum status episcopalis de quibusdam solum titulatis episcopis mendicantibus et giravagis.

Item (51v) quia mali praelati raro de suis excessibus corriguntur, quia non cito etiam contra notorie malos profertur sententia, sed per multos annos differtur, et saepius eorum punitio totaliter neg-

---

8. *Om. A.*

9. Cf. *Conc. Trid.,* Sess. 6, De Reform., c. 1, p. 55; Sess. 7, De Reform., c. 1, p. 68; Sess. 22, De Reform., c. 2, pp. 209–10; Sess. 24, De Reform., c. 1, pp. 252–54.

1. For a discussion of this and of parallel statements see above, pp. 163–65.

2. Cf. *Conc. Trid.,* Sess. 25, De Reform., c. 1, pp. 298–99.

3. *Om.* et esse *C; Add.* ratione *C.*

4. Matt. 5:14.

5. Matt. 5:13.

6. Cf. Eph. 5:8; Philipp. 2:15.

7. facit *A.*

ligitur, idcirco absque timore mala perpetrant, et plerique eorum suspensionis, excommunicationis, irregularitatis, et alias juris poenas contemnunt. Ideo providendum erit quod circa talia (36v) visitatio et inquisitio fiat, ut talium vita et fama in provincialibus conciliis, vel si opus sit, quandoque in generali concilio Summo Pontifici referantur, et ad eorum depositionem seu aliam condignam correctionem procedatur.[8]

Et licet hodie concilium non deponat vel restituat episcopos, sed solus Papa, ut. 2, q. 6, *Ideo*,[9] sicut notat glossa, 11, q. 3, cap. *Episcopus*,[1] super verbo *synodo*,[2] tamen forte nunc expediret ad antiquum morem illius capituli reverti ut a generali synodo damnarentur vel absolverentur episcopi, vel saltem quod hoc fieret in praesentia synodi, ut sic magis cessarent inordinatae affectiones quae solent in talibus justam sententiam impedire. Item si non placet servare illum antiquum rigorem (86) Carthaginensis Concilii quarti: [3] *Ut episcopus vilem supellectilem et mensam ac victum pauperem habeat, et dignitatis suae auctoritatem fide et opere et vitae meritis quaerat*, saltem placeat moderare quod excessivo pompa praelatorum in vestibus, ornamentis, familiaribus, equis, conviviis, et ferculis ad congruam temperantiam restringatur, et quod expensae in talibus superfluae, sicut fieri debet, pauperum necessitatibus applicentur.

Item tollatur monstruosus ille abusus quo quidam praelatorum, armis spiritualibus depositis, arma corporalia sumunt in campis pugnantes sicut principes (115v) saeculares, et saepe cum oppressione pauperum et crudeli effusione sanguinis, cum tamen David ab aedificatione templi, quia vir sanguinum erat, prohibitus sit. Item si non placet servare illum juris rigorem quod non liceat episcopis a sua ecclesia plus tribus hebdomadis abesse, saltem provideatur quod sine speciali licentia et rationabili causa diu ecclesias suas in praejudicium animarum non deserant,[4] sicut hodie multi praelati faciunt,[5] etiam, quod monstruosius est, religiosi et monachi, qui plus

---

8. Cf. *Conc. Trid.*, Sess. 13, De Reform., c. 8, p. 126; Sess. 24, De Reform., c. 5, p. 259.

9. C. 2, q. 6, c. 10.

1. episcopis *C*.

2. C. 11, q. 3, c. 65, *in v.* Synodo.

3. Hinschius, p. 304, *xv*.

4. Cf. *Conc. Trid.*, Sess. 6, De Reform., c. 1, pp. 54–56; Sess. 23, c. 1, pp. 222–25.

5. Evidence for this contention is, ironically enough, the fact that d'Ailly himself never visited his own diocese of Puy, to which he was appointed in April 1395 and which he relinquished in May 1397.

sunt officiales fisci quam Christi in curiis principum, (37r) in cathedris judiciorum, in cameris compotorum, et aliis actibus saecularibus, militantes contra statuta canonum, ut 11, q. 1, cap. *Te quidem,* cum suis similibus.[6]

Item providendum erit quod praelati in suis synodis et eorum officiales in suis curiis non ad repletionem bursarum intendant, sed ad correctionem (52r) vitiorum, emendationem morum, et aedificationem animarum, et quod exactiones pro sigillis et litteris moderentur, et poenae pecuniariae vel tollantur vel temperentur, aut in totum (87) vel partem ad pios usus notorie applicentur, et quod poena excommunicationis non leviter, ut supra tactum est, feratur, et quod litium prolixitates, quae pauperes spoliant, et multos de suae justitiae persecutione desperare faciunt, modis congruis rescindantur, et quorundam advocatorum et procuratorum insolentia intolerabilis reprimatur.

Item si obstante consuetudine non placet servare illam rigorosam regulam contra simoniam a jure humano impositam ut nihil pro ordinatione vel pallio vel cartis vel pastillo detur aut accipiatur, ut habetur cap. 5, epistolae tertiae Gregorii Papae,[7] et multa alia similia quae scribuntur in antiquis juribus,[8] saltem super his esset aliqua moderatio adhibenda, et pro conscientiarum sedatione, et multitudini errantium pie [9] condescendendo,[1] aliqua declaratio facienda juxta illud Nicolai Papae,[2] qui praesidens Synodo Constantinianae,[3] dixit: *Quia ergo usque adeo verenda simoniaca pernicies hactenus inolevit, ut vix quaelibet Ecclesia valeat reperiri, quae hoc morbo non sit aliqua ex parte corrupta, et tanta talium multitudo est, ut dum rigorem canonici juris super eos servare non possumus, necesse sit ut dispensatorie ad piae condescensionis studium* (116r) *animos nostros ad praesens inclinemus a simoniacis consecratos in* acceptatis (37v) *ordinibus manere permittentes. Hoc enim temporis nimia necessitas permittendum a nobis extorsit* etc. Similiter etiam

6. C. 11, q. 1, c. 29.

7. Gregory I, (590–604) *Epistolarum Lib. IX*, Indict., 2, Ep. 106; PL 77, 1028 ff. Also in *Decretum,* C. 1, q. 1, c. 27.

8. C. 1, q. 1–4, passim.

9. pro *C.*

1. condescendo *A.*

2. Nicholas II, 1058–61. In Mansi, *19*, 899, this decree is attributed to the Council of Rome of 1059, but it is probable that it was promulgated at the Lateran Council of 1061; cf. Hefele-Leclercq, *4*, 1169.

3. Read Constantiniensis?

eadem vel majori ratione permissio et condescensio facienda esset super pluribus aliis juribus et constitutionibus quae communiter in scandalum plurimorum non servantur, ut, Verbi gratia,[4] quod nihil omnino liceat accipere in distributione graduum, ordinum administratione,[5] vel sacramentorum, vel sepulturarum, aut hujusmodi spiritualium (88) vel spiritualibus annexorum, quod non liceat quemcunque episcopum vel clericum die dominico absentem esse serviciorum solemniis quod clerici ad matutinum et vespertinum officia venire teneantur,[6] quod non liceat clericis ante tertiam horam prandere, quod nullus sacerdotum a quinquagesima usque ad Pascha carnes comedat; quod sacerdotes adventum jejunent. Et sic de multis aliis similibus, de quibus videretur expediens declarare quod non essent praecepta, sed consilia.

Et similiter de observantia jejunii quadragesimalis quantum ad aliquas personas, et quoad aliquas circumstantias, esset moderatio adhibenda. Item quia praelatis de divino cultu specialis cura esse debet,[7] circa hujusmodi (52v) reformationem quae necessaria est providendum esset, et[8] quod in divino servitio non tam onerosa prolixitas quam devota et integra brevitas servaretur, quod in ecclesiis non tam magna imaginum et picturarum varietas multiplicaretur, quod non tot novi sancti canonizarentur, quod non tot nova festa solemnizarentur, quod tot novae ecclesiae non aedificarentur, quod praeterquam diebus dominicis et in majoribus festis ab Ecclesia institutis liceret operari post auditum officium, tum quia in festis saepe[9] magis[1] multiplicantur peccata in tabernis, choreis, et aliis lasciviis, quas docet otiositas, tum quia dies operabiles vix sufficiunt pauperibus (38r) ad vitae necessaria procuranda, et quod in hujusmodi festis scripturae apocryphae aut hymni novi vel[2] orationes seu aliae voluntariae novitates non legerentur omissis antiquis et authenticis et jam in Ecclesia consuetis, et quod generaliter omnis novitas et varietas ac usuum diversitas in horis ac[3] aliis divinis serviciis quantum fieri posset vitaretur juxta decretum

4. *Om.* Verbi gratia *ABC.*
5. Cf. *Conc. Trid.,* Sess. 21, De Reform., c. 1, pp. 189–90.
6. *Add.* et *C.*
7. *Om. B.*
8. *Om. B.*
9. *Om. C.*
1. *Add.* et saepe *C.*
2. aut *C.*
3. et *C.*

Toletani Concilii XI, de quo 12 dist., cap. *De his.*[4] Et multa alia utilia essent per praelatorum diligentiam providenda, quae per singula discurrere (116v) longum esset. (89)

Quarta consideratio erit de his quae reformanda essent circa statum religiosorum. Et primo videtur quod tanta religiosorum numerositas et varietas non expediat, quae inducit ad varietatem morum, et quandoque ad contrarietatem et repugnantiam obser-vationum, et saepe ad singularitatem, et ad[5] superbiam et vanam extollentiam unius status super alium. Et maxime videtur neces-sarium quod diminuerentur religiones ordinum[6] mendicantium; quia tot sunt et in numero conventuum et in numero suppositorum quod eorum status est onerosus hominibus, damnosus leprosariis et hospitalibus ac aliis vere pauperibus et miserabilibus indigentibus, quibus convenit jus et verus titulus mendicandi, ipsis quoque curatis parrochialibus, et, si bene consideretur, etiam praejudicialibus om-nibus Ecclesiae statibus, et specialiter hujusmodi religiosis intolera-bilis, et eorum religiosae professioni contrarius.[7] De qua materia et eorum variis excessibus pauca loquor, quia sunt plures doctores qui de hoc abunde scripserunt.[8]

Item providendum esset super correctione[9] quaestuariorum prae-dicantium, sive religiosorum, sive saecularium, qui suis mendaciis et immunditiis maculant Ecclesiam et eam (38v) irrisibilem reddunt, et officium praedicationis maxime honorandum jam contemptibile efficiunt.[1] Unde praedicatio, quae propter sui reverentiam ad prae-latos (53r) pertinet, non esset tot et talibus vilibus quaestuariis et mendicantibus permittenda. Item cum in Chalcedonensi Concilio statutum sit (ut habetur 16, q. 1, *Qui vere)*[2] quod monachi tantum-modo intenti sint jejuniis et orationi in locis ubi renuntiaverunt

---

4. D. 12, c. 13.

5. *Om.* et ad *AB.*

6. ordines religiosorum *A.*

7. et maxime in multiplicatione Magistrorum Bullatorum, et saepe indignorum, ipsis Religionibus onerosum, *in marg. V.*

8. Cf. Richard Fitzralph, Archbishop of Armagh (d. 1360), *Defensorium Cura-torum contra eos qui privilegiatos se dicunt;* Goldast, 2, 1392 ff. For a useful (if diffuse) discussion of Fitzralph's relations with the Friars, consult J. J. Greaney, "Richard Fitzralph of Armagh and the English Franciscans," *Catholic University Bulletin, 11* (Washington, 1905), 68 ff.; 195 ff.

9. correctio *B.*

1. Cf. *Conc. Trid.,* Sess. 5, De Reform., c. 2, pp. 29–31.

2. C. 16, q. 1, c. 12.

saeculo remanentes, nec ecclesiasticis nec saecularibus negotiis propria monasteria deserendo insistant,[3] providendum esset ne ipsi,
etiam occasione studii, claustra relinquerent, vel saltem moderandum
quod solum ratione studii theologiae, cum nimis multi saeculares
hodie studeant in litium facultate, ipsa quoque (90) theologia in
statu saecularium paucos habeat sectatores propter abusum Romanae Curiae, quae theologos contempsit et in omni ecclesiastico
gradu lucrativarum scientiarum studiosos praeposuit, cum tamen
primitivi theologi Ecclesiam aedificaverint, quam (117r) aliqui bara-
tratores destruxerunt, et nunc eam quasi ad extremam ruinam de-
ducere videntur, adeo ut jam horrendum quorundam proverbium
sit ad hunc statum venisse Ecclesiam ut non sit digna regi nisi per
reprobos.

Item nunc maxime opus esset, ad obviandum insultibus infidelium, quod reformarentur religiones militares et ad servandum
fidem, mores, et patrum regulas ac priores institutiones cogerentur.
Item circa claustra monialium, quae jam, proh dolor! ultra quam
dicere audeam dehonestata sunt, esset correctio adhibenda. Et inter
alias provisiones hoc videretur expediens, quod nulla religio mulierum sustineretur nisi tales haberent redditus unde possent sufficienter sustentari in suis domibus reclusae sine mendicitate et
discursu,[4] et quod de earum ecclesiis seu quorumcunque aliorum
religiosorum monasteriis vel prioratibus seu domibus, (39r) vel spiritualiter in moribus destructis vel in rebus temporaliter desolatis
fieret applicatio ad alia claustra in quibus religio servaretur, ut per
talem religiosarum domorum unionem superflua numerositas reli-
gionum restringeretur, et residua paucitas bonorum et devotorum
commodius sustentaretur.

Item in monasteriis esset inviolabiliter observandum quod nullus
nisi infirmus vel debilis aut hospes comederet extra refectorium;
quia experientia docet quod ubi hoc servaretur, aliae religionis
observantiae tenerentur facilius. Item pro serenandis [5] conscientiis
devotorum religiosorum summopere cavendum est eis ne a principibus aut aliis redditus suos aut alia ad eorum sustentionem pertinentia procurent ex injustis exactionibus aut quodomo-(91)-libet illicite
acquisitis, ne [6] etiam jura praelatorum ecclesiarum, et sacerdotum

---

3. Cf. *Conc. Trid.*, Sess. 6, De Reform., c. 3, pp. 57–58.
4. Cf. *Conc. Trid.*, Sess. 25, De regularibus et monialibus, c .5, pp. 285–86.
5. servandis *BC*.
6. nec *C*.

parrochialium indebite occupent, sive in decimis, sive in aliis proventibus ecclesiasticis, ne etiam in praejudicium ordinariorum ab eorum (53v) subjectione juri divino consona et in Chalcedonensi Concilio sanctorum patrum decreto firmata (ut patet 16, q. 1, cap. *Qui vere*)[7] per importunam humanorum privilegiorum impetrationem et violentam exemptionem damnabiliter se subducant. Nam secundum aliquos non est mediocriter (117v) dubitandum an tales sint in statu salvandorum, ut patet ex deductione Cantoris Parisiensis in Verbo Abbreviato, capitulo 37,[8] ut supra allegatum est in quinta consideratione primae partis.

Item in quibusdam religionibus devotis, quae regulae Beati Benedicti rigorem superaddunt in prolixitate vigiliarum et orationum et in austeritate jejuniorum et abstinentiarum et aliis variis observanciis afflictivis, videretur providendum de discreta[9] moderatione, et maxime circa infirmos, quod salva Christi lege nihil eis, quod discreti medici consulerent negaretur, sive in esu carnium, sive (39v) in aliis quibuscunque commoditatibus humanae fragilitati et naturali indigentiae opportunis. Alioquin non dixisset Christus: *Non est opus sanis medico*,[1] si non concessisset opus esse infirmis medicorum consilio.

Quinta consideratio erit de his quae reformanda sunt circa statum inferiorum ecclesiarum et ecclesiasticorum virorum. Et primo generaliter est providendum quod in ecclesiasticis beneficiis juxta eorum eminentias ponantur personae benemeritae, ut non praeferantur fatui et ignari scientificis et sapientibus, nec juvenes senibus, nec illis de una patria quorum vita et conversatio nota est et probata alii extranei et alieni in moribus, linguis, et consuetudinibus, nec potentes aut nobiles pueri clericis probatis et famosis doctrina atque moribus, nec advocati aut (92) intenti scientiis lucrativis, vel curiales, aut dominorum temporalium[2] servitores sacrae scripturae doctoribus, sicut a multis jam retroactis temporibus Romana Curia facere consuevit. Et ideo erit expediens quod ordinarii, qui in suis locis habere possunt et debent benemeritarum notitiam personarum, juxta earum merita beneficia conferant;[3] ita tamen quod, ut ob-

---

7. C. 16, q. 1, c. 12.
8. Peter Cantor, *Verbum abbreviatum*, cap. 44, § 114; PL *205*, 139–40.
9. districta *AB*.
1. Cf. Mark 2:17.
2. saecularium *A*.
3. vel saltem quod eorum non omnino tollata, *in marg. V*.

vietur eorum abusibus, potestas ordinaria limitetur; ut, Verbi gratia! quod non possint dignitates et beneficia majora conferre nisi doctoribus in theologia vel in jure quandocunque in suis vel propinquis dioecesibus erunt aliqui hujusmodi, quod non possint praebendas cathedrales conferre nisi graduatis in aliqua scientia, quod non possint habentibus duo beneficia tertium conferre nisi sint doctores aut in theologia (118r) vel in utroque jure licentiati, (40r) quod non possint etiam nisi graduatis [4] conferre curas, personatus, aut alia beneficia valoris centum librarum vel ultra in portatis.[5] Et ita de multis similibus provisionibus per quas et digni promoverentur, et multi nobiles et alii ingeniosi ad studium litterarum provocarentur, et universitates studiorum florerent, et, quod valde optandum est, importunae et violentae preces dominorum (54r) temporalium pro indignis cessarent, quae hodie quam periculose fiant docet experientia.[6, 7]

Item providendum esset quod universitates studiorum reformarentur et per praelatos scientificos visitarentur, ut gradus distribuerentur dignis sine favore aut acceptione personarum, et cum rigore examinis in scientia et moribus, ut doctrinae utiles resecatis, superfluis aut minus utilibus legerentur, ut instructores rhetoricae et linguarum Graecae et Latinae,[8] quarum ignorantia multipliciter ecclesiae damnosa est haberentur, et ut aliis studiosis, actibus rei publicae tam spirituali quam temporali utilibus juvenum ingenia [9] exercerentur.

Item adhibenda esset correctio circa mores ecclesiasticorum, qui jam nimis, proh dolor! sunt corrupti, in gula, luxuria, pompa, prodigalitate, otio, et aliis generibus vitiorum, (93) quod cedit in grave laicorum scandalum. Et maxime obviandum esset illi scandalosissime consuetudini seu potius corruptelae qua plures hodie non verentur tenere etiam publice concubinas. Et quia adversus eos poenae juris suspensionis, excommunicationis et irregularitatis

---

4. vel nobilibus vel alias bene meritis, *in marg. V.*

5. *Om.* in portatis *ABC.*

6. Et haec de graduatis dicta sunt, per modum exempli ponuntur, quae etiam moderari possunt, et alia addi, ad provisionem aliorum, sed non graduatorum, *in marg. C.*

7. Haec autem quod de graduatis dicta sunt etc., *in marg. V.*

8. In all these matters d'Ailly was drawing upon his experience as Chancellor of the University of Paris. The importance of Rhetoric was clearly a topic dear to him; cf. E. Gilson, *La Philosophie au moyen âge* (Paris, 1944), pp. 745–47.

9. utilia *AB.*

non proficiunt, contra tales in hac vel aliis inhonestatibus publicis incorrigibiles haberet locum poena depositionis ab officio et beneficio. Item quia archidiaconi ab Ecclesia instituti sunt ut serviunt episcopis, ut habetur originaliter (40v) Actuum sexto,[1] et specialius declarantur eorum officia 93 dist., quasi per totum,[2] ideo providendum erit quod debita officia exerceant, vel cum sint Ecclesiae onerosi, penitus extirpentur, sicut supra de chorepiscopis dictum est.[3] Item quia dicit Hieronymus: *Pauci sacerdotes, multi sacerdotes, pauci merito, multi numero,*[4] ideo[5] contra hanc scandalosam multitudinem esset summopere obviandum per hoc quod non promoverentur nisi digni et bene moriginati habentes scientiam ligandi et solvendi et intelligentiam divini servitii.

Item ad obviandum ignorantiae (118v) sacerdotum jam promotorum in ecclesiis cathedralibus et notabilibus collegiatis essent scribendi aliqui breves tractatus et etiam in synodi publicandi tam in Latino quam in vulgari super instructione necessaria de virtutibus et[6] vitiis, de articulis fidei, de sacramentis, de[7] modo confessionis et hujusmodi.[8] Similiter in hujusmodi ecclesiis deberet esse aliquis lector theologiae, qui legeret secundum, tertium et quartum Sententiarum, vel recipiendo utiliores materias dictorum librorum, eas sub brevitate applicaret ad expositionem et intelligentiam Epistolarum et Evangeliorum quae in Ecclesia per anni circulum recitantur. Similiter in dictis ecclesiis, et maxime in metropolitanis, deberent esse notabiles librariae theologiae et juris canonici ac librorum moralium, (54v) et maxime quod Magnus Liber Conciliorum Generalium, qui jam rarus est, licet sit perutilis et necessarius a metropolitanis in magnis ecclesiis haberi procurarentur. Item quia (94) correctio subjectorum saepe per eorum appellationes impeditur et datur peccandi audacia, esset circa eas adhibende moderatio, ne in earum nimis facili receptione et admissione inferiores praelati a metropolitanis vel Romana Curia in ordinaria excu-(41r)-satione justitiae gravarentur, sicut jamdudum Beatus Bernardus conquerebatur in Libro de Consideratione ad Eugenium Papam.[9] Qui liber in

1. Acts 6:1–7.
2. D. 93, esp. c. 6.
3. D. 12, c. 11, *in v.* intelligi.
4. St. Jerome?
5. idcirco *AB*.
6. *Add.* necessariis *C*.
7. et *C*.
8. *Om.* et hujusmodi *AB*.
9. St. Bernard of Clairvaux, *De Consideratione, III,* 2; PL *182,* 761–64.

hoc et aliis multis pro reformatione Ecclesiae non mediocriter utilis est, sicut et plures ejus libri et epistolae.

Sexta et ultima consideratio[1] erit de reformanda circa statum laicorum Christianorum, et maxime principum, a quorum moribus dependet moriginatio populorum; quia, ut dicit poeta:[2]

Regis ad exemplum totus formabitur orbis,
et iterum:

Mobile mutatur semper cum principe vulgus.

Et ideo provideant principes Christiani ut titulum suae Christianitatis, quem verbo confitentur, opere non negent contra Christi doctrinam, et per vias ei contrarias in conspectu sui populi corruptis moribus incedentes, et, ut quidam ait, delitias et divitias et honores saeculi cum altitudine cordis et fervore animi quaerentes et amplectentes non minus quam barbari vel pagani, quia cum rex Christianus, ut Christianus est, non debeat[3] pro se regere populum, sed (119r) pro Christo, scilicet ut illi vivat et deserviat. Et si aliter regit, non facit ut Christianus, sed ut paganus. Quae abnegatio cum sit publica vel notoria, pro constanti est in se ipsa magis abominabilis quam ea quae fit occulte, nec est minus stupenda quam illa, nisi solum quia est assueta magis communi notitiae. Supradictae vero apostasiae Christianorum notoriae tanto sunt magis abominabilis quanto majorem blasphemiam et illusionem construunt filio virginis: quoniam qui praedictis modis abnegant veritatem et sanctitatem Christianae religionis efficacius movent infideles ad blasphemandum eum (41v) et ad respuendum quaecunque de ipso dicuntur et praedicantur, ratio-(95)-nabiliter arguentes quod si talis et tantus esset Jesus Nazarenus qualem praedicant Christiani, non facerent universaliter et palam quaecunque illi contrariantur. Immo de facto praedicant quod ipse, qui docuit omnia terrena despicere, fuerit mendax vel indiscretus vel fatuus. Illudunt vero turpiter in eo quod missas audiunt et sermones, et in festis multiplicant (55r) sonitus campanarum et rasiones capitis et barbarum, et induunt splendida vestimenta, sed quicquid missis et sermonibus et solemnitatibus festorum in moribus et affectibus suis est contrarium cotidianis operibus publice solemnizant. Quae blasphemia necnon illusio est in superioribus magis pestifera, quia trahit ad corruptionem multipli-

---

1. This passage is cited above, pp. 42 and 103.

2. Claudian, *Panegyricus de Quarto Consultu Honorii Augusti,* lines 299, 300, and 302, but 299–300 in fact read thus: ". . . componitur orbis/Regis ad exemplum . . ."

3. debet *AB*.

citer subditos, inter quos idiotas plebis ad infidelitatem impellit: [4] sicut legitur de quodam principe publico adultero, qui cotidie missas audiebat solemnes, et frequenter confitebatur, quod plebs communiter asserebat adulterium non esse peccatum mortale, cum eorum princeps, qui saepe confitebatur et magnus ecclesiasticus erat, non cessaret publice fornicari. Similiter in aliis vitiis est exemplum superiorum nimis pestiferum. Propter quod opus est ut principes Christiani provideant ne suis malis exemplis subditorum mores corrumpant. Item quod liberos suos in bonis moribus et [5] in litterarum scientiis informari faciant. Item ut non solum a se, sed a suis familiaribus et domesticis superfluam et superbam vanitatem, avaritiam, et tyrannidem abiciant. Item quod populum eis subjectum bonis moribus aedificare studeant, eos a luxuria, avaritia, otio et a cunctis (119v) vitiis rei publicae contrariis retrahant, et specialiter a Dei et sanctorum (42r) blasphemia, quae saepe in juramentis et perjuriis committitur, arceant. Item quod malas consuetudines juri divino vel humano contrarias in suis subjectis per consilium theologorum et aliorum prudentum repellant. Item quod artes magicas et alias (96) superstitiones divina lege damnatas, et omnes errores et haereses fidei contrarias diligentius evellant et destruant. Item quod ad fidei exaltationem divini cultus honorem, Ecclesiae reformationem invigilent, et ad ea quae superius et inferius pro hujusmodi reformatione notata sunt et alia quaecunque [6] utilia diligenter laborent. Item quod zelo justitiae contra persecutores et oppressores [7] Ecclesiae, pauperum, et debilium excandescant, et eorum injurias propulsare non tardent, vicinis quoque et peregrinis fidem catholicae fraternitatis observent. Item quod contra Sarracenos et alios fidei adversarios potenter insurgent, et nunc dum maxime opus est, post unitam et reformatam Ecclesiam, infidelium insultibus viriliter se opponant, ac propter hoc quod guerras et bella, quae jam, proh dolor! et in Imperio et in regnis Christianis in contumeliam Christiani nominis crudeliter saeviunt, misericorditer compescant et ad Christianam pacem et unionem reducant. Alioquin infallibiliter verificabitur verbum Christi: *Omne regnum in se divisum desolabitur.*[8] Item quod Judaeis propter vilem quaestum turpiter non fave-

4. compellit *C.*
5. ac *C.*
6. quaeque *AB.*
7. *Om.* et oppressores *AB.*
8. Luke 11:17.

340

ant, eos scilicet inter eorum (55v) subjectos morari permittendo, nisi vel Christianis serviendo, agros colendo, vel alias mechanice laborando, et non usuras damnabiles in damnum Christianorum exercendo. Item quod Judaeorum conversorum bona non rapiant, sed ad vitae necessitatem eis possidere permittant, ne egestate compulsi apostatent et Christianos (42v) impietatis arguant.

Item multa alia essent per principes cum generali concilio Ecclesiae circa statum Christiani populi reformanda: quae si impediant, immo si ea diligenter non promoveant, timendum est eis ne contra ipsos manus Domini, prout jam incepit, gladium sui furoris exerceat.[9] Item quia Ecclesia non potest (97) principes ad praedicta reformanda temporaliter cogere, expediens erit ut per generale concilium ipsos ad ea monitis (120r) salutaribus exhortetur ut si faciendo quod in se est, apud supremum judicem excusetur. Nec solum opus erit exhortatoriis verbis, sed etiam bonorum morum et in melius reformatorum actuum exemplis; quia plus movent exempla quam verba. Ideo *coepit Jesus facere et docere.*[1] Unde nihil est quod tam efficaciter possit sive ad bonum sive ad malum principes et alios laicos inducere sicut facta exemplaria ecclesiasticorum. Ideo super illud Matthei 21: *Et intravit Jesus in templum* etc.,[2] dicit Chrysostomus:[3] *Sicut de templo omne bonum egreditur, ita de templo omne malum procedit. Si enim sacerdotium integrum fuerit, tota Ecclesia floret. Si autem corruptum fuerit, omnium fides et virtus marcida est. Sicut cum vides arborem pallentibus foliis, intelligas quod vitium habet in radice. Sic cum videris populum indisciplinatum, sine dubio cognosce quia sacerdotium ejus non est sanum.* Et inde patet quam necessaria sit ecclesiasticorum reformatio, cum morum suorum deformatio tam periculosa sit et cunctis fidelibus populis tam damnosa. Avertat autem misericors Dominus ab Ecclesia sua hanc contumeliam ut omnes praelati, sacerdotes, aut alii

9. Vide Appendix IV.

1. Acts 1:1.

2. Matt. 21:12.

3. The reference is in fact to the so-called *Opus imperfectum* of pseudo-Chrysostom, *Operum Divi Joannis Chrysostom, 3* (Basel, 1530), 663–64. The quotation seems to have been a popular one and appears in Henry of Langenstein's *Consilium pacis,* Dupin, 2, 53, as well as in Gerson (who took it from him) and also later on in Christopher St. German and Sir Thomas More. See R. J. Schoeck, "The Use of St. John Chrysostom in Sixteenth-Century Controversy: Christopher St. German and Sir Thomas More in 1533," *Harvard Theological Review, 54* (1961), 21–27.

ecclesiastici hujus lamentabilis, deformationis reperiantur (43r) culpabiles; sed sicut olim ipse sibi in *Israel septem milia virorum* reservavit *quorum genua non sunt curvata ante Baal,* sicut legitur 3, Reg., 19 capitulo,[4] sic hodie in omni statu Ecclesiae aliquos reservasse credendus est qui zelo Christianae legis accensi deformatos mores in melius reformabunt et suis salutaribus verbis et exemplis alios informabunt. Quod ipse praestare dignetur, (98) qui Ecclesiam suam pretiosi filii sui sanguine redimere dignatus est. Amen.

EXPLICIT [5] ⟨TRACTATUS DE MATERIA CONCILII GENERALIS⟩

4. 3 Kings 19:18 (Vulgate) or 1 Kings 19:18.
5. *Om. AB.*

APPENDIX IV

Critique of the Meller Edition

B. Meller's edition of the first two parts of the *Tractatus de materia* is printed in his *Studien,* pp. 290–336. It is based upon the same four manuscripts as the edition above, and, like it, follows *Ms. V* (Meller's *V* is *Ms. V,* his P is *Ms. A,* his P2 is *Ms. B,* and his P3 is *Ms. C*).

The numerous mistakes and omissions in Meller's edition can be ascertained by comparison, and it would be tedious as well as unnecessary to list them. They may be said, however, to fall into five main categories:

(1) Meller adopts no clear policy toward indicating the variants and omissions that are to be found in P, P2, and P3. Sometimes unimportant variants are indicated (e.g. p. 299, n.b.: *aut* for *vel;* p. 314, n.a.: *inthronizatus* for *inthronisatus*), sometimes important ones go unmentioned (e.g. p. 293, l. 7–8: P and P2 both omit *suae vocationi;* pp. 296 bottom line—297: P and P2 both omit *tali exercitio administrationis temporalium, sicut expedit immo sicut necesse est unum solum praeesse*—an extraordinary variant to ignore!). The only generalization that can be made on this matter is that the majority of the variants in P, P2, and P3 are not indicated, and that the choice of those which are mentioned seems to bear little relation to their significance.

(2) Marginalia in *V* are sometimes included in the text without any indication that they do not appear as part of it in any of the manuscripts—a startling duplication of the type of scribal error responsible for many a corrupt and unreliable medieval manuscript (e.g. p. 331, l. 17–18 *quae quantum ad potestatem ordinis sacramentalis* is in fact only a marginal annotation in *V;* the same is true of p. 331, l. 2–6: *Tamen secundum aliquos, hoc est speciale privilegium*

*Universalis Ecclesiae quod non potest errare in fide, licet hoc idem
pie credatur de concilio generali, videlicet quando innititur divinae
scripturae vel auctoritati, quae a Spiritu Sancto inspirata est. Alias
saepe errasse legitur).*

(3) Although the edition follows *V*, its departures from it in favor
of readings contained in one or more of the other manuscripts are
not always indicated (e.g. p. 296, l. 36: *V* reads *per* not *pro,* as is
printed in the text; p. 299, l. 1: *V* reads *destitutionem* not *restitutionem* as in text).

(4) Abbreviations are sometimes misinterpreted (e.g. p. 302, l. 16:
ecclesiasticae historiae for *ecclesiasticis historiis*), and incorrect emen-
dations are made against the evidence of all four manuscripts (e.g.
p. 292, l. 2: where *reintingi*—which appears in *V*, P, P2, and P3—is
emended to *reintegrari,* despite the fact that *reintingi* is also used by
Peter Cantor whose words d'Ailly is, in fact, quoting.

(5) The confusion evident in the transcription of the text is fully
paralleled in the citation of the references. At least twenty-five per
cent of the references given in Part I are either incorrect or inade-
quate. Sometimes a quotation is incorrectly attributed (e.g. p. 290,
n. 1: the correct reference is Proverbs 1:5, not Proverbs 9:9), but
more usually it is simply a matter of d'Ailly's obsolete and misleading references finding their way unchanged into the footnotes. This
occurs with considerable frequency and one wonders if much of an
attempt has been made to check d'Ailly's quotations against the
sources (e.g. p. 291, n. 7: the reference to Cantor is to Ch. 79 in the
modern edition, not to Ch. 72 as d'Ailly says, and therefore should
be to PL *205,* 235, not 3 ff. 213; similarly, p. 295, n. 16: the reference
is in fact to Ch. 44 and not Ch. 37, and is therefore to PL *205,* 139–40).

The dangers attendant upon this lack of interest in checking the
sources which d'Ailly is quoting become very clear when it combines
with a notable lack of respect for the actual readings in the manuscripts to produce an emendation such as appears on p. 292, l. 1,
where against the evidence of all four manuscripts *Johannes Carnotensis* is emended to read *Ivo Carnotensis.* Now Ivo of Chartres was
no doubt a famous man, but he died in 1117. The reference is to the
Third Lateran Council of 1179 at which John, Bishop of Chartres
—no lesser a person than John of Salisbury—was present (cf. above,
n. 5, p. 255). The manuscripts then are right, the editor is wrong,
and the mistake could have been avoided had he actually run down
the passage from Ch. 79 of Cantor's *Verbum abbreviatum,* which

d'Ailly ascribes to Ch. 72 and which he is, in fact, quoting word for word.

Taking into account this and the many other errors which occur in it, Meller's text of the *De materia* and in particular his notes to the text, should be used with caution. His edition cannot be regarded as definitive.

APPENDIX V[1]

On the Cardinalate

Hic autem, propter dictos excessus, dudum quandum opinionem recitavi, quam nuper in tractatu *De ecclesiastica potestate*, tanquam erroneam reprobandam esse declaravi: [2] videlicet, quorundam detractorum Romanae Ecclesiae, qui in ejus odium, praetextu quorundam abusuum, statum Cardinalium, quasi inutilem vel damnosum, nec ab Apostolis, vel Conciliis institutum, et sine causa rationabili usurpatum, tanquam onerosum Ecclesiae, extirpandum esse dixerunt, sicut olim de statu Chorepiscoporum factum esse legitur.[3]

Hunc autem errorem in hac Synodo Constantiensi quodammodo resuscitare aliqui praesumpserunt: [4] qui utinam attenderent, juxta doctrinam Christi, prius trabem de oculo suo ejicere, quam festucam de oculo fratrum, imo partum suorum. Utinam attenderent, statum episcoporum, et aliorum praelatorum, caeterorumque ecclesiasticorum, ac etiam laicorum, innumeris abusibus et vitiis deformatum: nec tamen ideo hujusmodi status dissipandos esse, atque perdendos, quoniam in multis offendimus omnes. Sed vitium atque abusus corrigi debet et non status destrui, vel debitis juribus defraudari; sicut boni medici officium est, ab infirmo morbum tollere, et non infirmum corpus destruere.

Utinam denique considerarent, qualiter domini cardinales, pro reformatione Romanae Ecclesiae, ac status ipsorum, se effectualiter paratiores obtulerint, quam quicunque alii cujuscunque status:

1. Dupin, 2, 908; for the significance of this passage see above, n. 20, p. 119.
2. Dupin, 2, 947.
3. Cf. D. 68, c. 5.
4. Cf. Salembier, *Schisme*, pp. 374–75.

346

imo plura membra Ecclesiae huic suae reformationi restiterunt, cum tamen reformationem capitis importune peterent.

Quia ergo Romana Ecclesia, in capite et membris suis, se cum ratione temperare studuit, justum est ut subditae Ecclesiae eidem, suoque regimini rationabiliter obtemperare et subesse debeant.

347

APPENDIX VI[1]
On Voting by Nations

Item, propter praemissa, expedit ut Reges et Principes mittant ad Generalia Concilia, non ad onerandum et confudendum, sed ad honorandum, et confortandam Ecclesiam, et ad ea quae ibi decreta fuerint, quantum in eis est, exequendum.

Item, quia juxta Evangelicam sententiam, quam etiam experientia rerum magistra docet, inter reges gentium, et principes saeculi, saepe sit contentio, quis eorum videatur esse major, quam contentionem Christus inter discipulos suos vitari docuit: ideo non videtur expediens, ut de caetero in generalibus conciliis, pro deliberando, ad partem, super rebus gerendis fiat divisio per Nationes vel Regna: quia talis modus dividendi magis est saecularis quam ecclesiasticus, et ad contentiones de majoritate vel superioritate dispositivus; sed juxta ecclesiasticas sanctiones et sanctorum Patrum observantias, magis videtur esse procedendum per Provincias Ecclesiastico more distinctas.

Tamen quia hujusmodi Provinciae valde inaequaliter sunt divisae in diversis mundi regionibus, ideo expediens videretur hanc moderationem observari, ut ad constituendam Provinciam in Concilio Generali, non sufficeret minor numerus quam xii notabilium personarum: quarum sex ad minus essent praelati, vel Ambasiatores Regum, Principum vel Universitatum generalium studiorum, aut Doctores in Theologia, vel in Jure: et illorum sex ad minus duo essent Episcopi, non Titulares, aut girogavi; alii vero sex sint in minoribus dignitatibus Ecclesiasticis constituti, vel in aliqua Facultate graduati.

1. Dupin, 2, 915–16; for the significance of this passage see above, n. 46, p. 152.

348

Quando vero in aliqua Provincia non esset talis numerus, aut talium personarum, ut suppleretur de aliis vicinis provinciis, et constitueretur una ex pluribus, quae denominaretur ab illa cujus ibi essent plura, aut notabiliora supposita, et ut hujusmodi personarum electio fieret in conciliis provincialibus, generale concilium praecedentibus: et ibidem ordinaretur de stipendiis, pro expensis et sumptibus eorundem, per modum subsidii charitativi, ecclesiastico more, et non saeculari autoritate vel potestate imponendi et exsequendi.

Bibliographical Note

Although there exists no fully satisfactory general study of d'Ailly, interest in his life and writings is by no means a recent development, and the lengthy list to be found in Ulysse Chevalier, *Répertoire des sources historiques du moyen âge,* new ed. (New York, 1960), *1,* 79–80, is an adequate guide to the relevant literature down to the end of the nineteenth century. Gallican writers kept d'Ailly's name alive until well into the eighteenth century, and as early as 1824, Arthur Dinaux wrote a *Notice historique et littéraire sur le Cardinal Pierre d'Ailly* (Cambrai, 1824). This was but the first of a series of similar endeavors in the nineteenth and twentieth centuries. The most recent and most reliable of these is the biography by Louis Salembier, *Le Cardinal Pierre d'Ailly* (Tourcoing, 1931). Salembier also wrote the brief but useful sketches in the *Dictionnaire de théologie catholique* and *Dictionnaire d'histoire et de géographie catholique* (both s.v. "Ailly, Pierre d' "), and the bibliographies appended to these provide, if taken in conjunction with the bibliographies in Chevalier and F. Uerberweg and B. Geyer, *Grundriss der Geschichte der Philosophie,* 11th ed. 2 (Berlin, 1928), 784–85, a reliable listing of the secondary works written on d'Ailly's life or about aspects of his thought up to the year 1928.

The years since then have seen the publication of one full-length biography, one noteworthy biographical sketch, and several studies concerned with individual aspects of his career and thought. The biography is Salembier's *Le Cardinal Pierre d'Ailly* and the sketch by A. Coville in the *Dictionnaire de biographie française,* s.v. "Ailly, Pierre d'." Of the detailed studies, those most relevant to the subject of this book are A. E. Roberts, "Summary of an M.A. thesis on the theories of Cardinal Pierre D'Ailly concerning forms of government in Church and State, with special reference to his interest in suggestions made by William of Ockham," *Bulletin of the Institute of Historical Research, 9–10* (1931–33), 44–46 (the thesis is deposited in the University of London Library), and the same author's "Pierre D'Ailly and the Council of Constance: a study in 'Ockhamite' theory and practice," *Trans. Royal Hist. Soc.,* 4th ser. *18* (1935), 123–42; M. Patronnier de Gandillac, "De l'usage et de la valeur des arguments probabiles dans les questions du cardinal Pierre d'Ailly sur le 'Livre des Sentences,'" *Archives d'hist. doct. et litt. du moyen âge, 8* (1933), 43–91; J. P. McGowan, *Pierre D'Ailly and the Council of Constance* (Washington, 1936); I. W. Raymond, "D'Ailly's 'Epistola Diaboli Leviathan,'" *Church History, 22* (1953), 181–91; B. Meller, *Studien zur Erkenntnislehre des Peter von Ailly* (Freiburg i. Breisg., 1954); George Lindbeck, "Nominalism and the Problem of Meaning as illustrated by Pierre d'Ailly on Predestination and Justification," *Harvard Theological Review, 52* (1959), 43–60; Francis Oakley, "The 'Propositiones Utiles' of Pierre d'Ailly: An Epitome of Conciliar Theory," *Church History, 29* (1960), 398–403, and "Pierre d'Ailly and the Absolute Power of God: Another Note on the Theology of Nominalism," *Harvard Theological Review, 56* (1963), 59–73 (criticizing Lindbeck).

Less immediately relevant but worthy of note are E. Buron ed., *Ymago mundi de Pierre d'Ailly,* 3 vols. (Paris, 1930); E. Vansteenberghe, "Un 'programme de vie' de la fin du moyen âge. Le 'De exercitio proficiencium' de Pierre d'Ailly," in *Aus der Geisteswelt des Mittlelalters, Festgabe M. Grabmann* (Münster i. W., 1935), *2,* 1231–46; and Max Lieberman's series of articles: "Chronologie Gersonienne: V Gerson et d'Ailly," *Romania, 78* (1957), 433–62; "Chronologie Gersonienne: VI Gerson ou d'Ailly: 'Annotatio doctorum aliquorum qui de contemplatione locuti sunt'," ibid., *79* (1958), 339–75; "Chronologie Gersonienne: VII Gerson et d'Ailly (II)," ibid., *80* (1959), 289–336; "Chronologie Gersonienne: VIII Gerson et d'Ailly (III)," ibid., *81* (1960), 44–98.

Of the biographies, Salembier's *Le Cardinal Pierre d'Ailly* may be said to be standard. It is concerned almost exclusively, however, with d'Ailly's public career, and the most valuable overall treatments of his life and thought remain, then, Salembier's first work, *Petrus de Alliaco* (Insulis, 1886), and the earlier book which it failed to supercede, Paul Tschackert, *Peter von Ailli* (Gotha, 1877). Neither is wholly satisfactory but Tschakert's is probably the better book and is valuable especially for the extracts from hitherto unpublished works which are printed in its lengthy appendices. Salembier's work is marred particularly by a somewhat *paleo*-neo-Thomistic horror of the "errors" of nominalism. But it is still the most comprehensive attempt to deal with d'Ailly's life and thought, and it gives (pp. XXII-XLIV) very full information concerning the editions and manuscripts of his works.

Of the works devoted to aspects of d'Ailly's thought other than the political, Meller's *Studien* is a comprehensive study of d'Ailly's epistemology, and Gandillac's lengthy article is the best treatment of his general philosophico-theological position. With the exception of Roberts's articles, little information is available on d'Ailly's ecclesiological and political thinking other than the fragmentary material contained in the biographies of Tschackert and Salembier, and the brief sections devoted to him in such works as K. Hirsch, *Die Ausbildung der Konziliaren Theorie im XIV Jahrhundert* (Vienna, 1903); R. W. and A. J. Carlyle, *A History of Mediaeval Political Thought in the West, 6* (Edinburgh and London, 1936); E. F. Jacob, *Essays in the Conciliar Epoch*, 2nd ed. (Manchester, 1953); John B. Morrall, *Gerson and the Great Schism* (Manchester, 1960); and Paul E. Sigmund, *Nicholas of Cusa and Medieval Political Thought* (Cambridge, Mass., 1963). Of these two most recent discussions, Sigmund's is the more satisfactory. To Roberts must go the distinction of having revealed the full range of d'Ailly's borrowings from Ockham, but her brief discussions, though they illustrate some of the salient features of his political thought, do not articulate it fully either with his ecclesiology or with his general philosophico-theological position. Without the considerable work of the last thirty years in late-medieval ecclesiology, philosophy, and theology, to do so would, of course, have been a truly formidable task.

D'Ailly's own writings have been listed several times: in Tschackert's biography, in the earlier work of Salembier, and also in the latter's *Le Cardinal d'Ailly: bibliographie de ses oeuvres* (Compiègne, 1909). The most recent and up-to-date listing is, however, the one appended to Salembier's later biography. The titles and locations of those tracts that have been found relevant to the present study are indicated in the footnotes. It will be sufficient here to comment that of d'Ailly's many Conciliar tracts, the most valuable are the *Tractatus de ecclesiastica potestate* (in Jean Gerson, *Opera omnia*, ed. Louis Ellies Dupin, 2 [Antwerp, 1706], 925–60), the

Tractatus de materia edited above, and the work entitled *Propositiones utiles* (in Dupin, *2*, 112–13)—this last brief tract being an extremely valuable epitome of Conciliar theory. By themselves, however, these Conciliar tracts would give an incomplete picture of d'Ailly's political thought, and they should be read in conjunction with his earlier scholastic disputations, written sometimes in more universal terms, and usually in an atmosphere at least a little more insulated from the persuasive pressure of events. Of these the most valuable have been found to be his *De legitimo dominio* (in Dupin, *1*, 641–46), *Utrum indoctus in jure divino* (in Dupin, *1*, 646–62), *Utrum Petri ecclesia lege reguletur* (in Dupin, *1*, 662–72), *Utrum Petri ecclesia rege gubernetur* (in Dupin, *1*, 672–93), and, of course, the *Quaestiones super I, III et IV Sententiarum* (Lyons, ed. Nicolaus Wolff, 1500), which is the principal source for his general theological and philosophical point of view.

If we turn now to "background" material, clearly only a fraction of that found useful in preparing a study of this type can be mentioned. The relevant works may, however, be classified in accordance with the three broad perspectives from which it is necessary to view d'Ailly's political thought: that of the history of the Great Schism and of the University of Paris; that if the history of medieval political and ecclesiological thought and of social and legal developments; that of the history of medieval philosophy and theology. For our purposes, the second is the most important, but none of these perspectives should be ignored.

Many works have been written on the history of the Conciliar movement, but the area is dominated by the massive studies of Noël Valois, *La France et le Grand Schisme d'Occident*, 4 vols. (Paris, 1896–1902), and *Le Pape et le Concile*, 2 vols. (Paris, 1909). These are the indispensable secondary studies, but, in addition, the short work by L. Salembier, *Le Grande Schisme d'Occident*, 5th ed. (Paris, 1921), is most useful because of the amount of attention paid to the activities of d'Ailly. Nor should the most recent account of the events leading up to the Schism, Walter Ullmann's *Origins of the Great Schism* (London, 1948), be ignored; it is especially noteworthy for the stress it lays upon the rôle and ideas of Cardinal Zabarella. And the most recent and most valuable treatment of the origins of Conciliar theory is, fittingly, that of a pupil of Ullmann's: Brian Tierney, *Foundations of the Conciliar Theory: The Contribution of the Medieval Canonists from Gratian to the Great Schism* (Cam-

353

bridge, 1955). A brief but useful survey of the earlier works on Conciliar theory is to be found at the beginning of this book (pp. 7–13), the main thesis of which, as the subtitle suggests, is that the foundations of Conciliar theory are to be sought, not in the doctrines of antipapal publicists or heretics, nor in the example of secular constitutional developments, but rather in the theories fomulated in the course of centuries by the glossators on the *Decretum* and *Decretals*. Finally, the revised version of Hastings Rashdall, *The Universities of Europe in the Middle Ages*, ed. F. M. Powicke and A. B. Emden, 3 vols. (Oxford, 1936) is, with its extensive notes, a good jumping-off ground for most questions concerning the universities and their history.

Of the works concerning the social, legal, and esslesiological developments which may be included in the second category of relevant background material, the following are basic: M. Bloch, *La société féodale*, 2 vols. (Paris 1939–40); F. L. Ganshof, *Feudalism*, trans. P. Grierson (London, 1952); and Walter Ullmann, *Medieval Papalism: The Political Theories of the Medieval Canonists* (London, 1949). This last should be read in conjunction with the critical review article of A. M. Stickler, "Concerning the Political Theories of the Medieval Canonists," *Traditio, 8* (1949–51), 450–63. Also of immediate relevance are Jean Leclercq, *L'Idée de la Royauté du Christ au Moyen Age* (Paris, 1959); Henri de Lubac, *Corpus Mysticum: L'Eucharistie et l'Église au Moyen Age* (Paris, 1944); Fritz Kern, *Kingship and Law in the Middle Ages*, trans. S. B. Chrimes (Oxford, 1939); and P. Gillet, *La personnalité juridique en droit ecclésiastique* (Malines, 1927). On particular specific issues, standard works such as the following are useful: A. Esmein, *Cours élémentaire d'histoire du droit français*, 14th ed. (Paris, 1921); Émile Chénon, *Histoire générale du droit francais public et privé des origines à 1815, 1* and *2* (Paris, 1926); R. Huebner, *A History of Germanic Private Law*, trans. F. Philbrick (Boston, 1914); F. Pollock and F. W. Maitland, *The History of English Law before the Time of Edward I*, 2 vols., 2nd ed. (Cambridge, 1911); A. van Hove, *Prolegomena ad codicem juris canonici*, Commentarium Lovaniense in Codicem juris canonici, *1*, tomus 1 (Mechlinae-Romae, 1945); P. Giraud, *Manuel élémentaire de droit romain*, 7th ed. (Paris, 1924). And for a critical listing and discussion of the extensive and important literature on the theory and practice of medieval representation see H. M. Cam, A. Marongiu and G. Stöckl, "Present Work and Present Views on the

Origins and Development of Representative Assemblies," *Relazioni del X Congresso Internazionale di Scienze Storiche, 1* (Florence, 1955), 1–101. Of the literature since 1955, Yves M.-J. Congar's "Quod omnes tangit, ab omnibus tractari et approbari debet," *Revue d'histoire de droit français et étranger*, 4me ser. *36* (1958), 210–59, is especially worthy of attention.

The histories of political thought may be said to bridge the gap between the above type of literature and the third category, in which we have placed the works concerning medieval philosophy and theology. These histories are found to be ranged between two opposed and "polar" positions. The first of these views political theory primarily as an expression or reflection of the political life of a given period, and the recent work of J. B. Morrall, *Political Thought in Medieval Times* (London, 1958), is perhaps a good illustration of this. From this point of view, the history of medieval political thought can be expected to be of interest to the medieval historian alone, but from the opposed position it is something that should possess a more universal significance and appeal. From this position, political thought appears above all as a branch of philosophy, a sustained rational attempt to solve the problem of political obligation and the related questions which cluster around it, and A. P. d'Entrèves, *The Medieval Contribution to Political Thought* (Oxford, 1939), may serve as an illustration of this approach. Each position has its own validity, but neither, by itself, is wholly satisfactory, and most of the standard works occupy ground somewhere in between —the mean being struck perhaps most effectively by Charles H. McIlwain, *The Growth of Political Thought in the West* (New York, 1932). From the many others should be singled out the encyclopaedic R. W. and A. J. Carlyle, *A History of Mediaeval Political Theory in the West*, 6 vols. (Edinburgh and London, 1903–1936), valuable especially for its extensive citations of the texts; the classic Otto von Gierke, *Political Theories of the Middle Age*, trans. F. W. Maitland (Cambridge, 1938); the recent useful collection of extracts, arranged topically with interpretative essays: Ewart Lewis, *Medieval Political Ideas*, 2 vols. (New York, 1954); and Ernst H. Kantorowicz, *The King's Two Bodies: A Study in Medieval Political Theology* (Princeton, 1957), a work of more wide-ranging importance than its title might suggest.

In addition to the general surveys, the following works devoted specifically to later medieval political thought are most important:

355

Alan Gewirth, *Marsilius of Padua, 1* (New York, 1951)—the first full-scale analysis of Marsilius to have appeared in English, and Georges de Lagarde, *La naissance de l'esprit laïque au déclin du moyen âge,* 6 vols. (Paris, 1942–46). Despite the adverse criticism of J. B. Morrall, "Some Notes on a Recent Interpretation of William of Ockham's Political Philosophy," *Franciscan Studies, 9* (1949), 335–65, the penetrating analysis contained in vols. 4–6 of Lagarde's book remains the most thorough-going examination of Ockham's political thought yet to be undertaken. A new edition of *Naissance* is being issued, and in it Lagarde has added a new volume on Ockham, *La Naissance de l'esprit laïque au déclin du moyen âge: Guillaume d'Ockham, défense de l'Empire, 4* (Louvain-Paris, 1962) and announced a new fifth volume to be devoted to Ockham's ecclesiology.

Little need be said, in conclusion, about our third category of background materials, those concerned with the history of medieval philosophy and theology, for full bibliographies are given in the extensive notes to Étienne Gilson, *History of Christian Philosophy in the Middle Ages* (New York, 1955), pp. 550–804. Gilson's treatment of the fourteenth century reflects the pioneer state in which the study of late medieval philosophy has lingered until very recently. His analysis of Ockham's thought is, however, to be preferred to that presented by Maurice de Wulf in his *Histoire de la philosophie médiévale, 3* (Paris, 1947), another standard history which on this point has been severely and convincingly criticized by Philotheus Boehner, *Franciscan Studies, 9* (1949), 443–56. The review has since been reprinted in Boehner's *Collected Articles on Ockham* (New York, 1958), and this book may serve as an introduction to the type of work which, in recent years, has led to radical revisions in the traditional estimate of Ockham's thinking. Similarly Heiko Augustinus Oberman, *The Harvest of Medieval Theology: Gabriel Biel and Late Medieval Nominalism* (Cambridge, Mass., 1963), which contains a useful "nominalistic Glossary" (pp. 459–79) and a first-rate bibliography (pp. 431–56), may serve as a guide to current ideas on late medieval philosophy and theology in general and to the growing bulk of work now being devoted to it.

Index

Abelard, Peter, 17, 19
Aegidius Romanus, 57–58, 71, 76, 78, 85, 100, 125 n., 134, 200 n.
Al Ash'ari, 17 n.
Alanus, 37, 218 n.
Albertus Magnus, 134
Alexander III, Pope, 255 n., 285, 289
Alexander V, Pope, 3, 13
Almain, Jacques, 9, 203–04, 207, 211, 213–16, 219–20, 222–23, 224 n., 225 n., 229
Alvarus Pelagius, 58 n., 72
Ambrose, St., 96 n., 259
Ames, William, 186 n.
Andreas de Novo Castro, 212 n.
Anselm, St., 19
Antiquus. *See* Bernardus Compostellanus
Aquinas, St. Thomas, 19, 35 n., 39, 51, 71 n., 82, 92, 101 n., 118, 128, 134, 140, 157, 162, 189, 199; and Aristotelian view of political society, 39–40, 98; on Mystical Body, 57; on forms of government, 117; on right of resistance, 156; on natural law, 168–70
Archidiaconus. *See* Guido de Baysio
Aristotle, 2, 36, 39, 53, 71, 97–98, 114, 134, 191
Armachanus. *See* Richard Fitzralph

Atomism (Asharite), 17 n.
Augustine, St., 18–20, 24, 71, 96 n., 155, 199, 298, 308, 319–20
Augustinus Triumphus, 147 n.
Averroës, 16–17
Avicenna, 17

Baldus de Ubaldis, 275 n.
Barclay, John, 223 n.
Barclay, William, 220 n., 223 n.
Bartholomaeus Brixiensis, 209–10, 268
Bartolus, 69 n.
Basel, Council of, 212 n., 221–22
Bekenntnis of Magdeburg, 227 n.
Bellarmine, 41
Benedict, St., 336
Benedict XIII, Pope, 3, 12, 212, 248–49, 256–57, 265, 280, 288–89, 291–93, 295, 297–300
Bernard, St., 164, 314–15, 327, 338
Bernardus Compostellanus, 290
Bernardus Parmensis, 37 n., 209 n.
Beza, Theodore, 227–30
Blackwell, The Archpriest, 223 n., 225 n.
Bonaventure, St., 19, 57, 298 n.
Boniface VIII, Pope, 36
Boniface IX, Pope, 3, 286
Bossuet, 9, 215–16
Boucher, Jean, 225

DATE DUE